P9-DFD-686

Beyond the Hiss Case

THE FBI, CONGRESS, AND THE COLD WAR

Beyond the Hiss Case

THE FBI, CONGRESS, AND THE COLD WAR

Edited by Athan G. Theoharis

 Temple University Press

Philadelphia

Temple University Press, Philadelphia 19122
©1982 by Temple University. All rights reserved
Published 1982
Printed in the United States of America

Library of Congress Cataloging in Publication Data
Main entry under title:

Beyond the Hiss case.

Includes index.
Contents: In-House coverup / by Athan G. Theoharis—
FBI break-in policy / by Anthony Marro—The case of
the National Lawyers Guild, 1939–1958 / by Percival
Bailey—[etc.]
1. Internal security—United States—History—20th
century—Addresses, essays, lectures. 2. United States.
Federal Bureau of Investigation—Addresses, essays,
lectures. 3. Hiss, Alger—Addresses, essays, lectures.
I. Theoharis, Athan G.
E743.5.B43 363.2′5 82-3309
ISBN 0-87722-241-X AACR2

Thomas Emerson and
Carey McWilliams

Contents

Abbreviations

AAP U.S., Senate, Select Committee to Study Governmental Operations with respect to Intelligence Activities, Interim Report, *Alleged Assassination Plots Involving Foreign Leaders*, 94th Cong., 1st sess., 1975.

ABAJ *American Bar Association Journal.*

AFSC U.S. Senate, Committee on the Judiciary, Subcommittee on Administrative Practice and Procedure, *Appendix to Hearings on FBI Statutory Charter*, Pt. 3, 95th Cong., 2d sess., 1978.

AH Alger Hiss Papers, Harvard University Library (presently accessible at the New York City offices of the National Emergency Civil Liberties Committee).

ALP FBI Files, American Labor Party, J. Edgar Hoover Building.

ALP Papers American Labor Party Papers, Tamiment Library, New York University.

COHC Columbia Oral History Collection, Columbia University.

COINTELPRO-CPUSA FBI COINTELPRO-Communist Party Files, J. Edgar Hoover Building.

CPJ FBI Files, Committee for Public Justice, Marquette University Archives.

Criley FBI COINTELPRO-Communist Party, Richard Criley Files (accessible through permission of Richard Criley, Carmel, California).

FMI U.S. Senate, Select Committee to Study Governmental Operations with respect to Intelligence Activities, Final Report, *Foreign and Military Intelligence*, Book I, 94th Cong., 2d sess., 1976.

GL *The Guild Lawyer.*

HFBIO U.S., House, Committee on the Judiciary, Subcommittee on Civil and Constitutional Rights, *Hearings on FBI Oversight*, Serial No. 2, Pt. 1, 94th Cong., 1st sess., 1975.

HIA   U.S., Senate, Select Committee to Study Governmental Operations with respect to Intelligence Activities, *Hearings on Intelligence Activities*, 94th Cong., 1st sess., 1975.

HIDFBI   U.S., House, Committee on Government Operations, Subcommittee on Government Information and Individual Rights, *Hearings on Inquiry into the Destruction of Former FBI Director J. Edgar Hoover's Files and FBI Record Keeping*, 94th Cong., 1st. sess., 1975.

HISG   U.S., Senate, Committee on the Judiciary, Subcommittee on Internal Security, *Hearings on Interlocking Subversion in Government Departments*, Pt. 16, 83rd Cong., 1st sess., 1953.

HIVC   U.S., House, Committee on Government Operations, Subcommittee on Government Information and Individual Rights, *Hearings on Interception of Nonverbal Communications by Federal Intelligence Agencies*, 94th Cong., 1st and 2d sess., 1975–1976.

HRCE   U.S., House, Committee on Un-American Activities, *Hearings Regarding Communist Espionage in the United States Government*, 80th Cong., 2d sess., 1948.

HRCE, II   U.S., House, Committee on Un-American Activities, *Hearings Regarding Communist Espionage in the United States Government—Part Two*, 80th Cong., 2d sess., 1948.

IARA   U.S., Senate, Select Committee to Study Governmental Operations with respect to Intelligence Activities, Final Report, *Intelligence Activities and the Rights of Americans*, Book II, 94th Cong., 2d sess., 1976.

KM   Karl Mundt Papers, Karl E. Mundt Archival Library, Dakota State College, Madison, South Dakota.

LGR   *Lawyers Guild Review.*

LN   Unserialized Official and Confidential Files, FBI Assistant Director Louis Nichols.

Marcantonio Papers   Vito Marcantonio Papers, New York Public Library.

NCARL   FBI Files, National Committee Against Repressive Legislation (accessible at NCARL offices, Los Angeles, California).

NLG   FBI Files, National Lawyers Guild (accessible at National Lawyers Guild offices, New York, New York).

O&C   Official and Confidential Files, FBI Director J. Edgar Hoover, J. Edgar Hoover Building.

RABA   *Reports of the American Bar Association.*

SAPP   U.S., Senate, Committee on the Judiciary, Subcommittee on Administrative Practice and Procedure.

SDF Papers   Social Democratic Federation Papers, Tamiment Library, New York University.

SDSR   U.S., Senate, Select Committee to Study Governmental Operations with respect to Intelligence Activities, Final Report, *Supplementary Detailed Staff Reports on Intelligence Activities and the Rights of Americans*, Book III, 94th Cong., 2d sess., 1976.

SDSRFMI   U.S., Senate, Select Committee to Study Governmental Operations with respect to Intelligence Activities, Final Report, *Supplementary Detailed Staff Reports on Foreign and Military Intelligence*, 94th Cong., 2d sess., 1976.

Sugar MSS   Maurice Sugar MSS, Meiklejohn Civil Liberties Institute, Berkeley, California.

VM   FBI Files, Vito Marcantonio, J. Edgar Hoover Building.

Beyond the Hiss Case

THE FBI, CONGRESS,
AND THE COLD WAR

1

Introduction

On January 21, 1950, Alger Hiss was convicted of perjury. Five days later Congressman Richard Nixon addressed the House of Representatives to commend the role of the House Committee on Un-American Activities (HUAC) in effecting Hiss's indictment and to condemn the Truman Administration's unwillingness to confront this serious threat to America's internal security.

Sympathizers praised the speech. Even critics denounced it only as a partisan attempt to exploit Hiss's conviction. Both critics and supporters, however, had missed Nixon's unintentional revelation of his close but covert relationship with the FBI. In his speech Nixon disclosed that he had had privileged access to confidential FBI investigative files, that he had known of the FBI's confidential interview with Igor Gouzenko and of the Justice Department's prosecutive strategy of late 1948, and that HUAC had been aware, prior to subpoenaing Whittaker Chambers in August 1948, of Chambers's 1939 interview with Assistant Secretary of State Adolf Berle. (See Chapter 7 and accompanying Hiss-Chambers Chronology for a detailed review of the extremely complicated evidence and chronology of the Hiss case.)

"Since December of 1948," Nixon asserted, "I have had in my possession photostatic copies of eight pages of documents in the handwriting of Mr. White which Mr. Chambers turned over to the Justice Department on November 17, 1948" (actually, Chambers's lawyer gave them to FBI agents on December 3, 1948). Nixon summarized the contents of this eight-page memorandum and the full text was then reprinted in the *Congressional Record*. Nixon further disclosed that as early as 1946 Igor Gouzenko (a former Soviet embassy employee who, having defected that winter, briefed Canadian officials about Soviet espionage activities in Canada) "had been questioned by intelligence agents of the United States and had furnished information dealing with espionage activities in this country." Nixon then quoted from "a secret memorandum, dated November 25, 1945," based on the testimony of another ex-Communist, Elizabeth Bentley, "dealing with Soviet espionage in the United States and prepared by an intelligence agency [the FBI] of this Government, which was circulated among key Government departments and was made available to the President."

The Truman Administration, Nixon lamented, had failed to act on this information in 1945 and 1946. Even after November 19, 1948, when Hiss's attorneys turned over to Justice Department officials typed and handwritten State Department memoranda which Chambers claimed he had received from Hiss in 1938, the Administration did nothing. Instead, the Justice Department apparently decided to discontinue the investigation of Hiss and to seek Chambers's indictment for perjury, to the intense frustration of FBI officials, notably FBI Director J. Edgar Hoover.

The Justice Department's strategy was thwarted however. On December 2, 1948, HUAC subpoenaed and Chambers turned over to HUAC investigators the so-called Pumpkin Papers, microfilm copies of State Department documents dated January 1938. In the widely publicized hearings of December 6–9, 1948, HUAC portrayed these microfilm documents as confirming Hiss's espionage activities. These HUAC hearings in turn impelled the Justice Department to seek Hiss's indictment for perjury.[1]

When commending HUAC's December 1948 hearings, Nixon impressively recounted the Justice Department's original handling of Chambers's November 1948 revelations:

I have learned from personal investigation that no agents of the Department of Justice even approached Mr. Chambers [between November 17 and December 3, 1948] let alone questioned him about the highly important evidence which he [sic, Hiss's attorney] had turned over [on November 19, 1948] to the Justice Department. In view of the [Washington Daily News] story which appeared on December 1, [1948] stating that the Justice Department was ready to drop the investigation [into Chambers's allegations about Hiss] for lack of new evidence, the only conclusion which can be drawn . . . is that it was the intention of the Department not to make an investigation unless they were forced to do so.

[HUAC] was able to force the Department to institute an investigation and [indict] . . . Hiss. . . . Even as late as December 5, members of the committee learned from an unimpeachable source that Justice Department officials before proceeding with further investigation of Mr. Hiss were considering the possibility of indicting Mr. Chambers for technical perjury due to his failure to tell the whole story when he first appeared before the committee and the grand jury.

The relationship between Nixon-HUAC and the FBI underscores the need for historians and other researchers to go "beyond the Hiss case"—and Hiss's innocence or guilt—to examine other questions, questions centering on the FBI's investigative and political roles during the Cold War years. How extensive were FBI leaks of derogatory personal and political information to "friendly" congressmen and reporters? Was the FBI-Nixon relationship atypical or representative? How extensive was covert FBI assistance to the politics of red-baiting during the Cold War years? Had the FBI become so politicized, and so immune to responsible oversight, that Bureau officials unhesitatingly collaborated with HUAC, conservative reporters, and other anti-Communist groups?

The essays in *Beyond the Hiss Case* do not focus on the question of the innocence or guilt of Alger Hiss. Instead, they examine the critical issues involved in the abuse of power, particularly the methods FBI officials, HUAC, and conservative reporters and congressmen employed to effect Hiss's indictment and conviction and to harass and discredit other dissident activists and organizations—and on also FBI officials' political activism. In the 1940s and 1950s, FBI officials had sought to shape public opinion and undermine opposition to untrammeled bureaucratic power. FBI investigative tactics in the Hiss case were not atypical, it should be emphasized, as other Bureau activities, chronicled here, confirm.

Beyond the Hiss Case does not survey all FBI investigative and political activities during the Cold War years. Sacrificing comprehensiveness for detailed analysis, the essays focus, first, on representative FBI investigative techniques, investigative priorities, and filing procedures and, second, on the Hiss case itself and Allen Weinstein's book, *Perjury*.

Beyond the Hiss Case emphasizes FBI break-ins and filing procedures for two reasons: they highlight the Bureau's disdain for the law and they formed the basis for its success in neutralizing responsible oversight. Recently released FBI documents demonstrate how, at least since 1940, high-level FBI officials blatantly circumvented legal restrictions (concomitantly devising separate filing procedures to preclude public discovery of their illegal activities). Nor were FBI officials content only to amass information on dissident activists. Instead, under the direction of J. Edgar Hoover and Assistant Director Louis Nichols, derogatory information from FBI files was purposefully disseminated to "friendly" reporters and congressmen.

In leaking such information, FBI officials had two complementary objectives. They sought to lend credence to the efforts of conservative activists like Congressman Richard Nixon, Senator Joseph McCarthy, HUAC, and Don Whitehead (*New York Herald-Tribune* reporter and author) to establish the "seriousness" of the internal security threat confronting American society. They further sought to neutralize potential challenges to the Bureau's investigative activities and independence. FBI officials successfully dissuaded President Truman from appointing a special presidential commission in 1949 and 1950 to investigate FBI practices and later contained the Long Subcommittee's investigation of the Bureau in 1965 and 1966. Aroused by the potentially damaging revelation of illegal FBI activities during the Judith Coplon trial, FBI officials assisted in the preparation of Morris Ernst's article "Why I No Longer Fear the FBI" and arranged for its publication in the *Reader's Digest* December 1950 issue, through *Digest* Senior Editor Fulton Oursler.

Five FBI investigations, one illegal investigative program, and one aspect of the FBI's covert relationship with HUAC are examined in the following chapters. The specific subjects are the National Lawyers Guild, Congressman Vito Marcantonio, the American Labor Party, Alger Hiss, Harvard University, FBI break-ins during an investigation of the Weather Underground, the Committee for Public Justice (CPJ) and the National Committee to Abolish HUAC (NCAHUAC). Not covered are the FBI's role in other investigations—for example, those involving Ethel and Julius Rosenberg, William Remington, Judith Coplon, J. Robert Oppenheimer, Owen Lattimore, the American Civil Liberties Union, the American Friends Service Committee, the Institute for Pacific Relations, the National Association for the Advancement of Colored People, the Southern Christian Leadership Conference, the Ku Klux Klan, the Socialist Workers Party, the Communist Party, the Black Panthers, the Congress of Industrial Organizations, and the John Birch Society. The five investigations, the harassment of NCAHUAC and of CPJ, and break-ins are representative of FBI officials' priorities, disdain for legal restrictions, and political activism. The FBI clearly overstepped its authority when investigating a radical political party (the American Labor Party), a radical congressman (Vito Marcantonio),[2] a radical lawyers' organization (the National Lawyers Guild), and a radical opponent of HUAC (NCAHUAC) because of their dissident activities. The FBI also investigated liberal activists like the founders of the CPJ.

The FBI's resort to illegal break-ins and investigative techniques was not confined to the Weather Underground, the National Lawyers Guild, and Judith Coplon. In January 1942, for example, FBI agents illegally entered the New York City offices of the American Youth Congress (AYC) to photocopy Mrs. Eleanor Roosevelt's correspondence with AYC officials. Copies were forwarded to FBI headquarters in Washington, where Hoover ordered them "carefully reviewed & analyzed." To prevent disclosure of its activity, the Bureau prepared the resultant report under a Do Not File procedure[3] and placed the copies themselves in FBI Assistant Director Louis Nichols's unserialized Official and Confidential file.

In July 1940, and this time at the direction of President Roosevelt and Assistant Secretary of State Adolf Berle, the FBI initiated an investigation of Herbert Hoover. Having been advised by reporter Marquis Childs that the former Republican President and his personal secretary Lawrence Richey had allegedly "addressed certain cablegrams to former Premier Laval of France," Roosevelt directed the FBI to "determine what messages, if any, of the type were sent by Mr. Hoover and Mr. Ritchey [sic] and what replies were received." The FBI conducted an investigation of "trans-Atlantic communications," but "failed to disclose that any such messages were sent."[4] Significantly, this FBI investigation—like later investigations of New Left organizations—stemmed from Herbert Hoover's opposition to Administration foreign policy. As in the 1960s and 1970s, the rationale was "national security": Hoover's and Richey's alleged contacts with Laval were subject to "official inquiry" because they had "injected themselves into international entree . . . so related to the operation of the Federal Government."

Whether or not coincidentally, on November 2, 1940, the FBI also prepared a thirty-nine-page "blind memorandum" (that is, not listing the names of sender and recipient) on labor leader John L. Lewis, who in that year had broken with President Roosevelt over his bid for a third term and his foreign policy toward Germany and had endorsed the candidacy of Republican presidental nominee Wendell Willkie. This November 2, 1940, report confirmed that the FBI had followed Lewis's and the United Mine Workers' activities closely since the 1920s and had intercepted, on April 18 and 27, 1938, at least two of Lewis's telephone conversations with Mexican official Alejandro Carrillo.

The second focus of *Beyond the Hiss Case* is the Hiss case itself and, concomitantly, *Perjury*, Allen Weinstein's account of it.[5] In the words of Alistair Cooke, the case symbolized a generation on trial and was a key element in the emergence of McCarthyite politics. American intellectuals endorsed the guilty verdict at the time and, later, uncritically praised Weinstein's book as conclusively establishing Hiss's guilt. None of *Perjury*'s sympathetic reviewers even commented on Weinstein's indifference to the abuse of power issues documented in the released FBI files.

Beyond the Hiss Case admittedly raises more questions than it answers. Our findings are tentative and, given the limited release of FBI files, our research into the role of the FBI, the Congress, and the conservative media during the early Cold War years is incomplete. We are not confident, however, that these questions can be better answered in the future, considering the Bureau's reluctance to permit research into its files—witness the recent efforts of FBI Director William Webster and other FBI officials to amend the Freedom of Information Act (FOIA), the Bureau's attempt to secure National Archives approval of two of its record-destruction plans,[6] and the incompleteness of the already released FBI files (either because of deletions or because of separate filing and record-destruction procedures dating from 1940).

But we have not raised doubt for its own sake. A study of FBI practices has obvious relevance today, given the Reagan Administration's policy priorities and congressional consideration of FBI charter legislation. What should the proper limits be on FBI investigative authority? Should its investigations be strictly limited to violations of federal statutes? How loosely should its "national security" powers be defined? Is it reasonable to base reform on administrative discretion rather than on tightly defined legislative prohibitions?

These are not questions of merely historic importance. As recently as 1975 Bureau officials misled congressional investigators about the scope of its past illegal activities. On September 22, 1975, the Senate Select Committee on Intelligence Activities had requested from FBI officials statistics on all "domestic security" break-ins conducted by the Bureau since 1942. Responding on September 23, 1975, the FBI had said that it could not provide an accurate accounting because there was "no central index, file, or document listing surreptitious entries conducted against domestic targets" and any reconstruction would have to depend upon "recollections of Special Agents." But FBI officials were disingenuous. They could have specified the number of such break-ins, since, until July 1966, surreptitious entries authorized by FBI headquarters were recorded "in a symbol number sensitive source index maintained in the Intelligence Division."[7] FBI headquarters also maintained another file, 66-2542, containing "correspondence relating to the number of installations, mail covers, informants, etc., in all field offices," and released FBI documents pertaining to break-ins involving the National Lawyers Guild and the Fair Play for Cuba Committee had been assigned "control" file numbers 66-1899 and 66-8160.[8] The existence of the index and of documents pertaining to break-ins and originally assigned 66 file numbers was known to responsible FBI officials in 1975. They could have been fully responsive to the Senate Select Committee's request for statistics. That they were not is an important fact.

Nor was this September 23, 1975, response the sole instance of FBI dissembling about its past break-in activities. During the period 1973–1976, the Bureau also misled the House Select Committee on Intelligence Activities; it misled a federal court (in responding to Judge Thomas Griesa's ruling on a suit brought by the Socialist Workers Party); it misled responsible Justice Department officials (when preparing responses to court-ordered discovery motions); and it misled the General Accounting Office (then conducting an audit of FBI investigative activities at the request of the chairman of the House Committee on the Judiciary).

Taken together, the FBI's disingenuousness during the 1970s and its investigative and political activities during the Cold War years prompt close scrutiny of the two FBI charter bills introduced in 1979 and 1980.

The first FBI charter bill, S. 1612, had been introduced on July 31, 1979, by Senator Edward Kennedy on behalf of the Carter Administration. S. 1612 does not limit FBI investigations to uncovering evidence of criminal activity. It includes a major exemption to the restrictive provisions—"except as to foreign intelligence and foreign counterintelligence investigations"—and authorizes the FBI to obtain "information" as well as to ascertain whether an individual "will engage" in criminal activities. It empowers the Bureau to investigate whether alleged "terrorist" activities would "influence" government policy and whether civil disorders are "threatened." It also permits FBI access to "third party records"—including telephone toll, insurance and credit, and bank records—and authorizes FBI assistance to other federal agencies and to state and local governments without determining whether such agencies may lawfully receive such information.

Senator Paul Laxalt introduced a second FBI charter bill, S. 2928, on July 2, 1980. Laxalt's bill abandons any pretense of applying criminal standards to FBI investigations. It repeats the "foreign intelligence" and "foreign counterintelligence" exception, and further authorizes the FBI to "conduct such investigations, and collect and maintain such intelligence and information, as may be necessary for the security of the United States and its defense, and to facilitate the operations of the FBI in carrying out investigations authorized by this chapter." Under the Laxalt bill, the FBI may investigate "activity which is likely or has the potential of violating the criminal laws of the United States"; individuals and groups seeking to "influence or bring about a change in the policy of the United States or any State or subdivision thereof"; "civil disorders or threatened civil disorders or public demonstrations which have a potential for violence, disruption, or disorder"; and "terrorist activity," defined as including "influencing or retaliating against the policies or actions of the Government of the United States or of any State or political subdivision thereof or of any foreign state, by intimidation or coercion." The FBI would further be empowered to disclose "information to the private sector" if that information "relates to potential terrorist activity" or concerns individuals "seeking employment of a type in which prior criminal history would indicate that such individual's conduct would constitute a clear and present danger to his employer or to persons with whom he would come into contact as a result of such employment." Furthermore, and particularly in view of the FBI's covert relationship with HUAC and the Senate Internal Security Subcommittee during the Cold War years, the Laxalt Bill authorizes the Bureau to "provide investigative assistance . . . to those committees of the Congress for which it is authorized to conduct background investigation of staff members, . . . if the chairman of the committee requests, and the Attorney General or his designee approves, the provision." Even Alfred Regnery, an aide to Senator Laxalt, conceded that S. 2928 "would theoretically leave the way open for those [recently disclosed] FBI abuses"; he offered the palliative that "we don't think those things are likely to happen again."

Not content with even S. 2928's proposals, the Heritage Foundation (a right-wing research organization) in November 1980 released a three-thousand-page report urging the newly elected Reagan Administration and the Ninety-seventh Congress to adopt a harder line toward dissident organizations and activists. Its major premise was that "individual liberties are secondary to the requirements of national security and internal civil order." Accordingly, the Foundation recommended reviving HUAC and the Senate Internal Security Subcommittee; rescinding Attorney General Edward Levi's March 1976 guidelines and President Carter's Executive Order 12036 of January 24, 1978, limiting Bureau investigations of "terrorist" and "potentially subversive" organizations; authorizing the FBI to use "such standard intelligence techniques as wiretapping, mail covers, informants and (at least occasionally) illegal entries"; exempting intelligence agencies from the disclosure provisions of the Freedom of Information and Privacy Acts; and abolishing the secret court, created under the 1978 Foreign Intelligence Surveillance Act, that reviewed and authorized all "foreign intelligence" and "foreign counterintelligence" electronic surveillance.

Although Reagon Administration officials denied that presidential policies governing the intelligence agencies and internal security would follow the Heritage Foundation recommendations, the report nonetheless offers insights into the priorities of conservative Republicans for the 1980s. Not surprisingly, on December 5, 1980, the newly elected Republican majority on the Senate Judiciary Committee voted to revive the Internal Security Subcommittee (terminated in 1978 in reaction to the abuses of civil liberties perpetrated under the rubric of "internal security"). As an aide to Judiciary Committee Chairman Strom Thurmond confided, the subcommittee "could keep watch over communist activities within the United States." In a companion effort, Congressman John Ashbrook introduced two bills in January 1981: H.J.R. 18 to create a Joint Committee on Internal Security and H.R. 14 to reestablish the House Committee on Internal Security (the former HUAC, so renamed in 1969).

Meanwhile, the Freedom of Information Act (FOIA) came under attack. In March 1981 the CIA repeated an earlier request for a legislative exemption from the FOIA's disclosure provisions. The FOIA, Deputy CIA Director Max Hugel claimed, hindered the Agency's "ability to perform its vital mission" while only rarely producing information of public interest. "While we do not question the principle that U.S. citizens should have the right to know what their government is doing and has done in the past," Hugel added, "we firmly believe that an exemption should be made in the case of the CIA." Then, on May 4, 1981, Attorney General William French Smith rescinded Attorney General Griffin Bell's May 1977 rule governing FOIA suits whereby the Department of Justice would defend in court only those exemptive claims of federal agencies in which disclosure of information would be "demonstrably harmful" to the national interest. Smith concurrently announced that the Reagan Administration had initiated a formal review of the FOIA to "assess the need for legislative reform." Such a review was required, he emphasized, because of the FOIA's administrative costs and the further consequence that "informants are more reluctant to share information with U.S. intelligence agencies, . . . and other impediments to effective government are created."

The Administration formally submitted its proposed amendments in October 1981. In testimony before the Senate Select Committee on Intelligence Activities, CIA Director William Casey demanded that the files of the CIA, the Defense Intelligence Agency, and the National Security Agency be totally exempted from the Act. Introducing the FOIA amendments, Assistant Attorney General Jonathan Rose recommended, among other changes, increasing the fees to cover all costs for processing FOIA requests (to include as well the salaries of officials who were reviewing documents for possible deletions), limiting judicial review of "national security" claims to determining whether withholding of such information was "arbitrary or capricious," and authorizing the attorney general to withhold whole categories of information relating to "terrorism," "foreign counterintelligence," organized crime, and ongoing investigations.[9]

In a further assault on the First Amendment, on May 8, 1981, the Reagan Administration proposed the Intelligence Identification Act, which would impose jail sentences of up to ten years for those who, having access to classified information, disclosed the names of agents and of up to three years for those not having such access, including reporters and scholars, who merely published the names, even if they had obtained them from public sources. This legislative proposal is currently pending—the measure never having been cleared for a floor vote in the Senate in 1981 despite passage in the House in October.

After meeting with intelligence agency officials early in 1981, President Reagan also ordered a review of existing regulations governing intelligence activities, ostensibly to improve antiterrorist capabilities. In response, an interagency working group, headed by the CIA's general counsel, drafted an executive order revising many of the restrictions instituted under President Carter's Executive Order 12036 of January 24, 1978. Under this draft, intelligence agencies, including the CIA, would have been authorized to spy on American citizens within as well as outside the United States—permitting the use of electronic surveillance, break-ins, and infiltration of domestic organizations. Although Carter's order had restricted the collection of intelligence information and the use of intrusive techniques, the proposed Reagan order would authorize such practices: Section 2 of Carter's order was appropriately titled "Restrictions on Intelligence Activities" with a subcategory "Restrictions on Certain Collection Techniques," but the comparable section in the proposed Reagan order is titled "Conduct of Intelligence Activities" and the subcategory, "Use of Certain Collection Techniques." The proposed Reagan order would, inter alia, downgrade the attorney general's oversight and review roles; broaden the type of surveillance intelligence agencies could conduct when investigating "unauthorized disclosure" of intelligence information; authorize the CIA to "engage in electronic surveillance activity within the United States only for the purpose of assisting, and in coordination with, another agency" having the authority to conduct such surveillance; drop the "probable cause" standard and requirement of presidential approval for use of searches and break-ins and substitute approval by the attorney general or (with his authorization) the head of the intelligence agency; and permit the collection, storage, and dissemination of information about individuals if it is merely "believed" (in contrast to the requirement of Carter's order that it be "reasonably believed") that the person was acting on behalf of a foreign power or engaging in international terrorist or narcotics activities.

Leakage of the text of the proposed executive order to the *New York Times* on March 9, 1981, resulted in extensive publicity, mostly adverse, and forced the Reagan Administration to downgrade the status of the proposed order to merely a "first draft" by a "working group" of intelligence agency officials. FBI Director William Webster, it was reported, thought that the FBI neither needed nor wanted the proposed changes, and so responsibility for these particular recommendations was attributed to lower-level intelligence officials, particularly within the CIA, and to conservative Republicans committed to unleashing the intelligence agencies. Throughout the week-long furor, the White House remained silent. Finally, on March 17, 1981, White House aide Edwin Meese told reporters that "I don't contemplate any change in the direction of loosening the reins on the CIA in domestic spying. The White House is absolutely opposed to the CIA getting into domestic spying." Meese, nonetheless, confirmed that within the next two to three weeks a new executive order on inteligence activities to combat terrorism would be issued.

The promised executive order did not materialize. In May 1981, a revised draft, written by the interagency task force, was circulated within the White House, the National Security Council (NSC), the intelligence agencies, and the congressional intelligence committees, but it was promptly opposed by the National Security Council staff. According to Reagan Administration officials, National Security Adviser Richard Allen and other NSC staff complained that the second draft would not give the intelligence agencies the mandate or structural changes required to bolster their intelligence-gathering activities.

In October 1981, the Reagan Administration submitted a third draft of its proposed executive order for review by the House and Senate intelligence committees. This draft gave the intelligence agencies (including the CIA) broad authority to infiltrate domestic organizations and to review bank, medical, telephone, and other personal records of American citizens and residents (specifically lifting the Carter order's ban on the CIA's conduct of "special activities" within the United States); freed intelligence agency officials from reporting possible federal crimes by their employees; authorized the agencies to conduct warrantless searches, including opening the mail, of American citizens and residents; and permitted the intelligence agencies to "cooperate with appropriate [state and local] law enforcement agencies for the purpose of protecting [their] employees, information, property, and facilities." Key congressmen and a congressional staff analysis of the order raised serious concerns about the scope of the order, but Administration spokesmen undercut these criticisms by citing the provision that "nothing in this order shall be construed to authorize any activity in violation of the Constitution or statute of the United States." They further asserted that the Department of Justice was currently drafting guidelines to clarify the powers of the intelligence agencies.

On December 4, 1981, President Reagan issued the new executive order 12333. In response to the congressional criticisms, Executive Order 12333 had deleted the sections permitting the CIA to infiltrate and influence domestic organizations without a warrant; freeing intelligence agency heads from reporting to the attorney general any possible federal crimes committed by their employees; affirming the president's "inherent" powers to authorize warrantless electronic surveillance; and permitting the intelligence agencies to conduct investigations within the United States into the unauthorized disclosure of classified information and sources. Nonetheless, the Reagan order radically expanded the intelligence agencies' permissible activities. They were now authorized to "conduct administrative and support activities within the United States and abroad necessary for the performance of authorized activities," as well as "such other intelligence activities as the President may from time to time direct." While their principal responsibilities were overseas, the CIA and the Defense Department intelligence agencies could conduct "counterintelligence activities" within the United states if coordinated with the FBI. In turn, the FBI was empowered to "conduct within the United States, when requested by officials of the intelligence community designated by the President, activities to collect foreign intelligence or support foreign intelligence collection requirements." The breadth of the order's definitions of "counterintelligence" and "foreign intelligence" would permit potentially broad domestic investigations. Such investigations were seemingly limited by the stipulation that they could not be undertaken "for the purpose of acquiring information concerning the domestic activities of United States persons." Other sections qualified this restriction, however, permitting: the acquisition and dissemination of "information obtained in the course of a lawful foreign intelligence, counterintelligence, international narcotics or international terrorist investigation," if necessary to protect "the safety of any persons or organizations, including those who are targets, victims or hostages of international terrorist organizations"; "incidentally obtained information that *may* indicate involvement in activities that *may* violate *Federal, state, local or foreign law* [emphasis added]"; and information "necessary for administrative purposes."

What are we to make of these events? What is the trade-off between individual freedom and national security? The essays in *Beyond the Hiss Case* provide an historical standard for appraising the wisdom of these recommendations to "unleash" the intelligence agencies and as well as the "worst case" scenarios advanced in their support. No less important, it highlights the limitations of conventional interpretations about McCarthyism which have stressed cultural and not political factors.

Notes

1. Later, as an embattled President, Nixon recognized HUAC's potential usefulness. On July 2, 1971, following the Supreme Court's decision upholding the *New York Times*'s right to publish the Pentagon Papers, he conferred with White House aides John Ehrlichman, H. R. Haldeman, and Charles Colson on future tactics. Nixon suggested approaching HUAC (then renamed the House Committee on Internal Security, HISC) to publicize the existence of a conspiracy harmful to the national security. Could Committee chairman Richard Ichord of Missouri handle this task, Nixon queried; who were the Committee's Republican members? "Our men," Nixon ordered, should "push HUAC and the bureaucracy [FBI, CIA, USIA, Defense Department]." Following up on this directive, Colson advised Ehrlichman on July 13, 1971, that "I am making contact with the key Ichord staff member [Bill Hecht] in the morning and will report the progress to you." On July 14, 1971, Colson briefed Ehrlichman on this meeting. Hecht was "enthusiastic over the prospect... and is in all respects a good Hill counterpart for the [H. L.] Hunt operation," but Ichord, having decided to run for governor of Missouri, was "very reluctant to start any sensational HISC hearings." Because Ichord was a patriot, however, Hecht believed that if the President "personally were to tell Ichord that this was a matter 'important to the national security' Ichord would order the hearings immediately." Colson recommended that the White House assess first "how good our information is and how effective we think we can be in putting our case together" before pressing Ichord to hold hearings. Eventually the Nixon White House decided not to pursue the matter, in part because of doubts about Ichord, its belief that Senator James Eastland of Mississippi was "more dependable," and its conclusion that congressional hearings could be harmful "due to HAK's [Henry Kissinger's] exposure."

2. The FBI did not confine its interest in members of Congress to the radical Marcantonio. Between 1950 and 1972, FBI agents collected information on all congressional candidates. Their monitoring of the political activities of congressmen predated even this 1950-initiated program. For reasons still unknown, on November 14, 1946, FBI officials prepared a five-page memorandum summariz-

ing "information in [FBI] files" concerning Senator Henry Cabot Lodge. Owing to its sensitivity, the memorandum was filed in Hoover's unserialized Official and Confidential file.

3. This report, however, was not filed with the photocopies of the correspondence in Nichols's Official and Confidential file. Unless held in another separate file, it apparently has been destroyed.

4. Monitoring cable messages was apparently not exceptional. In 1940, cable messages between the Soviet Union and prominent American Communists were also intercepted. See Beatrice B. Berle and Travis Jacobs, eds., *Navigating the Rapids, 1918–1971: From the Papers of Adolf A. Berle* (New York: Harcourt Brace Jovanovich, 1973), pp. 298, 339. During 1940 and 1941, moreover, FBI officials pressured the Federal Communications Commission (FCC) to monitor all international radio, cable, and telephone messages to and from Germany, Japan, Italy, and the Soviet Union. In a November 1940 meeting with FBI Assistant Director Edward Tamm, FCC Chairman James Fly conceded the FCC's technical ability to perform this mission—if granted additional funds and personnel. Fly nonetheless insisted upon a specific presidential directive. Bureau officials again approached the FCC in January 1941, but were advised by FCC attorneys that such practices were illegal—violating Section 605 of the 1934 Federal Communications Act. Accordingly, in February 1941, FBI Director Hoover raised this matter with Attorney General Robert Jackson, stressing this information's importance for "national defense" investigations. There is no available written record of Jackson's response to Hoover's request for advice "as to what further action can be taken by the Federal Bureau of Investigation with respect to this lack of coverage."

5. *Perjury: The Hiss-Chambers Case* (New York: Knopf, 1978).

6. In May 1975, FBI officials submitted to the National Archives a proposed plan to destroy FBI field office files, claiming that the most important information contained in them was duplicated in the FBI's headquarters files. On March 26, 1976, the National Archives approved this plan, sight unseen, without having independently ascertained whether in the process documents of "historic value" would be destroyed. The plan was subsequently challenged in court, and in January 1980 federal judge Harold Greene enjoined the National Archives and the FBI from further destroying Bureau records. Judge Greene directed the National Archives, after consultation with historians and archivists, to draft an alternative plan which would preserve documents of historic value.

7. The "symbol number sensitive source index" does not identify the nature of the "informant"—whether a break-in, wiretap, bug, or mail intercept. The

index cards list the assigned symbol number and then the location, date, and target of this particular surveillance.

8. Responding to my FOIA request for the 66-1899 and 66-8160 files, the FBI admitted that headquarters file 66-1899 had been destroyed on an unknown date prior to 1973. The FBI could also not identify the subject description of this file. The title of the comparable Washington Field Office file (wherein the memorandum reporting a December 1949 break-in involving the National Lawyers Guild was filed) is "Information Concerning Technical and Microphone Surveillance." Moreover, 66-1899 was a "control file" and not a National Lawyers Guild case file; that is, it contained all correspondence pertaining to authorization of such sensitive investigative techniques regardless of the target. Equally important, the FBI now concedes that break-in documents are contained in various headquarters files. These documents are presently being consolidated into a single "surreptitious entries" file, 62-117166. Telephone conversations, Athan Theoharis and Garland Schweickhardt, Oct. 9 and 22, 1981; Letter, James Hall to Athan Theoharis, and enclosures, Oct. 23, 1981.

9. In October 1981, the Reagan Administration circulated within the executive branch a proposed executive order on classification policy. Reversing the Carter Administration's policy which required declassification unless unauthorized disclosure "reasonably could be expected to cause at least identifiable damage to the national security," the proposed order stipulated: "If there is reasonable doubt about the need to classify, the information should be considered classified."

In-House Cover-up: Researching FBI Files

Athan G. Theoharis

Until recently, historians had not extensively researched the policies and activities of the federal intelligence agencies—but not because they were unimportant. There is a simpler reason: the records of federal intelligence agencies, most notably those of the FBI, were closed to historical research. "Friendly" journalists like Don Whitehead, Andrew Tully, and Harry and Bonaro Overstreet may have secured limited access to FBI files. Access to these same files, however, was denied to scholarly and other independent researchers—as all FBI documents were classified. Historians were denied access even to dated records, such as those documenting the FBI's surveillance role during World War I and the August 1923 investigation of the fraudulent Zinoviev Instructions.[1]

Congressional enactment of the Freedom of Information Act (FOIA) of 1966 seemed to resolve the research problem by mandating the citizen's right to secure federal agency files. Relying on the Act's provisions, on March 22, 1972, Smith College historian Allen Weinstein requested FBI files pertaining to the Alger Hiss and the Julius and Ethel Rosenberg cases. When Attorney General Richard Kleindienst denied Weinstein's petition on May 15, 1972, the historian brought suit under the FOIA, receiving legal assistance from the American Civil Liberties Union (ACLU). (The ACLU's principal interest was less to further historical research than to challenge the FBI's claimed exemption from the FOIA's disclosure requirements.) Protracted negotiations ensued—apparently amicably resolved on July 11, 1973, when Attorney General

The author expresses his appreciation to the Field Foundation and Warsh-Mott Funds for support of his research.

Elliott Richardson, Kleindienst's successor, authorized access by serious scholars to FBI files over fifteen years old.

Richardson's October 1973 resignation during the Watergate imbroglio, complicated the research problem even though his July order was never formally rescinded. Over the next year-and-a-half, the FBI episodically released batches of heavily censored documents. Frustrated by the apparent effort to undercut Richardson's order, on May 15, 1975, Weinstein resumed litigation. Armed with the stronger provisions of the (November 1974) amended FOIA, Weinstein's suit effectively broke down the Department of Justice's, and hence the FBI's, resistance, within months he received thousands of pages of FBI files pertaining to the Hiss case. FBI officials, nonetheless, employed the privacy and national security exemptions of the amended FOIA to censor, if less extensively and capriciously, the released documents. These deletions, however, could be challenged in the courts—under the 1974 amendments, a national security exemption claim was subject to judicial review. During the mid-1970s, then, the national security barrier to research seemed to have been breached.[2]

But was the national security barrier the principal obstacle to historical research? Only if the materials behind the barrier were intact—in other words, only if the Bureau had complied with the record retention requirements of the Federal Records Act of 1950—and the later Code of Federal Regulations of 1976.[3] These assumptions, however, were erroneous.

FBI Files

As early as 1940, FBI officials had devised rather sophisticated "Do Not File" procedures. Under these procedures, extremely sensitive FBI documents were not serialized and were filed separately, so that they could be destroyed or denied. Under a "Do Not File" procedure, FBI officials could affirm that a search of the central files disclosed no additional documents (particularly pertaining to the Bureau's illegal and "embarrassing" activities). The genius of this procedure was that no record had originally been created of their existence. In addition, such "sensitive information" was maintained separate from other FBI files either in the offices of the director and of assistant directors or "in a limited access area referred to as the special file room."[4]

On April 11, 1940, FBI Director J. Edgar Hoover advised other FBI officials how to prepare memoranda which were not to be filed in the bureau's central records system and, in cases, which were not to be retained permanently.[5] In time, this procedure was further refined. FBI officials were to use blue paper when writing such memoranda; FBI memoranda that were to be serialized were to be prepared on white paper. (When the Department of Justice unknowingly required the use of blue paper for interdepartmental correspondence, Hoover ordered that "Do Not File" memoranda be prepared on pink paper.)[6] These memoranda also contained the following notation on the bottom of the page: either "This Memorandum is for Administrative Purposes—To Be Destroyed after Action is Taken and Not Sent to Files Section" or "Informative Memorandum—Not to be Sent to Files Section." By employing this reporting procedure, FBI officials could submit sensitive information in writing to the FBI director or other high-level FBI officials with the assurance that the information would not be compromised. An internal FBI memorandum of September 23, 1958, describes how these memorandums were handled: FBI Assistant Director "Nichols had a stop up in the Records Branch and he reviewed all mail . . . and decided whether it should be kept in [Nichols's] OC file . . . or up in Records." Pink paper should be employed, Hoover stipulated in a March 1, 1942 memorandum, for those "memoranda prepared solely for the benefit of the Director which will possibly be seen by the Director and other officials and eventually be returned to the dictator [of the memorandum] to be destroyed or retained in the Director's office." Similar sensitive documents were filed separately in FBI field offices (whether in the SAC's "personal folder," the 62 file classification, or in the special file room) and were marked variously "Not for Files" or "ADM" in the lower right hand corner with a black stamp.[7]

Not surprisingly, FBI officials employed the Do Not File procedure (1) whenever formally authorizing illegal activities, (2) to preclude recurrence of embarrassing instances when documents recording illegal

FBI activities had been publicly compromised, or (3) whenever receiving illegally obtained information.

Conceding that break-ins were "clearly illegal," FBI officials nonetheless concluded in 1942 that such "black bag jobs" were an invaluable means for gaining otherwise unobtainable information—whether by acquiring membership and subscription lists, correspondence, and financial information about targeted individuals and organizations or by installing microphones. FBI Director Hoover intended to preclude discovery of the Bureau's use of illegal techniques and, accordingly, directed that all documents requesting authorization to conduct break-ins be prepared under a Do Not File procedure. Hoover's order insured two results. First, FBI officials could monitor when and under what circumstances FBI agents conducted break-ins, precluding frivolous instances and insuring that sufficient precautions had been undertaken to avert discovery. Second, FBI agents could convey information obtained through break-ins to FBI headquarters without risking disclosure. Authorized break-ins were recorded in a "symbol number sensitive source index" maintained in the Intelligence Division. Documents pertaining to break-ins were later conveyed through the "June mail" procedure (the information could also be disguised in other FBI reports as having been obtained from an "anonymous source" or a "confidential informant") and transmittal and authorization documents were filed in the sensitive and tightly controlled 66 file. In 1977, moreover, the section chief in the FBI's Intelligence Division destroyed one of the FBI's files that purportedly contained a large number of break-in documents.

FBI Assistant Director William Sullivan described the procedure for authorizing break-ins in a July 19, 1966, memorandum to FBI Assistant Director Cartha DeLoach:

We do not obtain authorization for "black bag" jobs from outside the Bureau. Such a technique involves trespass and is clearly illegal; therefore, it would be impossible to obtain any legal sanction for it. . . . The present procedure followed in the use of this technique calls for the Special Agent in Charge of a field office to make his request for the use of this technique to the appropriate Assistant Director. The Special Agent in Charge must completely justify the need for the technique and at the same time assure that it can be safely used without any danger or embarrassment to the Bureau. The facts are incorporated in a memorandum which, in accordance with the Director's instructions, is sent to [Assistant to the Director Clyde] Tolson or to the Director for approval. Subsequently this memorandum is filed in the Assistant Director's office under a "Do Not File" procedure.

In the field the Special Agent in Charge prepares an informal memorandum showing that he obtained Bureau authority and this memorandum is filed in his safe until the next semi-annual inspection by Bureau inspectors, at which time it is destroyed.

Concomitantly, the six-month destruction procedure governed the files maintained by FBI assistant directors. At a March 5, 1953, FBI Executives Conference, FBI officials agreed that all documents maintained by FBI officials in "personal files" were to be destroyed every six months (60 days for Supervisors in each Headquarters Division). With two exceptions, this record destruction was apparently done—that is, if FBI assistant directors did not take their "personal files" with them upon retirement. The two known exceptions to this record destruction rule involved FBI Director Hoover's "Personal Files" and FBI Associate Director Clyde Tolson's "Tolson File."

Hoover's "Personal File" was maintained in his office until his death in May 1972, at which time it was destroyed by his secretary, Helen Gandy. Gandy has testified (discussed further later in this essay) that she had destroyed this file on the explicit earlier order of the deceased FBI Director. Documents encompassing the period between 1965 and 1972 remain extant in the Tolson File. There is no way of ascertaining whether additional documents involving the 1965–72 period had originally been filed in the Tolson File, and were destroyed, and further why no document from the pre–1965 period remains extant. The extant documents, moreover, consist of the original copy of memorandums from Hoover to Tolson and to other FBI officials concerning major policy matters.

This commitment to avert possible public discovery of sensitive FBI records underlay as well FBI officials' response to Attorney General Elliot Richardson's August 8, 1973, decision requiring, among other provisions, that all departmental employees record all their contacts with "outsiders" (e.g., congressmen, White House officials, journalists) and retain a personal record of these contacts. FBI officials protested Richardson's order, fearing that if applied to FBI agents that this:

requirement that an employee who engages in [such] a discussion . . . must prepare a record, a copy of which would be his personal record, would place under the custody and complete control of the employee classifiable information which might frequently be of a highly sensitive nature. It would further permit an employee desirous of carrying such material and any other material with him upon departure from the FBI by merely preparing a series of recordings . . . in which he would incorporate material for his personal use at a later date. . . . This wrecks the need-to-know doctrine, plays havoc with the classification act, and . . . the maintenance of such personal records, which admittedly are uncontrollable, would be at least a technical violation of the espionage statutes.

Demanding that FBI agents be exempted from the Attorney General's order, FBI officials secured the requested modification: FBI agents could not maintain a personal copy of their contacts with "outsiders" and could not disseminate official information to persons outside the Department of Justice.

Concurrent with their refinement of these procedures to avert the public discovery of the FBI's covert use of sensitive investigative techniques and of far-reaching investigations, FBI officials concluded a similar arrangement with officials of the American Telephone and Telegraph Company (AT&T) for requests for leased lines whenever used for electronic surveillance interceptions. Under this procedure, AT&T "treated [FBI requests for leased lines] with the utmost discretion because they related to national security." Accordingly, "no records were kept [of these requests] in order to maximize the security of the operation." When the telephone company after 1969 required that each request for a leased line be submitted in writing, the FBI request form (from the FBI director to the participating Bell Telephone Company) specified that "you are not to disclose the existence of this request." AT&T was not informed of the name of the individual to be tapped, a company official later testified, in order to "insure that there is no leak in this supposedly sensitive area by one of our employees." In addition, when the Nixon Administration's so-called Plumbers Group requested installation of four wiretaps to ascertain the source of leaks involving the

Administration's Pakistan "file" during the India-Pakistan war, FBI records concerning the authorization of and reports on these taps were created under a Do Not File procedure.

FBI field office personnel also employed separate submission procedures when reporting politically sensitive information to FBI officials in Washington. Thus, in 1944, when the Albany, New York, field office formally requested policy guidance on whether to initiate an investigation and open a case file on the American Labor Party (ALP), FBI Director Hoover responded with a disclaimer: "The Bureau is not investigating the activities of the American Labor Party as such, in view of the fact that it is a recognized political party." Hoover, however, directed the Albany SAC to open a case file on the ALP and in the future to report any information "in letter form" (disguising the source as an "informant" and not an investigation conducted by the FBI). In addition, in 1955 Hoover authorized two additional reporting procedures: "blank" and "blind" memoranda. "Blank" memoranda were to be employed whenever FBI field offices reported information to FBI headquarters on the belief that it "is of possible interest to other Government agencies and is not within the jurisdiction of the FBI." (In 1957, the "blank" memorandum terminology was changed to "letterhead memorandum.") "Blind" memoranda, in contrast, were to be "used in those instances where the Bureau's identity must not be revealed as the source." Blind memoranda were to be typed on "plain white bond, unwatermarked paper" and transmitted by "cover letter."[8]

FBI officials could not always anticipate potential problems of embarrassment. Accordingly, whenever the FBI's involvement in illegal or questionable activities was publicly compromised, new separate filing procedures were devised. One such instance occurred during the Judith Coplon trial.

An employee of the Department of Justice's alien registration section, Judith Coplon was arrested on March 4, 1949, as she allegedly was about to deliver twenty-eight FBI documents to Valentin Gubitchev, a member of the Soviet Union's United Nations staff. Indicted for unauthorized possession of Government documents, Coplon was first tried in Washington, D.C. During her trial, Coplon's attorney demanded the production as evidence of the full text of the twenty-eight FBI documents found in her handbag at the time of her arrest—a motion which the Government opposed (at the particular urging to the FBI) on "national security" grounds. Ruling that the government could not seek to convict Coplon of a national security offense without producing in an adversary proceeding the evidence to support that charge, Judge Albert Reeves ordered the release of the twenty-eight documents.

When released, these FBI investigative reports disclosed no national secrets; they were, however, highly embarrassing to the FBI. For one, they highlighted that FBI investigations focused on liberal and radical activists. The subjects of these reports included prominent New Dealers Edward Condon and David Niles, Hollywood actors Frederick March and Edward G. Robinson, supporters of Henry Wallace's 1948 Progressive Party campaign, opponents of the House Committee on Un-American Activities, and the author of a master's thesis on the New Deal in New Zealand. Second, the released reports suggested that the FBI wiretapped extensively: fifteen of the twenty-eight containing information acquired through wiretaps.

To avert the recurrence of this embarrassment, on July 8, 1949, FBI Director Hoover issued Bureau Bulletin No. 34. Three months earlier, Hoover had issued new regulations governing the writing of investigative reports. Bureau Bulletin No. 34 revised and clarified the regulations, stipulating that FBI agents not include in the text of their reports "facts and information which are considered of a nature not expedient to disseminate, or which would cause embarrassment to the Bureau, if distributed." The information should instead be forwarded on "administrative pages at the conclusion of the report, which will be detached before distribution." Whenever reports having administrative pages were "distributed to any agency outside the Bureau," Hoover further specified, "the administrative pages should be detached."[9]

The Coplon trial had underscored the FBI's additional vulnerability because FBI agents had extensively used questionable investigative techniques. Accordingly, to avert discovery that the FBI resorted to break-ins, wiretaps, bugs, and sensitive confidential sources ("such as Governors, secretaries to high officials who may be discussing such officials and their attitude"), on June 29, 1949, FBI Director Hoover authorized another filing system, "June mail." All reports derived from "highly confidential" sources of such a "confidential character that the information should not appear in the file of a case" were to be captioned "June" and were to be filed in "separate confidential" files at FBI headquarters and field offices maintained under "lock and key."

Further developments in the Coplon case, in turn, led to the refinement of this procedure. During December 1949 pre-trial hearings, it had been disclosed that FBI agents had dissembled about FBI wiretapping practices and had recently destroyed wiretap records. To preclude such future embarrassment, FBI officials decided that it was not sufficient simply to devise separate filing procedures to limit knowledge of FBI wiretapping. In addition, all FBI supervisors, heads of field offices, and agents to whom a particular case had been assigned "should not be permitted to engage in any searches, physical surveillances, interviews with subjects or other types of work which may make him a competent witness in the event . . . it should be decided to proceed with prosecution. Thus, the Agent who might in these instances be competent witnesses would have no specific testifiable knowledge of the existence of a technical surveillance [wiretap] in that particular case."

By Hoover's further orders of December 22 and 28, 1949, all wiretap logs and all "administrative correspondence" relating to wiretaps (such as field office request and headquarter authorization memorandums) were to be captioned "June" to insure that they were "retained and filed separate and apart from the main file room in a confidential office" under "lock and key." Then, on July 19, 1950, FBI Assistant Directors D. M. Ladd and Alan Belmont "telephonically issued instructions to all SAC's regarding the utilization of microphones involving trespass and the SAC's were informed that microphone surveillance which involved trespass were to be considered as June mail." All the instructions regarding "June matters," moreover, were to be "transmitted orally."

To safeguard information obtained through intercepting and opening letters, additional separate filing procedures were employed. During the 1940s and 1950s, the FBI instituted a number of mail opening programs. In January 1958, moreover, FBI officials learned about the CIA's ongoing mail program in New York City wherein CIA agents monitored all mail to and from the Soviet Union. The next month a formal FBI-CIA agreement was concluded whereby the CIA serviced

FBI requests for copies of letters opened under the CIA's mail program. Information obtained from the CIA's program and the FBI's mail programs was not to be disseminated outside the Bureau or cited in any investigative report, and was stored in the FBI's "special file room." Should information obtained through these mail opening programs have to be disseminated to FBI field offices or other divisions, it was to be paraphrased to disguise the source. The information was transmitted to FBI field offices on FBI form 5-127, marked "Personal Attention." This notation insured that this transmittal was not processed in the FBI's normal channels, but was handled by field office supervisory staff. Copies of the intercepted letters were either to be destroyed (if of no value) or filed in a secure area separate from other FBI files. Retained copies were never stored in the case files of the individual whose mail had been opened, but could be retrieved through cross referencing.[10]

Other separate filing procedures safeguarded additional illegal or questionable FBI activities. We know of the following examples because (1) FBI officials had intentionally decided to preserve these documents; (2) other policy memoranda record this practice; or (3) even though the documents had already been destroyed, FBI officials subsequently testified to their past existence and use. Thus, FBI Assistant Director William Sullivan employed in 1969 a Do Not File procedure to report to FBI headquarters information he had obtained in Paris, France, from physical surveillance of syndicated columnist Joseph Kraft and from a bug which a French security agency had installed in Kraft's hotel room. The FBI also maintained an "obscene file" in the FBI Laboratory under FBI Director Hoover's strict supervision. Information in this file, for example, had been shared with the CIA in 1951, and in other "rare instances" the file "had been viewed by outsiders" without having been "specifically authorized by [FBI Associate Director Clyde] Tolson or myself [FBI Director Hoover]." Moreover, FBI agents assigned to congressional investigative staff forwarded "personal derogatory information" about members of Congress either orally or through Do Not File memoranda. Similarly, the wiretap records on the seventeen individuals (White House and National Security Council [NSC] aides and four Washington-based reporters) whom the FBI had wiretapped between 1969 and 1971, allegedly to uncover the source of leaks of "national security" information, were not filed with other FBI national security wiretap records. Nor, contrary to Attorney General Katzenbach's 1966 order, were the names of those whose conversations had been intercepted under this program included in the FBI's ELSUR Index. Owing to the "extreme sensitivity of the request from the White House," these wiretap records were kept in the office of Assistant Director Sullivan. An October 1971 memorandum highlights why this separate filing procedure was employed: "Knowledge of this coverage represents a potential source of tremendous embarrassment to the Bureau and political disaster for the Nixon administration. Copies of the material itself could be used for political blackmail and the ruination of Nixon, Mitchell, and others of this administration." The FBI memorandum recording President Nixon's May 1970 order to Hoover to submit future FBI reports based on these wiretaps to White House aide H. R. Haldeman (and not, as earlier, to National Security Adviser Henry Kissinger) was stamped "Do Not File" and "June." The same separate filing and non-serialization procedure was employed for FBI wiretap records on Charles Radford, a military aide assigned to the NSC staff. Radford's phone had been tapped because Nixon Administration officials suspected that he might have leaked NSC documents to the Joint Chiefs of Staff. In addition, in a November 7, 1963 memo to Hoover, the Chicago SAC wrote that the Bureau letter of September 13, 1963, "was destroyed after it was read by the agent assigned to the Counterintelligence Program." Other Bureau letters dated September 8, 1961, and September 18, 1962, were also destroyed under the separate filing procedure; and this action was duly reported by the Chicago SAC to Hoover.[11]

In October/November 1968, responding to Johnson White House requests, the FBI followed prominent Republican Anna Chennault. (Johnson Administration officials suspected that Chennault was using her contacts with the South Vietnamese embassy in Washington to sabotage the President's efforts to effect a Vietnamese peace settlement.) The reports resulting from Chennault's physical surveillance were also "protected and secured" to ensure that they could not be discovered and thereby affect the 1968 presidential election. In an October 30, 1968, memorandum, FBI officials acknowledged the political sensitivity of the action: "It was widely known that [Mrs. Chennault] was involved in Republican political circles and, if it became known that the FBI was surveilling her this would put us in a most untenable and embarrassing position."[12]

FBI Director Hoover's decision in 1939 to initiate a "custodial detention" program in time posed similar political problems. When briefed in 1940, Attorney General Robert Jackson approved the program. Under its provisions, individuals were included on a "custodial detention" list if investigations of their activities confirmed that "their presence at liberty in this country in time of war or national emergency would be dangerous to the public peace and safety of the United States Government." Because the investigative criteria employed to reach that judgement were clearly political—the investigations focused on American citizen's participation in dissident activities—the FBI's Custodial Detention program posed potential political problems for Bureau officials, problems that intensified when Congressman Vito Marcantonio was investigated and then recommended for a Custodial Detention listing. Because the initiative for this listing recommendation derived from the congressman's public criticisms of the Roosevelt Administration's foreign policy and, more important, his "position as a member of the House of Representatives," FBI officials urged Hoover to submit copies of Marcantonio's Custodial Detention card "for approval" to "Matthew F. McGuire, the Assistant to the Attorney General, in place of sending copies to Mr. L. M. C. Smith, Chief, Special Defense Unit." Hoover concurred with this recommendation, explaining in a July 28, 1941, memorandum to McGuire, "In view of the special circumstances in this case, I am transmitting the dossier to you rather than to the Special Defense Unit and I should appreciate your advice as to whether a copy should be furnished to the Special Defense Unit." (Significantly, recently released FBI files do not include Marcantonio's Custodial Detention dossier and Hoover's February 17, 1941 memorandum to Attorney General Jackson.) Responding on August 7, McGuire advised Hoover not to furnish a copy to the Special Defense Unit since, as a citizen, Marcantonio was "not subject to internment as an alien enemy in the event of war." Marcantonio could be prosecuted, McGuire added, "at that time" if he violated a criminal statute. McGuire had not specifically prohibited listing Marcantonio, and thus the FBI included his name in the Custodial Detention Index. [13]

FBI officials also employed separate filing procedures to obscure their own insubordination. When, on July 13, 1943, Jackson's successor as attorney general, Francis Biddle, ordered that Custodial Detention listings be terminated, Hoover technically complied, at the same time exploiting Biddle's failure to prohibit explicitly the compilation of a preventive detention list. Hoover simply renamed the program Security Index. To ensure that the attorney general could not learn of his insubordination, on August 14, 1943, Hoover advised all FBI officials:

The fact that the Security Index and Security Index Cards are prepared and maintained should be considered as strictly confidential, and should at no time be mentioned or alluded to in investigative reports, or discussed with agencies or individuals outside the Bureau other than duly qualified field representatives of the Office of Naval Intelligence and the Military Intelligence Service, and then only on a strictly confidential basis.[14]

With the September 1945 appointment of Tom C. Clark, a more sympathetic attorney general, Hoover recommended (in February 1946) and eventually secured (in August 1948) formal approval of a Security Index program. (At the time Hoover did not apprise Clark that the FBI already had an ongoing Security Index program in violation of Biddle's 1943 order.) If Clark only authorized a Security Index program, FBI officials unilaterally instituted a number of other listings: a "Comsab" program (concentrating on Communists with a potential for sabotage), a "Detcom" program (a "priority" list of individuals to be arrested), and a "Communist Index" (for those not qualifying for a Security Index listing because FBI investigations did not "reflect sufficient disloyal information," but whom FBI officials concluded were "of interest to the internal security"). Because these programs were politically sensitive and also were not all authorized by the attorney general, Hoover once again ordered that "no mention must be made in any investigative report relating to the classifications of top functionaries and key figures, nor to the Detcom or Comsab Programs, nor to the Security Index or the Communist Index. These investigative procedures and administrative aids are confidential and should not be known to any outside agency." As in Marcantonio's case, a separate submission procedure was established for "prominent persons." Security Index cards on these American citizens were to be "maintained in the Prominent Individuals

Subdivision of the Special Section of the Security Index," because "their apprehension might be attended by considerable publicity tending to make martyrs of them and thereby embarrassing the Bureau."[15]

To preclude discovery of other sensitive information, FBI officials created additional separate files. For example, while intensively interrogating Whittaker Chambers after Alger Hiss's December 15, 1948, perjury indictment, FBI officials received information having no bearing on the Hiss case which they wished to protect from court discovery. Thus they opened a "62 file" ("Administrative Inquiry") on Chambers "wherein should be filed information supplied by [Chambers] not having reference to the [Hiss] case file." Among other documents contained in the 62 file[16] were control files for sensitive investigative techniques (e.g., break-ins); liaison with local and state police officials, other federal agencies, and foreign intelligence agencies; liaison with congressional committees; and files "for information" or "information concerning" individuals (including derogatory information on Congressmen and prominent personalities). One could not "always know what action, if any was taken [by the FBI] with respect to these files, " Attorney General Edward Levi admitted during testimony before the House Subcommittee on Civil and Constitutional Rights. The "66 (Administrative Matters) file" and the unserialized "Official and Confidential" file maintained by FBI Assistant Director Louis Nichols in his office contained other equally sensitive documents. Included in the 66 file were break-in documents (reporting and transmittal memoranda), June mail authorization memoranda, control files on informants and on each FBI administrative unit, policy directives (Bureau Bulletins, SAC Letters, Executive Conference minutes), detention and security index program documents, files on persons "not to be contacted" and on congressional committees, memoranda describing the blank, blind, and letterhead memoranda procedures, the FBI's American Legion contact program, and reports concerning individuals "formerly connected with Soviet intelligence and who are now cooperative with the Bureau." Still other FBI files held highly sensitive information made available on a "confidential basis," information that was neither disseminated nor made part of an investigative report. Generally such information had been acquired from an "informant"—though FBI officials employed the "confidential informant" phrase to disguise the source of illegally obtained information (wiretap, bug, mail intercept, break-in).

The FBI continues to safeguard sensitive information. Thus, on April 12, 1977, when complying with Attorney General Griffin Bell's directive for "strict measures against personnel at any level of government who are found to be responsible for the unauthorized disclosure of official information," FBI Director Clarence Kelley admonished FBI officials to guard against "unnecessary discussion" of "sensitive investigative techniques" which "could result in disclosures which could seriously damage the effectiveness of the FBI and possibly endanger highly sensitive sources." Elaborating further, Kelley specifically cautioned: "Although certain techniques of operations were used many years ago, some were long range in scope and there is current and continuing need to protect information concerning such matters since they may still be useful." Then, on December 29, 1977, FBI Director Willam Webster advised all Special Agents in Charge how alias and false identification files in the organized crime area were to be maintained. Each field office was to establish a "66 classification control file" for all such documents; these files were not to be accessible to all FBI employees; were to receive "confidential and restrictive handling"; and their existence and accessibility were to be on a "strict need-to-know" basis. Webster further ordered: "In the interest of increased security and confidentiality, a SAC may remove all index cards from the main indexes and maintain them in a more secure area."

On November 7, 1978, moreover, while formally discontinuing the "June" mail procedure,[17] Webster authorized continued use of special filing procedures. The FBI Director specified the two categories of documents which "should receive special storage preferably in the same space designated for 'Top Secret' national security material" and "apart from" field office and headquarters "general files." These categories were:

(a) FBI national security electronic surveillance (ELSUR) material which identifies the target, reveals extraordinary technical devices being used, or where the subject is particularly sensitive.
(b) FBI communications identifying subjects of recruitment cases in which re-

cruitment appears probable or other sensitive communication dealing with penetration or double agent matters.

In addition, although prohibiting the use of "ambiguous terms such as 'anonymous source' and 'highly confidential source'" in "internal FBI communications" to disguise the resort to break-ins, Webster continued the practice of not identifying sources of information (whether break-ins or other "investigative technique[s] requiring special authorization") by means of "a permanent symbol or control record." Independent of these actions, between 1974 and 1976 FBI officials had attempted to preclude public knowledge of past FBI break-ins and, in the process, had misled a federal court, the Congress, and Department of Justice officials.

Attempting to understand the scope and nature of the FBI's past use of break-ins, in September 1975 the staff of the Senate Select Committee on Intelligence Activities requested from the FBI a statistical listing of its past "domestic security" break-ins. In response, FBI officials claimed that only approximate figures could be provided and explained:

There is no central index, file, or document listing surreptitious entries conducted against domestic targets. To reconstruct these activities, it is necessary to *rely upon recollections* of Special Agents who have knowledge of such activities, *and review of those files identified by recollection* as being targets of surreptitious entries. Since policies and procedures followed in reporting of information resulting from surreptitious entry were designed to conceal the activity from persons not having a need to know, information contained in FBI files relating to entries is in most cases incomplete and *difficult to identify*. (Emphasis added.)

These claims that there is no "index, file, or document" were misleading. In May 1977, FBI officials reportedly discovered "a number of documents" authorizing and approving thirteen break-ins in a "safe contained in the Office of the Executive Assistant to the Deputy Associate Director." (This safe had formerly been used to store FBI Director Hoover's Official and Confidential files, carbon copies of COINTELPRO (Counterintelligence Program) documents, and foreign counterintelligence documents.) That same year, Robert Shackelford, section chief of the FBI's Intelligence Division, destroyed forty-seven files pertaining to the FBI's investigation of Weather Underground members. Yet the newly discovered documents, did not comprise the totality of extant FBI break-in documents—there were other documents pertaining to the FBI's Weather Underground break-ins. Additional documents, pertaining to other break-ins were filed in the 66 file. Moreover, "prior to July 1966, surreptitious entries which were authorized by FBI Headquarters were recorded in a symbol number sensitive source *index* maintained in the Intelligence Division." [Emphasis added].

Nor was this the sole instance wherein FBI officials had dissembled about past break-ins. Responding to a General Accounting Office (GAO) audit of FBI domestic security investigations, initiated in June 1974 at the request of the chairman of the House Committee on the Judiciary, FBI officials did not report a break-in in their summary of a Weather Underground case. (The GAO had randomly selected certain cases and the FBI had agreed to prepare written summaries on these cases rather than permit GAO auditors direct access to case files.) The FBI also did not brief the Senate and House Select Committees on Intelligence Activities about the Weather Underground break-ins. And, when responding to court-ordered discovery motions of 1973, 1974, and 1975 for documents pertaining to any FBI break-ins involving the Socialist Workers Party (SWP), FBI officials falsely denied to the Department of Justice, and in turn to the federal court, that the Bureau had broken into SWP offices.[18] (On March 24, 1976, the Justice Department advised the court and the SWP that the FBI had in fact conducted ninety-four break-ins against the SWP.)

FBI officials also created falsified records to safeguard from public discovery the Bureau's assistance to conservative politicians. Whenever receiving written requests from conservative congressmen for FBI files on particular individuals, FBI Director Hoover formally declined these requests in writing. An FBI agent hand-delivered Hoover's letter of declination to the congressman, who brought with him the requested file, and was prepared to answer any of the congressman's questions about its contents.[19]

The United States attorney prosecuting the Hiss case employed a separate filing procedure to isolate information from the regular files which had been obtained from Horace Schmahl, a former investigator for the Hiss defense. In 1949, Schmahl informed the FBI and Assistant

Attorney Thomas Murphy (the chief prosecutor) about "defense activities and plans of which he learned in the course of his employment with Hiss's lawyers." Troubled by Schmahl's offer, an FBI agent wrote that "inasmuch as the Hiss case is presently in trial it appears that any contact with Schmahl at this time could be later construed adversely." Prosecutor Murphy, however, did not share agent Corcoran's reservations about communicating with Schmahl. Murphy met Schmahl on June 6 and, at a subsequent date, received at least one six-page memorandum outlining the Hiss defense strategy. Murphy's confidence derived from his use of a separate filing procedure to avert court discovery should defense attorneys suspect Schmahl of being a double agent. An FBI memorandum of September 22, 1949 describes this procedure: "It will be recalled that Horace Schmahl did, so far as it could be ascertained, all of the legal work for [John] Broady [for the Hiss defense], and as it will also be recalled, *confidentially through Armand Chankalian*, administrative assistant to the United States Attorney, SDNY [Southern District, New York], turned over the results of his investigation [emphasis added]."[20]

NSA Files

The National Security Agency (NSA) also employed separate filing procedures to preclude discovery of its illegal activities. In 1967, NSA began to intercept the international electronic communications of American citizens and organizations, targeted because of their anti-war or civil rights activities. Sensitive to the adverse political ramifications of the illegal program, NSA officials required that all such NSA-intercepted communications (1) be hand-delivered to the requesting agencies (military services, FBI, CIA, Secret Service); (2) be classified "Top Secret"; (3) include no identification that they had originated with the NSA; (4) be disseminated with the notation "For Background Use Only"; and (5) neither be assigned serial numbers nor filed with other NSA intercept reports.

This NSA interception program was refined in 1969 and code named

MINARET. MINARET's formal charter describes the specific procedures devised to preclude discovery of the NSA's role:

MINARET (C) is established for the purpose of providing more restrictive control and security of sensitive information derived from NSA-intercepted communications. . . . An equally important aspect of MINARET will be to restrict the knowledge that such information is being collected and processed by the National Security Agency. . . . MINARET information will not be serialized, but will be identified for reference purposes by an assigned date/time. . . . Further, although MINARET will be handled as SIGINT [Signals Intelligence, the task and mission of the NSA] and distributed to SIGINT recipients, it will not . . . be identified with the National Security Agency.

Officials who received "MINARET information," in addition, were specifically admonished to destroy or return these reports to the NSA with two weeks.[21]

The military intelligence agency responsible for conducting yet another illegal interception program, Operation SHAMROCK, initiated during World War II and reauthorized during the period 1945–1949, devised yet another separate filing procedure. Although in September 1975 NSA officials had advised the Senate Select Committee on Intelligence Activities that all documents pertaining to SHAMROCK had been provided to the Committee, on March 25, 1976, they informed the Committee that another file containing additional SHAMROCK documents had been "discovered." These files, NSA officials contended, had been held by a lower level NSA employee who brought them to his superiors' attention on March 1, 1976. Additional documents pertaining to SHAMROCK were independently uncovered. Conducting a simultaneous inquiry into this illegal interception program, the House Subcommittee on Government Information and Individual Rights requested a National Archives search of its holdings for any documentation pertaining to SHAMROCK. National Archives staff discovered an additional nine documents in the records of the Office of the Secretary of Defense (James Forrestal). The Department of Defense refused on "national security" grounds to release to the Subcommittee either these documents (which detailed Forrestal's December 1947 meeting with officials of the international telegraphic companies and an abortive Administration legislative effort of 1948 to legalize SHAMROCK) or other documents

pertaining to SHAMROCK's initiation in the period, 1945–1946. Responding to the Subcommittee's subpoena of these documents, the international
telegraphic companies affirmed that they had retained no copies.[22]

CIA Files

The CIA employed similar procedures. In September 1977 testimony
before the Senate Subcommittee on Administrative Practice and Procedure, Acting CIA Director John Blake admitted that the CIA maintained "soft files," which he characterized as "files of convenience or
working files." These files, Blake observed, were not easily retrievable
"because they are not official records and they are not indexed as such."
Blake also affirmed that "within the Agency, there is no single central-
ized record system. For reasons of security and need to know, there are a
number of records systems designed to accomplish the information retrieval needs of the various Agency components and the Agency's
clients."

For example, in December 1971, when confronting the delicate
political problem of how to handle the mail of "Elected or Appointed
Federal and Senior State Officials (e.g. Governor, Lt. Governor, etc.)"
intercepted under the Agency's New York City mail program, CIA
officials stipulated that these "special category items" were not to be
"carded" for inclusion in the mail program's highly classified files, but
were to be "filed in a separate file titled 'Special Category Items.'" All
cables and dispatches pertaining to the CIA's illegal domestic surveillance program, CHAOS, were also to be "specially handled" by the
Agency's counterintelligence staff. Such documents were to be "slugged"
CHAOS to limit distribution to the counterintelligence staff or to high-
level CIA officials on an "eyes only basis." In addition to other carefully
defined procedures to restrict the dissemination of sensitive information,
in February 1962 CIA Director John McCone had initiated a further
procedure: "Background Use Only." This notation was to be employed
"to preclude the inclusion of the information in any other document or
publication." Former CIA agent John Stockwell claims that the Agency
used three other sensitive record practices: "Eyes Only" and "Pro-

scribed and Limited" to control the distribution of cables reporting sensitibe operations, and "Back Channel," wherein information was conveyed orally, hand-carried, or limited to single copies to avoid creating a permanent written record.

During September 1975 testimony before the Senate Select Committee on Intelligence Activities, CIA Director William Colby maintained that "only a very limited documentation of [the CIA's drug program and poisonous toxin testing] activities took place." The desire for compartmentation when sensitive matters were involved "reduced the amount of record-keeping." Former CIA project director Sidney Gottlieb also admitted during October 18, 1975, testimony on the drug program that no written records were kept on the transfer of toxic agents "because of the sensitivity of the area and the desire to keep any possible use of materials like this recordless." (CIA memoranda and the testimony of other officials confirm that this same practice was employed during CIA consideration of plans to assassinate foreign leaders.) Colby's and Gottlieb's description of the intentional incompleteness of CIA files is confirmed by an internal CIA report of 1963: "Present practice is to maintain no records of the planning and approval of [drug] test programs." A 1957 report by the CIA's inspector general on the Agency's drug testing program also emphasized that "precautions must be taken not only to protect operations from exposure to enemy forces but also to conceal these activities from the American public in general. The knowledge that the Agency is engaging in unethical and illicit activities would have serious repercussions in political and diplomatic circles and would be detrimental to the accomplishment of its mission."

In July/August 1977, however, CIA Director Stansfield Turner in effect repudiated Colby's contention that a fuller record of the CIA's drug testing program could not have been provided to the Congress. Testifying before the Senate Select Committee on Intelligence, Turner conceded that material given to the Congress in 1975 had been "sparse in part because it was the practice of the CIA at that time not to keep detailed records in this drug-testing category." After an "extraordinary and extensive search," Turner continued, additional CIA documents pertaining to the Agency's drug programs had been located in retired CIA archives filed under financial accounts. The newly discovered documents revealed a far more extensive program than Colby had described.[23]

Presidential Deniability

The objective of ensuring that no permanent and retrievable written record would be created detailing illegal or questionable activities extended to the presidential bureaucracy. For example, a December 29, 1953 memorandum from FBI Director Hoover to Attorney General Herbert Brownell reported that a proposed presidential directive on the FBI's investigative authority had been discussed and approved at a December 15 National Security Council (NSC) meeting; however, the NSC minutes of this meeting recorded neither the discussion nor the decision. In his May 13, 1954, diary entry, presidential press secretary James Hagerty reported the NSC discussion and decision of that day on Attorney General Brownell's recommendation concerning the FBI's investigative authority. The NSC minutes on this meeting again recorded neither fact.[24]

Former NSC officials Robert Johnson, Marion Boggs, and James Lay, moreover, have testified to the intentional incompleteness of NSC minutes. Responsible for writing the minutes of an August 18, 1960, NSC meeting, Johnson consulted with senior NSC staff (either Boggs or Lay) to determine how to report Eisenhower's order to assassinate Congolese leader Patrice Lumumba. "Quite likely," Johnson advised the counsel of the Senate Select Committee on Intelligence Activities, the president's statement "was handled [in the memorandum Johnson wrote on this meeting] through some kind of euphemism or may have been omitted altogether." Queried about Johnson's testimony, Boggs could not recall having been consulted and then added: "I would almost certainly have directed Mr. Johnson to omit the matter from the memorandum of discussion." Lay was even more descriptive of NSC minute taking: "If extremely sensitive matters were discussed at an NSC meeting, it was sometimes the practice that the official NSC minutes would record only the general subject discussed without identifying the specially sensitive subject of the discussion. In highly sensitive cases, no reference to the subject would be made in the NSC minutes."[25]

This commitment to sanitize the record was apparently unexceptional. The reports of the Senate Select Committee on Intelligence Activities recount numerous instances wherein: (1) secretive procedures were devised to safeguard recognizably sensitive projects; (2) intelligence officials could not produce documents pertaining to questionable activities that the Select Committee had independently learned about through testimony or referenced documents; (3) incomplete records were intentionally created to ensure "plausible deniability" or to confine knowledge to those "who need to know"; and (4) documents were destroyed contemporaneous with their creation. A January 14, 1977, Department of Justice report justifying the decision not to prosecute former CIA officials for illegally opening the mail of American citizens highlights the extent of this practice. Executive approval of the CIA's mail opening program could not be established, the report maintained, because under the practice of "plausible deniability" or "presidential deniability" no "written records [were made] of presidental authorizations of sensitive intelligence-gathering operations. It was thought that the conduct of foreign affairs frequently required the practice of non-recordation of such presidential authorizations."[26]

Document Destruction

Were the vast majority of extremely sensitive FBI and other intelligence agency documents simply filed separately? Are these documents still available for research purposes—despite the intent of Do Not File procedures to permit the undiscoverable destruction of sensitive documents? Is our present knowledge of these procedures itself evidence of the existence of a rather complete record of the intelligence agencies' activities? The answer to all these questions is no. First, we have only fortuitously learned of these programs and activities—in most cases, because intelligence agency officials had consciously decided to preserve *certain* records. Second, the types of records that we now know have been destroyed strongly suggest that the most sensitive documents have also been disposed of.

For example, in a January 16, 1973, letter to CIA Director Richard

Helms, Senate majority leader Mike Mansfield requested that the Agency retain "any records or documents which have a bearing on the Senate's forthcoming investigation into the Watergate break-in, political sabotage and espionage, and practices of agencies in investigating such activities." (At the time Helms was preparing to leave the directorship to begin serving as ambassador to Iran.) In response to Mansfield's order, Helms's secretary asked the CIA Director what should be done about the tapes and transcripts recording all of his office telephone and room conversations. On January 24, Helms ordered the destruction of the tapes and transcripts. (There were approximately three file drawers of transcripts covering Helms's tenure as CIA Director.) In addition, in January 1973, documents pertaining to the CIA's drug programs were destroyed, as other unspecified CIA tapes had been in November 1972. Helms had also ordered the destruction of CIA drug program records in January 1973. Queried by the staff of the Senate Select Committee on Intelligence Activities whether destruction of sensitive records was a regular CIA practice, Helms elliptically admitted that the CIA had "regular procedures" for destroying records "monitored by certain people and done in a certain way" but conceded that the January 1973 document destruction had not followed these procedures.[27]

Following congressional repeal in September 1971 of the emergency detention title of the Internal Security Act of 1950, FBI Director Hoover asked Attorney General John Mitchell how to handle policy documents pertaining to the Justice Department's independently authorized and broader detention program. Responding on February 19, 1972, Assistant Attorney General Robert Mardian ordered Hoover to destroy these documents. Twenty-five intelligence agency reports detailing Korean CIA activities within the United States, as well as reports of the military attache in Chile for the period September/October 1970, have also apparently disappeared. The working notes used to prepare a 1967 CIA report on planned assassinations were also destroyed at CIA Director Richard Helms's specific order.

Released FBI files pertaining to the Bureau's electronic surveillance of Alger Hiss from 1945 to 1947 confirm that Bureau files have been purged. For example, Hoover's memorandum requesting Attorney General Tom Clark's authorization to tap Hiss is extant but not Clark's approval of that request. The tapes and reports based on the wiretaps of 1945–46 have not been preserved, although the fact that the FBI had wiretapped Hiss during these months is confirmed by Bureau memoranda submitted every sixty days requesting reauthorization to continue the wiretap and summarizing information obtained through it. When Hiss moved to New York City in 1947, the FBI continued to tap his phone. These records, as well as other subfiles designated A through E in New York Field Office file 69-14920, moreover, were "destroyed at a date unknown."

Following National Archives approval in March 1976 (reauthorized in August 1977 following the lifting of a moratorium against any file destruction for the duration of congressional investigations of the intelligence agencies) of an FBI records plan to destroy "closed files of the Federal Bureau of Investigation Field Division," the FBI on October 15, 1977, began systematically to destroy all field office files. Contrary to FBI officials' assurances to the National Archives in 1975, the information in field office files was not always duplicated in the FBI's headquarter's files. Indeed, in a March 14, 1980, deposition, Robert Scherrer (then unit chief of the FBI's Records Management Unit) admitted as much. Responding to a question from counsel as to how the FBI could retrieve information obtained from a "highly confidential source," Scherrer affirmed: "If it was a so-called black bag job, the only way to do so would be to go to the field office to retrieve it. Headquarters doesn't get copies of the substance of the information." In fact, documents pertaining to FBI break-ins of the offices of the Socialist Workers Party (SWP) in New York City and of the Chicago Committee to Defend the Bill of Rights in Chicago were extant only in the personal safes of the special agents in charge (SACs) respectively of the New York and Chicago field offices. These documents had been filed in the SACs' "Personal Folders." Furthermore, released FBI headquarters files on the Hiss and Rosenberg cases, on Clifford Durr, and on Martin Luther King, Jr. did not contain many of the released documents filed in FBI field offices.

In 1974, the NSA's Office of Security destroyed the files on American citizens it had compiled since the Agency's creation in 1952. In June 1970, on Hoover's direct order, all working copies of the so-called Huston Plan were destroyed. (This plan authorized the intelligence

agencies to employ a variety of "clearly illegal" investigative techniques.) The Post Office Department had also devised a Do Not File
procedure for all mail cover request and reporting forms. Postal Form
2008 (used by federal agencies when requesting a mail cover) contained
the notation: "Under no circumstances should the addressee or any unauthorized person be permitted to become aware of this action. Destroy
this form at the end of period specified [two years]. Do not retain any
copies of form 2009 [the form used by the Post Office to transmit the information obtained through the mail cover to the requesting agency]."[28]

Hoover's Personal and Confidential Files

During an interview with Washington journalist and author David
Wise, former FBI Assistant Director William Sullivan claimed that at
the time of FBI Director Hoover's death in May 1972 Assistant to the
Director John Mohr removed "very mysterious files" from Hoover's
office. These were "very sensitive and explosive files," Sullivan maintained; Attorney General Edward Levi did not locate them when he reviewed the 164 file cases which had constituted Hoover's Official and
Confidential file. Levi "didn't locate the gold," Sullivan averred—
although it is unclear whether the former FBI assistant director believed
that this "gold" had been filed in Hoover's Personal and Confidential file
and were then destroyed by Hoover's personal secretary Helen Grady in
May/June 1972 or still remained extant.[29]
Hoover had maintained two sets of confidential files in his office.
These files contained highly sensitive documents which were not to be
placed in the FBI's central files. One of these was Hoover's Personal and
Confidential file. The other, a "confidential" file "in which are kept
various and sundry items believed inadvisable to be included in the
general files of the Bureau," had been created in the 1920s. Then, in an
October 1, 1941, "Informative Memorandum—Not to be Sent to the
Files Section," Hoover advised other FBI officials of his decision to
create yet another "confidential file" to be maintained in the office of
FBI Assistant Director Louis Nichols. This file, Hoover reported, was
to "be restricted to items of a more or less personal nature of the Direc-

tor's and items which I might have occasion to call for from time to time such as memoranda to the Department of Justice on the Dies Committee, etc."[30]

Shortly after Hoover's death on May 2, 1972, however, Helen Gandy (Hoover's executive assistant) first reviewed in the FBI director's office (until May 12) and then in his home (until July) documents contained in Hoover's Personal and Confidential file. At this time, and pursuant to the deceased FBI director's earlier order, Gandy destroyed this file and the accompanying index cards. (Testifying in December 1975 before the House Subcommittee on Government Information and Individual Rights, Gandy claimed to have found no official policy documents during her review of Hoover's Personal and Confidential file.) On May 4, 1972, Hoover's Official and Confidential file was transferred to FBI Deputy Associate Director W. Mark Felt's office and eventually was incorporated in FBI central files. (When these files were inventoried, FBI officials discovered that three folders were missing. Listed on an October 1971 inventory, the folders were captioned with the names of three high-level FBI officials.)[31]

Hoover's October 1941 order may have resulted in the creation of at least three sets of confidential files. This did not mean that two of the confidential files contained "official" and the third "personal" documents (the implied testimony of Helen Gandy and other FBI officials to the contrary). When researching Hoover's Official and Confidential file, Mark Gitenstein, staff counsel for the Senate Select Committee on Intelligence Activities, discovered eight file cases that had originally been kept in Hoover's Personal and Confidential file. In October/November 1971 the file cases had been transferred, on Hoover's orders, to his Official and Confidential file. Sullivan's July 16, 1966, memorandum to DeLoach outlining the Do Not File procedure for break-ins was among the eight transferred files. This was undeniably an official policy document. The other transferred files were also official policy documents of varying degrees of political sensitivity. Because they recorded the biases and political activities of FBI officials, the public release of these documents could have compromised the FBI director and other FBI officials.[32]

One of these other transferred files was a November 20, 1953, cover memorandum captioned "Elizabeth Bentley" to which were appended twenty-eight glossy and color-coded charts. The charts detailed how FBI reports based on Bentley's November 1945 FBI interview had been distributed to Truman Administration officials in 1945 and 1946. FBI staff personnel had prepared these charts to supplement Hoover's November 17, 1953, testimony before the Senate Subcommittee on Internal Security, at which time the FBI director in essence had confirmed Attorney General Brownell's partisan condemnation of the Truman Administran's lax security procedures. In a speech in Chicago on November 6, 1953, Brownell had criticized the former president's failure to withdraw Harry Dexter White's nomination as a director of the International Monetary Fund after having received FBI reports questioning White's loyalty. The reports had been based on Bentley's unsupported charges. Truman's subsequent defense of his Administration's handling of the White nomination and condemnation of Brownell's resort to "McCarthyism" precipitated the joint congressional testimony of Brownell and Hoover. Apparently, Hoover had ordered FBI officials to compile the twenty-eight charts, intending to introduce them as visual exhibits to dramatize his November 17 testimony. The Elizabeth Bentley file might not have been as compromising to the Bureau's and FBI director's interests as the July 1966 memorandum describing the Do Not File procedure for break-ins. Nonetheless, because his testimony serviced a Republican administration's partisan interests, Hoover's second thoughts about releasing the glossy charts contributed to his decision to isolate this particular Bentley file from the FBI's central files.

If another of these seven folders had been publicly accessible, Hoover's Fred B. Black Personal and Confidential folder—consisting of three July 6, 1966 memoranda from FBI Assistant Director Cartha DeLoach to FBI Associate Director Clyde Tolson; a July 6, 1966, Hoover memorandum to Attorney General Nicholas Katzenbach; and a July 18, 1966 Hoover letter to all FBI special agents in charge—it could also have compromised the FBI director and high-level Bureau officials. The documents pertain to a brief the Department of Justice was then preparing in a federal criminal case, *Black v. United States*. Apprised when reviewing defendant Fred Black's appeal of conviction that the FBI had "bugged" Black's conversations, the Supreme Court ordered government attorneys to outline the legal authority for this microphone installation. In the course of responding to the court order, Attorney General Nicholas Katzenbach and Deputy Attorney General Ramsey Clark reviewed a draft brief submitted by FBI Director Hoover affirming that attorneys general since 1954 had authorized such FBI microphone surveillance. This FBI claim ran counter to Katzenbach's experiences.[33] Accordingly, the Attorney General consulted his predecessors Robert Kennedy, William Rogers, and Herbert Brownell, who all disputed the FBI contention. They had never authorized the use of microphones outside of the internal security area, Brownell and Rogers advised Katzenbach, and were completely unaware that the FBI had broken in to install any microphone. Thus briefed and acting on Katzenbach's behalf, Clark informed Hoover that when responding to the court's order the Department of Justice intended to state that the use of microphones had been a "departmental *practice* of long usage" and "the FBI consistently interpreted and understood our [the various attorneys general] decisions to apply to major crimes."

Prior to February 1952, FBI officials had not advised the attorney general of their unilateral decisions to authorize microphone surveillance, including those installed through break-ins. Having been briefed by FBI Director Hoover in October 1951 about FBI microphone surveillance policy, on February 26, 1952, Attorney General J. Howard McGrath informed Hoover that "I cannot authorize the installation of a microphone *involving a trespass* under existing law." McGrath had not prohibited this practice; he had nonetheless created a paper record of his conclusion that it was illegal.

Accordingly, the FBI did not totally cease use of this technique. On June 6, 1952, Hoover advised McGrath's successor, Attorney General James McGranery, that "we discontinued some of the microphone installations" instituted through break-ins. Apprised of the FBI's "limited" use of this technique in cases "which directly affected the internal security," McGranery (according to Hoover's memo on this meeting) concluded that such installations were proper and that "in such instances where [Hoover] felt that there was need to install microphones, even though trespass might be committed, that he would leave it to my judgement as to the steps to take."

McGrath's conclusion that an attorney general could not authorize illegal bugs, in any event, was effectively reversed in May 1954. At that time, Attorney General Herbert Brownell authorized FBI microphone installations, including those accomplished by means of break-ins. Although not Brownell's intent, FBI officials interpreted the Attorney General's directive as authorizing FBI break-ins to install microphones during criminal investigations. In addition, FBI officials did not seek the attorney general's prior authorization in each case of use. In late April 1954, for example, FBI agents in Chicago installed a microphone in Stanley Levison's hotel room on the authorization of FBI Assistant Director Alan Belmont. (Belmont briefed FBI Director Hoover of his decision on April 24, 1954.) And, whereas the FBI had installed a total of 738 microphones between 1960 and 1966, FBI officials notified the Justice Department and U.S. attorneys of only 158 of these installations. The FBI memoranda reporting these statistics do not clarify whether this notification (1) was after the fact (and then only when prosecution was pending); (2) made clear that the intercepted messages had been obtained from microphones and not wiretaps; or (3) was confined to those instances when microphones had been legally installed. The FBI had consistently been unwilling to brief Justice Department officials about its microphone surveillance practices, having concluded that "the Department lacks security, leaks confidential information to the press and has a propensity for going forward and advising the courts whenever they have knowledge of microphone coverage regardless of whether or not this coverage had any bearing on the case under consideration."

The FBI's independent practices constituted its immediate problem in light of the Justice Department's response to the Supreme Court's order in the Black case. Concerned over "the gravity of the issues presented by the Department's actions in the Black Case," FBI officials sought documentation "in connection with our continuing search for authorization for the Bureau's use of these devices." Among these efforts: (1) the Chicago and New York SACs wrote FBI Assistant Director James Gale that they had played tapes from microphone intercepts involving criminal investigations during meetings with Attorney General Robert Kennedy; (2) FBI Assistant Directors Gale and Cartha LeLoach interviewed Courtney Evans, the FBI's liaison with Attorney General

Kennedy, to establish that Evans had briefed Kennedy about FBI microphone uses; (3) DeLoach contacted former Republican Attorneys General Rogers and Brownell to neutralize their opposition to the FBI's claimed authority; and (4) DeLoach and Gale solicited Internal Revenue Service Commissioner Sheldon Cohen's support for the FBI's claim of authorization for microphone surveillances.

DeLoach's memoranda of July 6, 1966, recording these contacts were particularly sensitive. First, these memoranda indirectly confirm the FBI's inability to establish that attorneys general had directly authorized microphone surveillances. Second, the memoranda record DeLoach's attempt to exploit the partisan biases of former Republican Attorneys General Herbert Brownell and William Rogers. Briefing Tolson on his conversations with Rogers, DeLoach reported having told the former Republican attorney general that, "it was obvious that Katzenbach was attempting to state that FBI usage of microphones began with the Republicans and that Bobby Kennedy merely inherited the situation. [Rogers] stated he felt this was absolutely true and all the more reason why he and Brownell should not be brought into the matter." Rogers further assured DeLoach "that under no circumstances would [Rogers] or Brownell say anything that would injure the FBI in any manner." DeLoach concluded with this recommendation:

We are preparing . . . a memorandum to counterproposals which . . . the [FBI] Director [should] allow me to discuss with Deputy Attorney General Clark. In this memorandum we are suggesting that the brief merely cover the period of the Kennedy and Katzenbach Administrations and not go back beyond 1960. We are not retreating from the original premise that the FBI had authority to utilize microphones during the Rogers and Brownell administrations; however, in order to defeat Katzenbach's purpose of bringing the Republicans into this matter, we are making certain suggestions for the Director's consideration, which would adequately protect the FBI and at the same time point out that authority was definitely given by Kennedy and Katzenbach.[34]

When originally filing these documents in his Personal and Confidential file, Hoover intended to "protect the FBI." Why, then, in October/November 1971 did he transfer these and other documents to his Official and Confidential file? While this explanation is admittedly speculative, because at that later date the FBI director wanted to preserve a written record of his July 1966 written order prohibiting break-ins. Why, then, in July 1966 had Hoover formally prohibited the continued use of break-ins?

In 1965, the Subcommittee on Administrative Practice and Procedure of the Senate Committee on the Judiciary began investigative hearings into the Internal Revenue Service's invasions of privacy. In time, the Subcommittee's hearings broadened to include all federal investigative agencies (including the FBI). In detailed questionnaires to the agencies, the Subcommittee specifically requested information concerning their investigative techniques and filing systems. Fearing the adverse consequences should ongoing FBI practices be publicly disclosed, in 1965 and 1966 FBI Director Hoover abruptly ordered termination of FBI mail-opening programs, break-ins, and trash covers, and imposed numerical limits on the installation of wiretaps and microphones. In addition to the political risks that this Subcommittee inquiry posed, the Department of Justice's brief in the Black case publicly conceded that the FBI had been conducting break-ins to install microphones for a number of years without the attorney general's direct authorization. The same concerns which had led DeLoach to prepare the July 6, 1966, memorandum recording his efforts to "confirm" that FBI break-ins to install microphones had been responsive to orders also led Sullivan to prepare the July 16, 1966, informative memorandum describing how break-ins had been authorized since 1942 and outlining the Do Not File procedure. Upon receipt of this briefing memorandum, FBI Director Hoover had written on the bottom of its last page: "No more such techniques must be used."

We cannot presently resolve whether Hoover actually ordered the termination of break-ins in July 1966, or simply intended to create a paper record of his termination order. We do know that FBI agents continued to employ break-ins after 1966. Specifically, in August 1970, responding to President Nixon's demand that the FBI investigate alleged terrorist killings of New York policemen with "no punches pulled," Hoover telephoned Assistant to the FBI Director Sullivan to order use of "any practical means" during FBI investigations of the radical Weather Underground.

Hoover's verbal order had been relayed through a trusted aide. By early 1971, however, Sullivan's relations with Hoover had begun to deteriorate, almost reaching a breaking point by July 1971. Sullivan worsened an already tense relationship on August 28, 1971, by writing an extremely abrasive letter to Hoover criticizing the FBI director's policies and management. Hoover relieved Sullivan of his duties as FBI Assistant Director on September 30, 1971, an action prompting Sullivan to resign on October 6.

In the interim, Sullivan had briefed Assistant Attorney General Robert Mardian about the blackmail potential of the seventeen wiretap logs which Sullivan kept in his office. Mardian thereupon flew to San Clemente to inform the vacationing President Nixon about the problem. On his return to Washington, Mardian directed Sullivan to deliver the wiretap records to him. After retaining the records for a couple of days, Mardian gave them to White House aide John Ehrlichman for safekeeping. Hoover, however, did not learn about the absence of these "Sensitive Files" from Sullivan's office until sometime after Sullivan's October 6 resignation. He thereupon ordered an inquiry into their disposition. At first advised that the "Sensitive Files" had been destroyed, on November 1, 1971 Hoover learned from Attorney General John Mitchell that they had in fact been "sent to Mr. John Ehrlichman at the White House to be kept there." This was done, Mitchell reported, "in view of the fact that should any Congressional inquiry be made and a subpoena issued to the Department of Justice or the FBI, we would not have such files in our custody and the White House, under Executive Privilege, would be in a position to refuse availability to the files."[35]

Following Mitchell's revelation, the FBI director apparently became concerned about Sullivan's direct knowledge of his August 1970 verbal authorization of FBI break-ins during the investigation of the radical Weather Underground. Accordingly, Hoover reviewed his Personal and Confidential file later that month, concentrating on the B entry (in FBI parlance, break-ins were termed "black bag jobs"), and then had the July 16, 1966 memorandum transferred to his Official and Confidential file. In effect, Hoover preserved a paper record of his order to terminate break-ins—in the process, if not intentionally, preserving a record of the FBI's break-in practices and the Do Not File procedure. Significantly, an inventory of the folders which had comprised Hoover's Official and Confidential file was prepared in October 1971.

Because, in accordance with his order, Hoover's Personal and Confidential file was destroyed following his death in May 1972, we cannot ascertain whether this file contained other sensitive policy documents. According to FBI officials, Hoover had reviewed the A–C alphabetical entries of his Personal and Confidential file by the time of his death. No additional policy documents were uncovered by Helen Gandy during her post-mortem review of the remaining alphabetical entries. Did the first three alphabetical entries alone contain official documents, and were there only eight such folders in the A–C entries?

During December 1975 testimony before the House Subcommittee on Government Information and Individual Rights, Gandy and other FBI officials sought to allay suspicions that the remaining alphabetical entries of Hoover's Personal and Confidential file contained policy documents. Hoover's executive assistant since the 1930s, Gandy had physical control over the FBI director's Personal and Confidential and his Official and Confidential files (including, by her testimony, the responsibility for deciding to which of these confidential files to assign specific documents). Yet Gandy claimed not to know where Do Not File documents had been filed. Documents filed in the Personal and Confidential and in the Official and Confidential files, she nevertheless conceded, had neither been serialized nor recorded in the FBI central files. Former FBI Assistant Director John McDermott also professed ignorance as to where Do Not File documents had been filed. He admitted having discovered four volumes labeled Do Not File covering the 1942-1946 period in the FBI's Investigative Division but not a single Do Not File document for the post-1946 period. Hoover's Official and Confidential file might contain Do Not File documents,[36] McDermott conceded, but there were "no special files labeled 'Do not file.' " In his companion effort to refute any suspicions that Do Not File documents had been filed in Hoover's Personal and Confidential file, former Assistant to the Director John Mohr described how such documents were handled:

A thing that is marked "Do Not File" is returned normally to the dictator [of the document]. It is up to the dictator then to destroy that particular memorandum or to record thereon "File in the regular file." In other words, if after the thing has served its purpose and he determines that it ought to go to a regular file, and it's not material that may be destroyed, then he can designate it for a regular file. Otherwise, it's up to him to maintain it for a reasonable period of time and then destroy it. It is usually ninety days.[37]

Mohr's testimony inadvertently described the genius of the Do Not File system: FBI officials could transfer Do Not File memoranda to the central files whenever it was convenient or desirable to do so. However, Mohr's testimony, as that of Gandy and McDermott, was not fully accurate; namely, his contention that the decision to retain or destroy these documents was made within ninety days by the dictator of the memorandum. Some Do Not File memoranda "eventually [were to] be returned to the dictator to be destroyed or retained in the Director's Office." In the latter case, they were safeguarded in "personal" files—Sullivan's July 16,1966 memorandum in Hoover's Personal and Confidential file, field office break-in request and authorization documents in the New York and Chicago SACs Personal Folder, and numerous other Do Not File documents in FBI Assistant Director Louis Nichols's Official and Confidential file or FBI Associate Director Clyde Tolson's "personal file."

Gandy and McDermott, moreover, could have described the procedures employed to file break-in documents so that these documents could not be publicly compromised.[38] The FBI maintained a "June mail control file" and at least three files (66-2542, 66-1899, 66-8160) wherein documents pertaining to break-ins were filed (but not the documents obtained through a break-in—these were filed in the case file of the individual or organization). In 1977, Robert C. Shackelford, Section Chief of the FBI's Intelligence Division, destroyed another file containing break-in documents.[39] Nor were Gandy and McDermott alone when dissembling about break-in documents and filing procedures. In a September 23, 1975, response to the Senate Select Committee on Intelligence Activities, the FBI had also denied that FBI headquarters retained any break-in "file or document."[40]

The File on the Hiss Case

Included among the FBI's fifty-four thousand pages of documents on Alger Hiss were three memoranda written by FBI Director Hoover dated March 19, 20, and 21, 1946, bearing the notation, "This Memorandum is for Administrative Purposes—To Be Destroyed after Action is Taken and Not Sent to Files Section." Released in the 1970s, these Do Not File memoranda were discovered in the FBI's Administrative Inquiry file 62-116606-1. Because these documents contained this notation and were found in the 62 file, Allen Weinstein claims to have researched all of the FBI's Do Not File documents on Alger Hiss.[41]

Weinstein is wrong. Owing to their political sensitivity, Hoover's March 1946 memoranda had originally been prepared under the Do Not File procedure. They record the FBI director's recommendation to Attorney General Tom Clark of a strategy to force Alger Hiss's resignation or dismissal as director of the State Department's Office of Special Political Affairs: leak derogatory information about Hiss to conservative congressmen. Yet, the 62-116606 file does not contain any memoranda from the recipients of the FBI director's March 1946 memoranda— Clyde Tolson, Edward Tamm, D. Milton Ladd, and Hugh Clegg—reporting their actions on Hoover's briefing. In particular, this file contains no memoranda from Clegg, the FBI's congressional liaison who apparently hand-delivered the FBI's file on Hiss to Mississippi Senator James Eastland (in response to Eastland's telephoned request).

Hoover's March 1946 memoranda, moreover, had not originally been filed in the 62-116606 file. With the inception of HUAC's December 6-9, 1948, hearings. Hoover ordered Tolson, Ladd, and Nichols to compile a "carefully prepared and indexed overall" memorandum recording all reports on Hiss that the FBI had sent to the State Department. On December 10, 1948, FBI Assistant Director D. Milton Ladd forwarded the requested information to Hoover. Upon receipt of this memo, Hoover queried "Just where were these [Hoover's Do Not File memoranda of March 19, 20, and 21, 1946] found? They are not included in attached memo of Ladd's of December 10. I want a complete memo of the Hiss continuity prepared." Responding on December 13, 1948, Ladd advised Hoover that the March 19, 20, and 21 memoranda had been "located in Mr. Tolson's personal file in his office by [FBI Assistant Director Louis] Nichols."[42] Thereupon Hoover ordered: "I think the pink [Do Not File memos] or whites [a reference to Ladd's March 20, 1946 memoranda cited in footnote 41] attached should go into the regular files." On December 28, 1948, Ladd advised Hoover that the "pink and white memos have been included in the regular files in this matter." The pink and white memoranda were transferred to the 62-116606 file on January 5, 1949.[43] Thus, as Mohr later testified, Do Not File memoranda could subsequently be incorporated (not necessarily within ninety days) in the "regular files;" in this instance, Hiss's December 15, 1948 indictment meant that the March 1946 memoranda were no longer politically sensitive and the FBI director had reason to preserve a record of his earlier strategy to effect Hiss's dismissal. The existence of these memoranda in the 1970s was thus a happenstance result of Hoover's political decision of December 1948.

When released, moreover, the 62-116606 file on Alger Hiss contained eleven separate documents (ten FBI memos plus a copy of Attorney General Herbert Brownell's November 6, 1953 speech). The ten FBI documents were dated: October 8, 11, 1945; March 19, 1946; March 20, 1946 (three); March 21, 1946; an undated routing slip (probably December 1948); and June 21, and 26, 1956. Despite this chronological variance, all documents bear the same serial number, 62-116606-1. Because they were not numbered consecutively (as the normal case for documents filed in the FBI's central files), it is impossible to ascertain whether or not there had been still other FBI documents involving Hiss which had also at one time been filed in the 62-116606 file.[44]

Were, then, sensitive Do Not File documents filed in the personal files of FBI officials? There is an apparent pattern, confirmed by the fact that (1) Hoover's March 1946 memoranda had been located in "Tolson's personal file"; (2) Sullivan's July 1966 memorandum, clearly an official policy document, had originally been filed in Hoover's Personal and Confidential file; (3) Hoover had prepared a memorandum for his Personal Files reporting his June 1, 1971, briefing of Attiorney General John Mitchell on derogatory information contained in FBI files on a member of Congress;[45] (4) the New York and Chicago SACs had filed break-in request and authorization memoranda in their Personal Folders, and (5) photocopies of correspondence obtained through a break-in, the Do Not File memorandum pertaining to this break-in, and numerous other politically sensitive reports were filed in the unserialized Official and Confidential file which FBI Assistant Director Louis Nichols maintained in his office.[46] Still other released FBI memoranda involving the Alger Hiss case raise the possibility that additional sensitive documents have been destroyed or have not yet been released. As in the case of the March 1946 Hoover memoranda, we learned of this destruction only through happenstance.

Thus, in an October 13, 1949, memorandum, FBI Director Hoover called the Boston SAC's attention to a sentence in FBI agent Francis O'Brien's August 24, 1949 investigative report. This sentence, Hoover wrote, was not in compliance with Bureau Bulletin No. 34 requiring that FBI agents include on their report's administrative pages "facts and information which are considered of a nature not expedient to disseminate or would cause embarrassment to the Bureau, if distributed." The FBI director then insisted, "In view of the above, page 4 of the aforementioned report has been rewritten and copies thereof are being furnished to the offices receiving this letter. In addition, the objectionable sentence afore-mentioned has been placed on page 10A which is also being enclosed herewith." Hoover's memorandum formally chastizing O'Brien, and his Boston supervisor, for failing to comply with Bureau Bulletin No. 34 thereby disclosed the FBI director's earlier authorization of this separate filing procedure. The release of the October 1949 Hoover memorandum alone publicly compromised Bureau Bulletin No. 34.[47]

Released FBI files on the Hiss case, more importantly, do not fully recount the nature and scope of the Bureau's relationship with HUAC and Congressman Richard Nixon during 1948. Our knowledge of the incompleteness of released FBI files once again was gained fortuitously from references in other released FBI reports or the admissions of participants John Cronin and Richard Nixon.

For example, during an interview with Garry Wills, Father John Cronin admitted that "Ed Hummer was one of the FBI agents I had worked with [since 1945]. He could have got in serious trouble for what he did [in 1948], since the Justice Department was sitting on the results of the Bureau's investigation into Hiss—the car, the typewriter, etc. But Ed would call me every day, and tell me what they had turned up; and I told Dick [Nixon], who then knew just where to look for things and what he would find." In his memoirs Nixon obliquely confirms the FBI/HUAC relationship: "Because of Truman's executive order [of March 13, 1948] we [HUAC] were not able to get any direct help from J. Edgar Hoover or the FBI. However, we had some informal contacts with a lower-level agent that proved helpful in our investigations.[48]

The Cronin interviews and Nixon's account confirm that, dating at least from August 1948, FBI agents leaked information about Hiss to then-Congressman Nixon. Nixon was also assisted by FBI Assistant Director Louis Nichols. Thus, a December 9, 1948, FBI memorandum reports Nixon's "voluntary" assertion to several former FBI agents "that he had worked very close with the Bureau and with Nichols during this past year on this [the Hiss] matter."[49]

Despite this corroboration of a close FBI/HUAC relationship during 1948, with the exception of FBI memoranda of August 2 and 18, 1948, and September 2, 1948 (recording perfunctory FBI contacts with HUAC members), FBI documents released to date do not recount its nature and extent.[50] We cannot presently ascertain whether documents recording this relationship have been destroyed or remain extant. Our recent knowledge of at least one instance wherein the FBI destroyed documents pertaining to the Hiss case, and of the destruction of FBI documents pertaining to the ongoing trial of former FBI officials Gray, Felt, and Miller, strongly suggest that the FBI's most sensitive records have been destroyed.

Having sued to secure the release of FBI files on the Alger Hiss case, researcher Stephen Salant learned that in 1958 the FBI had destroyed a December 5, 1950, letter from Whittaker Chambers to Henry Julian Wadleigh and an accompanying check made out by Chambers to Wadleigh. The destruction of this letter and check is not without significance, since these documents raise questions about why Chambers wrote and sent Wadleigh a check in December 1950.[51] (Because these materials were not prepared under a Do Not File procedure, FBI officials had been obliged to compile an inventory listing the destruction of the Chambers letter and check along with other less sensitive court exhibit documents.) In addition to revealing another instance of the FBI's destruction of documents, Salant's suit illustrates the current knowledge about past separate filing procedures possessed by lower level FBI officials handling FOIA requests.

Responding on January 9, 1978, to Salant's interrogatories, FBI agent

Martin Wood (a supervisor in the FBI's Management Division responsible for processing FOIA requests) affirmed that all the FBI's Hiss files had been released or were being processed for release excepting two instances: "Four (sub) files of a main file in New York were destroyed;" and "a main file in one of the field offices was 'stripped,' that is, *duplicate copies only* of documents were destroyed." (Emphasis added.) Asked whether the FBI maintained "separate" files on Chambers and Wadleigh, Wood evasively stated that files on Chambers and Wadleigh "do exist." Whenever responding to questions about FBI files or documents on particular individuals, Wood consistently qualified his denial either by asserting that there was no record in "our central indices" or that all documents had been released which were "retrievable through a search of our central indices."

Wood responded less confidently during his April 28, 1978, deposition. The FBI supervisor reaffirmed that all FBI documents pertaining to the Hiss case which were retrievable through "our central indices" had been or were to be released. The insistent questioning of David Levitt, Salant's counsel, forced Wood to clarify these assertions. Queried about FBI separate filing systems and procedures as described in some detail in my October 22, 1977, *Nation* article, Wood admitted ignorance of these procedures. Such Do Not File documents were not indexed in the central files, Wood conceded. He did not know where these files were kept and whether all such files had been released or still existed. Wood also admitted that "all of the bulky exhibits concerning the Hiss case were destroyed on January 17, 1974, by authorization of Chicago supervisor James W. Fox." Significantly, this record destruction occurred while Allen Weinstein's FOIA suit, initiated in November 1972, was pending, and during the period when Congress was in the process of amending the FOIA. This disclosure directly contradicted the Department of Justice's written assurances that, "since receipt of FOIA requests for records relating to the Hiss case, and the advent of litigation regarding such requests, no records destruction has taken place."[52]

The recent trial of former FBI officials L. Patrick Gray, W. Mark Felt, and Edward Miller further revealed that whenever extremely sensitive investigative programs were initiatiated the FBI routinely instituted separate filing and record destruction procedures.

Owing to their direct knowledge of FBI filing procedures, and the relationship of the FBI's investigative activities to the policies of the Nixon Administration, Gray, Felt, and Miller could and did submit a series of discovery motions. These motions, and in turn the Government's responses, highlight the extent of the Bureau's intentionally incomplete record-retention practices. FBI documents released to Miller's attorneys disclose that during the early 1970s several FBI assistant directors had concluded that a discussion of "investigative techniques ranging from clearly legal to illegal, should not be disseminated to the Department of Justice in writing, but should be discussed orally on a need-to-know basis only, with a responsible official of the Attorney General's staff." The Government's responses to other defense motions suggest that sensitive documents were frequently destroyed: at least one White House memorandum was missing, and fifteen hundred–plus FBI documents were destroyed by an FBI official after they had been returned by the Department of Justice to the Bureau. During a November 30, 1978, trial hearing, Robert C. Shackelford, the retired FBI section chief who destroyed these documents (and himself a possible target of this Department of Justice investigation), admitted destroying these documents allegedly because of the need to protect sensitive information. "The section I headed was being broken up and no one was occupying my office," Shackelford claimed. "A lot of the material was highly classified and very frankly that was my major concern."[53]

Can, then, the researcher seeking the files of federal intelligence agencies on controversial Cold War internal security cases expect to receive a full record of FBI, CIA, and NSA documents? The bulk of these agencies' files on these cases can be obtained through the FOIA. Because of these agencies' past record-keeping procedures, researchers should be extremely wary before accepting assurances that all files have been released. The possibility remains that the most sensitive FBI, CIA, or NSA documents either have been destroyed or, if extant, are not retrievable through a name search of the agency's "central indices." For this reason the most troubling questions about these cases may never be resolved.

Notes

1. In *The Price of Vigilance*, Joan Jensen recounts how, during the 1960s, FBI officials successfully pressured the National Archives to withdraw those FBI documents and copies of FBI documents pertaining to the Bureau's surveillance activities of the World War I period that were in already accessible Department of Justice and American Protective League files. Jensen's experience succinctly captures the research problem of access confronting historians of federal surveillance policy. See Joan Jensen, *The Price of Vigilance* (Chicago: Rand McNally, 1968), p. 314. See also Melvyn Dubofsky, *We Shall Be All* (Chicago: Quadrangle, 1969), p. 539; Sanford Ungar, *FBI* (Boston: Atlantic Monthly Press/Little, Brown, 1976), pp. 373–75, 383–86, 571; Paul Blackstock, *Agents of Deceit* (Chicago: Quadrangle, 1966), pp. 96–97; and Joan Jensen, "Military Surveillance in Two World Wars: Watching the Workers" (paper given at an April 10, 1980 session of the Organization of American Historians; San Francisco, California, copy in author's possession), p. 26.

2. First Amended Complaint for Declaratory, Injunctive and Mandamus Relief, John Shattuck and Melvin Wulf (ACLU attorneys for Allen Weinstein), Dec. 4, 1974, and accompanying exhibits, *Weinstein v. Saxbe*, Ca 2278-72. Plaintiff's Memorandum of Law in Support of Motion for Summary Judgment and *in camera* Review, John Shattuck, Melvin Wulf, and Hope Eastman (ACLU attorneys for Weinstein), May 15, 1975, *Weinstein v. Levi*, Ca 2278-72. Athan Theoharis, "Classification Restrictions and the Public's Right to Know: A New Look at the Alger Hiss Case," *Intellect* (Sept.-Oct. 1975), p. 89. *New York Times*, Nov. 12, 1973, p. 30; Jan. 28, 1974, p. 45; Oct. 27, 1974, p. 8E; Feb. 16, 1975, p. 16E; Feb. 1, 1976, p. 9E. *Milwaukee Journal*, Nov. 12, 1973; Nov. 13, 1973, p. 3; March 30, 1975, p. 3; June 26, 1975, p. 6; Sept. 4, 1975, p. 11; Sept. 12, 1973, p. 28; Feb. 19, 1976, Accent p. 12. *St. Louis Post-Dispatch*, Aug. 17, 1975, p. 19A. Allen Weinstein, "Open Season on 'Open Government,' " *New York Times Magazine* (June 10, 1979), p. 74. Because executive orders 11652 and 12065 required federal agencies to review and declassify nonsensitive documents over thirty years old, the National Archives finally accessioned FBI records pertaining to the Bureau's formative years, 1908 through 1924. See also, John Scott, "The Freedom of Information Act: Its Significance for the History Teacher," *The History Teacher* (November 1980), pp. 73–85.

3. The Act required agency and department heads to "make and preserve records containing adequate and proper documentation of the organization, functioning, decisions, procedures, and essential transactions of the agency, and

to furnish the information necessary to protect the legal and financial rights of the Government and of persons directly affected by the agency's activities." Reiterating these requirements, the Code detailed how compliance was to be ensured. The relevant sections of the Act and Code are quoted in *Final Report of the National Study Commission on Records and Documents of Federal Officials* (Washington: GPO, 1977), pp. 17, 82–84.

4. I have discussed these procedures and the problems they pose for scholars who research FBI files in "Bureaucrats above the Law: Double-Entry Intelligence Files," *Nation* (Oct. 22, 1977), pp. 393–97; "Abuse of Power: What the New Hiss Suit Uncovers," *Nation* (Oct. 7, 1978), pp. 336–40; and "The FBI and the FOIA: Exempting Files," *First Principles* (Sept./Oct. 1981), pp. 1, 5–8. See also, John Rosenberg, "The FBI Shreds Its Files: Catch in the Information Act," *Nation* (Feb. 4, 1978), pp. 108–11, and "Follow-Up: The F.B.I.'s Field Files," *Nation* (March 3, 1979), pp. 231–32. *AFSC*, p. 201.

5. Hoover's order did not mean that the maintenance of separate files began in 1940. Dating at least from the 1920s, the FBI maintained separate files for specified documents. In 1929, FBI Director Hoover directed that file room officials "maintain a separate and distinct" file for the names of confidential informants whose names "must not be placed in the regular investigative files." In addition, in 1916 the Bureau created a separate filing system for case files concerning investigations of enemy aliens and other World War I matters. Index cards, for example, on the Industrial Workers of the World, National Association for the Advancement of Colored People, Harry Weinberger, and Eamon DeValera—who were subjects of this investigative program—cite documents bearing the notation "confidential files." The FBI apparently maintained discrete "confidential files" as late as the 1970s. In a Nov. 12, 1971, memorandum to FBI Deputy Associate Director W. Mark Felt, Hoover wrote that he was returning Felt's Nov. 2, 1971 memorandum "in order for it to be placed in the Confidential Files." The National Archives has not been able to locate this Confidential File. W. Mark Felt, *The FBI Pyramid from the Inside* (New York: Putnam's, 1979), p. 144. National Archives and Records Service, "Appraisal of the Records of the Federal Bureau of Investigation," Nov. 9, 1981, Volume One, p. 2–1; Volume Two, 134 Security Informants and Appendix F Special Studies.

6. In February 1950, FBI Director Hoover ordered the termination of use of these pink memoranda—nonetheless, FBI officials continued to resort to Do Not File procedures for sensitive documents and to maintain separate "personal" files in their offices. National Archives and Records Service, "Appraisal of the Records of the Federal Bureau of Investigation," Nov. 9, 1981, Volume One, pp. 2–5. Memorandum, Executives Conference to Tolson, March 10, 1953, and

Memorandum, Hoover to Tolson *et al.*, March 19, 1953, both in 66-2095-100; Memorandum, J. J. McDermott to Jenkins, June 11, 1975, FBI 66-17404-94.

7. This instruction, specified in Part II, Section 2–4.2.1 of the FBI Manual "regarding surveillance files," apparently was intended to insure that FBI field offices maintained separate files for sensitive wiretap and microphone documents—as they were required to do for the "names of confidential informants." The ADM reference, an abbreviation for Administrative Matters, file classification 66 in the FBI's records system, conceivably provided the basis for the "Do Not File" notation: "This is for Administrative Purposes . . . ." *HIDFBI*, pp. 96–99, 103–4, 116–18, 123–46, 154–70, 173. *AFSC*, p. 175. Blind memo, fml, Sept. 23, 1958, Morris Ernst folder, *LN*.

8. In 1975, FBI officials in testimony before and in memoranda to the Senate Select Committee on Intelligence Activities confirmed that Sullivan's 1966 memorandum accurately described how break-ins had been authorized and monitored since 1942. Former FBI Assistant Director Charles Brennan conceded the record-destruction advantages of the "Do Not File" procedure: because not serialized like other FBI documents, break-in documents could be safely destroyed without this becoming known. *HIA*, Vol. 2, The Huston Plan, pp. 97–99, 129–31, 273–80. *HIA*, Vol. 6 Federal Bureau of Investigation, pp. 12–14, 352–59. *SDSR*, pp. 355–71. *HIVC*, pp. 26–27, 29–31. *New York Times*, Aug. 9, 1973. *Washington Post*, June 7, 1981, p. A6. Letter, Charles Dollar to Athan Theoharis, Dec. 11, 1981, and telephone conversation, Athan Theoharis and Charles Dollar, Dec. 10, 1981. Memo, J. J. McDermott to Jenkins, June 11, 1975, FBI 66-17404-94. Memos, Executive Conference to Tolson, March 10, 1953 and Hoover to Tolson *et al.*, March 19, 1953, FBI 66-2095-100. Memo, Legal Counsel to FBI Director, Aug. 15, 1973 and Addendum, Intelligence Division, Aug. 17, 1973; Memo, Legal Counsel to FBI Director, Aug. 23, 1973; Memo, FBI Director to All SACs, Aug. 23, 1973; Memo, FBI Director to Attorney General, Aug. 25, 1973; Memo 35-73, Aug. 28, 1973; Memo, Legal Counsel to FBI Director, Dec. 7, 1973; Memo 55-73, Dec. 4, 1973; all in FBI 66-19022. U.S., House, Committee on the Judiciary, *Hearings on White House Surveillance Activities and Campaign Activities*, 93d Cong., 2d sess., 1974, pp. 1437–40. Letters, SAC Albany to FBI Director, February 14, 1944, FBI 100-1262 and reply February 29, 1944, FBI 100-25869-84, *ALP*. Memo, Proposed Change in Manual for Field Stenographer, Oct. 12, 1955, FBI 66-1934-7393 and Memo, H. B. Fletcher to Tamm, Dec. 10, 1957, FBI 66-2435-2052. FBI officials employed blind memoranda whenever reporting information obtained through microphone surveillance or when revising microphone surveillance policy. Microphone Surveillance folder,

Synopsis of Hoover's O&C Files, *O&C*. Blind memoranda were used, for example, to furnish information to HUAC counsel during the 1960s, FBI officials being directed to employ "terminology . . . such that the memorandum cannot be identified as a Bureau document." Airtel, FBI Director to SAC New York, Nov. 12, 1969, FBI 100-358086-34-75.

9. Frank Donner, "Electronic Surveillance: The National Security Game," *Civil Liberties Review* 2 (Summer 1975): 21–23. Victor Navasky and Nathan Lewin, "Electronic Surveillance" and Thomas Emerson, "The FBI as a Political Police" in *Investigating the FBI*, Pat Watters and Stephen Gillers eds. (Garden City: Doubleday, 1973), pp. 241, 243, 245, 322. *New York Times*, June 2, 1949, p. 3; June 3, 1949, p. 2; June 4, 1949, p. 2; June 8, 1949, p. 1; June 9, 1949, p. 1; June 10, 1949, p. 10; June 11, 1949, p. 6; June 12, 1949, p. 1; June 16, 1949, p. 15. Bureau Bulletin No. 34, Series 1949, July 8, 1949.

10. *SDSR*, pp. 562, 628, 632, 658–59, 675–76. SAC Letter No. 69, June 29, 1949, FBI 66-1372-1; Memo, Tolson to FBI Director, Dec. 7, 1949, FBI 66-8160-1579x; Memo, W. A. Branigan to A. H. Belmont, May 28, 1954, FBI 66-1372-11; Memo, SAC New York to FBI Director, Aug. 3, 1954, FBI 62-10026A; and Memo, W. R. Wannall to W. C. Sullivan, Jan. 17, 1969, FBI 66-1372-49. For further testimony on how these sensitive records were handled, see Deposition, Robert Scherrer (Unit Chief, Records Management Division, FBI) March 14, 1980, *ACLU et al. v. City of Chicago et al.*, Ca 75-C-3295, pp. 11, 12–39, 42–44, 51–52.

11. *SDSR*, pp. 304–6, 343–44. Memos, Nichols to Tolson, April 14, 16, and 21, 1953, Joseph Bryan III folder, *LN*; Telephone interview, Joseph Bryan III, July 18, 1981. David Wise, *The American Police State* (New York: Random House, 1976), p. 76; Frank Donner, *The Age of Surveillance: The Aims and Methods of America's Political Intelligence System* (New York: Knopf, 1980), p. 116; Christy Macy and Susan Kaplan, eds., *Documents* (New York: Penguin, 1980), pp. 203–4. Memos, Chicago SAC to FBI Director, Sept. 12, 1961, FBI 100-32864-1005; Oct. 5, 1962, FBI 100-32864-1263; and Nov. 7, 1963, FBI 100-32864-1722; discovered in FBI files of one or more of the plaintiffs in *Alliance to End Repression et al. v. James Rochford et al.*, Ca 74-C-3268. I thank Kenneth O'Reilly for calling these memos to my attention. On May 4, 1979, I wrote archivist James Rhoads to urge that before the National Archives's Records Disposition Division agrees to any FBI field office and headquarters files record destruction plans, it first become fully apprised of the FBI's separate filing and record destruction procedures. I submitted these memos of 1961–63 as examples. The National Archives referred my letter to the FBI. On June 15, 1979, FBI Director William Webster responded that copies of these documents

were in the FBI's "Central Records System" in Washington, adding: "Instructions for destruction of the letters were contained in the field office copies and were based on the fact that these letters were strictly informational, without continuing value, and *for security reasons*, should be restricted to only those personnel directly involved in that program [emphasis added]." Letters, Athan Theoharis to James Rhoads, May 4, 1979; Jean Fraley to James Awe (copy to Athan Theoharis), May 15, 1979; William Webster to Athan Theoharis, June 15, 1979.

12. *HIA*, Vol. 6, Federal Bureau of Investigation, pp. 164–65, 193, 195–96, 251–53, 483–84. *IARA*, pp. 120, 228, 228 n11. *SDSR*, pp. 314–15.

13. Athan Theoharis, *Spying on Americans: Political Surveillance from Hoover to the Huston Plan* (Philadelphia: Temple U. Press, 1978), pp. 40–42. Letters [name deleted] to FBI Director, May 30, 1941, and reply, June 21, 1941; Memo [name deleted] to Hoover, July 21, 1941; Memo, Hoover to McGuire, July 28, 1941; Letter, McGuire to Hoover, August 7, 1941, all in *VM*. (I thank Kenneth Waltzer for sharing his research.) Athan Theoharis, "The Problem of Purging FBI Files," *USA Today* (Nov. 1978), p. 50.

14. Theoharis, *Spying on Americans*, pp. 43–44.

15. Theoharis, *Spying on Americans*, pp. 44–48. *SDSR*, p. 443. Memo [name deleted] to FBI Director, Jan. 10, 1952, Security Index Files, J. Edgar Hoover Building.

16. The 62 file was also employed to isolate sensitive documents in field office files. In 1948, the heads of FBI field offices were directed to use the "62 classification" for "confidential data or information which pertains to no particular file or case and which due to its nature should be retained under the exclusive control of the Special Agent in Charge, such as information coming to the attention of the office relating to public officials or individuals with whom the Bureau has official business contacts and concerning whom no investigation is contemplated." National Archives and Records Service, "Appraisal of the Records of the Federal Bureau of Investigation," Nov. 9, 1981, Volume Two, 62 Miscellaneous Subversive.

17. On January 24, 1978, FBI official M. S. Ramsey recommended discontinuance of the "June mail" procedure "in today's environment, with compartmented intelligence classifications and the overall attention given to handling sensitive data as well as FOIPA [Freedom of Information-Privacy Acts] considerations." Memo, M. S. Ramsey to Bassett, Jan. 24, 1978, FBI 66-1372-52; see also, Memo, R. J. Gray to W. O. Cregar, June 27, 1978, FBI 66-1372-53.

18. Memo, Special Agent F. X. Plant, Feb. 21, 1949, FBI 65-14920; Memo [name deleted] to FBI Director, Jan. 31, 1948, FBI 66-2542-8-6; Memo, Miami

Field Office to FBI Director, Jan. 7, 1944, FBI 66-2542-3-29-294; Memo, W. A. Branigan to A. H. Belmont, Sept. 14, 1953, FBI 5549, all in *AH*. Memo, Special Agent William Ryan to SAC Chicago, July 31, 1950, FBI 100-3466-66, *NLG*. Motion, Alan Baron *et al.* (counsel for L. Patrick Gray), May 22, 1978, *United States v. Gray, Felt, and Miller*, Cr 78-00179, pp. 4, 13. *HFBIO*, pp. 8–11. *AFSC*, p. 183. See also, Synopsis of Hoover's O and C Files, Feb. 16, 1975, *O&C*. U. S., Senate, Committee on the Judiciary, Subcommittee on Administrative Practice and Procedure, *Hearings on FBI Statutory Charter*, P. 2, 95th Cong., 1st sess., 1978, pp. 212–13. "June mail" documents were filed in FBI 66-1372. Memo, Webster to All SACs, Oct. 18, 1978, FBI 66-04-4241x8 and Memorandum 52-78, FBI Director William Webster, Nov. 7, 1978, FBI 66-04-4241x. Employing the Freedom of Information Act, I have received Nichols's unserialized Official and Confidential file. FBI memos describing the "blank," "blind," and "letterhead" memoranda procedures are Memo, Proposed Change in Manual for Field Stenographers, Oct. 12, 1955, FBI 66-1934-7393, and Memo, H. B. Fletcher to Tamm, Dec. 10, 1957, FBI 66-2435-2052. The referenced FBI memo discussing the FBI's strategy to circumvent the FOIA is A. J. Decter to Jenkins, June 7, 1976, FBI 66-3286-1197x. *HIA*, Vol. 2, Huston Plan, pp. 278–80. Memo, J. H. Gale to DeLoach, Dec. 29, 1965, folder 114, *O&C*. Deposition, Robert Scherrer (Unit Chief, Records Management Division, FBI), March 14, 1980, *ACLU et al. v. City of Chicago et al.*, CA 75-C-3295, pp. 74–75. *Washington Post*, June 7, 1981, p. A6. Letter, Wesley Swearingen to Michael Shaheen, Nov. 16, 1978. Memos, re: Surreptitious Entries to Assistant Attorney General, Civil Rights Division, Dec. 1, 1975 FBI 66-8160-3790, and March 22, 1976 FBI 66-8160-3833. The FBI's break-in index is cited in Report, FBI Director William Webster to Attorney General Benjamin Civiletti, Feb. 19, 1980, pp. 3–6, 8–16, 18–25, A5; see particularly pp. 22, 25, and A5. See also James Reynolds and Daniel Freedman, "Summary of [Justice Department] Inquiry into the Nondisclosure of FBI Bag Jobs in the Socialist Workers Party Civil Litigation," June 25, 1980, pp. 9, 11, 15, 16, 32. Letters, James Hall to Athan Theoharis, May 7 and 29, 1981.

19. Memo, Hoover to Tolson, Tamm, Ladd, and Clegg, March 19, 1946, FBI 62-116606-1, *AH*. Interview, Kenneth O'Reilly with Robert McCaughey (administrative assistant to Karl Mundt), Madison, South Dakota, Feb. 28, 1979. I thank O'Reilly for sharing this revealing interview. During his research into the Mundt Papers, O'Reilly had reviewed a number of Mundt to Hoover letters requesting FBI files of identified individuals and Hoover's written letters of denial. In a later interview with McCaughey, O'Reilly asked about Mundt's apparently obtuse persistence. Mundt was not stupid, McCaughey responded,

and then described this covert practice. Willing to cooperate with favored individuals by leaking information from FBI files, FBI officials purposefully created a paper record of denial to camouflage their action. See also Letters, Bishop G. Bromley Oxnam to FBI Assistant Director Louis Nichols, March 10, 1949, Feb. 16, 1950, Oct. 14, 1955; Letter, Nichols to Oxnam, Oct. 19, 1955; Memo, G.B.O. [G. Bromley Oxnam], Oct. 20, 1955, all in G. Bromley Oxnam Papers, Manuscript Division, Library of Congress, Washington, D.C.

20. Athan Theoharis, "Abuse of Power: What the New Hiss Suit Uncovers," pp. 336–37. Allen Weinstein, *Perjury: The Hiss Chambers Case* (New York: Knopf, 1978), pp. 301, 304, 585. Memo, D. E. Shannon, Dec. 29, 1948, FBI 65-14920-537; Memo, W. W. Corcoran, June 1, 1949, FBI 65-14920-4072; Memo, T. G. Spencer, June 8, 1949, FBI 65-14920-3606; Memo, D. E. Shannon, June 13, 1949, FBI 65-14920-6617; Memo, W. W. Corcoran, June 14, 1949, FBI 65-14920-4023; Memo, T. G. Spencer, Sept. 22, 1949, FBI 65-14920-4379, all in *AH*.

21. *HIA*, Vol. 5, National Security Agency and Fourth Amendment Rights, pp. 7–24, 31–33, 145–63. *SDSR*, pp. 736–64, 781–82.

22. *SDSR*, pp. 767, 769. *HIVC*, pp. 209–10, 323–24.

23. *HIA*, Vol. 1, Unauthorized Storage of Toxic Agents, pp. 6, 11, 21–23, 245. *FMI*, pp. 390, 394, 402–06, 408, 408 n90. *AAP*, pp. 54, 61, 162, 165. John Stockwell, *In Search of Enemies: A CIA Story* (New York: Norton, 1978), pp. 46, 160n, 168–69, 228n, 273. *Milwaukee Journal*, July 16, 1977, pp. 1, 3; July 21, 1977, p. 2; Jan. 7, 1979, Accent 2; Jan. 9, 1979, Accent p. 5. U.S., Senate, Select Committee on Intelligence and Committee on Human Resources, Subcommittee on Health and Scientific Research, *Joint Hearings on Project MKULTRA, the CIA's Program of Research in Behavorial Modification*, 95th Cong., 1st sess., 1977, pp. 2–5, 8–10, 14–15, 21–23, 25, 38, 45–55, 65 n2, 65–66, 70–71, 74, 82–88, 84 n75, 84 n76, 84 n77, 88 n90, 103–107, 134, 137. U.S., Senate, Committee on the Judiciary, Subcommittee on Administrative Practice and Procedure, *Hearings on Oversight of the Freedom of Information Act*, 95th Cong., 1st sess., 1977, p. 68; see also pp. 73–85, 93, 525–32. Deputy CIA Director Frank Carlucci further amplified Blake's testimony about the CIA's "compartmentalized" files. U.S., House, Committee on Government Operations, Subcommittee on Government Information and Individual Rights, *Hearings on the Freedom of Information Act: Central Intelligence Agency Exemptions*, 96th Cong., 2d sess., 1980, pp. 28–30, 62, 67. See also the recent testimony of Deputy CIA Director Bobby Inman in U.S. Senate, Select Committee on Intelligence, *Hearings on Intelligence Reform Act of 1981*, 97th Cong., 1st sess., 1981, pp. 13–14. Macy and Kaplan, *Documents*, pp. 213–15, 223.

Brief for the Use of the (FBI) Director in Appearance before the Presidential Board to Review Periodically U.S. Foreign Intelligence Activities, pp. 15–16, 18, Jan. 20, 1956, folder # 149, O&C. Director of Central Intelligence Directive No. 117, Feb. 21, 1962, Center of National Security Studies Library. See also, Director of Central Intelligence Directive No. 11/2, Allen Dulles, Nov. 15, 1954, Center for National Security Studies Library, Washington, D.C.

24. *SDSR*, pp. 458 n336, 464. May 13, 1954 Entry, James Hagerty Papers-Diary Entries, May 1954, Dwight Eisenhower Library, Abilene, Kansas.

25. *SDSRFMI*, pp. 138–141, 199 n106a, 141 n108. See *AAP*, pp. 55–60, 56 n2.

26. *Report of the Department of Justice Concerning Its Investigation and Prosecutorial Decisions with Respect to Central Intelligence Agency Mail Opening Activities in the United States* (Jan. 14, 1977), pp. 11–12, 471. *FMI*, pp. 45–46, 51–52, 54–56, 59, 60, 86, 107, 112, 283, 294, 309–10, 360, 385 n2, 386–391, 394, 398–99, 401, 403–8, 404 n77, 406 n83, 409–11, 410 n95, 418–19, 421, 423, 427, 428, 440, 447, 459–60, 471–74, 475 n1, 480–81, 483 n34, 499 n100. *AAP*, pp. 3, 6–7, 10–12, 25–26, 33, 44–45, 53, 55–64, 67–70, 93, 95–96, 98–108, 114–35, 148–80, 182–88, 246–54, 261–79. *SDSR*, pp. 596, 599, 623, 689, 743 n27, 745 n33, 746, 761, 762, 768–70, 783, 800–9, 808 n148, 811, 813. *SDSRFMI*, pp. 28, 30, 35, 46, 50–51, 70–71, 128–31, 128 n134, 129 n144, 132–33. Seymour Hersh, "The Angleton Story," *New York Times Magazine* (June 25, 1978), p. 15.

27. Commission on CIA Activities Within the United States, *Report to the President* (Washington: GPO, 1975), pp. 203–4. Wise, *American Police State*, pp. 253–57. *HIA*, Vol. 1, Unauthorized Storage of Toxic Agents pp. 21–23, 245. *FMI*, p. 404 n76.

28. *HIA*, Vol. 2, Huston Plan, pp. 218, 223; *IARA*, p. 147 n43; *SDSR*, pp. 545, 777–78, 940, 945, 955–60; *AAP*, pp. 3, 136 n1, 182–84, 237–38. Nelson Blackstock, *COINTELPRO: The FBI's Secret War on Political Freedom* (New York: Vintage, 1976), pp. ix, 204–11. Affirmation, Marshall Perlin, July 26, 1979 *American Friends Services Committee et al. v. William H. Webster, et al.* Ca 79-1655, pp. 10–11. Theoharis, "The Problem of Purging FBI Files," p. 48; John Rosenberg, "The FBI Would Shred Its Past," *Nation* (June 3, 1978), pp. 653–55, and "Follow-Up: The F.B.I.'s Field Files," pp. 231–32; Theoharis, "Bureaucrats above the Law: Double-Entry Intelligence Files," p. 394. *New York Times*, April 4, 1976, p. 29, April 25, 1976, p. 28; June 27, 1976, pp. 16, 3E; July 11, 1976, pp. 20, 2E; Aug. 1, 1976, pp. 1, 33, 3E; Aug. 15, 1976, pp. 28, 4E; Aug. 22, 1976, pp. 26, 3E. *Chicago Sun-Times*, Feb. 3, 1979, p. 10. "Not for File" Memo, Jan. 10, 1966, Chicago SAC Personal Folder,

Chicago Committee to Defend the Bill of Rights. *SAPP, Hearings on Invasion of Privacy (Government Agencies)*, 89th Cong., 1st sess., 1965, p. 90; U.S. Senate, Select Committee on Intelligence, *Report on Activities of "Friendly" Foreign Intelligence Services in the United States: A Case Study*, 95th Cong., 2d sess., 1978, pp. 15–16, 16 n4, 21. Fred Cook, "The *Coram Nobis* Appeal: Alger Hiss—A New Ball Game," *Nation* (Oct. 11, 1980), p. 341. Edith Tiger, ed., *In Re Alger Hiss*, (New York: Hill and Wang, 1980), II, 120, 122–24, 129–33, 280, 286–87, 374. Letter, Barry Lynn et al. to Senator Edward Kennedy, May 9, 1979. Deposition, Robert Scherrer in *A.C.L.U. et al. v. City of Chicago et al.*, Ca 75-C-3295, March 14, 1980, p. 80.

    29. Wise, *American Police State*, p. 282.

    30. *HIDFBI*, pp. 154–55. *HFBIO*, pp. 4–11, 15–19, 34. The Nichols file contains memoranda pertaining to his contacts with favored reporters, sensitive FBI investigations (including the resort to break-ins) of, or assistance to, prominent Americans (such as Eleanor Roosevelt, Herbert Hoover, Charles Fahy, John D. Rockefeller III, and Kermit Roosevelt), and "Informative" and "Administrative Purposes" memoranda. The "confidential file" administered by Felt in 1971, moreover, is no longer extant. Felt, *FBI Pyramid*, p. 144. Letter, Charles Dollar to Athan Theoharis, Nov. 19, 1981.

    31. *HIDFBI*, pp. 2–19, 34–74, 84–146, 173–77, 203–5. *HIA*, Vol. 6, Federal Bureau of Investigation, pp. 12–14, 351–59. Furthermore, an FBI memo on Fred Cook contains the notation that a carbon copy was filed in Hoover's "Personal File." See, Memo, M. A. Jones to Bishop, July 14, 1971, folder 52, *O&C*.

    32. *HIDFBI*, pp. 39, 44, 46–47, 49–50, 55, 57, 60–61, 63, 95, 173. HIA, Vol. 6 Federal Bureau of Investigation, pp. 12–14. Nor was this the sole known instance wherein politically sensitive policy documents were transferred from Hoover's "Personal File" to another tightly controlled "official and confidential" file. In February 1950, a series of memoranda prepared in 1936 by then Harvard Law School Professor Felix Frankfurter for the Roosevelt Administration on a Louisville housing case, at the time on *certiorari* before the Supreme Court, were transferred from Hoover's Personal File to the Otto N. Frankfurter folder in Nichols's Official and Confidential files. See Letter, Felix Frankfurter to President Roosevelt, Feb. 25, 1936; Memo, Suggested Treatment of Remaining Constitutional Cases before the Supreme Court by Corcoran and Cohen, no date; Memo, President Roosevelt to Attorney General and Solicitor General, March 2, 1936; Memo, Nichols to Tolson, Feb. 14, 1950; Routing Slip, Nichols to Lurz, no month or day, 1950; all in Otto N. Frankfurter folder, *LN*.

    33. At various times during 1965, FBI Director Hoover had briefed Katzenbach that the FBI had broken in to install microphones during its investigation of

Martin Luther King, Jr. In every instance, the attorney general was informed *after* the bugs had been installed and their use terminated. Rather than question the FBI's authority for this independent action, in January 1966 Katzenbach wrote Hoover: "Obviously these are particularly delicate surveillances and we should be very cautious in terms of the non-FBI people who may from time to time necessarily be involved in some aspect of installation." Memos, FBI Director to Attorney General, May 17, 1965, Oct. 19, 1965, Dec. 1, 1965; Memo, Katzenbach to Hoover, undated but stamped received by FBI Jan. 10, 1966; see also, Memo, Sullivan to DeLoach, Jan. 21, 1966; all in folder 24, *O&C*.

34. Fred B. Black folder (Memo, DeLoach to Tolson, July 6, 1966; Memo, DeLoach to Tolson, July 6, 1966; Memo, FBI Director to Attorney General, July 6, 1966; Letter, Hoover to SACs, July 18, 1966; Memo, DeLoach to Tolson, July 6, 1966), *O&C*. Elizabeth Bentley folder (Cover Memo, Elizabeth Bentley Testimony, FBI Director Hoover to Helen Gandy, Nov. 20, 1953 and attached twenty-eight pages of charts titled Distribution of Investigative Information by the FBI to the White House, Attorney General, and Other Executive Departments), *O&C*. For background to Hoover's and Brownell's testimony, see Memo, Assistant Attorney General Warren Olney III to FBI Director, Nov. 10, 1953, FBI 5588 and Data re: Raymond Murphy, Nov. 17, 1953, State Department 52; both in *AH*. Theoharis, *Spying on Americans*, pp. 125–29. David Garrow, *The FBI and Martin Luther King, Jr.* (New York: Norton, 1981), pp. 41, 240 n50; see also, pp. 46, 104, 107–10, 114, 115, 117–18, 120, 139, 150. Memo, J. H. Gale to DeLoach, May 27, 1966; Memo, Attorney General to FBI Director, Jan. 13, 1966; Memo, FBI Director to Attorney General, Jan. 5, 1966; Memo, A. H. Belmont to Tolson, July 2, 1959; Memo, FBI Director to Attorney General, Oct. 6, 1951; Memo, Attorney General to FBI Director, Feb. 26, 1952; Memo for Files, J. Edgar Hoover, June 9, 1952; Memo, Attorney General to FBI Director, May 20, 1954; Memo, A. H. Belmont to L. V. Boardman, May 21, 1954; Memo, FBI Executives Conference to Tolson, July 20, 1959; Memo, FBI Director to Deputy Attorney General Byron White, May 4, 1961; Memo, C. A. Evans to Belmont, March 13, 1962; Memo, A. H. Belmont to Tolson, Aug. 17, 1961; Memo, C. A. Evans to Belmont, Aug. 17, 1961; Memo, FBI Director to Attorney General, April 5, 1965; Memo, FBI Director to Attorney General, May 27, 1965; Letter, SAC (Chicago) Marlin Johnson to James Gale, Dec. 20, 1965; Memo, John J. Danahy to Gale, Dec. 22, 1965; Memo, J. H. Gale to DeLoach, July 1, l966; Memo, DeLoach to Tolson, Dec. 24, 1965, all in folder 164, *O&C*. The other folders originally filed in Hoover's Personal and Confidential file and transferred to the Official and Confidential file pursuant to the FBI Director's order are: Agreement between the Federal

Bureau of Investigation and the Secret Service concerning Presidential Protection, Feb. 3, 1965; Memo, General Investigative Division, March 4, 1971, and attached teletype, Washington Field Office to FBI Director, March 3, 1971, re: Bombing at U.S. Capitol; Memo, W. F. Glavin to FBI Director, Feb. 25, 1941, re: FBI recording instruments; Letter, E. R. Butts to FBI Director, April 2, 1951.

35. Theoharis, *Spying on Americans*, pp. 115–16, 125–29; Wise, *American Police State*, pp. 77–78; Ungar, *FBI*, pp. 304–11; Felt, *FBI Pyramid*, pp. 144, 308. U. S. Senate, Committee on the Judiciary, Subcommittees on Administrative Practice and Procedure and on Constitutional Rights, Committee on Foreign Relations, Subcommittee on Surveillance, *Joint Hearings on Warrantless Wiretapping and Electronic Surveillance—1974*, 93d Cong., 2d sess., 1974, pp. 365–69. *New York Times*, Aug. 12, 1977, p. A12; June 23, 1976, p. B2. *Detroit News*, June 22, 1978, p. A10. Defendant's Reply to Government's Response Opposing Supplemental Discovery Motion, Edward Bennett Williams (counsel for John Kearney), June 28, 1977, *United States v. Kearney*, Cr 77-245, pp. 8–9; Defendant's Supplementary Motion for Discovery and Inspection, Edward Bennett Williams, Oct. 5, 1977, *United States v. Kearney*, Cr 77-245, pp. 3, 9, 16; Government's Response to Defendant's Supplementary Motion for Discovery and Inspection, Stephen Horn (Attorney, Department of Justice, submitted for Assistant Attorney General Benjamin Civiletti), Oct. 31, 1977, *United States v. Kearney*, Cr 77-245, pp. 6–15. Memorandum of Points and Authorities in Support of Defendant Miller's Motion to Dismiss the Indictment Because of Pre-Indictment Delay, Thomas Kennelly and Howard Epstein (counsel for Edward Miller), May 22, 1978, *United States v. Gray, Felt, and Miller*, Cr 78-00179, pp. 3–9; Motion for Discovery and Inspection on behalf of Defendant Gray, Alan Baron *et al*, (counsel for L. Patrick Gray), May 22, 1978, *United States v. Gray, Felt, and Miller*, Cr 78-00179, pp. 4–11, 13; Memorandum in Support of Defendant Gray's Motion to Dismiss Indictment for Legal Insufficiency, Alan Baron *et al*, May 22, 1978, *United States v. Gray, Felt, and Miller*, Cr 78-00179, pp. 5–8, and Defendant Gray's Response to Opposition of the United States to Defendant's Motion for Severance and Relief from Prejudicial Joinder, Alan Baron *et al*, June 21, 1978, *United States v. Gray, Felt, and Miller*, Cr 78-00179, pp. 2–6.

36. Some Do Not File documents were filed in the unserialized Official and Confidential file that FBI Assistant Director Louis Nichols maintained in his office. (See, for example, the American Youth Congress and Department of Justice folders.) Break-in policy documents, in most cases, were filed in the 66 file.

37. *HIDFBI*, pp. 37–47, 49, 54–57, 74–84, 100–101, 103–6, 116–20, 123–

26. In contrast to Mohr, FBI agent Martin Wood expressed a "hazy" knowledge about where Do Not File documents had been retained. Claiming that there was "never a do-not-file file," Wood added: "Certain documents in the past were prepared with the instruction do not file, which meant they were not to go into the regular files. As far as I know, they were kept in folders in certain offices, like in the Director's office, that sort of thing" (Deposition, FBI Agent Wood, April 28, 1978, *Salant v. U.S. Department of Justice et al.*, Ca 77-873, p. 45). Acting FBI Director L. Patrick Gray, however, contradicted Wood's assertions. In a pre-trial discovery motion of May 22, 1978, Gray requested "all FBI documents in the Government's possession, custody or control marked either 'June' and/or 'Do Not File' from the period January 1, 1960 to the present." In this motion, Gray pinpointed where these documents had been filed: "pertinent documents from F.B.I. files designated as '66-1686' (the 'June' file)." Motion for Discovery and Inspection on behalf of Defendant Gray, Alan Baron et al. (counsel for L. Patrick Gray), May 22, 1978, *United States v. Gray, Felt, and Miller*, Cr 78-00179, pp. 4, 13. The FBI claims that Gray erred when citing 66-1686 as the "June" file.

38. Indeed, in 1942 FBI Assistant Director Louis Nichols asked Gandy as to where photostatic copies of Mrs. Eleanor Roosevelt's 1940–41 correspondence with American Youth Congress (AYC) officials should be filed. The FBI had obtained this correspondence through a break-in of the AYC's New York office. Nichols wrote: "Do you wish to keep or should I place in Official Conf. file." Routing slip, Nichols to Gandy, undated 1942, American Youth Congress folder, *LN*.

39. In a pre-trial discovery motion, former Acting FBI Director L. Patrick Gray requested the release of all June and/or Do Not File documents pertaining to FBI break-ins conducted since 1960 and cited the 66-1686 file number as the " 'June' file" where such documents were maintained. Gray erred when citing this file number, the FBI claims: 66-1686 contained payroll and annual leave reports and had been destroyed in 1951. FBI officials nonetheless concede that a "June mail control file" and index cards referring to break-ins exist; it is not known, however, whether these were the 'June' file Gray cited in his discovery motion. Another FBI memorandum records that one "June" file, 66-2542, contains "correspondence relating to statistical information as to the number of installations, mail covers, informants, etc., in all field offices. . . . furnished by the field. . . periodically so that [headquarters] may be aware of developments in the various field offices on a continuing basis." Some break-in documents, moreover, were filed in the 66 file. These include a memorandum transmitting documents obtained during a December 1949 break-in in Washington, D.C. of the

office of the National Lawyers Guild (66-1899-445) and memoranda pertaining to an October 1963 break-in in New York City of the Fair Play for Cuba Committee (66-8160-3790 and 66-8160-3833). Employing the FOIA, I requested the release of the "symbol number sensitive source index" and of all break-in documents filed in the 66-8160 and 66-1899 files. In October 1981, the FBI advised me that headquarters file 66-1899 had been destroyed at an undetermined date prior to 1973 and that there was no extant record of the subject of this file. (This was contrary to Bureau practice: whenever FBI files had been destroyed, the FBI had always maintained a record of the date of the destruction and the subject matter of the destroyed files.) Further responding to my specific identification of file numbers, and the press's and the Congress's interest in whether break-in documents existed, the FBI then conceded that break-in documents existed in various headquarter's files. Following an intensive search, the FBI was in the process of collecting and then integrating these documents in a single "surreptitious entries" file, 62-117166.

In its settlement to a suit filed in Chicago, *A.C.L.U. et al. v. City of Chicago et al.*, moreover, the Justice Department admitted that between 1948 and 1966 the FBI had committed "at least 500 black bag jobs [in the Chicago area] directed against approximately 50 targets." These statistics, Justice Department officials conceded, "include only those black bag jobs for which documentation still exists. There may have been additional black bag jobs [in the Chicago area], the documentation of which has been destroyed or cannot be located."

Letters, Athan Theoharis to David Cook, Oct. 29, 1980; to Donald Smith, Feb. 10, 1981; and to James Hall, May 19, Sept. 8, and Oct. 30, 1981. Letters, James Hall to Athan Theoharis, May 7 and 29, Sept. 3, and Oct. 23, 1981. *Washington Post*, May 30, 1981, p. A9. *Detroit News*, Aug. 14, 1981, p. 7A. Telephone conversations, Athan Theoharis and Donald Smith, May 28, 1981; Athan Theoharis and Garland Schweickhardt, Oct. 9 and 22, 1981; Athan Theoharis and Douglass Cassel, June 1 and 10, 1981; Athan Theoharis and Katherine LeRoy, June 3 and 12, 1981. Memo, Domestic Intelligence Division Inspection to A. H. Belmont, Nov. 18, 1960, FBI 66-1372. Memo, William Ryan to SAC Chicago, July 31, 1950, FBI 100-3466-66, *NLG*. Memos, Re: Surreptitious Entries, Assistant Attorney General, Civil Rights Division, Dec. 1, 1975, FBI 66-8160-3790 and March 22, 1976, FBI 66-8160-3833. Motion, Alan Baron *et al.*, May 22, 1978, *U.S. v. Gray, Felt, and Miller,* Cr 78-000179, pp. 4, 13. The following documents from *A.C.L.U. et al. v. City of Chicago et al.*, Ca 75-C-3295 and *Alliance to End Repression et al. v. Joseph DiLeonardi et al.*, Ca 74-C-3268: Deposition, Robert Scherrer (Unit chief, Records Management Division, FBI), March 14, 1980, pp. 60–67, 74; Federal Defendants' Opposition to Alliance Plaintiffs' Motion to Compel Production of Material from the FBI Files of Richard Criley and the Chicago Committee to Defend the Bill of Rights, April 24, 1980; ACLU Plaintiff's First Supplemental Interrogatories to Federal Defendants Civiletti, Webster and Ingram Concerning Black Bag Jobs, May 14, 1980; and Joint Motion and Stipulation, Oct. 29 and Nov. 3, 1980, p. 17. Athan Theoharis, "The Importance of F.O.I.A.: New Light on Old Black-Bag Jobs," *Nation* (July 11–18, 1981), pp. 46–47. Memo, SAC, Washington Field Office to FBI Director, July 23, 1950, FBI 66-1899-445.

40. *HIA*, Vol. 2, Huston Plan, pp. 277–80.

41. Memos, Hoover to Tolson, Tamm, Ladd, and Clegg, March 19, 1946; Hoover to Tolson, Tamm, and Ladd, March 20, 1946; and Hoover to Tolson, Tamm, and Ladd, March 21, 1946; all in FBI 62-116606-1, Alger Hiss Folder, *O&C*. See also Memo, Bannerman to Russell, March 22, 1946, State Department 151, *AH*. In addition, see Memos, Ladd to Tamm, March 20, 1946, and Ladd to FBI Director, March 20, 1946; both in *O&C*. In contrast to the Hoover memoranda, Ladd's memoranda were not written on pink paper and did not contain the Do Not File notation. Weinstein's assertions were made on William Buckley's television show see transcript "Firing Line: The Guilt of Alger Hiss," April 7, 1978 (Southern Educational Communications Association), p. 15, and in his book, *Perjury*, p. 358n.

42. The National Archives' FBI Records Appraisal Project Staff located only a portion of the file which Tolson maintained in his office and confined to the period 1965 to 1972. Apparently, the pre-1965 documents maintained by Tolson had been destroyed. Letters, Charles Dollar to Athan Theoharis, Nov. 19, 1981, and Dec. 11, 1981.

43. Undated routing slip, Hoover to Tolson, Ladd, and Nichols, FBI 1478; Memo, Ladd to FBI Director, Dec. 10, 1948, FBI 1478; Memo, Ladd to FBI Director, Dec. 13, 1948, FBI 1479; Undated routing slip, Hoover to Tolson, Ladd, and Nichols, FBI 1479; Pink Memo, Ladd to FBI Director, Dec. 28, 1948, FBI 1480; Memo, Ladd to FBI Director, Dec. 28, 1948, FBI 1733; all in *AH*. The transfer of Do Not File documents to the regular files was apparently not unexceptional. We know of at least two other such instances. In a June 28, 1949 memorandum to FBI Associate Director Clyde Tolson (captioned like Hoover's memoranda of March 19, 20 and 21, 1946: "This Memorandum is for Administrative Purposes—To Be Destroyed After Action Is Taken and Not Sent to Files Section"), FBI Assistant Director Nichols reported how UPI Washington bureau chief Lyle Wilson succeeded in extracting a commitment from presidential press secretary, Charles Ross, that Truman would not act favorably on a National Lawyers Guild's request that he initiate an investigation

of the FBI. Nichols's June 1949 memorandum was transferred to the regular files on August 19, 1958 (Memo, Nichols to Tolson, June 28, 1949, FBI 1669, *NLG*). The second involved an instruction from Helen Grandy to transfer a memorandum dated May 26, 1960 to Hoover's O&C file (File Case 143 [name deleted], Synopsis of Hoover's O&C files, February 17, 1975, *O&C*).

44. Tamm to Director, Oct. 8, 1945; Memo, Hoover to Tolson, Tamm, Ladd, Carson, Oct. 11, 1945; Memo, Hoover to Tolson, Tamm, Ladd, Clegg, March 19, 1946; Memo, Hoover to Tolson, Tamm, and Ladd, March 20, 1946; Memo, Hoover to Tolson, Tamm, and Ladd, March 21, 1946; undated routing slip, Hoover to Tolson, Ladd, Nichols; Speech, Attorney General Herbert Brownell, Nov. 6, 1953; Memo, Nichols to Tolson, re: Chapter 29, June 21, 1956; and Memo, Nichols to Tolson, re: Chapter 29, June 26, 1956; all FBI 62-116606-1, *AH*. The 62-116606 file on Alger Hiss apparently did contain other FBI memoranda. On November 7, 1953, the FBI director ordered the preparation of a "memorandum brief" on the "Alger Hiss case as it concerns the [Igor] Gouzenko angle and [Hoover's] conferences with the Secretary of State [James Byrnes]." Such a memorandum was prepared and was submitted to [Hoover] on November 13, 1953. It summarized "the dissemination of monographs on Soviet espionage, summaries on Alger Hiss, liaison contacts and various conversations [Hoover] had with Secretary of State Byrnes, Under Secretary of State Dean Acheson and the Attorney General [Tom Clark] regarding Hiss." The memorandum ran at least forty-eight pages (only pp. 1, 34–43, and 48 have been released) and consisted of summaries of contemporary FBI memoranda. All the released memoranda in Hoover's Official and Confidential file on Hiss predating 1953 were summarized in this memorandum brief. In addition, the released portion of the November 13, 1953 memorandum summarized three other (as yet unreleased) FBI memoranda which were not included in the released Hoover Official and Confidential file on Hiss. These concerned: (1) a June 3, 1946 meeting between FBI agent Ralph Roach and White House aide George Allen; (2) a summary dated July 25, 1946, entitled "Soviet Espionage in the United States," prepared in response to a July 18, 1946 request from White House Special Counsel Clark Clifford to Attorney General Clark, and (3) a November 19, 1946 Hoover letter to State Department Security official Frederick Lyon reporting the results of a wiretap on Hiss's office phone. See memos, Ladd to FBI Director, Nov. 7, 1953, FBI 101-2668-48, and Ladd to FBI Director with attached memo brief, Nov. 13, 1953, FBI 101-2668-52; both in *AH*.

45. File case 106 [name deleted], Synopsis of Hoover's O and C Files, Feb. 16, 1975, *O&C*.

46. See, for example, Memo, Nichols to Director, Sept. 5, 1941, American Magazine folder; Memos, Tamm to Director, Jan. 22 and 24, 1948, American Mercury folder; Photocopies of letters from Mrs. Eleanor Roosevelt to Joseph Cadden and to Frances Williams, and replies; Memo, D. M. Ladd to Director, Feb. 4, 1942, plus three cover memoranda, American Youth Congress folder; Memo, Nichols to Tolson, Feb. 3, 1944, Frances Biddle folder; Memo, Ladd to Director, Sept. 18, 1944, and Memo, Richard Auerbach, July 25, 1944, Styles Bridges folder; all in *LN*.

47. Memo, FBI Director to Boston SAC, Oct. 13, 1949, FBI 4062; Report, Special Agent Francis O'Brien, Aug. 24, 1949, FBI 4027; both in *AH*.

48. Garry Wills, *Nixon Agonistes* (New York: New American Library, 1971), pp. 36–47; Richard Nixon, *RN: The Memoirs of Richard Nixon* (New York: Grosset & Dunlap, 1978), p. 58; Allen Weinstein, "Nixon vs. Hiss: The Story Nixon Tells, and the Other Story," *Esquire* (Nov. 1975), p. 76. Other documents confirm that Cronin maintained direct contact with FBI and State Department security officials; see Memo, Laughlin to Fletcher, March 8, 1949, FBI 2327, and Data, re: Raymond Murphy, Nov. 13, 1953, State Department 52; both in *AH*.

49. Memo, Nichols to Tolson, Dec. 2, 1948, FBI 101; Memo, Ladd to FBI Director, Dec. 9, 1948, FBI 157; Memo, M. A. Jones to Nichols, Dec. 28, 1948, FBI 055; all in *AH*.

50. Memo, Guy Hottel (SAC, Washington Field Office) to FBI Director, Aug. 2, 1948, FBI 3433; Memo, Nichols to Tolson, Aug. 18, 1948, FBI 3502; Memo, New York SAC to FBI Director, Sept. 2, 1948, FBI Ah 34; all in *AH*. Nichols's close relationship with HUAC continued beyond December 1948. See Memo, L. Whitson to H. B. Fletcher, Dec. 9, 1948, FBI 150; Memo, Guy Hottel to FBI Director, Dec. 21, 1948, FBI 617; Memo, Laughlin to Fletcher, March 8, 1949, FBI 2327; Memo, Guy Hottel to FBI Director, March 31, 1949, FBI 2728; Memo, Nichols to Tolson, June 28, 1949, FBI 3470; Memo, Nichols to Tolson, July 11, 1949, FBI 3661; Memo, Nichols to Tolson, Jan. 11, 1950, FBI 4478; Memo, Ladd to FBI Director, Oct. 9, 1952, FBI 5403; all in *AH*. Memo, Nichols to Tolson, July 18, 1950, *NLG*.

51. Inventory, Baltimore, Md., Sept. 13, 1949, ad. 123, FBI 65-1642-1B, Sect. 5 (destroyed by Special Agent Bernard Norton, June 4, 1958); Memo, Baltimore SAC to FBI Director, Dec. 18, 1951, FBI 4707; Memo (registered mail), FBI Director to Baltimore SAC, Dec. 27, 1950. Defendant Federal Bureau of Investigation's Answers to Plaintiff's First Series of Interrogatories to the United States Department of Justice, Special Agent Martin Wood, March 8, 1978, *Salant v. U.S. Department of Justice et al.*, Ca 77-893, pp. 14, 15–16,

23–26. Supplemental FBI response to Plaintiff's Interrogatories, Special Agent Martin Wood, March 30, 1978, *Salant v. U.S. Department of Justice et al.*, Ca 77-893. Apparently, the FBI's destruction of the Chambers-Wadleigh letter and check was not atypical. Through discovery motions involving the litigation brought · by Michael and Robert Meeropol to secure the FBI files on their parents Julius and Ethel Rosenberg, legal and research staff uncovered sixty-four files (numbering thousands of pages) the existence of which the FBI had not formerly acknowledged. The staff also discovered another forty-two files which the FBI conceded had been destroyed despite an August 1, 1975 court order enjoining the FBI from destroying any files pertaining to the Meeropols' FOIA request. *FOIA, Inc. Update*, Vol. 1, No. 2 (Feb. 1979), p. 2.

52. Defendant Federal Bureau of Investigation's Answers to Plaintiff's First Series of Interrogatories to the United States Department of Justice, FBI Agent Martin Wood, March 8, 1978, *Salant v. U.S. Department of Justice et al.*, Ca 77-893, pp. 7, 8, 11, 12, 14–28. Deposition, FBI Agent Martin Wood (by David Levitt, counsel for Stephen Salant), April 28, 1978, *Salant v. U.S. Department of Justice et al.*, Ca 77-893, pp. 5, 23–26, 40–47, 51, 64–69, 75–76, 85–87, 89– 91. See also Theoharis, "Bureaucrats Above the Law: Double-Entry Intelligence Files," pp. 393–97.

53. *New York Times*, April 16, 1978, p. 2E; June 23, 1978, p. B2; Dec. 1, 1978, p. A25; Dec. 6, 1978. *Milwaukee Journal*, April 11, 1978, pp. 1, 11; April 12, 1978, p. 3; April 13, 1978, p. 2; Nov. 16, 1978, p. 12; Nov. 23, 1978, p. 3; Nov. 30, 1978, p. 6; Dec. 19, 1978, p. 2; Jan. 6, 1979, p. 2; Jan. 16, 1979, p. 3; Jan. 21, 1979, p. 18. *Detroit News*, June 22, 1978, p. A10. Memorandum of Points and Authorities in support of Defendant Miller's Motion to Dismiss the Indictment because of Pre-Indictment Delay, Thomas Kennelly and Howard Epstein (counsel for Edward Miller), May 22, 1978, *United States v. Gray, Felt, and Miller*, Cr 78-00179, pp. 3–9; Memorandum in support of Defendant Gray's Motion to Dismiss Indictment for Legal Insufficiency, Alan Baron *et al.*, May 22, 1978, *United States v. Gray, Felt, and Miller*, Cr 78-00179, pp. 5–8; Defendant Gray's Response to Opposition of the United States to Defendant's Motion for Severance and Relief from Prejudicial Joinder, Alan Baron *et al.*, June 21, 1978, *United States v. Gray, Felt, and Miller*, Cr 78-00179.

3

FBI Break-in Policy

Anthony Marro

Early in January 1978, George Koelzer traveled from his law office in Red Bank, New Jersey, to the Department of Justice in Washington, D.C., on behalf of an FBI agent in Newark who, like several dozen other agents, had suddenly found himself in need of a lawyer. Koelzer was forty at the time, a big (6'7") man, with the impish looks of a Barry Fitzgerald and the build of an interior lineman gone slightly to seed. He had been a federal prosecutor in his early years as a lawyer, but had been out of the department for nearly a decade, becoming both well-known and moderately wealthy in private practice. But he also looked back fondly on his days as a prosecutor telling friends that it had been exciting and challenging work, and that some of his proudest moments had been when he stood before juries in federal courtrooms in Newark, telling them: "Ladies and gentlemen, my name is George Koelzer, and I represent the United States of America."

Koelzer had worked first in the Justice Department's criminal division in Washington and then had gone to Newark with the Organized Crime Strike Force. He had worked closely with FBI agents there, had partied with them, had come to know many of them well, and had stayed close to some of them after he left the government. He and many of the agents had come from the same mold: sons of ethnic, working-class parents, who had gotten through college largely on their own, without rich and influential relatives to help them through or help open doors for them after they graduated. If he had done better, financially and professionally, than many of them, he nonetheless identified with them and shared many of their values. Indeed, he even looked and dressed like an agent, wearing

This essay is based principally on extensive interviews with federal prosecutors, FBI agents, and former agents (given under the assurance of confidentiality), research into court documents (obtained during the author's coverage of these trials as a reporter for *The New York Times* and *Newsday*), and identified published sources.

his dark hair clipped short at a time when even federal judges were wearing it long, and showing a preference for the clothing that had come to be almost an FBI uniform: subdued suits, white shirts, wing-tipped shoes and snap-brim hats. He knew the Bureau about as well as any outsider could, knew its strengths and its weaknesses, its procedures and policies, and how agents *really* went about their business, as opposed to the ways spelled out in the FBI Manual of Instructions. The agents in Newark and New York knew and trusted him, and considered him almost an insider. And so it was natural that when everything began to collapse, several of them called him for help.

The center of the furor was Squad 47 in the New York Field Office, which had been formed in the spring of 1970 specifically to track down a number of radical fugitives, most of them members of the Weather Underground movement. The Weather Underground had claimed credit for a rash of terrorist bombings, and had threatened more, sometimes taunting the FBI for its inability to catch its members and stop the explosions. Most of the fugitives were wanted on lesser charges, however, for antirioting and firearms violations. The fugitives had gone into hiding, and in its attempts to find them, Squad 47 had located a number of friends, relatives, and associates who the agents thought might be in contact with them—and might be able to point to their whereabouts—and had then, without warrants or authority from any court, tapped their phones, opened their mail, and entered their apartments in search of clues.

The Bureau had tapped phones, opened mail, and entered apartments without warrants in the past, although the break-ins were supposed to have ended in 1966, when the then-director J. Edgar Hoover had scribbled "no more such techniques must be used", that seemed to prohibit them. But the Squad 47 case was different in at least three important ways. First, the agents got caught. They had created a retrievable written record and thus the break-ins could later become known to Justice Department prosecutors. Second, the break-ins had came to light in the aftermath of the Watergate scandals and two years of Congressional investigations of abuses by the nation's intelligence agencies, mainly the FBI and the CIA. Hoover was dead, public opinion polls showed huge drops in the numbers of people who had a high regard for the Bureau, and, as Clarence M. Kelley, the new FBI director, told his agents, the "sanctuary from criticism" that the Bureau had enjoyed in the past no longer existed. Third, many of the break-ins by Squad 47 had been made subsequent to a June 1972 decision by the Supreme Court in *United States v. United States District Court* (known as the *Keith* decision) in which the court had ruled that the government could not conduct electronic surveillance without a warrant in domestic security cases.

The Omnibus Crime and Safe Streets Act of 1968 permitted two types of electronic surveillance. In criminal cases, FBI agents could go to a court and get permission for a so-called Title III wiretap authorization, if there was probable cause to believe that a crime was being committed. In "national security" cases, wiretaps could be installed simply by getting the permission of the attorney general, who was considered to have authority to approve wiretaps whether the target was a foreign intelligence agency, such as the KGB, or a domestic political group, such as the Weathermen.[1]

The *Keith* decision did not address the question of whether the attorney general could continue to authorize warrantless wiretapping in foreign intelligence cases. But it made clear that such wiretapping and bugging couldn't be done in domestic security cases without court approval. And the Justice Department investigators assigned to probe the Squad 47 break-ins were taking the view that break-ins, at least as intrusive as electronic surveillance, clearly required a warrant as well. In short, without addressing the question of the legality of warrantless entries and wiretaps in the past, the Justice Department investigators started from the assumption that the *Keith* decision clearly prohibited them, and that the agents who had made them had committed felony crimes.

Moreover, Justice Department investigators had some of the records to prove it.

On March 17, 1976, an agent reviewing the files in the FBI's New York office came across a series of twenty-five folders hidden away in a safe. The safe, it turned out, had belonged to John Malone, a handsome former firearms instructor who had run the New York office for a decade before his retirement in 1975, and who, despite his unquestioned bravery, and despite the real affection that many agents had for him, was known within the office as "Cementhead."[2]

The agent had no particular interest in Squad 47, or in John Malone. He was merely following a court order to search FBI files as part of a discovery process in a civil suit that had been brought against the government by the Socialist Workers Party, a small Trotskyist group, which was charging (with considerable justification, as it turned out) that it had been the subject of illegal surveillances over the years. The first twenty-four folders contained files about break-ins that had been committed in the distant past, each file covering a six-month period in the years 1954 to 1966. The twenty-fifth file, however, was labeled "July 1, 1966." This file contained material indicating that break-ins had taken place long after 1966, despite Hoover's supposed ban, and had been done by members of Squad 47, and perhaps by other units as well, during the search for the Weather Underground fugitives.

Suddenly, Justice Department officials had to deal with the reality that there had been break-ins by FBI agents, that they had occurred after a Supreme Court decision that made clear that such acts were illegal, and that the agents had left a written record behind. Moreover, the five-year statute of limitations on criminal acts had not yet expired.

Justice Department investigators descended on New York, on Newark, and several other field offices, and dozens of FBI agents, once they got over the shock of being named targets in a criminal investigation—no agent in the FBI's fifty-year history ever had been charged with a crime committed in the course of his work—went looking for lawyers.

The reason for Koelzer's trip to Washington dated back to January 10, 1973, when FBI agents in Newark and elsewhere were looking for a fugitive named Judith Flatley. An anti-war activist, Flatley was wanted on a so-called eighty-eight violation—that is, for an unlawful flight to avoid prosecution—stemming from Weather Underground activities in Madison, Wisconsin, and in Chicago. The specific charges included mob action, federal firearms violations, and forgery. Her parents, Benjamin and Rosa Cohen, were living in Union, New Jersey, and the agents handling the case had decided to break into their home, hoping to find evidence that might point to her whereabouts. Such entries, which are known in the Bureau as "black bag jobs," or simply "bag jobs," were generally illegal. (The term "black bag job" comes from the black laundry-type bags in which agents carried the bulky camera equipment that was used to copy documents in the 1940s and 1950s; today, the cameras are small enough that they can be concealed in attache cases.) They were relatively common, or had been in the 1950s and early 1960s, particularly in investigations of alleged organized crime figures, and of people whom FBI officials considered subversive.

All the details of what happened that January morning still aren't known, and some of them probably aren't terribly important. But what is known is this: Sometime after the Cohens had left for work, Weaver and several other agents entered their house, searched the premises, found an address book and photographed its contents. The search was quick, the exit clean, and the FBI agents were back in the Newark office by about 8:30 A.M.

In many cases, FBI agents had broken into homes and offices and, if they found nothing of interest, made no record to indicate that an entry had been made. Agents and former agents have conceded this privately, and Koelzer agrees. "They'd bag these places and never say or write a word about it, if nothing came out of it," he admits. "But because they found something in Cohen's house that they wanted to copy, they had to open a file. And and this meant that the vaunted FBI paper machine had to go to work." More specifically, the Newark office telephoned FBI Headquarters in Washington, and J. Wallace LaPrade, the Special Agent in Charge (SAC) in Newark, assured FBI officials that if "special investigative techniques" could be used in the Flatley case, he could guarantee (1) that they would be productive, and (2) they would not cause any embarrassment or harm to the Bureau. The memo that resulted from this call documented that an entry had taken place, and later, when the Justice Department began investigating such break-ins and department investigators descended on the Newark office, one of the supervisors there telephoned Koelzer, and requested his help.

The supervisor himself was a minor, or at least peripheral, figure in the case, a man who recently had been assigned to internal security work. The Justice Department apparently never had any real intention of prosecuting him, since he had little or nothing to do with the break-in. But some of the paperwork had crossed his desk and the Justice Department team, which was threatening to prosecute lower level agents in order to pressure them into testifying against FBI officials who authorized or ordered the break-ins, listed him among the subjects of the investigation. Because of this prospect Koelzer was returning to the Justice Department building on Pennsylvania Avenue, where two young attorneys told him they had a memo that made his client important to their case—a link in the chain-of-command that stretched between the officials who had authorized the entry and the agents who had actually carried it out.

The Justice Department prosecutors, for the most part, still are not talking publicly about their role in the case, but Koelzer's somewhat biased recollection of the meeting is detailed and precise. "They were a couple of kids," he says of the lawyers. "Very bright, but green as grass." The prosecutors showed him the memo which reported that LaPrade had called Edward Miller, the head of the FBI's Intelligence Division, on the morning of January 10, assuring him that a break-in would be both productive and fail-safe. The memo never used the term "break-in," but anyone who knew anything about the Bureau, and knew how to read between lines, knew what it meant. The memo also indicated that Miller then had gone to Acting FBI Associate Director W. Mark Felt, and had received Felt's approval.

Koelzer says that he asked the two attorneys if that was the crucial memo they had been telling him about, and they replied that it was. He then asked what they thought the memo documented. They replied that it showed Miller and Felt authorizing the agents to stage a bag job. "I told them to read it again," Koelzer says. They read it again, and again concluded that Miller and Felt had authorized the agents in Newark to enter the house.

"No, that's not what it shows," Koelzer says he told them. "What it shows is that it's already been done."

And indeed, it had been. The call from LaPrade apparently hadn't been made until about 9:00 A.M., which was after the agents had returned to the office. "They looked as though it had never occurred to them before that this was the way things were done," Koelzer said. "It was like watching the light bulb go on in the Saturday morning cartoons. It takes about eight people to do even the most routine break-in. It would take two to follow the Cohens to work, and sit outside to make sure they didn't suddenly return home. It would take two more to sit outside the house and make sure others didn't approach it. And it would take three or four to go in for the search. It takes a couple of days' planning to do this. There was no way they could get authorization from Miller and Felt and do the job the same day. . . . The only way they could guarantee they would get something out of it and not get caught was if it had already been done." He paused and shrugged. "The department had been working on the case for more than a year, and they still didn't know how to read an FBI file."

Koelzer's last observation is not entirely true, and even if it were, would not be as harsh a judgment as it might at first seem. Learning to find one's way through FBI files is no easy chore, for the Bureau traditionally has been reluctant to share information with outsiders, unless it was to its advantage; in many ways the Justice Department, of which the Bureau technically is a part, was considered both foreign and hostile, viewed by many FBI agents with suspicion and sometimes even disdain. And one of the most important lessons the Justice Department investigators learned early in their probe of the break-ins was that FBI files often were of limited use: incomplete, self-serving, protective of the Bureau, and not to be trusted. "You couldn't take them at face value," said one of the Justice Department investigators who worked on the Squad 47 case. "Sometimes agents on the street were hiding things from people at headquarters, and sometimes people at headquarters were hiding things from each other. They were a starting point [for an investigation], but nothing more."

In some cases, no records of break-ins had been made, or had been made but later destroyed. In other cases, as Koelzer had suggested, records had been created only after the fact, and in such a way as to make it difficult to sort out just who had done what, when, and under what authority. In many other cases, the information had been hidden away in the Bureau's Do Not File file, a filing system designed to keep certain information out of the FBI's central records system, thus allowing the Bureau to tell the Congress, the courts, and even superiors in the Justice Department that a check of a given matter had been made and any information about it had not been found "in the central files."

And in other cases, the Bureau, or its agents, had simply withheld information, or lied about it, as it did to investigators from the General Accounting Office (GAO) in 1974. The investigative arm of the Congress, the GAO at the time was conducting an investigation for a House Judiciary Subcommittee headed by Representative Don Edwards

(D.,Cal.), which had oversight responsibility for the Bureau. The purpose of this GAO audit was to evaluate the effectiveness of the Bureau's domestic security investigations both in terms of information obtained and crimes uncovered. A former agent and an outspoken liberal, Edwards is not only critical of many Bureau practices and procedures, but, unlike many critics, knew where to look for the information. However, the Nixon Administration did not permit the GAO to look in the files. Instead, GAO auditors were permitted only to select case names at random, and then randomly select an agent who would inspect the files and report back on the investigative techniques used in each case, and on the results of the investigation.

Having decided by sheer chance to look into the FBI's investigation of two anti-war activists living in upstate New York, the GAO also picked by sheer chance as its agent to inspect the files a man who had worked on that very case. The agent, according to federal investigators, went to his superiors and warned, in effect, that "there were bag jobs up there." And while it still hasn't been established just who told him what, this agent never relayed the information about the bag jobs to the GAO team. The result was that the GAO, and hence the Congress, was never told about these break-ins. These entries into the one-room cabin of Stewart Albert and Judith Clavier, in Hurley, New York, became known several years later during the Justice Department investigation of bag jobs—only then did the subcommittee learn that the Bureau had misled the GAO team. Later, the FBI, by its own admission, seriously undercounted the number of pre-1966 bag jobs in its September 23, 1975, report to the Senate Select Committee on Intelligence Activities and had also withheld entirely information about the post-1966 bag jobs committed while searching for the Weather Underground fugitives. In the words of FBI Director William H. Webster, who ordered an internal investigation of the matter several years after the fact, the information given to the Senate Committee was "grossly inaccurate."

Other things were done that make it difficult to discover the extent of this deception and the FBI's use of bag jobs. Former FBI agents have admitted that it was not unusual for agents to stage bag jobs and then to report the information they obtained as having come from "highly confidential sources," "anonymous sources," or "confidential informants," particularly informants who had disappeared from the streets, as informants often do, and thus couldn't be tracked down by FBI inspectors to verify the claims. The result was that information from bag jobs ended up in FBI files, but without any honest accounting in those same files about the true source. And one former agent, Anthony Villano, has publicly admitted that agents working organized crime cases sometimes staged break-ins to get the information needed to go back to a judge and apply for a Title III wiretap. There was pressure on agents to install Title III wiretaps, he said, and this sometimes led them to stage break-ins to get enough information—which they then claimed to have obtained from a "reliable informant"—to demonstrate to a court that there was probable cause that a crime had been committed, and that a wiretap was needed to solve it. In his book *Brick Agent*, Villano also wrote that if Hoover had really prohibited bag jobs, in 1966, not all of the agents had been briefed about this directive. "Perhaps that was true for the Bureau's internal security squads," Villano wrote of the order, "but if the ban included agents dealing with ciminals, they kept that a secret from me."

The reports that FBI agents had staged warrantless break-ins to obtain information later presented to a court in support of a warrant have never been fully investigated. To some prosecutors, this contention is one of the most troubling aspects of the whole controversy because it suggests that some criminal prosecutions may have been tainted. But some former prosecutors privately concede that they at least suspected that information from illegal break-ins was being presented to courts as justification for search warrants or for court-authorized wiretaps. "They would do it on truck hijacking cases all the time," said one former prosecutor, who did not want to be quoted by name, but whose claim is supported by numerous present and former agents and prosecutors. "They'd bag a place, find the truckload of goods, then come back and say that an 'informant of proven reliability' had given them a tip, and if they could get a search warrant they could come up with the stuff. You'd ask if it was a live informant, and they'd hem and haw and scratch their heads. But the fact was that everybody knew, and nobody cared."

It is not clear that "everybody" knew. Many prosecutors and Justice Department officials insist they did not. And it is not true that nobody cared. Some prosecutors and Justice Department officials have since said they would have tried to stop such break-ins if they had known about them, particularly if they had resulted in tainted evidence—the "fruit of the poisoned tree," as lawyers like to say—being introduced into court as justification for a warrant.

What all this makes clear, however, is that the full scope of the FBI's bag jobs probably never will be known. Too much of the evidence has been hidden or scrambled, and it's unlikely that congressional committees, GAO investigators, historians, or journalists ever will be able to reconstruct it entirely. It's not likely that we'll ever know just how many crimes had been committed or how much mischief had been done by FBI agents making warrantless entries, or just whose civil liberties had been violated along the way. But enough has emerged in recent years—from congressional investigations, Justice Department investigations, news reporting, and civil suits—to establish that bag jobs were common, at least in the 1950s and 1960s, and that the victims included a broad cross-section of American society, many of them persons never indicted for, or even suspected of, committing a crime.

Most of the persons whose homes had been entered during the search for Weather Underground fugitives in the early 1970s, for example, were not themselves fugitives, and in some cases not even political activists. Many had never been accused of any crime. Most of them had no involvement at all with any foreign government, let alone been the tools of foreign intelligence agencies. They were, in the main, merely friends, relatives, and associates of the fugitives, people who FBI agents thought might be in contact with them and whose homes might contain information—a postmark on a letter, or a telephone number, for example—that might lead to their capture. "These bag jobs were done on innocent people who had nothing to do with foreign powers," John Neilds, the prosecutor in the Miller-Felt case, told the jury. "I say to you that the people whose homes were searched were not only innocent of collaborating with hostile foreign powers—they were innocent, period."

It has been seven years since the FBI first admitted to the Senate Select Committee on Intelligence Activities that bag jobs had been committed, although the initial admission was limited to foreign counterintelligence work, and the then FBI Director, Clarence M. Kelley, insisted that they pretty much had stopped with Hoover's ban in 1966.

Since then, the nation has learned that the bag jobs involved far more than just a few foreign embassies, and that, Kelley's statement and Hoover's supposed ban to the contrary, FBI break-ins had continued well into the early 1970s. The result of the disclosures was heavy criticism from civil liberties groups, embarrassing stories in the press, congressional hearings, civil suits filed by some of the persons whose homes were ransacked by agents, and a full-scale investigation by the Justice Department. There has not, however, been any new specific legislation, or legislative charter, that would outlaw warrantless entries in the future, or even limit them in specific ways. (To the contrary, President Reagan's Executive Order 12333 authorizes break-ins during "foreign intelligence" and "counterintelligence" investigations.) Several agents have been given letters of censure; not one has been fired, fined, or sentenced to jail. One agent involved in the break-ins of the early 1970s, James Vermeersch, not only escaped prosection and administrative discipline, but was transferred to St. Louis, where he was assigned to the office of legal counsel, instructing younger agents about the law on search and seizure and, as he testified in the Miller-Felt trial, trying to "keep agents up to date on constitutional principles, and this type of thing."

William H. Webster, the new director, has issued detailed guidelines aimed at limiting break-ins in the foreign counterintelligence area, and virtually prohibiting them in domestic cases. But these are only guidelines, not laws. As such, they are subject to the whims of new directors and attorneys general, who can reverse them as quickly and as easily as William French Smith, Reagan's attorney general, in May 1981 reversed the policy set in 1977 by Carter's first attorney general, Griffin Bell, stipulating that government agencies couldn't withhold public records from the public unless they could prove that disclosure would cause serious harm.

The results of the long and controversial Justice Department investigation into FBI break-ins have been mixed. Sixty-eight agents and officials were targeted for possible disciplinary action, most of them members of Squad 47. FBI Director Webster decided to let the street agents, for the most part, off with a warning, and took disciplinary action against just four agents and officials. Later, he reconsidered one of the cases, and reduced the punishment.

The Justice Department had in 1977 indicted John Kearney, one of the supervisors of Squad 47, but in April 1978 dropped the charges, saying it wanted to prosecute only FBI officials who gave the orders. In April 1978, the Department secured the indictments of three high level officials for having authorized the Weather Underground break-ins: L. Patrick Gray (the former Acting FBI Director), former Acting FBI Associate Director W. Mark Felt (the Number Two official in the Bureau since 1972 until his retirement), and FBI Assistant Director Edward Miller (who headed the Intelligence Division during the early 1970s). Gray's trial was first postponed and his indictment eventually dismissed. Felt and Miller, however, were tried and, in November 1980, were convicted, only to be pardoned in March 1981 by President Ronald Reagan. The President short-circuited normal pardon procedure by not consulting with the Justice Department, and by granting the pardons before Miller and Felt had even applied for them. John Neilds, the chief prosecutor in the case, criticized the pardons and Reagan's accompanying statement as indicating that Reagan didn't know what the case was all about. (In Neilds's view, it was about whether the Fourth Amendment means what it says about prohibiting unwarranted searches and seizures.) Reagan's pardon decision was applauded, however, by such different personalities as Bob Hope, the comedian, who said that "convicting Mark and Ed for trying to protect this country from some pretty unsavory characters who are out to do us a lot of harm [is] like throwing Reggie Jackson out of a game for hitting a grand slam home run," and by former President Richard Nixon, who sent the two men champagne and a note saying, "justice ultimately prevails."

Meanwhile, even as Miller and Felt were standing trial, the Carter Justice Department's office of legal counsel, in one of its last official acts, issued an opinion reaffirming the President's inherent power to order warrantless entries in national security cases.

But while few agents were disciplined and no one was jailed, the various investigations were not without value. Among other things, they gave the public an unprecedented look inside the workings of the nation's largest police force, and dramatically pinpointed the great dangers to constitutional government and individual rights in letting a law enforcement agency operate outside the law. In many cases, it now is clear, the

FBI had been virtually unaccountable to anyone—FBI officials having decided on their own whose homes would be entered, without any approval or authorization either by the courts or by their nominal superiors in the Justice Department. In some cases, the FBI was an organization run amuck with agents and operatives conducting so-called wildcat wiretaps and break-ins on their own, without even the knowledge of their immediate supervisors, let alone the FBI director or the attorney general. Mark Cummings, an attorney for Felt, made this point at a bench conference during the Miller-Felt trial, complaining that, on at least some occasions, "this agent and some of the other agents on Squad 47 conducted local wiretaps on their own, without Bureau authority," and that "there is no indication, and not one iota of evidence, that Bureau headquarters was aware of this wildcat tapping that these agents were doing." And this is particularly worrisome because, as prosecutor Neilds told the jury: "You just can't have our nation's largest police force deciding for itself who is a spy and who isn't a spy, whose home should be searched, and whose home shouldn't."

One of the most basic lessons from all this is that the Bureau, when operating out of the public eye, has willingly short-circuited the Constitution, particularly when it was under heavy political pressure to get results. While much of what was done probably was the FBI's own doing, some of the most blatantly illegal actions against political activists, alleged gangsters, and, most recently, the Weather Underground fugitives, came when both the public in general and the White House in particular were clamoring for results. Pressure from the Nixon White House was a big factor in the great emphasis given the search for the Weather Underground fugitives, and the Bureau resorted to break-ins when the usual—and legal—methods of investigation had failed.

If the targets of the break-ins had been foreign agents or fugitives themselves, the Bureau could have obtained a legitimate search warrant about as quickly as it could have typed up the request. But it never sought any search warrants because it had no legitimate cause and knew that even the most pro-prosecution judge would have been hard-pressed to grant them. "There was no way we could have gotten warrants for the break-ins because there was no justification," an agent who was a member of Squad 47 conceded. "It was a total fishing expedition. Most of these people [whose homes were broken into] had only a marginal connection with the Weathermen. . . . No judge would have let us have warrants for this sort of thing."

Having decided to sidestep the courts, the Bureau then had to hide its actions from the courts, and from everyone else. Another of the lessons to be learned from the investigation into the break-ins is that FBI officials, at least in the past, went to great lengths to keep secret things they wanted kept secret. The FBI lied to the GAO about the break-ins at the Albert-Clavier cabin up in Hurley, New York and misled the Senate by withholding information about the so-called WEATHERFUG (as in Weather Fugitives) break-ins, telling the Senate Select Committee on Intelligence Activities that bag jobs had ended, for the most part, in 1966. Several ranking officials lied to Justice Department investigators and to a grand jury that was hearing evidence about the break-ins. And there is strong evidence that senior FBI officials were misled; Clarence Kelley insisted to the day he left the FBI directorship that he hadn't known about the post-1966 break-ins, which, if he's telling the truth, suggests that there were many people in the Bureau who knew about them but, for whatever reason, decided not to tell even him. "I can assure you that Clarence Kelley didn't know anything about it," one sympathetic FBI official said, after the disclosures about the WEATHERFUG break-ins had embarrassed the FBI director. "He was saying [they ended] in 1966, and that was what he was told. This means there had to be people who knew about it and knew what he was saying, and didn't tell him not to say it. Not a God-damned soul. So they've got Clarence Kelley out there with his neck out a mile . . . trying to explain why he doesn't know what's going on in his own Bureau."

The Justice Department investigation leading to the indictments of Felt and Miller also confirms that, to justify its actions, the Bureau was willing to overstate the evidence, and the threat. The agents who conducted a bag job at the home of Leonard Machtinger, whose younger brother, Howard, was a Weather fugitive, argued that they were pressured, in part, by the necessity of ending the bombings for which the Weather Underground was claiming credit. The FBI's standard line in recent years is that during the early 1970s there were forty thousand bombings and bomb threats—with no breakdown of actual bombings and threats. But by April 1973, when FBI agents made the entry into Leonard Machtinger's apartment on Manhattan's East 86th Street, there had been only one bombing in the previous year and a half for which the Weather Underground had claimed credit.

The details that emerged from the Justice Department investigation into the break-ins also shows that the Bureau has been quick to redefine and exaggerate the nature of the "internal security" threat. In the WEATHERFUG case, Miller and Felt and their attorneys argued that the break-ins could be justified without court warrants because the Weather Underground had close ties to foreign governments. This was a foreign counterintelligence investigation, Felt and Miller claimed, and thus one in which warrants weren't needed. The Supreme Court has never specifically ruled on whether warrants are needed in wiretaps and break-ins that are part of an authentic foreign counterintelligence investigation. But even if they aren't, the authority to order the break-ins would lie with the President, and not the head of the FBI's Intelligence Division (Miller) or an FBI assistant director (Felt). Yet L. Patrick Gray III denies that he ever told Miller and Felt to authorize break-ins, and — while they clearly were sympathetic to Miller and Felt — both former President Nixon and Richard Kleindienst, the former attorney general, testified that they hadn't either.

But the important point is that while Miller and Felt and agents at every level were citing the supposed foreign ties of the Weather Underground as justification for the warrantless entries, the testimony in the Miller-Felt trial shows that the investigation, from start to end, was handled strictly as a domestic criminal case. The charge, in most instances, was "unlawful flight to avoid prosecution," not espionage, and the possible ties to foreign government were at best incidental and at bottom irrelevant.

By ransacking their files, the FBI and CIA managed to compile a ninety-eight-page report suggesting that the Weather Underground was extensively involved with the Albanians, the Cubans, the North Vietnamese, the North Koreans, the Soviets, and the Chinese, not to mention the Viet Cong. Yet during Vermeersch's two-day testimony before the grand jury investigating the break-ins (he was the street agent who took part in a number of Weather Underground break-ins), according to

Justice Department prosecutors, he never once used the words "foreign," "intelligence," or "security" to describe the investigation. Instead, he repeatedly described it as a "fugitive" case.

Finally, the Justice Department investigation showed that while the agents, in the main, professed to have only the highest of motives, there were some things done in the course of the break-ins that suggested that they sometimes were conducting bag jobs for kicks, for a lark, just for the hell of it. The members of Squad 47 never found a fugitive as a result of the break-ins, or as a result of the mail openings and wiretaps that went hand-in-hand with them. Indeed, there was a time when two of the fugitives surrendered and the FBI didn't find out until several weeks later, keeping their search active while the pair were in the custody of local police. FBI agents did copy personal correspondence, valentine cards, love letters, and poems. They copied the Hebrew lessons they found in Leonard Machtinger's apartment because, as Special Agent Michael Kirschenbauer later said, they appeared to be "in a foreign tongue of some type" and he wanted the FBI lab to check this out. They copied and sent to the FBI laboratory for a cryptoanalysis examination a list of initials and numbers found in the apartment of Jennifer Dohrn, the sister of Weather fugitive Bernardine Dohrn, thinking they were some sort of code. The lab reported back that they appeared to be initials and birthdates of some of her friends.

Generally, the agents wouldn't take anything from an apartment, because they didn't want to raise suspicions that the place had been entered. But on one occasion they stole a pair of panties from Jennifer Dohrn's room, and presented them as a going-away gift to an agent who was leaving the squad. Some of the agents apparently thought this was funny, but it infuriated some of the Justice Department investigators when they learned about it, and undercut some of the sympathy they had had for the agents.

"I thought it was childish and offensive," said one of the Justice Department attorneys involved in the case, who did not want to be quoted by name. "The panties thing really offended me. It undercut all their arguments that they were just trying to get real evidence. They were going in and copying love letters and stealing panties. That put a whole different coloration on it. To some extent, these guys were just having a good time.

And that's not the way law enforcement agencies should treat citizens."

He paused briefly, and then added: "They had a real personal animosity towards Jennifer Dohrn and . . . some others. It was almost as though they took personal pleasure in violating the privacy of these people. And that bothered me."

All of these things could take place because the FBI had been able to do things in secret, to hide its own records, to deal in winks and nods and coded language, rather than direct orders, and, in general prevent outsiders (even federal investigators) from reconstructing just what had happened, and just who was to blame. One of the new guidelines which Webster put into effect requires agents to spell out precisely and clearly in their reports what sorts of investigative techniques have been used.

But there were other issues involved in the indictments of Gray, Felt, and Miller, issues that were raised by defense lawyers like Koelzer, William Hundley, Brian Gettings, Thomas Kennelly, Jack Solerwitz, Edward Bennett Williams, and Greg Craig, about the pressures put on street agents to produce, about the willingness of Justice Department officials over the years to give the FBI such a long leash to set its own rules, and about the fairness of prosecuting agents for things they had been rewarded for in the past—for changing the rules, in effect, after the game had been played.

The supporters of the FBI agents who had participated in the Weather Underground break-ins noted the great pressure from the Nixon White House to find the fugitives. They complained that the Justice Department, despite a memo telling the Bureau to terminate some of the "national security" wiretaps after the *Keith* decision, never told the agents directly that the decision meant that bag jobs couldn't be done in domestic cases without a court order. They groused about the unfairness of putting some FBI agents on trial when the people most responsible, Hoover and his long-term lieutenants, were either dead, or safely outside the statute of limitations.

"You can't give agents incentive awards for thirty years for pulling bag jobs and then turn around and try to put them in jail," said Koelzer, who ended up representing nearly a half-dozen agents caught up in the investigation. "And you can't blame it just on the agents. These things didn't start with the Weathermen. They've been going on since World War II, and there were a lot of people in the Justice Department over those years who either told the bureau to go ahead and do it, or turned and looked the other way."

Although the FBI is a stickler for record-keeping, it is not certain just where or when the Bureau's first bag job took place, or against whom it had been committed. In a way, this is a shame, because an exhibit depicting the event would be an interesting addition to the museum in the J. Edgar Hoover Building, which contains such other Bureau memorabilia as the death mask of the late John Dillinger (ambushed by FBI agents in Chicago) and the hollow nickel in which a Russian spy had hidden some microfilm. The exhibit, for example, might contain the first black bag ever used in a break-in, along with a set of lock picks and a tiny, easily concealable microphone. It could contain a copy of the orders setting up the Do Not File files, which made it possible to record break-ins without leaving any official record, and perhaps photostats of some of the letters of commendation—known within the Bureau as M.V.P. (for Most Valuable Player) Awards—that routinely were given to agents who successfully conducted warrantless entries. It might also, of course, include photographs of agents reenacting the historic event.

While there is, unfortunately, no such exhibit, bag jobs nonetheless are a big part of FBI lore. Among themselves, or with friends, veteran agents talk about break-ins the way Army veterans sometimes talk about their particular war, spinning out tales that are sad, funny, and, at bottom, often disturbing. They tell of the agent who died of a heart attack one night, while inside the diplomatic mission of a Communist country. His fellow agents not only had to get him out of the mission, but then had to break in again and clean up a mess on the carpet that was caused when he fell. They tell of the agent who, while trying to plant a bug in a mob hangout in Chicago, slipped off a joist in the attic and jammed his leg through the ceiling, requiring a frantic effort to repair the hole and plaster it over before dawn. They talk about the bug planted in the office of a mob attorney who was having an affair with his secretary; agents monitoring the meetings that took place in the office are said to have found themselves privy—on two separate occasions—to conception, distressed conversations about the resulting problem, and arrangements for the subsequent abortion.

There are tales of bag jobs being disrupted by the sudden return of the person whose property was being searched, or, occasionally, by local police. "You hit the cop and you ran," said one former agent when asked what happened in such cases. A former New York City policeman recalled a time, a generation ago, when FBI agents pulling a bag job at the apartment of a Russian official were surprised by the official, who had returned unexpectedly and somehow had slipped past the agents on watch outside. The agents knocked him out, and then ransacked the place, to make it look like a robbery. Later, when the Russian reported it to the police, an FBI emissary urged the police not to investigate the matter too thoroughly, and it remained an "unsolved" burglary in the police books.

Some of this retelling of bag jobs came into public light during the Miller-Felt trial, as former agents, testifying for the defense, became a sort of passing parade of bag jobs past, describing their activities against different groups in different decades. Elmer Lindberg, a former agent, told how he had performed bag jobs against foreign nationals, resident aliens, and United States citizens while investigating German espionage cases in the 1942–1945 period. David Ryan, a long-term Bureau official, testified that in the 1950s he had done bag jobs against foreign diplomatic missions in New York, including one that the Bureau was so proud of that Hoover described it in detail to President Eisenhower and the entire cabinet. George Burley told how he had done bag jobs against Communist Party members and organized crime figures. And John Gordon recalled how he had conducted surreptitious entries against the Ku Klux Klan in Mississippi in 1964, and had received an official commendation for his work.

To a man, these FBI agents seemed not only comfortable with what they had done, but rather proud of it. And this, too, was only fitting, for as a rule the better agents were selected for bag jobs, agents who were cool and tough and not easily panicked, and ready to fight their way out of a jam. "We picked only the top people for bag jobs," said the late William Sullivan, formerly the Number Three official in the Bureau. "We picked men with nerves of steel. We didn't send lunkheads off on those jobs."[3]

Although there probably were earlier break-ins, the best evidence is that they became institutionalized sometime around 1940, which was the year that—on April 11—Hoover outlined the record-keeping procedures that allowed the agency to keep track of such things internally, without worrying about the records getting in the wrong hands. This procedure, the predecessor of the Do Not File records system, called for the use of blue paper (later, pink paper) for any memos intended for only the director and other ranking FBI officials, and which were not to be retained in the Bureau's regular files.

In 1942, the system was further refined, and the Do Not File system came into being, permitting the field offices and headquarters to exchange information about warrantless entries and wiretaps, and other sensitive matters, without worrying about leaving a retrievable record behind in the files. In the normal course of things, records were to have been put on white paper, were then given serial numbers, cross-indexed, and filed. Because they had index numbers, the regular files couldn't be removed without a gap having been left in the numbering system indicating that something was missing. But the Do Not File procedure avoided this. It permitted these files to be hidden, and even destroyed. It also permitted agents to testify—under oath, if necessary—that they had searched the "central files" and had found no evidence that a given person or organization had been bagged or bugged.

A person didn't have to be a criminal, or even a suspected criminal, to be targeted for a bag job. The FBI not only investigates crimes, but also gathers political intelligence of various sorts (although it claims to be doing much less political intelligence gathering now, at least where domestic groups are concerned), and since World War II has been heavily involved in foreign counterintelligence work. This is particularly true of the FBI field offices in Washington, where the foreign embassies are located, and New York, where the United Nations (commonly referred to by agents as "the Trojan horse") is based.

In 1975, FBI Director Clarence Kelley told the Senate Select Committee on Intelligence Activities that 239 agency-initiated break-ins had occurred between 1942 and 1968. He didn't claim that these were the *only* ones that had occurred, but did say that they were the only ones for which records could be found, and indicated that most had been against foreign intelligence operations.

Many of the break-ins were in the "intelligence" or "national security" field, and they point up one aspect of FBI operations that has bothered many students of the criminal justice system, including some ranking Bureau officials. The federal government's chief law enforcement agency, the FBI is (or at least was) the chief gatherer of intelligence about foreign spies and about those domestic groups that FBI officials considered dangerous or subversive. Most nations separate criminal investigation from intelligence gathering, but in the FBI these investigations are contained under one roof. And since many of the agents moved back and forth from criminal squads to security squads, they often found themselves—depending on their assignment of the moment—governed by very different sets of rules.

What often happened, some agents privately admit, is that agents assigned to a criminal investigation resorted to the same techniques that they had used while chasing foreign spies—illegal wiretaps, mail openings, break-ins. It was only a small step from a warrantless wiretap of a foreign mission to a warrantless wiretap of a Communist Party-U.S.A. office, and only a small step from there to a warrantless wiretap of a social club where alleged mobsters hung out.

A great many of the break-ins, many agents agree, were aimed at members of various radical political groups—the Communist Party-U.S.A., the Socialist Workers Party, Fair Play for Cuba Committee, National Lawyers Guild, American Peace Mobilization, Civil Rights Congress, Committee for the Protection of the Foreign Born—which FBI Director Hoover and other FBI officials considered "subversive." This practice continued for years, despite the fact that most of the groups had so small a following that it was hard to think of them as a threat to the Republic, and despite the fact that in many cases there was little or no evidence that they had any violent intent. "You look back at all those bomb throwers we were chasing and you'll see most of them didn't have any bombs," says William Hundley, a former Justice Department prosecutor now in private practice. "Most of those guys never threw anything but leaflets."

One case that illustrates this point is that of the Socialist Workers Party (SWP) a small, powerless, and probably harmless (not to say ineffective) Trotskyist group that eventually filed suit against the FBI and the Justice Department, claiming numerous violations of civil and constitutional rights. Court testimony in the suit, which finally went to trial early in 1981, indicates that between 1958 and 1966 FBI agents broke into SWP offices more than ninety times, looking for documents that might show that the organization was working to overthrow the United States government. For a time, the Bureau was staging break-ins against one SWP officer who was blind and had to have his mail read to him. Agents installed a tape recorder to listen in on the reading of the mail, and then went back repeatedly to install new batteries. The surveillance continued year after year, despite the fact that the Bureau— according to its own records—found no evidence of espionage, violence, or criminal wrongdoing. Indeed, in all their years of spying on the SWP, ransacking its offices, and planting informants in its ranks—thirty-four years' worth of surveillance that generated roughly eight million pages of files—the FBI never obtained enough information of wrongdoing to seek a single criminal indictment.

While the records concerning bag jobs are fragmentary, those that do exist, plus interviews with numerous agents and former agents, suggest that the bulk took place between 1950 and 1966, and that the large number in this period was due in part to the Cold War climate, and to a new, almost sudden, preoccupation with organized crime. M. Wesley Swearingen, a former agent, insisted that FBI offices in at least six major cities staged thousands of break-ins during the 1950s and 1960s (Justice Department investigators found evidence of break-ins in a minimum of sixteen cities), and that he personally had taken part in about 300 in the Chicago area alone. Moreover, he maintains, agents had encouraged their informants to conduct break-ins of homes and offices, and steal records or other evidence that could be used against the people and organizations they were being paid to provide information about.

Hoover and other FBI senior officials had long been staunchly anti-Communist, and the monitoring of subversives had been a high-priority item for the FBI in the post–World War II years. FBI agents went into Communist Party offices so routinely that one agent later remarked that the party headquarters in New York had been "burgled more than a fur company in the Bronx." But the focus on organized crime was relatively new. For years, Hoover and his lieutenants had belittled the notion that there was a Mafia-type criminal network, or that, if there was, it was of any great import. While agents in the Federal Bureau of Narcotics compiled detailed charts purporting to illustrate the structure and scope of such organized crime families, and while congressional investigators probed the alleged ties between organized crime and labor unions, the FBI paid little heed, marshaling its resources instead against bank robbers, draft dodgers, kidnappers, and virtually anyone who managed to wander across a state line in a stolen car. But the discovery of the so-called Appalachian Convention in 1957 gave credence to the notion of a nationwide criminal network, dominated by Italian-American gangsters, and suddenly Justice Department officials pressured the Bureau to identify its members and to disrupt their operations. And this, in turn, resulted in FBI officials pressuring street agents to develop sources within organized crime families and to gather everything that could be learned about them. Dossiers were compiled on the life-styles, business activities, travels, sex lives, and personal friendships of suspected mobsters. Information, much of it fragmentary, libelous, and of questionable veracity, was collected, in vacuum-cleaner fashion, from every possible source.

One of the earliest ways to get this information was through wiretaps and other eavesdropping devices, and all through the late 1950s and early 1960s, the FBI planted hundreds, perhaps thousands, of them in business offices and meeting places of known or suspected organized crime figures, and sometimes, but less frequently, in their homes. To plant the devices, they often made surreptitious entries—usually without court warants—and often paused while inside to photocopy whatever documents they could find. This practice was so widespread that many people outside the Bureau knew about it, including newspaper reporters, prosecutors, defense lawyers, and local police. Later, when it became known publicly and many Justice Department officials, prosecutors, and members of Congress (including many who once had been prosecutors) were professing outrage and claiming never to have heard about break-ins before, some others were quick to dismiss this with scorn. "They had bugs in mob apartments and offices all over New York," said James Kelly, a city policeman in New York in the 1950s, who later, as an investigator for various Senate committees, became familiar with many of the transcripts. "How do you think they got all those bugs in? The mailman didn't put them in."

No, it wasn't the mailman. It was, in the main, street agents working the Bureau's so-called Top Hoodlums project, a crash effort to gather as much information as possible as quickly as possible on people allegedly involved in organized crime. "We did hundreds of them against the mob—all of them illegal," says one former agent, who specialized in organized crime work and who claims to have taken part in more than fifty break-ins. "We were wired in on twenty-four [organized crime] families—bosses, under-bosses, all the way down the line. All of these were done through break-ins, and all were illegal as hell. . . . Jesus Christ, we had [Chicago crime boss] Sam Giancana buried" under warrantless wiretaps.

Not all of his colleagues agree that such entries were illegal. Indeed, many argue that before the *Keith* decision, there was no clear constitutional requirement for a court warrant to install an eavesdropping device, or for the surreptitious entry needed to install it. And the attorneys for Edward S. Miller and W. Mark Felt argued throughout their trial that the Bureau, through presidential directives, had ongoing authority to conduct warrantless entries in "national security" cases.

There is little question, however, that many FBI officials knew that break-ins without warrants probably were illegal (the FBI memo describing the Do Not File procedure states that black bag jobs were "clearly illegal") and that the great number of agents considered them, if not flatly illegal, at least highly improper. FBI agents knew that information from break-ins was inadmissable in court, and evidence of their knowledge that break-ins were wrong is found in the great lengths they went to try to hide them. Their reports did not state that information had been obtained from a break-in but from an "anonymous source." One report stated that pilfered material "is not evidentiary in nature" and that "Every effort must be made in utilizing this material to avoid disclosing its existence." Agents making break-ins usually went in without badges or identification of any kind, and fully understood that, if caught in the act, they would be disowned by the Bureau. "It was your ass if you got caught," said one agent, who admitted taking part in break-ins against organized crime figures. "You were told, 'If you get caught, you're on your own.' "

The reporting of break-ins, such as it was, was virtually in code, with such terms as "special techniques" or "sensitive investigative techniques" used in place of a clear description of what had been done. When included in the files, information from the break-ins often was reported as having come from an "anonymous source" or a "highly confidential source." Indeed, when Miller told Felt that he had authorized a break-in at the home of Murray Bookchin, he didn't say that agents had wanted to conduct an entry and that he had approved it. Rather, his February 13, 1973 memo to Felt stated: "Special Agent-in-Charge Arbor W. Gray . . . requested authority to contact an anonymous source at the residence of Murray Bookchin . . . . He assured me that such could be accomplished with full security and he was given authority to proceed."

Testimony in the Miller-Felt trial made clear that, over the years, Bureau officials had withheld information about warrantless entries from Special Prosecutor Archibald Cox, from several attorneys general, and from the courts. "They broke into the homes . . . of the American people for thirty years, and they did it in secret," John Neilds, the chief prosecutor in the Miller-Felt trial, told the jury. "And it's not an easy secret to keep, either. Thirty years of break-ins into the homes of the American people, and they kept it a secret from us.

"They kept it a secret from their own filing system, and even in their 'Do-Not-File' files, they wrote it down in such a way that it made it appear that the information had come fron an anonymous source. They even kept it a secret from attorneys general, but most important of all, they kept it a secret from us. And then when we find out—when we find out, they turn around and look at us and say, 'But nobody ever told us it was wrong.'

"Well, I suggest to you that they knew very well it was wrong, and they knew very well what the consequences would be if we found out what they had been doing."

But to many Bureau officials, over many years, the results were considered well worth the risk. And this was particularly true in the field of espionage and foreign counterintelligence, where the FBI was often called upon by other agencies to conduct break-ins at foreign embassies and consulates to obtain highly sensitive intelligence data. Much of this work remains highly classified. Indeed, during the Miller-Felt trial, neither defense lawyers nor prosecutors were permitted to describe it in detail, and only referred to such break-ins as "Program C" entries. By several reliable accounts, these were break-ins conducted largely at the request of the National Security Agency (NSA), an agency so secret that even President Truman's November 1952 executive order creating it had been and remains classified, and until recently the NSA was spared even the most routine sort of congressional oversight.

The NSA is structured to intercept foreign communications and then to try to decode the messages it has obtained. Its incredibly vast, complex, and sophisticated monitoring operation permits it to capture and record messages transmitted from points all over the globe, including those from foreign governments to their diplomatic offices here. Most of this information is coded and intercepting the messages is only the first, and often the easiest, part of NSA's job. Much of the FBI's work for the NSA, according to former agents and others in a position to know, involved break-ins at foreign embassies, consulates, and trade missions to obtain code books and other data that could be helpful in deciphering foreign codes. Soviet bloc embassies, but not the Soviet embassy itself, were said to have been among the chief targets, and on one occasion, with the help of an informant, FBI agents disguised as trash collectors drove a garbage truck right into the yard of the Czech embassy in Washington in the middle of the night, and carted away the embassy's coding machine.

"There was almost no way we could get into the Soviet embassy," said an agent who took part in some embassy and consulate break-ins, "the security was too tight. But we went into the Czech, Polish and Yugoslav embassies." In most cases, he said, the agents photographed coding and decoding equipment, from every possible angle. Then they photocopied every document that could be found, hoping that if the NSA had intercepted a message going in, and the FBI could then find and copy the decoded version, a resulting match-up would help break the code.

Others said that Arab embassies and consulates were constant targets, and fairly easy to enter. "All the Arab embassies were easy," said one agent. "The only problem was tripping over the Jews already inside." This is an exaggeration, of course, but there apparently was at least one case when agents in New York conducting a break-in at an Arab consulate came face to face with others, believed to be Israeli agents, already inside, and managed to get away only after some tense negotiations. And several agents who worked in New York said that on more than one occasion when FBI agents tried to tap a phone at an Arab consulate or mission, they discovered that Israeli agents already had installed a tap of their own.

Defense lawyers in the Miller-Felt trial argued that it was nonsense to tell the FBI that it could conduct such sensitive entries as these, but then turn around and say it was a crime to conduct a similar entry in search of a fugitive terrorist—and that it was unfair to applaud them for one sort of break-in but indict them for another. "Remember when Hoover went over and told Eisenhower and the whole cabinet what he was doing?" Frank Dunham, an attorney for Felt, told the jury. "And they didn't boo. They didn't hiss. They didn't say 'Who are these agents?' 'Who authorized this?' 'Indict him!' They didn't throw fruit at him. They cared. They said, 'Good work. We're glad the FBI's on the job.' "

The prosecutors argued, in response, that there is a great difference between legitimate national security work and criminal investigations of United States citizens, which—despite the defendants' attempts to link Weather fugitives with a number of foreign governments—the attempts to find the fugitives clearly had been. And, prosecutors argued, having known all along that bag jobs were illegal, Hoover ultimately decided to ban them in 1966.

It's not at all clear, however, that Hoover had prohibited bag jobs in 1966 because they were illegal. Most FBI officials had known that for years. Rather, it seems that Hoover formally banned them because the climate was changing—there was increasing criticism in the Congress and the courts about wiretapping—and because there was a real possibility that the FBI's resort to bag jobs would be made public.

During the 1966 trial of Fred Black, Attorney General Nicholas DeB. Katzenbach had advised Hoover that he had to disclose the existence of FBI bugging to the Supreme Court. Internal FBI memos indicate that FBI officials were angry about this decision, and fearful that Justice Department officials would claim to have had no knowledge of any bugs, or the break-ins often made to install them, and thus lay the whole blame on the Bureau. Within two weeks after Katzenbach had warned the FBI director of his decision to tell the Court about the lack of explicit Justice

Department authorization for this FBI bug, Hoover issued his edict, prohibiting bag jobs from then on.

The Hoover ban was not in the form of an announcement to the field offices, or even a specific memo. Rather, it came in the form of a handwriten notation scrawled on the bottom of a July 19, 1966 memo from William Sullivan, then the head of the Intelligence Division, to FBI Assistant Director Cartha DeLoach. Sullivan favored contuing bag jobs, but conceded their illegality. "We do not obtain authorization for 'black bag' jobs from outside the bureau," Sullivan admitted. "Such a technique involves trespass and is clearly illegal; therefore it would be impossible to obtain any legal sanction for it." In short, Sullivan was saying that the FBI never formally asked the Justice Department, or the courts, for authority for bag jobs, because the authority was not theirs to give.

Hoover's reply was that "no more such techniques must be used." But it's not really certain whether the FBI director was banning all break-ins, or just break-ins in domestic cases. And it's not clear whether he actually meant to prohibit them, or just make sure that no one sent him any paper seeking his personal approval.

In a January 6, 1967, memo to DeLoach and to FBI Associate Director Clyde Tolson, Hoover wrote: "I note that requests are still being made by Bureau officials for the use of 'black bag' techniques. I have previously indicated that I do not intend to approve any such requests in the future, and, consequently, no such recommendations should be submitted for approval of such matters. This practice, which includes also surreptitious entries upon premises of any kind, will not meet with my approval in the future."

The obvious question is whether Hoover actually did intend a flat prohibition on future break-ins, or whether he was just engaging in some sort of paper exercise intended to distance himself from any illegal acts that might be uncovered. It's also possible, because many of the break-ins had been staged for the NSA, Hoover was hoping that if he refused to let his agents do them, other agencies of the government, and perhaps even the White Hosue, would pressure the Justice Department to have him do them again, and in the process would assume responsibility for any resultant problems. The internal FBI report on bag jobs that was recently prepared for FBI Director Webster takes note of the Hoover ban, but also states that "it is unclear, however, whether this prohibition continued unaltered."

The reason for this uncertainty, the report continues, is that "notwithstanding Hoover's note . . . an instruction went out from Headquarters to the Chicago and New York City Field Offices on January 25, 1968, instructing them to conduct a survey determining the feasibility of technical surveillance on the Chicago National Headquarters and the New York regional headquarters of SDS." Furthermore, the report cites evidence that in mid-1968 a surreptitious entry was conducted in a domestic security case, and the results of the entry were forwarded to Headquarters.

Thus, at least a few bag jobs were done in the immediate post-1966 period, although many agents insist that they were stopped in the main, and that the 1966 prohibition was real. By 1970, the climate was changing again, and the Nixon White House was pressuring the FBI to resort to such techniques to deal with radical domestic groups, espionage rings, and fugitive terrorists.

On March 6, 1970, an event occurred in New York that brought the FBI back into the bag job business in a very real way. On this date, an explosion occurred in a townhouse at 18 West 11th Street, in New York's Greenwich Village, in which the bodies of two young anti-war activists were later found, along with more than sixty sticks of dynamite and more than one hundred blasting caps. Two women, believed to be Cathy Wilkerson and Katherine Boudin, were seen runing, naked, out of the smoke and rubble immediately after the blast, and a wave of news stories about young radical terrorists and a Greenwich Village "bomb factory" appeared in the nation's press.

The Bureau in 1970 was not only a disciplined and professional police force, but also a power in its own right, much respected in the country as a whole, and yet feared, in a way, by many in high places in the government, presidents included. Congressmen feared FBI Director Hoover, while attorneys general deferred to him. And Lyndon Johnson, in explaining his decision to allow Hoover to continue as FBI director past the normal retirement age, told his aides—according to Washington legend— that he'd "rather have him inside the tent pissing out, than outside the tent pissing in." So great was Hoover's power that his agency was given virtually a free hand in setting its priorities and allocating its resources as the FBI director saw fit. In his last twenty-one trips to the Congress with budget requests, Hoover was given precisely the budget he requested nineteen times. The other two times, the FBI's budget was increased by friendly Congressmen without Hoover even having to ask formally for the extra funds.

In its relationship with the Justice Department, the Bureau presented a textbook example of the tail that wagged the dog. In many areas of criminal law enforcement, the FBI set the priorities for the Department rather than the other way round. In *The Reform of FBI Intelligence Operations* (Princeton: 1979), John Ellitt observes that it made "little difference whether the attorney general was a liberal like Ramsey Clark or a conservative like John Mitchell . . . . Whatever their ideological bent, attorneys general usually preferred to let the FBI set its own guidelines or, when it sought direction, to give whatever investigative authority the bureau desired."

It was a mysterious agency, little known to outsiders, secretive about its operations, protective of its own, and quick to pull the wagons around when challenged by outsiders, no matter how minor the threat. It was almost lily white in its make-up (in 1970, only about fifty of its eight thousand special agents were black) and completely male. Women served as secretaries, telephone operators, and clerks, but none were special agents. The in-house joke was that Hoover didn't want any "Dickless Tracys" carrying a badge. The Bureau also was something of an anachronism. In as simple and basic a matter as clothing, it was out of touch with the times. Hoover insisted that his men wear white shirts and conservative suits long after fashions had changed, with the result that the whole idea of the FBI dress code—to be neat without being conspicuous—was stood on its head, and it became difficult for agents to conduct the most routine sorts of surveillance.

It was an anachronism in more fundamental ways. A look at the FBI's budget for 1971—Hoover's last full year as FBI director—suggests that he perceived the biggest law enforcement problems to include car thieves, draft-dodgers, and the Communist Party-U.S.A. The latter, he said, remained "under the complete control and domination of the Soviet Union," and because of this was "a menace to the security of our country." To many of the street agents, the Communist Party-U.S.A.

was considered something of a joke, and agents assigned to monitor it sometimes were referred to as the "geriatric squad," because much of the party membership had grown so old. Only modest resources were committed to fraud against the government, and various forms of white-collar and organized crime. Bank robberies, however, were high on the FBI's priority list, and the great emphasis placed on them was seen by some critics, both within the Bureau and without, as evidence of Hoover's unwillingness (or inability) to change with the times.

There was a time, back before the Federal Deposit Insurance Corporation was established, when bank robberies were a serious threat to large numbers of people, because a single robber could make off with much of the wealth of an entire small town. Good roads and fast cars enabled bank robbers to move quickly across state lines, out of the reach of local police, and there was no other agency able to deal with this sort of interstate crime. Moreover, much of the glamor that surrounded the FBI grew from tales of its shootouts with bank robbers. A half-dozen of the best-known bank robbers were shot to death during a six-month period in 1934, and the stories that resulted usually portrayed FBI agents as brave, heroic, and larger than life, such as Jack Lait's account of the shooting of John Dillinger for International News Service. "John Dillinger, ace bad man of the world, got his last night—two slugs through the heart and one through his head," Lait's story began. "He was tough and he was shrewd, but he wasn't as tough and shrewd as the Federals, who never close a case until the end."

By the 1970s, however, most big city police departments, and many state police agencies, were able to deal effectively with bank robberies, which tend to be routine, easily solved crimes. Most bank robbers leave physical evidence behind—a hand-written note, a fingerprint on the counter—and, even in the days before banks were equipped with cameras, there usually were witnesses to give a description of the robber or the get away car. But Hoover and his men liked working bank robberies, and they were still devoting major resources to them in 1970, despite the fact that about three times as much money was being lost to bank embezzlement each year. And bank embezzlement, like other white-collar crimes, was of scant concern.

The Bureau's intelligence operations also were flawed, as investigations subsequent to Hoover's death made clear. In many cases, agents seemed more intent on building dossiers than gathering legitimate intelligence, more intent on learning things that could be used against people than in learning about them. The GAO audit of FBI domestic intelligence operations showed that of the 676 cases it had studied, only sixteen were referred to the Justice Department for prosecution. Of these, only seven actually resulted in indictments and only four resulted in convictions.

In short, FBI resources were being wasted, and this was particularly troubling to persons who cared about the agency, and about law enforcement, because, with fewer than eight thousand special agents, it was a much smaller agency than most people realized and didn't have the resources to waste.

While its investigative force was small and stretched very thin, the FBI had developed a headquarters bureaucracy that many street agents found to be not only bloated, but distant, detached, and out of touch with the reality of the world that the agents were working in. It was top-heavy with men who had worked their way up the ladder in the administrative section, many of them agents who knew little of the problems of law enforcement, but who had mastered the skills of budget setting, personnel management, and record-keeping, as well as the Byzantine internal politics of the Bureau. It is a common gripe in government, and elsewhere, that many of the people who get to the top lack the qualifications to remain at the bottom; this was particularly true in Hoover's FBI. The number of sycophants was startling, even for Washington. Some sense of this was captured in a letter that Neil J. Welch, at the time the head of the FBI's Philadelphia Field Office, wrote in 1977 to a committee that was searching for a successor to Clarence Kelley. Welch was mistrusted at FBI Headquarters as a maverick in an organization dominated by team players. Among other things, he was known to hold the view that both the FBI and the nation would be better off if someone put sandbags around the headquarters building and disconnected the telephones. The headquarters structure, he wrote in his application for the top job, was a "ponderous, ineffectual, costly bureaucracy, which does not contribute substantially to the essential work of the FBI." It was, he added, "totally autocratic" in nature and scorned and distrusted by agents on the street.

Its top officials, he said, by and large lacked the "total investigative work experience necessary for top command."

Much of this was not known in 1970, at least not to the public at large. In the past decade, there has been a vast outpouring of information about Hoover and his Bureau, ranging from the fact that it harassed Martin Luther King to his grave and even beyond (the FBI lobbied mightly after his death to keep Congress from declaring his birthday a national holiday) to the fact that the Hoover slept in the nude. But in 1970, at the time Squad 47 was formed, there was no general concern that the Bureau was squandering its manpower on trivial crimes, any more than there was wide knowledge (although there always were suspicions, particularly on the part of defense lawyers, mobsters, and political activists) that it was, to be blunt about it, committing numerous crimes.

As Richard Harris wrote in the August 8, 1977, issue of *The New Yorker*, after more than a year of congressional inquiries into the Bureau:

Without any legal authorization, they have tapped telephones, they have opened and read private mail, they have planted electronic bugs in offices and bedrooms, they have written anonymous and false letters to spouses and associates and employers of people they wanted to harm, they have committed burglaries and other break-ins, they have paid informants who later have lied under oath, they have furnished funds and arms to paramilitary right-wing groups that have burned and bombed offices of left-wing groups . . . they have used *agents provocateurs* to entrap others by planning and encouraging criminal conspiracies, they have incited police violence, they have blackmailed and slandered critics, and they have driven opposing radical militants to attack one another.

Many of these activities had been going on for years, and still were going on in the spring of 1970. Indeed, a case can be made that they were fostered and encouraged by the whole attitude of the Nixon Justice Department, which was trying to get the Bureau even more involved in "domestic security" matters, and whose loudly trumpeted fight for law and order seemed to many, as journalist Russell Sackett once put it, "as calculatedly malign as anything this nation has seen since frontier lawmen stopped holding up stagecoaches on the side." Given all the different ways in which the FBI had been breaking the law, given the great pressure from the Nixon White House to catch the fugitives, and given the free hand that the bureau was allowed by the Nixon White House, the Congress, and the Department of Justice in the early 1970s, it's not surprising in the least that the members of Squad 47 did what they did, which was to operate, in some ways, like a secret police.

Squad 47 came into being almost immediately after the explosion in the townhouse. The designation meant that it was Squad No. 7 in Division No. 4 (the New York Field Office's Internal Security Division). At the start, it consisted of about twenty agents, but later, at the peak of the drive to catch the Weather Underground fugitives, it had as many as fifty agents. Most of the agents were rather young (the majority were in their twenties or early thirties), and most realized from the start that they were going to be under intense pressure to get results.

The division was stretched across a large open room in the Bureau's old offices on East 69th Street. Each agent had a desk of his own, with the various squads grouped together, about three rows of desks per squad. At the front of each squad, in a partially enclosed cubicle, was the supervisor, who was roughly the equivalent of an Army platoon sergeant, being the link between the officials at FBI headquarters and the "brick agents" on the street. Squad 47 shared the large room with the Communist Party-U.S.A. Squad, the Black Panther Squad, and several other security squads. But there were a number of things that set it apart.

For starters, it was the only squad that was searching for specific fugitives and had warrants outstanding for specific arrests. Partly because of this, it was known within the office as the "fugitive squad," or the "WEATHERFUG Squad." And this meant that while the other squads were doing mostly intelligence work, Squad 47 was doing not only intelligence work, but ordinary criminal investigation as well—a routine, straight-out, search for fugitives. From the start, then, the squad had a dual role, it had to gather intelligence on the Weather Underground while at the same time tracking down specific fugitives as part of an ordinary criminal case.

Another difference was that it worked mostly at night. While the usual Bureau work day was 8:00 A.M. to 5:00 P.M., the members of Squad 47 usually didn't arrive until near dark and stayed on the job until near dawn. The main reason was that—because having virtually no Weather

Underground informants—the Bureau had to try to penetrate the organization. Members of Squad 47 were thus allowed to dress in casual clothes, to wear their hair long, and to try to blend into the milieu of the East Village and other centers of the anti-war movement. This was a dramatic departure from normal Bureau operations. Hoover had rarely allowed his agents to work undercover, insisting instead that they use informants to penetrate such groups. The very fact that agents were allowed to wear dungarees on the job, and let their hair grow, was a sign of the pressure on the Bureau to get results.

A third difference was that the squad's supervisor was a veteran named John Kearney, a ruggedly handsome, much-respected agent, who was known through the whole FBI for his skill in organizing and performing break-ins. Kearney was forty-nine at the time, a veteran of more than twenty years in the Bureau. He was considered a sane and rational man, who had worked surveillance of various Communist Party-U.S.A. units for years, but doing it with professional detachment, rather than ideological zeal. (Later, after his indictment had made him a hero and martyr to many conservative groups, Kearney reportedly told friends that while he appreciated their support and was thankful for their contributions to his defense fund, he nonetheless felt uncomfortable as a conservative symbol. "I'm a Kennedy liberal," he said.) And there is little doubt that Kearney was given the job specifically to train the young agents of Squad 47 in the various break-in and wiretapping techniques that he had become so proficient in over the years.

In a special internal report compiled for William Webster after he became FBI director, FBI officials said that it not only was clear that the break-ins had taken place, but that many people at headquarters had known about them and had approved them. Indeed, the report noted, Kearney's appointment as supervisor of Squad 47 "can be viewed as inherent authorization to use extraordinary techniques," because that's what Kearney had spent his career doing. "Kearney was experienced and skilled in the conduct of these investigative techniques," the report continued. "He had utilized these techniques in investigations since the 1950s. In addition, when he was appointed to Squad 47, he was given the job of getting the squad into shape, and of developing investigative techniques with respect to Weather Underground fugitives."

A senior FBI official, who knows and admires Kearney, agrees, saying that Kearney was not only known for his skill, but also for his coolness in tense situations. "That's why they sent him up there," he said. "Little did he know the roof was going to come crashing in."

John Kearney was not the only one to supervise Squad 47 during its heyday. He was succeeded by Horace Beckwith and later by Leo Kelly. In the chain-of-command, the supervisor reported to the SAC who headed the division—in 1970, Joseph Gamble, and J. Wallace LaPrade (who ultimately became head of the whole New York office, before being fired by Attorney General Griffin Bell for not cooperating with Justice Department investigators probing the break-ins), John Morley, Andrew Decker, and Arbor Gray.

Agents rotated through the squad, as they do all FBI squads, some staying only a brief time, and several staying for more than four years. Among those who stayed long enough to become deeply involved in the search for the Weather fugitives were Vermeersch, John Glennon, Donald Strickland, James Reevesk, James Ross, Francis Jerrett, Robert Mason, John Curtin, Howard Denscott, Robert Vericker, Thomas Meyers, Vincent Alvino, Terry Roberts, Michael Kirschenbauer, and Bernard Stec.

Their superiors persistently emphasized the importance of Squad 47's job and went to some lengths to depict the Weathermen as a menace. For example, after several years had passed without the capture of a single fugitive, John Morley, who had become the SAC, posted a notice calling for additional agents to volunteer for the squad.

The Weathermen and related New Left subjects represent an admitted revolutionary combine whose stated objective is the destruction of organized society. As indication of their contempt for our government, they have claimed credit for the bombing of the United States Capitol and the Pentagon Building, both of which resulted in extensive property damage. They have also been associated with other bombings and criminal activities which have caused injury and death.

Seven of the Top Ten [persons wanted by the bureau] have a New Left and/or Weatherman background. They are wanted for a variety of felonious crimes, including sabotage and unlawful flight to avoid prosecution for the crimes of murder and bank robbery.

Until these heinous individuals are apprehended, they will be encouraged by their past criminal actions and could further engage in other bombings and criminal activity which could overshadow what they have caused to date.

While our investigative efforts concerning the location of the Weatheman and Top Ten fugitives to date have been extensive, results achieved have been minimal . . . . I am therefore reallocating additional manpower to the Weatherman investigations and the informant development program. I specifically want agents on this important project who have the initiative, imagination, and confidence to handle the extremely important investigative challenge inherent in this assignment.

The "heinous" persons being sought included some of the better known radicals of the day: Mark Rudd, who first became known nationally during the riots at Columbia University in 1968; Cathy Wilkerson and Katherine Boudin, who were thought to have been the two women who had run naked from the townhouse after the explosion on March 6, 1970; Jeffrey Jones, Lawrence Wise, and Howard Machtinger, and one of the leaders of the Weather Underground, Bernardine Dohrn, a former Girl Scout and University of Chicago Law School graduate, who had been indicted for inciting to riot.

The chief plan for locating the fugitives was to keep a close watch over people thought to be in touch with them. These included friends, relatives, lovers, and fellow anti-war activists. Since many of the fugitives were the children of wealthy parents, the assumption was that they might still be getting money and support from them while in hiding. The agents focused their attention on Jennifer Dohrn, the sister of Bernardine; Leonard Machtinger, the brother of Howard; and Benjamin and Rosa Cohen, the parents of Judith Flatley; and about twenty others, many of them political activists, including Dana Biberman, Brian Flanagan, Alvin Loving, Russell Neufeld, Phyllis Prentice, Jane Spielman, Steven Krugman, Joan Facher, Judy Greenbergh, Judith Clark, Sam Karp, James Worth, Natalie Rosenstein, and Sara Blackburn.

Aside from routine surveillance, Squad 47 used three major techniques, all of them—according to Justice Department prosecutors—illegal. The first was to steal and then open their mail. The second was to plant wiretaps on their phones or electronic bugs in their homes without a court order. And the third was break-ins.

In the past, the Bureau often had done so-called mail covers, intercepting letters at the post office or elsewhere, and copying the address, return address, and postmark from the envelope. But Squad 47 went two steps beyond this. With the help of mailbox keys that they obtained, sometimes from building superintendents, FBI squad members lifted the mail right out of the mailboxes, and took it to the squad room at East 69th Street. There the agents used a steamer to open the mail. (The steamer was a device that held a letter over a steam duct until the glue became loosened.) Then a small knife would be inserted under the flap to open the envelope without tearing it. The mail would be read and often photocopied, and then sealed back into the envelope and returned to the mail box. This became so routine that the trips to the mail boxes of some of the targets became known as the "mail run," and the assignments for the mail run were posted on the Squad 47 bulletin board.

These activities were known to everyone in the squad, including agents not directly involved. In addition, most agents in the squad knew that there was a headset in the squad room that was used to monitor the wiretaps, and that the supervisor had a key ring containing keys to the apartments and mailboxes of many of the targets of the break-ins.

Immediately after the *Keith* decision, in June 1972, the attorney general's office ordered an end to the wiretap on Jennifer Dohrn. The tap was removed because of the court ruling that warrants were required in domestic cases. Despite this order, the agents proceeded to stage a series of break-ins at her apartment, either unaware or unconcerned that the same court decision clearly held such intrusions illegal.

Who authorized these break-ins? The answer is uncertain, because several of the principals are dead, and many of the records are missing. The start-up of Squad 47 coincided with the development of the so-called Huston Plan. The inter-agency committee which drafted this plan had been created, pursuant to President Nixon's order, on June 5, 1970. The final report was presented to Nixon on June 25, 1970 and approved by him on July 14, 1970—although Nixon ordered the recall of the authorization memorandum on July 28, 1970. This authorization memo, sent out under the signature of White House aide Tom Charles Huston (and not President Nixon) on July 23, 1970, would have gotten the FBI back into the break-in business in a big way. Some of the pressure for this came from the NSA, Huston has since testified, but some also came from the

Justice Department, which had revitalized the Internal Security Division, under the command of Assistant Attorney General Robert Mardian. The forty-three-page memo specifically outlining the plan called for increased electronic spying on Americans and foreign diplomats, more extensive mail openings, and greater attempts to recruit informants on college campuses. It also called for "surreptitious entries" by the FBI, which Huston noted in the authorization memo would be "clearly illegal," but which he claimed were worth the high risk.

A number of FBI officials are known to have contributed to the plan's development, including William Sullivan, then the Number Three official, and a man who had been angry at Hoover's 1966 written order prohibiting such entries. But Hoover dissented from the proposal, and raised such a fuss that Attorney General John Mitchell recommended that Nixon rescind authorization. It is unclear, however, whether there was any direct connection between the formal approval of the Huston Plan and the Weather Underground break-ins.

Sullivan is dead now, shot while deer hunting in New Hampshire in 1977. And Hoover has been dead since 1972. But before he died, Sullivan blamed the Squad 47 break-ins on Hoover, who already was dead, saying that in 1970 Hoover had personally told him to relay the message to John Kearney that he should use "any practical means" to catch the fugitives. Sullivan told this to a federal grand jury in 1977, and told it to me in a long telephone conversation several weeks later.

The first call I received leading to this interview came not from Sullivan, but from a lawyer for one of the agents caught up in the investigation of the Squad 47 break-ins. The lawyers for the agents had been in contact with Sullivan, and had been trying to persuade hm to say something that would make clear that the agents had been under orders from Headquarters and had not been staging bag jobs on their own. The lawyer called me at the Washington Bureau of the *New York Times*, where I was working, and said that Sullivan had something he wanted to say about the case, and that, for whatever reason, he wanted to say it to me. He said Sullivan would be at his home in Sugar Hill, New Hampshire, at a given time, and wanted me to telephone him there.

Sullivan seemingly wanted to help the agents, but had to be careful how he went about it to make certain he didn't put himself in more of a bind. He had been forced out of the Bureau by Hoover in October 1971, and presumably was outside the statute of limitations on possible criminal charges. But he nonetheless was being named, almost automatically, in virtually every civil suit being brought against the Nixon Administration and its Justice Department for investigative misconduct, and he might be liable for more such suits if he admitted giving the order for the WEATHERFUG break-ins. So while he was anxious to help the agents, he was not anxious to increase his own liability, or say anything that would put himself out too far on a limb.

I telephoned Sullivan, whom I had interviewed before, and what followed during the next hour was one of the most unusual interviews I'd ever been involved in. In fact, it wasn't even an interview in any real sense, since Sullivan both asked *and* answered all of the questions, which he apparently had written out in advance. The reason, he made clear, was that he was trying to walk a very fine line, and didn't want to *ad lib* himself into more trouble than he already was in.

Sullivan was a short, peppery man, who had been raised in New England and still spoke with a trace of a Yankee twang. He also had a nineteenth-century speaking manner, avoiding contractions (he would say "would not" rather than "wouldn't" and "cannot" rather than "can't") and using such terms as "rascals" and "villains" that had long been out of vogue. I took notes on a typewriter as Sullivan dictated both sides of the "interview," raising questions himself and then answering them. While not a verbatim recounting, my notes are close. They also, I subsequently learned from Justice Department sources, match up pretty well with what Sullivan actually told the grand jury.

Sullivan's version is the only first-hand account charging Hoover with a direct involvement in the Squad 47 break-ins. As best as can be reconstructed from the notes, the "interview" went as follows, starting with the first question that he asked and then answered himself:

Q: Have you testified before a grand jury recently?

A: Yes, I testified before the grand jury on July 15, 1977.

Q: What was it related to?

A: It related to FBI operations of the past and to the indictment of Jack Kearney, a former agent in the New York office.

Q: How much time did you spend with the grand jury?

A: I do not recall the exact amount of time. It was about nine hours, I believe, with time out for luncheon, and a few other minor interruptions.

Q: Would you care to identify the prosecutors who interrogated you?

A: Yes. I see no reason why I should not identify the prosecutors who formulated the questions. They were three in number: Mr. [Paul] Hoeber, Mr. [William] Gardner, and Mr. [Frank] Martin. All three conducted themselves in a very professional and gentlemanly manner. I have no criticism of them whatsoever. Mr. Hoeber was in charge of the interrogation, and he impressed me most favorably as a very capable young man—professional, thorough, courteous, tenacious, forthright and with a sense of humor which I fully appreciated. There should be more young men like him in the government.

Q: Were the members of the grand jury really interested in the proceedings?

A: Yes, very much so, in the questions raised and in the answers given. I think it is a very fine grand jury.

Q: Will you discuss with me your testimony?

A: No, I do not wish to discuss or make known publicly the details of my testimony at this time. I have, of course, discussed it with my attorney, Joseph E. Casey, of Washington, D.C.

Q: Do you have any strong conviction about this whole affair which you are willing to discuss with me?

A: Well, yes. I will discuss with you some of my strongly held convictions concerning the FBI and the Kearney case. Along with thousands of people in this country, including lawyers, judges, and others from all walks of life, I consider the indictment of Mr. Kearney to be unnecessary, unwarranted, unjust, cruel, and outrageous. But such atrocious decisions and bungling and folly with the costly consequences at the taxpayers' expense are not unknown in our government. I have witnessed such decisions many times during my thirty-five years in the federal service . . . . There is indeed a ludicrous, even comic aspect, to this entire mess. However, we cannot limit our reaction to laughter because an innocent man, Jack Kearney, will be ruined for life, and his family damaged and forced to live in an atmosphere of despair by the kind of devastating action being now engaged in by the Department of Justice.

Q: Why do you say Jack Kearney is innocent?

A: I say this because I know that Jack Kearney, one of the most outstanding men in the history of the FBI, acted as he did on instructions from FBI Headquarters and not on his own decision or initiative. He followed orders.

Q: How do you know that he followed orders?

A: I know because I was involved in these orders, officially.

Q: Can you tell me why, how, and when you were so involved?

A: This is getting into my testimony, given before the grand jury, which as I have told you, I do not care to discuss at this time.

Q: Don't you think what you know should be given to the public—that the public should be entitled to it?

A: I agree. The public should know, and I intend to make all of this available to the public in detail when I testify on behalf of Mr. Kearney at his trial, should it ever come to this unjust and unnecessary point.

Q: Is there anything at all on which you are able to comment concerning this problem?

A: Well, I can give you the essence of what I know. It is this: In the fall of 1970, while talking with Mr. Hoover, he brought up the failure of the FBI to catch the underground security fugitives who had engaged over a long period of time in illegal and violent activities resulting in the destruction of buildings and even the loss of life.

Mr. Hoover was angry at the time, and it was very evident to me that he believed the failure to catch the fugitives was harmful to the reputation of the FBI. I told Mr. Hoover he had in effect shackled the hands of our field office men by taking away from them vital tools which for well over a quarter of a century he had trained them in using and had instructed them to use. He now was asking for the same results which the tools had been very important in providing by exerting on the FBI field agents tremendous and even unbearable pressure. His reply to me was: "These fugitives must be caught." He repeated this two or three times. Finally, he said forcefully: "Use any means necessary, practical or effective, because these fugitives must be caught."

[Note: I interrupted Sullivan here and asked if this was a direct quote or a paraphrase. He replied that it might be a paraphrase, but it was very close to being a direct quote. Then he continued describing his session with Hoover, apparently reading from some sort of prepared text.]

A statement of this kind was so clear it needed no interpretation from me. Subsequently, I passed on Mr. Hoover's statements to Mr. Kearney. This is why I say to you that Mr. Kearney operated on official instructions from FBI Headquarters, and therefore is an entirely innocent man.

Mr. Kearney may have received other similar instructions from other FBI officials.

Q: Do you think that other men in the FBI field offices acted upon this statement if it became known to them?

A: I do not wish to answer this question.

Q: Do you think other FBI men may be indicted?

A: I do not know. If we have learned anything from what has gone on in the past year, I would say no. However, we may not have learned anything. Sometimes we are very slow to learn, and will not learn. This reminds me of the old truth that "one must have more than mortal skills to convince another against his will." When or where this divine skill may appear in the case, I have no way of knowing.

Q: One last question. When you said, "If we have learned anything," who do you mean by we?

A: I mean the United States government, of which we are all a part of, and in particular the government officials who are handling this case, at enormous expense to the taxpayer—money which could be better used in assisting law enforcement, instead of weakening it, or money which could be better used for public housing, medical research, and for other constructive and progressive social purposes. If this was done, I'm sure that the taxpayers would be much better pleased. Also, I believe this would be far more in accord with the current Administration's positive goals.

Whether Hoover actually told Sullivan to use any means necessary to catch the fugitives may never be known. Kearney has told associates that he can't recall the specific conversation with Sullivan in which Hoover's order was conveyed, but that he had many conversations with him, and is certain that Sullivan knew the bag jobs were taking place. Hoover already was dead when Sullivan reported the director's statement, and since no one else was supposed to have been present during the Hoover-Sullivan discussion, no one can confirm the story. Sullivan himself has since died, his last official word on the subject being grand jury testimony blaming authorization for the break-ins on Hoover.

If Hoover did give the order, it would mean that he did it in the very same time frame in which he torpedoed the Huston plan. If he didn't, it might mean that Sullivan had given the order on his own and then blamed it on Hoover. But this would have been very risky—almost unheard of for a subordinate—because it is almost certain that Hoover would have found out. What is clear, however, is that it was done, and that some of the top people at Headquarters knew that FBI agents were conducting bag jobs.

While some agents of Squad 47 readily admit to taking part in the break-ins, some are a bit queasy about referring to them as "bag jobs." James Vermeersch, a member of the squad, testified in the Miller-Felt trial that "bag job" was a term used "by the older agents," but not by himself. John Glennon, a fellow member of Squad 47, said he not only didn't use the term but objected to it, because it suggested the agents were burglars, rather than gatherers of intelligence. Asked what he took the term to mean, he told prosecutor Neilds, "From what I can understand, it's something like a burglar running around with a little bag of tools or something, doing things he is not supposed to be doing."

NEILDS: Did you do a bag job on Jennifer Dohrn's home?
GLENNON: No. I did a surreptitious entry.

Whatever the term, agents from Squad 47 made several entries at Jennifer Dohrn's homes, both at an apartment in Manhattan, and at the house she shared with Judith Clark and Susan Roth at 501 8th Avenue, Brooklyn. They made entries on December 11, 1972, on February 13, 1973, and February 24, 1973, among other dates. Later, several agents claimed not to recall much about the residences, except that (according to one agent) the furniture was "ratty," and (according to another) there was no trouble telling Jennifer Dohrn's room because it was the "most ill-kept."

These and other comments in the Miller-Felt trial suggested that some of the members of Squad 47 not only disapproved of the politics of some of the people they had under surveillance, but disapproved of their life-styles as well. Glennon, for example, described a break-in at the home of

Murray Bookchin, a well-known lecturer who an informant of known unreliability had told FBI agents might have been in touch with some of the Weathermen. The agents copied some of his writings, his bank records, an address book, and also a picture of his daughter. But about all Glennon, who later left the Bureau to become a high school principal, could remember was that the place was, in his words, a bit of a mess.

"It was an aggregation of books and papers and periodicals and food and clothing, and in general it was a mess," he said. "It was embellished in early American asylum green—the color of the place it was painted. Horribly lighted. The main thing I remember about it was that it was over-run with reading material—on the floor, up the walls, books all over the place. No pun intended there—Bookchin, he certainly had a lot of books."

Staging a bag job was intrusive in many ways, because agents not only went into people's homes and searched their belongings, but also gathered information about their personal lives. Before a break-in could be attempted, agents would keep the subjects under surveillance, to find out as much as possible about their personal habits, where and when they worked, what their social lives were like, and, most importantly, when they might be certain to be away from home. Only after this sort of surveillance and dossier building was done could the planning for a break-in begin. In some cases, the intrusion was far more extensive. During one of their break-ins into the Albert-Clavier home in Hurley, New York, agents planted a listening device that they kept in place for more than a week. The home was little more than a one-room cabin, so the device, if operating effectively, presumably picked up everything they and their friends had to say. "My wife said she felt she had been raped," Albert said, after learning about the electronic bug. "It struck me as one of the most uncivilized acts imaginable."

According to records and court testimony, about ten to thirteen agents were required to stage one of these break-ins, about four of whom would actually enter the apartment.[4] The agents making the entry usually went in without guns, partly because under most state laws an armed break-in is considered a more serious crime than an unarmed break-in. They also would usually be without their FBI badges, although some carried phony I.D. cards, claiming to be state or city inspectors.

Once inside, the agents would search as quickly as possible, looking under the beds, in the closets, in desks and drawers and shoes. Using a documents camera that had been concealed in an attache case (when the case opened, the camera and two flash guns would pop up and be swung into place, in perfect pre-set focus for a document laid flat in the bottom of the case), they would photograph anything that they thought might provide them with a clue. If a typewriter was around, they'd take a typewriting sample, in order to have it compared with others in the FBI laboratory on the chance that it might match up with the type used in any of the notes claiming credit for a bombing. As Vermeersch explained it to the jury in the Miller-Felt trial: "There is a method that the bureau uses to take a typewriter sample and essentially you go to a typewriter and take a sample of the typewriter."

Agents also would look for any sign that the inhabitant had been on a trip—out-of-town matchbooks, road maps, or airplane tickets. They looked for telegrams, letters, diaries. On several occasions, they even scraped up soil samples from a bathtub, to have a lab check on where the soil might have come from.

A good example of the drill that agents went through on a typical bag job can be seen in the April 13, 1973 entry into the apartment of Leonard Machtinger, which was described in some detail in the Miller-Felt trial. Machtinger, a lawyer, was living in an apartment at 315 East 86th Street, in Manhattan, an apartment building near the FBI field office, in which several of the agents of Squad 47 also lived. One of the agents had obtained a key to the apartment (the usual sources of keys were doormen or superintendents, and the usual pay was fifty dollars), so there was no need to pick the lock.

When he left for work that morning, Machtinger was followed by an agent named Robert Vericker, who waited until he was sure Machtinger had settled in for a while, and then called agents waiting in another apartment in the same building. Those agents telephoned Machtinger's apartment to make sure no one else was inside, then they went to the apartment and, as a last precaution, knocked on the door, When no one answered, they used the keys they had obtained and, according to court testimony, four of them—Michael Kirschenbauer, James Vermeersch, Terry Roberts, and the supervisor, Horace Beckwith—went inside. Another agent, Vincent Alvino, waited out in the corridor, using a tape measure to pretend that he was measuring the windowsills and the drapes.

The normal practice was for the agents inside to immediately establish contact with the agents on watch outside and in the streets, to make sure the walkie-talkies were working so that they could be warned if anyone returned to the apartment. Then, as they did in Machtinger's apartment, they would begin the search.

Squad 47 operated pretty much full time from 1970 to 1975, and never caught a fugitive as a direct result of all its illegal mail openings, break-ins, and wiretaps. Ultimately, federal prosecutors found evidence of at least thirty-two surreptitious entries, seventeen illegal wiretaps, two unauthorized microphone installations, and numerous mail openings. The squad also left an unusually complete record of its activities behind, locked inside John Malone's safe.

When the word first got around about the material in Malone's files, many agents and officials shook their heads in wonder that the evidence was still around. "It's just like the Nixon tapes," said one ranking FBI official at the time. "You can't understand why he just didn't burn the damn things."

One possible answer was given by a member of Squad 47, who opined, that there was much pressure from above to catch the fugitives, and there was "a great bureaucratic effort" to show all the work that was being put into the search. The result, he said, was that a lot of stuff was put on paper, and was kept in the files, that probably wouldn't have been if the investigation had been short and successful.

The material became the basis of the Justice Department investigation, which began in 1975 and got fully under way in 1976. The investigation prompted cries of outrage by many agents and their supporters, although not every agent was wholly sympathetic to the plight of Squad 47. There were some, particularly on the organized crime squads, who thought the members of Squad 47 had been foolish to leave so much evidence behind. There were others, particularly younger agents, who thought that the break-ins had been wrong, and had further tarnished the Bureau's reputation. And there was at least one agent, near retirement age, who felt that Squad 47 had broken an FBI rule.

As one member of Squad 47 recounted it later, the man was virtually a stereotype of the old FBI agent of the 1950s. "He was a classic old-timer," the young agent said. "He even wore a straw hat and wing-tipped shoes." He listened to the younger agent complaining about the injustice of it all, and then shook his head in disagreement. "Mr. Hoover said in 1966 not to do it, so you've got to take your medicine," he said.

Within the FBI, however, this was a distinctly minority view.

Epilogue

The trial of Edward S. Miller and W. Mark Felt finally took place in autumn of 1980, a drama played out, for the most part, in a near-empty court room, the news coverage by and large relegated to the inside pages of those newspapers that bothered to report it at all. There was a brief flurry of excitement on October 29, when former President Nixon testified in the case. He had been called by the prosecution but was sympathetic to the defendants, claiming that while he had never personally ordered the Weather Underground break-ins he thought the FBI director probably had such authority if national security or foreign intelligence gathering was at issue. He seemed tired and old, and his nose seemed to have grown, like Pinocchio's, a result of his jowls having shrunk and his hairline having receded to the point where his face, always a cartoonist's delight, seemed almost a living caricature of the thirty-seventh President. As he began his testimony several women stood and began shouting "liar!" and "war criminal." The former president sat and stared straight ahead, drumming his fingers on the witness chair, while the women were removed by federal marshalls.[5]

By the time the trial started, much of the passion the case had generated seemed to have subsided. It had been about five years since the last known break-in, Squad 47 had long since been disbanded, and what public anger there had been over the entries seemed to have evaporated like a fog before a cool breeze. The first group of Justice Department investigators had quit the case after then Attorney General Griffin Bell had vetoed their plans to seek a string of indictments against a number of middle-level and top FBI officials. Bell insisted instead that the indictments be limited to only the topmost officials known to have been involved. The second team, headed by Barnet Skolnik, the prosecutor from Baltimore who had been instrumental in the development of criminal cases against Vice President Spiro Agnew and Governor Marvin Mandel, was more sympathetic to Bell's point of view, which seemed to be that (1) a crime had been committed and a prosecution must be brought to show that the FBI was not above the law, but that (2) some consideration should be given to the fact that bag jobs had been taking place for years and no one had ever objected.

By the time the trial had ended, with verdicts of guilty against Miller and Felt, even the *Washington Post* was urging in an editorial that these FBI officials not be sent to jail. Felt and Miller had been punished enough, *The Post* concluded, and no public good would be served by putting them behind bars. "The question that truly troubles us . . . is whether Messrs. Felt and Miller are the proper persons to be standing in front of Judge Bryant" the *Post* wrote on the day sentence was to be imposed, "or whether they are the fall guys for a system acquiesced in by countless others and that they themselves did not create."

But even while public support—and the support of the new Republican Administration—seemed to be swinging back to the Bureau, still new concerns about FBI operations were being raised. Among those raising them, ironically, was Koelzer, former prosecutor, friend of agents, and now defense lawyer for Senator Harrison Williams (D., N.J.) probably the biggest catch in the Bureau's ABSCAM net. During much of 1979 the FBI had run a major undercover operation in which agents and operatives, masking as front men for a fictitious Arab Sheik, offered large bribes to public officials, many of whom pocketed the cash and promised official help to the sheik. The ABSCAM operation (ABSCAM was an acronym for Arab Scam) itself became the focus of a serious debate over the limits to which the federal government should be allowed to go in luring persons into committing a crime. And Koelzer, while arguing that such things never would have happened if Hoover had still been in control, complained in hearing after hearing, in defense of his client, that the Bureau had gone far beyond the bounds of proper law enforcement, had tried to entrap innocent and unsuspecting officials, had overstated the evidence, had created crimes where no crimes had existed, and had allowed informants and operatives to run out of control.

The ABSCAM operation was "sickening," "revolting," and "despicable," Koelzer thundered. It had resulted in a case against Williams that was built upon "innuendo, suspicion, and easy slanders." The principal FBI agent in the case, Anthony Amoroso, was a "rather tasteless, crude, insensitive, vulgar FBI agent," he told the jury.

He paused, either for effect or reflection. These agents, he told the jury, were "not the agents you and I knew [when we were] growing up."

Notes

1. Later, feminists in the group would protest the sexist nature of the name, and the group would become known as the Weather Underground. But at the time Squad 47 was formed it was still known as the Weathermen, a radical, antiwar group that took its name from the line in a Bob Dylan song that said: "You don't need a weatherman to know which way the wind blows."

2. The FBI, in its Wanted posters and its press releases, is quick to point up nicknames of the people it is chasing, particularly alleged organized crime figures. What is less well-known to the public is that many FBI agents and officials have nicknames too. One official at FBI Headquarters was considered so vacuous that he was known as "Empty Suit." A Special Agent in Charge in upstate New York was known as "The Wedge"—the simplest tool known to man. James B. Adams, long a power in the FBI hierarchy, was known as "The Littlest Agent," because Hoover had waived the Bureau's 5'7" height requirement to let the 5'6" Adams join. And there were more. One agent was known as "Blue Eyes." Another was known as "Broadway Bill." Yet another was known as "The Rodent," and another "The Sheriff." An agent who sold white shirts at wholesale prices in the New York Field Office (he had a relative with a major shirt company and got them cheap) was known as "Frankie the Shirt." And there were a whole group of officials in the Administrative Division in Washington who were thought to have risen up through the ranks, in part, because they had cultivated the good graces of Hoover's long-time secretary, Helen Gandy. They were known as "The Gandy Dancers."

3. One veteran of many bag jobs, when told about Sullivan's comment, replied: "The problem was, they promoted the lunkheads."

4. The number of agents used could vary enormously. FBI agents staging a break-in at a mob-owned trucking office often could pull a bag job with only four or five persons. Agents trying to do one at a major embassy often needed forty or more, to maintain surveillance on all the officials known to have keys. In these

break-ins, agents would fan out all over the city, keeping the diplomats under surveillance, to make sure they didn't return while the bag job was under way. Sometimes, according to former agents, the agents doing the surveillance were not supposed to know officially that a break-in was taking place. But the men going in usually put out the word because, as one of them said, they wanted to make sure the agents outside knew it was an inportant job, and "didn't throw up a half-assed surveillance." Also, many of the Squad 47 break-ins were in the day time, when the subjects were at work. Most bag jobs of diplomatic missions or mob hangouts were done late at night, with the hours between three and five o'clock in the morning favored, because by then the bars were closed, even in New York, and there was less chance of bumping into people out on the street.

5. One of these women was identified at the time as Judith Clark, the former roommate of Jennifer Dohrn, and the subject of several of the FBI break-ins. One year later, in October 1981, she was arrested with Weather fugitive Katherine Boudin and several others, and charged with murder and robbery in connection with the hold-up of a Brinks armored car in Nyack, New York.

4

The Case of the National Lawyers Guild, 1939–1958

Percival R. Bailey

I

In late spring 1954, millions of Americans witnessed the televised confrontation between Senator Joseph McCarthy and the Department of the Army. A special Senate subcommittee was then investigating McCarthy's charges about the inadequacy of Army security procedures[1] in hearings that unexpectedly brought to a public climax McCarthy's own career. The dramatic peak of the hearings involved an exchange between McCarthy and Joseph Welch, the Army's specially appointed chief counsel and a senior partner at Hale and Dorr, the distinguished Boston law firm. The flow of the televised hearings had already turned against McCarthy when, on June 9, the Senator interrupted Welch with one of his frequent "points of order." The public had a right to know, McCarthy insisted, that Frederick Fisher, a member of Welch's law firm, "has been for a number of years a member of an organization which was named, oh years and years ago, as the legal bulwark of the Communist Party." McCarthy's unnecessary remark provoked Welch's celebrated riposte: "Senator, until this moment I had never really gauged your cruelty or your recklessness. . . . Have you left no sense of decency, sir, at long last? Have you left no sense of decency?"[2]

Newspaper accounts of the June incident carefully reported that while a student at Harvard Law School in the late 1940s Fisher had belonged to the National Lawyers Guild (NLG), but had resigned from the controversial organization early in 1950. Since then he had become a leader of the Boston Young Republicans, and was well established at Hale and Dorr. Fisher's youthful dalliance with the National Lawyers Guild, Welch assured reporters, had been his "one mistake," long since repented.

The House Un-American Activities Committee, these news stories invariably added, had cited the NLG in 1944 and again in 1950 as a "Communist front." The same charge had been reiterated by Attorney General Herbert Brownell, Jr., in 1953; even then the Guild was contesting in federal court Brownell's proposal to add the National Lawyers Guild to the Attorney General's list of "subversive" organizations.[3]

With ex-Communist informants and FBI undercover agents emerging regularly in 1954, no questions were then asked how McCarthy had uncovered Fisher's past history. The Senator's source was apparently the Federal Bureau of Investigation. Since 1951, the FBI had maintained an active "informant" in the Harvard Guild from whom on several occasions it obtained and then microfilmed the NLG's correspondence and membership lists. A photographed list had most recently arrived at the FBI's Boston Field Office on April 15, the day before Welch confirmed Fisher's withdrawal from the case.[4] The whole case, accordingly, was a minor, albeit typical example of the FBI's covert collaboration with anti-Communist politicians such as Joseph McCarthy.[5]

For the National Lawyers Guild, the Welch-McCarthy episode was the latest in a series of public attacks dating from 1950, when the Guild published a documented account of FBI wiretapping, burglaries, and unauthorized surveillance, and called upon President Harry S. Truman to instigate a thorough and independent examination of FBI practices. Chiefly in response to the Guild's January 1950 expose of Bureau lawlessness, FBI officials orchestrated a campaign of public and covert measures which, by 1954, contributed to the organization's virtual destruction. The history of those events highlights a stratum of the "McCarthy era" that, until now, has been safely buried in the FBI's tightly controlled files.

Founded in December 1936, the National Lawyers Guild was a national bar association for "liberal" lawyers, in explicit contradistinction to the conservative and racially exclusive American Bar Association. The new bar association proposed "to unite the lawyers of America in a professional association which shall function as an effective social force in the service of the people, to the end that human rights shall be regarded as more sacred than property rights."[6]

The three to four thousand lawyers who joined the Guild during its first two years spanned the political spectrum from liberal New Dealers to anti-capitalist radicals. Among its members were governors of at least two states, a few United States senators, several of the nation's most distinguished black attorneys, and a large number of government lawyers from all levels of the Roosevelt Administration. Not surprisingly, the Guild also enlisted a few socialists and perhaps a hundred lawyers aligned politically with the United States Comunist Party.[7]

Despite their small numbers, the Communist-oriented members played an important role in activating the new organization, as American Communists had in many of the broad-based "popular front" organizations created during the late thirties. Young Communist lawyers, who disclosed their Communist affiliations to few outside the Party, volunteered for those NLG chapter offices and committee assignments that required more than a casual attendance at meetings and regular payment of dues. Serving as chapter secretaries—and one briefly as the NLG national secretary—individual Communists could thereby guarantee that NLG organizational work would not lag, and that matters of particular importance to Communists received at least due consideration from the Guild's overwhelmingly non-Communist policy-making bodies. The coexistence of Communists and non-Communists in the NLG was further enhanced by the fact that many New Deal liberals shared the Party's pre-eminent political objectives of the late thirties—social reform, a strong labor movement, and a multi-class opposition to fascism.[8]

Until 1938, the Communists' presence in the National Lawyers Guild was either unknown to the broader public or a matter of no public concern. In that year, however, the newly formed House Special Committee on Un-American Activities (HUAC)—the so-called Dies Committee—began to hurl charges of "Communist influence" against New Dealers, their agencies, and their political associations. Reacting to these charges, certain influential anti-Communist Guild members attributed the NLG's failure to expand beyond its original thirty-five hundred members to rumors of Communist "influence" within its ranks. To reassure more cautious liberals whom they hoped to recruit, the Guild's anti-Communist faction demanded that the organization unequivocally oppose all forms of dictatorship, including communism, and as a condition for election to any NLG office candidates must personally endorse such a statement. The prospect of a political "test oath," however, did not sit well with the Guild's non-Communist but strongly civil libertarian majority. Proposals for an anti-Communist oath requirement were rejected in 1939 and again in 1940; and the resultant tales of the Guild's factional infighting received front-page national news coverage.[9]

In the heightened anti-Communist atmosphere enveloping the United States during the spring of 1940, a host of New Dealers (notably Attorney General Robert H. Jackson and Assistant Secretary of State Adolf A. Berle), prominent liberal lawyers, and politicians publicly denounced and abandoned the NLG. Thus stigmatized, the vulnerable organization lost at least half its remaining members in the next several months; by the end of 1940, no more than a thousand lawyers remained members in good standing. Only a stubborn effort, led by the Communist-oriented faction, prevented the four-year-old bar association from becoming defunct.[10]

For the next decade, the NLG's fortunes rose and fell with those of the American left generally. While the wartime Soviet-American alliance endured, the NLG gained in size, influence, and respectability. Its national president, Robert W. Kenny, for example, was elected attorney general of California in 1942, and was invited in 1945 to represent the Guild at the founding convention of the United Nations and at the Nuremberg war crimes trials. With the Soviet Union transformed at war's end from ally to potential enemy, the Guild again found itself part of an embattled and declining "progressive" minority.[11]

Resignations by former NLG members owing to the Guild's stand on the Federal Employee Loyalty Program, the Marshall Plan, and NATO, however, were partially offset by the increased participation in NLG affairs of liberal opponents of the Cold War such as Yale Law Professor Thomas Emerson, former Assistant Attorney General O. John Rogge, and Clifford Durr, who had recently refused reappointment to the Federal Communications Commission because opposed to Truman's loyalty program. For unreconstructed New Dealers Emerson, Rogge, and Durr, and for about two thousand other liberal and radical lawyers who chose not to cut their losses in the intensifying Cold War, the Guild served as a last outpost of the prewar liberal-radical alliance. As such, the NLG's survival assumed a symbolic importance independent of its diminished role as a bar association.[12]

II

The FBI began its modern program of domestic political intelligence in 1936, only coincidentally the same year the National Lawyers Guild was founded. In August of that year, FBI Director J. Edgar Hoover persuaded President Franklin D. Roosevelt to authorize FBI surveillance of those Communist and fascist activists within the United States whose international political ties might jeopardize the national security. FBI domestic intelligence operations were ostensibly based on this vague mandate until 1939. In that year, FBI officials interpreted another presidential directive issued in September 1939 as authorizing general investigations of "subversive activities." Additional authority for FBI political surveillance was provided through federal laws of 1939–1941, either barring Communists from federal employment, outlawing advocacy of the forcible overthrow of the government, or requiring the registration of those organizations that were agents of a foreign power. Beginning in 1939, FBI officials also began to compile a Custodial Detention list of persons whom they believed would constitute a danger to national security in the event of war.[13]

From the start, the National Lawyers Guild questioned the expanded scope of the FBI's publicly known activities. On more than one occasion Guild officials cited FBI Director J. Edgar Hoover's role in the infamous Palmer Raids of 1920 (which Hoover falsely minimized in 1939 and thereafter), and Guild conventions adopted resolutions critical of the Bureau. In 1941, for example, an NLG resolution denounced the FBI for its "gestapo activities," and demanded Hoover's removal as FBI director and the reduction of the Bureau's annual budget so as "to restrict its jurisdiction to the field of federal crime and to deprive it of authority to get in matters which affect labor or civil rights." A 1948 Guild resolution pointedly warned that "the FBI has taken upon itself the role of the political police on the continental model, and has enlisted for this purpose the aid of local police departments."[14]

FBI officials first became interested in the National Lawyers Guild in 1939 and 1940. In a 1940 memorandum to the Department of Justice, FBI Director Hoover queried whether Guild members who were government employees should not be considered "security risks" in the event of war. Justice officials demurred and continually rejected Hoover's recommendations for security checks on Guild members. FBI agents nonetheless apparently broke into the NLG's Washington National Office—an early Bureau "black bag job"—to photograph the Guild's national membership list and several hundred pages of minutes, correspondence, and other organizational documents.[15]

After World War II, the FBI helped engineer new mandates for its continuing surveillance of domestic radicals. In July 1946, President Harry Truman agreed, on the recommendation of Attorney General Tom C. Clark, to authorize FBI wiretapping in cases involving "national security." At the end of 1946, moreover, FBI officials exerted considerable influence during the Administration's planning of a loyalty program for federal employees. By the time Truman formally established the Federal Employee Loyalty Program in March 1947, the FBI had shouldered its way to the center of that operation, in the process securing another investigative "blank check."

From the Bureau's perspective, a key aspect of the Loyalty Program was its authorization of an "Attorney General's list" of "totalitarian, fascist, communist, or subversive" groups. Ostensibly, the list was to serve as a guide to enable Loyalty Review Boards to evaluate the political associations of a suspect government employee. Because the Attorney General elected to make such lists public, FBI officials correctly regarded the list as a powerful means for discrediting left-liberal and radical groups.[16]

Not surprisingly, therefore, FBI officials almost immediately nominated the National Lawyers Guild for the Attorney General's list. To buttress the case for listing the Guild, in August 1947 nineteen FBI field offices were directed to report all NLG activities in their area. In November 1947, in response to this order, FBI agents began to tap the telephone of the NLG's National Office in Washington; three to four months later, FBI agents again burglarized the Guild's Washington office to photograph membership records. These illegal activities uncovered no evidence that the NLG was foreign- or Communist-controlled, however, and the Attorney General did not include the Guild on the list of "subversive" groups released in December 1947 and May 1948.[17]

In response to several impatient requests from FBI officials to list the NLG, Attorney General Clark finally concluded: "Lawyers Guild not included on list—I have many friends in it and would give them a hearing before doing so." Stymied by Clark's refusal, the FBI nonetheless drafted a "thumbnail sketch" of the National Lawyers Guild, citing Adolf Berle's and HUAC's past allegations of Communist influence. A copy of this sketch was thereafter included in the FBI dossier on any Guild member who came up for review by a government loyalty board. The FBI, thus, unilaterally succeeded in establishing NLG membership as a criterion for questioning the "loyalty" of government employees.[18]

The Bureau, moreover, continued to monitor the Guild's Washington telephone. In January 1948, for example, the wiretap revealed NLG plans for a public forum on the Loyalty Program, featuring remarks by Guild members O. John Rogge, Thurgood Marshall, Arthur Garfield Hays, and Robert W. Kenny. Two FBI agents were thereupon assigned to "cover" the forum. In June, FBI officials learned that Yale Law Professor Thomas Emerson was preparing a study of FBI practices involving the Loyalty Program. Accordingly, the Bureau's New Haven Field Office was instructed to inquire about Emerson's project "in such a manner as to preclude the possibility of Professor Emerson learning of the Bureau's interest in this matter." After some delay, New Haven agents forwarded a photographic copy of Emerson's ninety-two-page draft to Washington, enabling Bureau officials to prepare replies to the Yale professor's criticisms long before publication of his article in the *Yale Law Journal*.[19]

In June 1949, the Washington wiretap forewarned the FBI about NLG interest in the Judith Coplon espionage trial. A Justice Department employee who had transmitted information about FBI intelligence to Valentin Gubitchev, a member of the Soviet Union's United Nations staff, Coplon was arrested in March 1949. Her arrest at first seemed to be a major FBI triumph. By June, however, the Coplon trial had become an embarrassment for the FBI. The catalyst to this stemmed from Coplon's trial strategy of disputing the government's contention that national security information had been passed to the Russians. Coplon's attorney demanded that the twenty-eight FBI investigative reports that his client allegedly had intended to transmit to Gubitchev be submitted as evidence. Arguing that the government could not indict Coplon on "national security" grounds and then refuse to have the evidence supporting this charge tested in court, Judge Albert Reeves warned government attorneys that he would dismiss the espionage charges unless the FBI files were produced as evidence.[20]

The basis for the FBI's resistance to the judge's order soon became evident when fragments of the eight-hundred-page exhibit were released to defense attorneys and then to the press. The files confirmed that FBI agents had regularly spied on private citizens, including such prominent Americans as actor Frederick March and Bureau of Standards Director Edward U. Condon. The files underscored the FBI's general interest, not in suspected criminal activities but in the political ideas and associations of American citizens. Many of the statements incorporated in the FBI files, the *New York Times* pointedly observed, resembled "the allegations so often made with a beating of drums and a tooting of trumpets by the Committee on Un-American Activities."[21]

The Bureau was not entirely defenseless in the face of the Coplon revelations, however. Congressman Harold Velde, a former FBI agent and current member of the House Un-American Activities Committee, blasted the Bureau's detractors, while Velde's HUAC colleague Richard Nixon charged that the Attorney General's order to make the FBI files public had "done irreparable harm to our entire security organization." The weak tide of any possible anti-FBI reaction had already been turned, therefore, when Clifford Durr, the new NLG president, on June 19, 1949, publicly called upon President Truman to examine the Bureau's questionable investigative procedures.[22]

Although Durr's call for a presidential inquiry received scant public notice, the hypersensitive Bureau hierarchy nonetheless regarded his proposal as a serious threat. FBI Assistant Director Louis Nichols was at first dissatisfied with Truman's jocular response to reporters' questions during a presidential press conference about the possibility of an investigation of the FBI. Exploiting his contacts with the Washington press corps, Nichols one week later advised FBI Director Hoover of his telephone conversation with United Press Washington bureau chief Lyle Wilson: Wilson and UPI reporter Merriman Smith had elicited from Truman's press secretary, Charles Ross, a firm denial that any investigation was contemplated. "It seems that Lyle [Wilson] and Merriman Smith got together," Nichols explained, "and really pinned this thing down." Nichols then drafted, and Hoover signed, a letter to Wilson conveying the FBI director's warm appreciation. This liaison relationship, moreover, was but one of many occasions when the FBI's contacts in the nation's mass media intervened either to defend the Bureau's carefully maintained reputation, or to smear its critics.[23]

Despite the obvious reluctance of the Truman White House to accede to its recommendation, the Guild was not easily discouraged. On June 24, 1949, FBI Inspector Howard B. Fletcher informed Hoover that the NLG had purchased the *Coplon* trial transcript containing the FBI investigative reports, "and are contemplating the issuance of an attack on the Bureau." Two weeks later Fletcher drafted a memorandum for Hoover's signature to advise Attorney General Clark that

you may desire to cause an examination and review of all the information [previously] submitted [by the FBI] concerning the National Lawyers Guild to determine whether some action should be taken by the Department to characterize this group publicly. Other suggestions may arise from additional activity on the part of the National Lawyers Guild as an organization or on the part of some of its individual officers, and it may offer an opportunity for some type of action.[24]

Clark remained unwilling, however, to "publicly characterize" the Guild, once again declining to add it to the Attorney General's list.

Through the summer and early autumn the FBI closely followed the National Lawyers Guild's activities. Telephone conversations between NLG Executive Secretary Robert J. Silberstein in Washington and NLG President Clifford Durr in New York revealed the Guild's formation of a special committee to analyze the *Coplon* documents. Included as members of this committee were Durr, Silberstein, Thomas Emerson, O. John Rogge, and Washington civil liberties lawyer Joseph Forer.[25]

Through this surveillance, FBI Assistant Director D. M. Ladd learned and informed FBI Director Hoover in October 1949 that the NLG

Special Committee was preparing a report on the *Coplon* documents that might be used "to obtain publicity critical of the Bureau." A draft of the report was to be presented to the NLG National Executive Board on October 8. Three days after the Guild Board meeting, the FBI's Washington Field Office managed to procure "photographic copies of a report on the activities of the FBI, being prepared by the Guild, and related correspondence." After analyzing the microfilmed document, in which the Guild condemned the FBI's illegal intelligence methods and extensive abuses of its investigative authority, Ladd advised Hoover:

This attack on us is merely a continuation of the campaign which the National Lawyers Guild is trying to put over in smearing the Bureau, and in arousing indignation against any investigation of Communists and their sympathizers. . . . This type of attack illustrates the need for our reports in security cases being carefully prepared. The reports must completely cover the investigating techniques used, and must only be disseminated in instances where we can stand behind the information set forth.

In response, Hoover wrote, "Very true. The Training Division and Investigative and Security Divisions should constantly and persistently bear down on this."[26]

FBI agents continued to monitor the evolving but as yet unpublished NLG report. For example, on November 15 NLG Secretary Silberstein phoned Clifford Durr to report the availability of a revised version; three days later FBI headquarters received from the Washington Field Office microfilm copies of the revised report and of the minutes of the Guild's October Executive Board meeting. The memorandum transmitting the film of this Guild report attributed it to "the highly confidential informant of the Washington Field Office"—a standard Bureau euphemism for an illegal break-in.[27]

Thus forewarned, FBI officials immediately instituted defensive measures. On November 29, Hoover warned the new Attorney General, J. Howard McGrath, of the impending NLG attack on FBI practices, and suggested that McGrath alert President Truman. Concurrently, the Bureau moved against the Guild through the press, planting a story with Lyle Wilson of United Press. On December 5, Wilson sent out a wire service story based on the minutes of the October NLG Executive Board meeting. The National Lawyers Guild—"a left-wing organization already suspect as a Communist front"—Wilson reported, was preparing a campaign to "weaken" the FBI and drive Hoover from office. Such a campaign would be "right down the party line." Two days later, Attorney General McGrath signed the memorandum to President Truman prepared for him by Bureau officials itemizing the Guild's charges against the FBI.[28]

Then, in late November, FBI Director Hoover ordered the preparation of "a complete memo on the Guild from its inception to date." Presented to Hoover on December 6, and transmitted two weeks later to Attorney General McGrath, the three-hundred-page document attempted to discredit the Guild as a "Communist front," thereby ensuring that the Attorney General would at last designate the NLG as "subversive." Anticipating McGrath's favorable action, FBI agents once more surreptitiously entered the NLG National Office on December 26, and microfilmed correspondence, a current membership list, and two appendices of the NLG's report on the FBI, the existence of which had just been revealed by the wiretap.[29]

The Bureau's three-hundred-page memorandum included biographical summaries of 125 NLG officers and Executive Board members. Of these, the Bureau report claimed, some had been "alleged at some time in the past to be Communist Party members," while others had exhibited "Communist sympathies." NLG President Clifford Durr and NLG Secretary Robert Silberstein had frequently attacked the FBI, while such "individuals as Thomas I. Emerson of Yale University and Thurgood Marshall of the National Association for the Advancement of Colored People, who have been particularly critical of the Bureau in the past, are current officers." The NLG, moreover, had opposed all legislation directed against Communists and "subversives," and had long sought abolition of the House Un-American Activities Committee. The Bureau's researchers detailed the Guild's other "subversive" activities: the NLG had "consistently favored measures beneficial to labor," reportedly recommended "an extension of social welfare measures," advocated "lower taxes for lower income groups and higher taxes on higher income groups and corporations," supported federal anti-lynching legislation, and sought an end to the poll tax, at the same time criticizing the Justice

Department's failure to protect the civil rights of black Americans.[30]

Bureau officials' attempts to smear the Guild coincided with potentially embarrassing developments in the second Coplon trial. Coplon's original conviction during her first trial in Washington the previous June had been overturned on appeal because the FBI had failed to obtain a search warrant. Pre-trial hearings for a second trial on roughly similar charges began in a New York federal court in November 1949. The hearings revealed that FBI agents had tapped Coplon's telephone, and had possibly overheard conversations between the defendant and her attorney. The result, as summarized by the *New York Times*, was an awkward period for the Bureau:

> For several weeks there was a parade of FBI agents through the courtroom. Their testimony was contradictory. Some said they didn't know anything about wiretapping, and then admitted they knew it had been done in the case. At first the FBI said there were no records of monitored conversations recorded by Washington. Some were unintelligible—and the defense implied that they had been damaged purposely.

On January 13, 1950, Judge Sylvester Ryan released, from among the documents the Bureau had been required to produce, a memorandum reporting that FBI Assistant Director Ladd and Inspector Fletcher had authorized destruction of Coplon wiretap recordings *after* their existence became known during the pre-trial hearings.[31]

The revelations of FBI wiretapping in the second Coplon trial precipitated high-level public criticisms of the Bureau. In letters printed in the *New York Times* and the *Washington Post*, James L. Fly, former chairman of the Federal Communications Commission and a respected liberal, protested the FBI's illegal wiretapping and destruction of evidence. "Private counsel guilty of such conduct would be called to account at the bar," Fly insisted, but the FBI appeared to recognize "no limitation of law." Attorney General McGrath responded to Fly's criticisms. Defending FBI wiretapping as closely controlled and legitimate, McGrath cited the authorizations of President Roosevelt and several Attorneys General for "limited" FBI wiretapping to protect "the national security."[32]

One such "limited . . . national security" wiretap—at this time in its twenty-sixth month of continuous use—intercepted a conversation of NLG officers Clifford Durr and Robert Silberstein with journalist I. F. Stone in which they discussed ways to maximize press coverage of the NLG's report on the FBI, scheduled for public release on January 23, 1950. This intelligence was relayed to the Department of Justice, to the White House, and possibly also to Congressman Richard M. Nixon. Whether or not the recipient of an FBI leak, Nixon telephoned the three national wire services on January 18, the eve of the Guild's planned press conference to read a letter he was sending to HUAC chairman John S. Wood demanding a special hearing on the National Lawyers Guild "to determine the truth or falsity of charges that it is being used as a Communist front organization."[33]

Nixon's ploy succeeded. The next day's Associated Press account of the Durr press conference was headlined, "House Committee Urged to Probe Lawyers Guild"; the news story included no mention of the NLG report to be released the following Monday. Lyle Wilson began his United Press account of the same event, "The campaign to drive FBI Director J. Edgar Hoover from office begins in earnest today under the auspices of an organization of lawyers officially tabbed as a Communist front." After briefly referring to the NLG report, Wilson's story detailed at length Nixon's letter, and contained an almost verbatim recital of the FBI's "thumbnail sketch" of the Guild's alleged Communist affinities.[34]

Only two of those in attendance at the NLG press conference wrote fully detailed accounts. One of these was FBI agent Steven A. Smith, who reported directly to FBI headquarters. The other was I. F. Stone, who suggested in his *New York Daily Compass* column that, despite poor press coverage, the FBI might have learned about the NLG report "while monitoring Durr's phone to make sure that he didn't kidnap the neighbor's baby." Noting that the full report was to be released on Monday, January 23, Stone cautioned his readers not to "be surprised if before then the House Committee [on Un-American Activities] learns from a highly confidential informant that a key officer of the Guild has been manufacturing atom bombs for Russia in his basement Bendix."[35]

The Guild's efforts to ensure maximum press coverage soon encountered difficulties of another kind. In a five-column, front-page headline, Sunday's *New York Times* emphasized: "Hiss Guilty on Both Perjury

Counts; Betrayal of U.S. Secrets is Affirmed."[36] Under these circumstances it would have been surprising had the American press highlighted the claims of a heretical lawyers' organization that the FBI endangered civil liberties.

Nonetheless the *Washington Post* and the liberal *New York Daily Compass* did devote a fair amount of space to the Guild's report on the FBI. Other newspapers, in contrast, relegated the NLG release to backpage wire service stories. These stories qualified the impact of the report's findings by citing Hoover's and Attorney General McGrath's previous defenses of FBI procedures and a 1944 HUAC report labelling the NLG a "Communist front." The following day the United Press reported that Attorney General McGrath continued to "stand behind" the FBI. This aroused the Groucho Marx side of journalist Stone, who suggested that McGrath's haste to stand behind the FBI was offered "in the hope that J. Edgar Hoover wouldn't creep up and stand behind him."[37]

The NLG's "Report on the Alleged Practices of the FBI" was based on the twenty-eight individual "investigative reports"—approximately eight hundred pages in the trial record—which the FBI had been compelled to produce during the Coplon trial. These documents, the Guild charged, confirmed that the Bureau was conducting an unannounced "loyalty program" on a scale much broader than the official Federal Employee Loyalty Program. Employing "subjective and reactionary" criteria when conducting security investigations, the Bureau had assumed a leading role in the "growing tendency to suppress civil liberties on the pretext that the action of suppression will protect the American people from 'subversive elements.' "

The scope of FBI domestic intelligence exceeded legal mandates, the NLG report continued, and included illegal surveillance techniques and apparently deliberate harassment of citizens and organizations. FBI agents had tapped "numerous phones over extensive periods of time," conducted covert, warrantless searches of private homes, and, on some occasions, intercepted and opened personal mail. Judging from the frequency of such evidence in the twenty-eight documents released during the Coplon pre-trial hearings, the NLG committee concluded, "on a strictly numerical basis, the FBI may commit more federal crimes than it ever detects."

The Guild's report further contended that the FBI's domestic intelligence work was both illegal and often directly injurious to innocent citizens. Agents' visits to landlords, neighbors, and employees could be socially and economically harmful and could "do a lawyer no good if an FBI agent questions a federal judge before whom the lawyer practices as to the lawyer's 'loyalty.' " Additionally, the Guild committee presciently doubted

that much of the material gathered by the FBI is not communicated, whether officially or unofficially, to employers, state and municipal organizations, newspapers, political groups, etc. Certainly it will seem almost incredible to those who follow the activities of the House Committee on Un-American Activities that it is not furnished large quantities of information by the FBI and what the Committee knows has a tendency to become public property.

To reverse these dangerous practices, the NLG report urged that FBI investigations be restricted to actual or suspected crimes, and that President Truman create a special committee, composed "of able and distinguished private citizens" having subpoena power and assured of full access to FBI files, to examine thoroughly Bureau policies and practices.[38]

Following release of the NLG report, the FBI watched closely for any repercussions that might focus unfriendly public scrutiny on the Bureau. When Guild member Joseph Forer discussed the NLG's findings at a New York forum, the FBI was there; and when the NLG National Executive Board discussed the report in Cleveland, four agents conducted "physical surveillance," which included taking photographs and moving pictures, as well as preparing an inventory of the trash outside the hotel where the Board had met. FBI wiretappers warned FBI Director Hoover that NLG President Durr intended to present the Guild's charges to the House Appropriations Committee when that committee reviewed the Bureau's current budgetary request. Upon learning of an NLG effort to have a United States senator introduce a resolution favoring an investigation of the FBI, FBI officials contacted sources in that senator's office, and eventually received assurances that he would not act. In March 1950, moreover, the FBI Field Office in Springfield, Illinois, apprised headquarters of a local Guild member's attempt to have the NLG report considered by the Illinois Bar Association's Civil Liberties Committee.

Bureau officials promptly supplied the FBI's "thumbnail sketch" of the Guild to a supporter in the Association, and local FBI field offices were ordered to report periodically over the next six months on any action taken by the Bar Association. No action was ever taken.[39]

In the weeks following publication of the NLG report, the FBI found occasional opportunities to strike back at its critics. During his annual appearance before the Senate Appropriations Committee in early February 1950, for example, FBI Director Hoover claimed that the NLG was Communist influenced and had long been conducting a campaign to undermine the FBI. Although the Committee did not publicly release Hoover's testimony until June, FBI Assistant Director Nichols publicly repeated the FBI Director's charges on February 4 in an address to a Washington civic association.[40]

FBI officials continued to pressure the Attorney General to designate the NLG as a "subversive" organization. In March, the head of the Justice Department's Internal Security Section conceded to FBI Assistant Director Ladd that the NLG had "just barely missed" being listed by the Attorney General earlier and "that there was some feeling, apparently in the Department and . . . among people on the Hill, that there were many innocent people who have been taken in by the organization." To this explanation Hoover penned a frustrated reply: "If that be true they should resign. It is all the worse to allow it to continue unbranded and serve as a trap for the gullible."[41]

To enhance its case for "branding" the Guild, FBI officials expanded the December 1949 "summary memorandum" detailing the NLG's "subversive" activities. After randomly checking the December 26 NLG membership list against FBI case files, searchers concluded that 6.6 percent of Guild members were Communists, and that another 25 percent either belonged to "organizations affiliated with or dominated by the Communist Party," or "associated with Communist Party members or [were] sympathetic toward Communism." With such flimsy evidence, the Attorney General was understandably unwilling to initiate a listing procedure that would certainly produce a courtroom confrontation with the Guild's accomplished constitutional lawyers.[42]

FBI officials clearly needed other means to discredit its small but persistent critic. One such opportunity was provided by the NLG correspondence microfilmed by FBI agents in December 1949.[43] (These Bureau actions suggest that the tactics later employed under the FBI's COINTELPROs had been employed by the FBI on an ad hoc basis against organizations deemed "subversive" well before the programs' formal initiation in 1956.) Included among the NLG documents was a letter which revealed that while serving as NLG delegate to the 1949 International Association of Democratic Lawyers (IADL) convention in Rome, NLG Secretary Robert Silberstein had supported a motion of the IADL's pro-Soviet majority to expel the Yugoslav delegation—Yugoslavia having recently broken with Stalinist orthodoxy. Yet, Silberstein had omitted any mention of the Yugoslav expulsion from his report to the Guild on the Rome convention. The Washington Field Office relayed these facts to FBI headquarters, adding "it is believed that considerable dissention in the ranks of the Lawyers Guild could occur if this matter became public." Two weeks prior to the Guild's May 1950 convention in New York City, the matter did "become public" in liberal journalist Murray Kempton's *New York Post* column. Bureau documents strongly suggest that whether Kempton knew it or not, the FBI was the source of his information.[44]

As the NLG report inferred, FBI officials in fact did use their friends in Congress and in the press. In May, conservative Senators Pat McCarran and Homer Ferguson invited Hoover to outline the Bureau's case against the Guild before a closed session of the Senate Judiciary Committee. Shortly thereafter, the Senate Appropriations Committee released Hoover's February anti-NLG testimony to the press, which was then given front-page coverage. The head of the American Legion promptly amplified Hoover's allegations, while HUAC Congressman Burr P. Harrison pointedly demanded that the Attorney General list the Guild as subversive and order it to register as an agent of a foreign power.[45]

Bureau officials particularly turned to the House Un-American Activities Committee for assistance. What transpired underscores Walter Goodman's description of HUAC and the FBI as "a pair of mischievously indiscreet lovers," maintaining a formal distance in public, "yet so fond were the glances they exchanged, so endearing the sentiments, that observers could hardly keep from speculating over what they did together when the lights went out." The Committee had considered initiating a hearing on the NLG in December 1949, following Lyle Wilson's first story on the forthcoming NLG report. In the spring of 1950, portions of the FBI's NLG dossier were leaked to HUAC and were in turn incorporated in a Committee report on the National Lawyers Guild. HUAC members Richard Nixon and Burr P. Harrison, moreover, fully briefed FBI Assistant Director Nichols about the progress of the Committee's report. "Congressman Nixon advised me today," Nichols informed FBI Associate Director Clyde Tolson on August 29, 1950, that the report had been delayed because "Congressman Walters [of HUAC] was a member of the Guild in 1939." Nixon promised that the Committee report would be released soon. "If and when the Committee Report is issued," Hoover commented, "we should call the Attorney General's attention to it and to our previous memos and suggest consideration again for designating it subversive."

The released fifty-page HUAC *Report on the National Lawyers Guild: Legal Bulwark of the Communist Party* incorporated "evidence" from the FBI's 1949 "summary memorandum" on the Guild. In some places, the HUAC report lifted passages verbatim, and in others, paraphrased passages from that FBI document. NLG criticism of the FBI, opposition to legislative attacks on Communists, and frequent intercession, as "friends of the court," during trials involving Communist defendants, the Committee report charged, confirmed its Communist allegiances. Many Guild members had also served as defense counsel for uncooperative witnesses subpoenaed by the Committee. Following a long series of incredibly strained comparisons of the Guild's positions with those expressed by the *Daily Worker*, the HUAC report recommended that the Attorney General list the National Lawyers Guild as "subversive," and compel it to register "as an agent of a foreign principal." The American Bar Association should also "consider the question of whether or not membership in the National Lawyers Guild, a subversive organization, is compatible with admissibility to the American Bar."[46]

The HUAC document was publicly released on September 17, 1950, without any hearings having been held. Its impact was devastating. HUAC's earlier (1944) assault on the NLG, issued as an appendix to the Committee's major "report" on the National Citizens Political

Action Committee, had done little damage to the organization. HUAC's 1950 charges, however, were made in a fundamentally altered context. The Soviet Union's successful A-bomb test in September 1949, the simultaneous revolutionary victory of the Chinese Communists, and the very recent North Korean invasion of South Korea had, in the words of historian Alonzo Hamby, "created a situation on which the most preposterous charges of Red subversion could gain attention." Such an atmosphere—further heightened by the confessions of Soviet atom spies in other countries, the convictions of Alger Hiss and Judith Coplon, Senator Joseph McCarthy's charges of Communist infiltration of the State Department, and the atomic espionage indictments of the Communists Julius and Ethel Rosenberg—nurtured support for repressing Communists and their defenders. Judges and lawyers were particularly reluctant to have any connection with an organization associated, in the public mind, with communism. (The FBI's wiretap on the Guild's National Office instantly apprised FBI officials of a wave of resignations from the Guild in the wake of the HUAC allegations.) [47]

NLG President Thomas Emerson vainly attempted to rebut HUAC's report; the FBI effectively neutralized his efforts. Thus, when Emerson met with reporters in November and released his rebuttal to HUAC, FBI Assistant Director Nichols could report that some of the Bureau's journalistic allies "just about broke up the Lawyers Guild press conference this morning." A few days later, the FBI leaked another IADL document, apparently retrieved from Robert Silberstein's trash, to HUAC stalwart Harold Velde. Velde in turn relayed the item to journalist Fulton Lewis, Jr., who announced in his December 8 column that Silberstein, then participating in a White House Conference on Children and Youth and "voicing his opinions on American youth," had recently received a letter from a prominent French Communist lawyer. A week later HUAC released a second report accusing the Guild of financing the work of a "Communist lobby"—the National Committee to Defeat the Mundt Bill. This latest HUAC document contained information that almost certainly originated from the FBI's tap of the NLG telephone. [48]

Although the HUAC report seriously damaged the Guild's public credibility, FBI officials still worried about further NLG sallies against the Bureau. On March 1, 1951, the NLG wiretap disclosed that a leader of the student Guild chapter at Harvard Law School was preparing an article on FBI wiretapping. The Boston Field Office was immediately alerted, and three days later the president of the Massachusetts Bar Association, Samuel Sears, publicly blasted the Law School for harboring the subversive NLG chapter. In an open letter to Harvard Law School Dean Erwin Griswold, Sears condemned Harvard for "playing host to the Communist party," and demanded the disbandment of the student group and the cancellation of a scheduled appearance by NLG Vice President Osmond K. Fraenkel, a well-known attorney for the American Civil Liberties Union. Dean Griswold refused to intervene, noting with unconscious irony that "the U.S. Attorney General, with the resources of the FBI at his disposal, has not yet seen fit to list the National Lawyers Guild as a subversive organization." Despite this failure to dislodge the NLG from Harvard, the Boston Field Office soon reported the recruitment of a member of the Harvard chapter as a "confidential informant" of the Bureau, with the assigned symbol number "BOS-627."[49]

The enlistment of BOS-627 soon proved to be fortuitous. Losses of membership and income had forced the Guild to close its Washington office in July 1951; reduced national operations thereafter were conducted from the New York chapter office. With the NLG wiretap defunct, the Bureau's new "informant" was an invaluable and prolific source of inside information about Guild activities. For example, when Washington FBI agents discovered the draft of yet another resolution critical of FBI procedures in Joseph Forer's trash, BOS-627 was promptly dispatched to the Guild's Chicago convention to report whatever action the NLG might take on Forer's proposal.[50]

III

In his public reply to HUAC's September 1950 "Report on the National Lawyers Guild," NLG President Thomas Emerson had claimed that one reason for the Committee's attack had been the professional activity of individual NLG members. Having first played a major role in harassing political dissidents, Emerson charged, HUAC now sought "to intimidate or eliminate the only lawyers who have had the courage to defend those at the whipping post. In short, the Committee is striking at the constitutional rights of one accused, to counsel of his own choice, and at the duty of every lawyer, under the code of ethics, not to reject a client's cause out of fear." Indeed, many of the lawyers who appeared as defense counsel before HUAC, state anti-radical committees, Loyalty Review Boards, and the Immigration Bureau were NLG members.[51]

The five attorneys representing the Communist Party leadership during the 1949 Smith Act trial in New York City were also long-time Guild activists. (The Act made it illegal to advocate the overthrow of the Government by force or violence.) This tumultuous trial concluded with the conviction of the eleven Communist leaders. Following the verdict, Judge Harold Medina summarily sentenced the five defense attorneys, with whom he had frequently clashed during the seven month trial, for contempt of court. More ominous than the contempt sentence, however, was the fact that two of the Smith Act attorneys were soon disbarred from practice. despite a professional tradition that over-zealous courtroom advocacy did not constitute grounds for disbarment. When testifying before the Senate Appropriations Committee two months after Medina's verdict, Hoover cited the conduct of these five attorneys as further evidence of the NLG's subversive character.[52]

Other radical lawyers, most of whom were Guild members, were threatened with disbarment in the late forties for refusing, during the course of their representation of clients in court and before legislative committees, to answer questions about their political affiliations. Attorney General Tom Clark in August 1949, and United States Solicitor General Philip Perlman the following April, further encouraged such harassment of left-wing lawyers by publicly suggesting that lawyers who belonged to the Communist Party, or who failed to deny such membership under oath, were categorically unfit to practice law before the federal courts.[53]

The American Bar Association (ABA) was also offended by the presence of radicals within the legal profession. The Association's 1948 convention had already resolved to expel any lawyer who failed, by invoking the constitutional privilege against self-incrimination, to deny Communist Party membership or who "publicly or secretly aids, supports or assists the world Communist movement to accomplish its objectives in the United States by participating in its programs, whether he be an avowed party member or not." That same convention, however, tabled a recommendation of the ABA Board of Governors to exclude all members of the National Lawyers Guild.[54]

The ABA's September 1950 convention went much further, calling upon all state and local authorities to impose a periodic anti-Communist oath on attorneys within their jurisdiction. This call for a lawyers' loyalty oath (the more so because lawyers were already compelled to swear allegiance to the Constitution) was sharply criticized by several prominent jurists and the New York City Bar Association. A lawyer might be a member of the Communist Party, Harvard Law Professor Zechariah Chafee asserted, and still be a perfectly competent practitioner of the lawyer's craft. Furthermore, Chafee observed, a dedicated seditionist would probably sign any such oath, whereas some non-radical lawyers were certain to balk at any examination of their private political beliefs. "Such men may be called over-conscientious," he concluded, "but excessive scrupulousness is not so common among lawyers that we can afford to drive it out of the Bar."[55]

The ABA refused to yield to such high-level rebukes. Instead, its House of Delegates requested that state and local bar associations disbar "all lawyers who are members of the Communist Party or who advocate Marxism-Leninism." A week later ABA stalwart Herbert O'Conor, a McCarthyite United States senator from Maryland, introduced a "sense of the Senate" resolution to bar Communist lawyers from practicing in federal courts.[56]

Then, on June 4, 1951, the Supreme Court upheld the Smith Act convictions of the eleven Communist Party leaders. Later that month, the Court refused to review Judge Medina's contempt sentences of the five defense attorneys. With the way cleared for additional prosecutions, the government quickly indicted fifty-two second-level Communist Party leaders in New York, California, Baltimore, Pittsburgh, and Honolulu. At a time, therefore, when lawyers able and willing to defend Communists in court were sorely needed, the professional hazards of doing so had increased sharply.[57]

Some lawyers cited reasons other than fear of reprisal for refusing to represent Communist clients. The well-known trial attorney Whitney

North Seymour complained that the Party insisted on dictating defense strategy under terms of which "no self-respecting lawyer would accept any kind of case for anyone." The Communist leaders had indeed insisted upon a militant "class struggle" approach to legal defense in the first Smith Act trial; in any event, at least four of the lawyers in that trial were politically oriented toward the Communist Party, and thus largely agreed with that approach. In subsequent trials, however, many Communist defendants sought to retain well-known non-Communist attorneys, and allowed them a considerably freer hand. Nevertheless, in New York, Philadelphia, and Baltimore, the defendants were unable to retain lawyers until the court itself formally intervened to appoint counsel, and by so doing, protected the lawyers from the stigma of having volunteered to defend Communists.[58]

As it turned out, Los Angeles Guild leader John McTernan, Guild President Thomas Emerson, and two active members of the New York NLG Chapter represented the seventeen Communist leaders tried in New York. The California Smith Act defense team was led by Ben Margolis, McTernan's partner, and included only one non-member of the Guild, a local labor lawyer whose practice declined drastically as a result of his involvement in the trial.[59]

The conduct of Los Angeles Judge William C. Mathes during the California trial seemed the reincarnation of Harold Medina. Mathes's insistence on impossibly high bail and unnecessary contempt citations against some of the defendants provided an opportunity for opponents of the trial to elicit public sympathy for the defendants. Remembering Judge Medina's treatment of defense attorneys during the earlier trial, the NLG in California sought to publicize as fully as possible within the California legal profession the nature of the Los Angeles proceedings. At the end of November 1951, therefore, the Guild announced its intention, when the trial began in February, to reproduce and mail long excerpts from the trial transcript to thousands of California lawyers.[60]

California FBI offices immediately notified Bureau headquarters of the Guild plan. Within two weeks HUAC investigators began preparing to open hearings into Communist activities within the California legal profession. At the end of January 1952, the Committee publicly interrogated five California lawyers who had formerly belonged to the Communist Party and to the National Lawyers Guild. These five cooperative witnesses named thirty-two other California Guild members, including Ben Margolis, John McTernan, and other current Smith Act counsel, and described them as active Communists. Robert Silberstein, the long-time NLG executive secretary, was additionally named as a Party intimate. The Committee promptly subpoenaed many of those so named to appear during scheduled hearings on February 18.[61]

As Walter Goodman observes, the HUAC decision to interrogate the Los Angeles Guild members at a time "when Communist lawyers were being threatened with disbarment and non-Communist lawyers were uneasy about taking on the defense of Party members, could only add to that political prudence which sapped the nation of its dissenting spirit in the early nineteen fifties."[62] HUAC, to be sure, had its own reason for discrediting an organization which had sought its abolition relentlessly for fourteen years, and whose members had counselled their clients not to cooperate with HUAC inquiries. Unquestionably, however, the Committee had acted on the basis of information which the FBI had covertly provided.

In October 1950, following release of the widely publicized HUAC report on the National Lawyers Guild, a lawyer who had formerly belonged to both the Los Angeles Guild Chapter and the Communist Party contacted the FBI's Los Angeles office. Presumably anxious to guard against adverse repercussions from his past, he furnished the FBI with a list of Guild members whom he described as Communist-affiliated; this list was almost identical to those named before HUAC in January 1952. Conceivably, then, upon learning of the Guild's efforts to develop sympathy from California lawyers by publicizing the questionable procedures employed during the Los Angeles Smith Act trial, Bureau officials again used HUAC to discredit those who challenged FBI designs. Just as the Bureau's earlier December 1949 "summary memorandum" on the NLG had become the HUAC report of September 1950, so apparently did the FBI's October 1950 non-public list of radical California lawyers become the highly visible January 1952 HUAC inquisition of those who had fought the Smith Act in court.[63]

FBI activities were not confined to leaking derogatory information to a friendly congressional committee. Thus, when the Guild's National

Executive Board met on February 2, 1952 to prepare a response to HUAC's subpoena of its executive secretary and thirty-two of its members, BOS-627 was on hand to observe and to advise FBI officials that Board members Leonard Boudin and Murray Gordon had been designated to prepare an official Guild statement for release on February 11. Thanks presumably to BOS-627's remarkable access to NLG deliberations, newspaper columnist Ogden R. Reid was able to pre-empt Boudin and Gordon. In a February 10 article, headed "The Red Underground: Lawyers Guild Decides Stand in case of Inquiry," Reid identified all those who had attended the February 2 National Executive Board meeting, reiterated the HUAC charges against NLG Executive Secretary Silberstein, and printed an itinerary of the Guild's new president, Earl B. Dickerson.[64]

HUAC and Reid were not alone in attempting to discredit the NLG. Austin Canfield was another willing accomplice. The chairman of a recently formed American Bar Association committee "to study Communist tactics, strategy, and objectives, particularly as they relate to the obstruction of proper court procedure and law enforcement," Canfield charged in a February 26 speech to the ABA House of Delegates that a small group of from fifteen to twenty lawyers had become the "masterminds" of the Communist party. The ABA official declined to reveal the source of his information, but a report of his committee stated that HUAC "in recent weeks has unearthed sufficient evidence against some few attorneys which evidence, in the opinion of your Committee, would justify consideration and action by the grievance committee of a state or local association." The ABA Committee report predicted "that many more attorneys will be exposed as members of the Communist party or as advocates of Marxism-Leninism" during future hearings.[65]

In its first year of existence the Canfield Committee sought to persuade state and local bar associations to purge themselves and the profession of Communist lawyers. The Committee's "Brief on Communism," which incorporated FBI Director Hoover's February 1950 Senate attack on the National Lawyers Guild, was widely distributed to assist bar groups in this effort. His committee, Canfield explained shortly after its formation, intended to "investigate certain organizations which use their members to defend Communists in court and in hearings before Congressional inquiry committees." To further this "investigation" Canfield contacted and in early 1951 received from the FBI four "blind memoranda" on NLG officers.[66]

A week after the five ex-Guild members' January 1952 appearance before HUAC, Canfield again contacted FBI Assistant Director Louis Nichols. "He said the National Lawyers Guild is whooping it up," Nichols informed FBI Associate Director Clyde Tolson, "and they have to decide whether to take them on or not. I told him he would probably have trouble as long as the National Lawyers Guild remained in operation." "Canfield likewise stated," Nichols later reported, "he is trying to get together basic facts [on the offensive nature of the Guild's weekly summaries of the California Smith Act trial] and there will be a special meeting of his Committee in an attempt to move the American Bar Association into action against the National Lawyers Guild." Nichols then leaked to Canfield the FBI report on the most recent NLG convention, based on information provided by the ubiquitous BOS-627.[67]

Although HUAC postponed its scheduled February 18 hearings, the Committee did interrogate Robert Silberstein in Washington in April. The NLG Secretary proved a thoroughly unhelpful witness, refusing on Fifth Amendment grounds to discuss his politics, and accusing the Committee of deliberately attempting "to discourage people from handling cases of unpopular causes." The Committee members' questions of Silberstein on this occasion conformed to the comparisons of Guild and Communist Party positions first developed in the FBI's "summary memorandum" of January 18, 1950.[68]

HUAC convened other hearings in Los Angeles in September 1952, subpoenaing the testimony of twenty-four lawyers, all of whom were uniformly defiant. Several witnesse were forcibly ejected from the hearing room, while others poured scorn on the "stool pigeons" who had named them in January. No one answered a question on political affiliation, even though some clearly were not currently close to the Communist Party. Most of the two-day hearing was clandestinely taped by sympathizers of those subpoenaed, and turned into a record—"Voices of Resistance"—which was sold to recoup the cost of legal defense.[69]

Resistance was not enough. ABA anti-Communists had devised a strategy to purge radical lawyers who refused to talk even though bar associations declined to require loyalty oaths of their members. Using lists provided by HUAC and by the Senate Internal Security Subcommittee, the Canfield Committee directly encouraged disbarment action against lawyers who stood silent on Fifth Amendment grounds. Congressional investigations, the ABA Committee concluded, "have rendered great public service in continuing to expose before the public the subversive activities of Communists."[70]

Besides pressuring state and local authorities, the ABA House of Delegates petitioned President Dwight D. Eisenhower's Attorney General Herbert Brownell to begin proceedings to exclude from practice before federal courts and administrative agencies any lawyer who was a Communist or who failed to deny under oath any Communist connections. In August 1953, the ABA adopted a report of its Special Committee, now chaired by former Senator Herbert O'Conor, which held that, since lawyers could decide which testimony was in fact incriminating, any lawyer invoking the privilege against self-incrimination had proved himself unfit to practice law. The following March, acting on another O'Conor Committee recommendation, the ABA House of Delegates endorsed Senator Pat McCarran's bill to skirt the Fifth Amendment, and compel testimony in court and before Congress by granting immunity to uncooperative witnesses.[71]

Alarmed by the American Bar Association's persistent efforts to purge radical lawyers from the profession, in the summer of 1953 the National Lawyers Guild issued a call for a "National Conference on Proposals to Impose Political Tests for the Right to Practice Law." Ironically, however, before the summer's end, the Guild was compelled to add to its conference title the phrase "or to Function as a Bar Association.[72]

For years FBI officials had sought to have some authority with more respectability than HUAC designate the NLG as "subversive." Disappointed in their repeated attempts to place the Guild on the Attorney General's list, Bureau officials first considered a more oblique attack: requiring the NLG to register under the Foreign Agents Registration Act because of its affiliation with the International Association of Democratic Lawyers. This scheme had to be abandoned when the NLG withdrew from the IADL in 1951. Next, FBI officials prepared materials to persuade the Subversive Activities Control Board to compel the Guild to register as a "Communist front group" under the terms of the McCarran Internal Security Act of 1950. This ploy was dropped in May 1953 when FBI Director Hoover learned that the new Republican Attorney General, Herbert Brownell, had agreed to include the Guild on an expanded version of the Attorney General's list.[73]

The National Lawyers Guild learned of Brownell's decision on the same day that he publicly announced it in a major address to the annual convention of the American Bar Association. It had become evident, Brownell told the ABA delegates, that "at least since 1946 the leadership of the Guild has been in the hands of card-carrying Communists and prominent fellow-travellers." The Guild had followed the party line on every major issue, the Attorney General continued, "excepting only those so notorious that their espousal would too clearly demonstrate the Communist control." That the Guild served as "the legal mouthpiece for the Communist Party and its members" was demonstrated by its opposition to all laws and investigations aimed at restricting or exposing Communist activity in the United States. A week later, in a speech to the Veterans of Foreign Wars, Brownell expanded his public indictment. The National Lawyers Guild had been initiated, proposed, and organized "under the direct supervision of the Communist Party," and had been used "to indoctrinate members of the legal profession." As further proof of the Guild's subversive character, Brownell cited its criticisms of United States foreign policy and of the FBI.[74]

The Attorney General's manifest prejudgement convinced NLG leaders of the need for a strong defense against the latest attack. Thomas Emerson publicly termed Brownell's announcement "a basic challenge to the whole right of association in this country," while the *Guild Lawyer* contended that the attack revealed

that the mentality and standards of the House Un-American Activities Committee now guide the highest legal office in our government. The purpose of the Attorney General is evidently to silence the one bar association which has consistently fought against all invasions of consitutionl rights and . . . to intimidate further that section of the Bar which has provided most of the legal counsel for the victims of repression.

To prepare its defense strategy, the NLG called a special National Executive Board meeting for the second week in September.[75]

Although any organization proposed for inclusion on the Attorney General's list was entitled to an administrative hearing to contest this ruling, the fifty Guild Board members who gathered on September 12 were nearly unanimous in concluding that such a hearing, before an obviously prejudiced Attorney General, would afford the Guild neither due process of law nor a clear standard of judgement. The Board resolved, therefore, to request a hearing only to stop Brownell from immediately designating the Guild and instead to seek in federal court a restraining order and contest the listing procedure there. Committees were appointed to raise $25,000 for legal fees and at least one prominent non-Guild attorney was retained to represent the Guild in federal court. Because issues involved in the case could have broad relevance for civil liberties, the Board also authorized employment of a public relations consultant, and proposed to prepare a mass-produced pamphlet to present to members of the Bar the Guild's side of the case.[76]

The FBI's BOS-627 was among those attending the NLG's September Executive Board Meeting. This "informant's" detailed accounts of these and later deliberations on legal and political strategy afforded privileged information to the Guild's courtroom adversaries—the FBI and the Department of Justice. In response to BOS-627's report on the non-Guild lawyers whom the Executive Board had hoped to retain, the FBI contacted at least one of them. While it cannot be confirmed that the Bureau directly interfered with NLG attempts to retain counsel, in any event, the Guild was represented in court by three of its own members, Joseph Forer, Osmond K. Fraenkel, and NLG President Earl B. Dickerson.[77]

The Department of Justice was nonetheless concerned by the Bureau's reckless use of BOS-627. Department officials were particularly worried about FBI intrusion on "the discussions of matters involving the preparation of the NLG's case now pending in District Court and its defense under E. O. 10450 [Eisenhower's April 1953 order outlining "security" dismissal standards] proceeding." Department officials twice warned F. J. Baumgardner, head of the Bureau's Internal Security Section, of "the dangers attendant to the informant's participation in such discussions and the reporting of information which may be privileged." Baumgardner assured Justice that the FBI was "aware of the problem." FBI officials, however, did not prevent BOS-627 from attending another Board meeting.[78]

On November 30, 1953, the Guild's attorneys filed suit in Federal District Court in Washington to enjoin the Attorney General from listing the Guild and to secure a judgement that the listing procedure constituted a denial of due process of law. Rebuffed by the District Court, the NLG successfully sought a restraining order from the Circuit Court of Appeals, which ordered the District Court to reconsider the NLG petition. The District Court remained unpersuaded, holding that the NLG must first exhaust its administrative remedies through a hearing before the Attorney General. After unsuccessfully petitioning the Circuit Court, on October 28, 1955, NLG attorneys applied to the Supreme Court for a review of its case.[79]

The drawn-out litigation compelled the Department of Justice to suspend administrative proceedings aimed at formally listing the National Lawyers Guild. In this way, the NLG momentarily avoided what Supreme Court Justice Hugo Black had termed "the practical equivalent of confiscation and a death sentence for any blacklisted organization." This suspension of proceedings did not prevent others from concluding, on the basis of Brownell's public pronouncement before the ABA, that the Guild had been officially designated as "subversive." The usually careful *Washington Post*, for example, headlined a story "Lawyers Guild Put on 'Subversive' List," while a *New York Times* story identified the NLG as being "on the Attorney General's list of subversive organizations." Even the American Civil Liberties Union's *Weekly Bulletin* commented on the Guild's "designation as 'subversive.' " It may have been an honest mistake, therefore, when ABA President Lloyd Wright publicly averred that the NLG was "on the Attorney General's list of alleged subversive organizations."[80]

During the mid-fifties, the ABA and the Guild frequently found themselves on opposite sides—the Association's anti-Communist Committee seeking to disbar radical attorneys, and the NLG attempting to defend them through public pressure and by intervention as "friend of the Court." The ABA Committee repeatedly implored state and local associations to move against radical lawyers. In addition, ABA Committee members conferred with Attorney General Brownell over the best method for initiating federal disbarment proceedings against left-wing attorneys. The ABA Committee discovered, however, that many state and local groups seemed reluctant to act, while the Attorney General maintained that federal disbarment could begin only after action had been successfully concluded in the state courts.[81]

Sensing the need for a firm precedent, ABA Committee chairman Herbert O'Conor announced his committee's intent to submit an *amicus curiae* brief to the Florida Supreme Court in support of the disbarment of attorney Leo Sheiner, a Guild member who had refused to discuss his political affiliations before the Senate Internal Security Subcommittee. "If the Supreme Court of Florida upholds the Association's position, that members of the Bar who seek protection of the Fifth Amendment are not qualified to retain their licenses," O'Conor explained, "then bar associations will be in a position to act against attorneys seeking that protection." The National Lawyers Guild also submitted an *amicus curiae* brief opposing Sheiner's disbarment.[82]

The Florida Supreme Court overturned Sheiner's disbarment and remanded the case to the lower court for rehearing. Deprived of this clear precedent, the O'Conor Committee reported little progress in its other efforts to secure disbarments in New York, California, and the District of Columbia. Accordingly, in September 1955, O'Conor asked the FBI for a membership list of the National Lawyers Guild. O'Conor's intent was to initiate disbarment action against the entire diminishing membership of a bar association officially designated as "subversive."[83]

The sour tone of the O'Conor Committee's subsequent reports bears witness to the fact that, by late 1955, the tide of legal harassment against Communists and the lawyers who represented them had begun to turn. In a Smith Act trial in Cleveland, for example, three local, non-radical attorneys recruited and paid by the Cleveland Bar Association represented the eleven indigent defendants. In February 1956, five of the defendants were acquitted. Having enjoyed almost complete success during six years of Smith Act prosecutions and appeals, the Department of Justice was obviously shocked by the Cleveland verdict. On March 5, the head of the Department's Criminal Division, Assistant Attorney General William F. Tompkins, publicly condemned the Cleveland Bar Association's action and claimed that the three defense attorneys had been "duped" by the Communists.[84]

Although criticized in some quarters, Tompkins's remarks were reaffirmed by the FBI. In testimony before the Senate Appropriations Committee, FBI Director Hoover contended that the Communist Party had secretly adopted a new strategy that "would include legal maneuvers—acquiring eminent counsel to defend the Party and its leaders—and the use of petitions, forums, mass meetings, and radio broadcasts."[85]

The National Lawyers Guild immediately challenged Hoover's implication that lawyers who defended Communists had made themselves instruments of a subversive strategy. In a public letter addressed to Hoover, President Eisenhower, and Attorney General Brownell, NLG President Malcolm Sharp affirmed "the high duty of lawyers to defend the rights of accused persons and that they should not be subject to attack or vilification as a result of pursuing this duty." In response, Hoover notified the Attorney General that he did not intend "to even dignify Mr. Sharp's letter with a reply, much less a statement."[86] Brownell, however, was apparently worried about the public outcry over the remarks of Tompkins and Hoover, and urged the FBI director to reconsider.

The Bureau hierarchy spent several days drafting a formal response to the NLG president's letter. In this effort, they were assisted by Justice Department officials. "I showed it to Warren Berger [sic]," FBI Assistant Director Nichols confided to FBI Associate Director Tolson. Nichols added that Burger, head of the Department's Civil Division and engaged in litigation with the NLG, at the time, was "quite enthusiastic over the letter after having read it. At first he thought the letter should not be answered, but after having read the letter stated this letter would hurt the Commies." After a final meeting with Brownell, who suggested further revisions, Hoover released his response to the press on April 9. [87]

The FBI director's letter categorically rejected Sharp's charges. The Communist legal campaign had been developed during "secret" Communist meetings. In addition to his own confidential informants, Hoover cited the recent report of the ABA's O'Conor Committee that "the Communist Party has been and today still is seeking to delay and if possible to defeat every phase of Judicial administration that offers any minimum or remote threat to the progress of the Communist movement in the United States." Hoover concluded with an almost epigrammatic rendition of the Bureau's thinking on political heresy and the right to counsel:

I shall always contend that every defendant is entitled to honest, skillful and highly principled counsel for his defense. The great majority of the legal profession has long ago established very sound adherence to American ideals of justice. The legal profession has also condemned the conduct of a small but vocal group of lawyers who have tried to twist the court procedures and protections and resort to methods of chicanery to turn our legal and judicial system into a mockery as part of their campaign to destroy our American way of life.

Radio and newspaper coverage of Hoover's reply, carefully monitored by Bureau headquarters, indicated that the FBI had won a resounding public relations victory over the unloved National Lawyers Guild.[88]

While it could still rely on a chorus of uncritical support from most of the national press, the FBI and its anti-Communist allies nonetheless suffered further court reversals. Under Chief Justice Earl Warren, the Supreme Court agreed to hear appeals of the California Smith Act convictions in October 1955. In 1956, the Court blocked an order which would have compelled the Communist Party to register with the Subversive Activities Control Board and agreed to hear appeals of the Pittsburgh Smith Act case. Frustrated in its plan to destroy the Communist Party in the courts, the FBI initiated in August 1956 what the Church Committee has termed "a sophisticated vigilante program against domestic enemies." Formally designated COINTELPRO, this program in essence expanded and formalized the media smear campaigns, illegal surveillance methods, and political sabotage which the Bureau had employed on an ad hoc basis for at least fifteen years against the National Lawyers Guild.[89]

The libertarian trend in the Supreme Court's decisions reached its peak on June 17, 1957—"Red Monday." On that day the Court reversed the contempt citation of a labor leader who had refused to discuss his politics before HUAC, reinstated a State Department employee fired under the Federal Employee Loyalty Program, and freed five of the California Smith Act defendants while ordering new trials for the rest. The Court also reversed two cases in which applicants had been denied admission to practice law on political grounds. The following year the Court overturned the 1949 contempt convictions of the original Smith Act lawyers, having earlier reversed the disbarments of two of them.[90]

The Supreme Court refused to intervene in the case of *National Lawyers*

Guild v. Brownell. On May 7, 1956, the Court announced that it would not hear arguments on the case until the Guild had exhausted its administrative remedies. The Justice Department, however, was reluctant to proceed to a hearing. In July 1958, FBI Director Hoover begrudgingly informed his subordinates of the Bureau's failure to have the Guild listed as "subversive." The Attorney General had decided, in the case of the National Lawyers Guild and another organization which had challenged its designation,

that the cases would ultimately be carried to the Supreme Court and it was likely the Supreme Court would throw out the entire Attorney General's list of subversive organizations, and he wanted to avoid this as he believed neither of the two cases was particularly strong and he did not think that the Attorney General's list should, therefore, be risked by pressing the two cases in question.

In September the Department of Justice announced its decision to stop proceedings, allegedly because of the death or unavailability of witnesses, "without in any way exonerating the National Lawyers Guild." As Osmond Fraenkel observed, this public explanation was an accusatory and "most ungracious" sort of concession.[91]

IV

The FBI files on the National Lawyers Guild reveal that the Bureau's, and its congressional and journalist allies', eight years of harassment—between 1950 and 1958—contributed to the Guild's loss of over four-fifths of its membership and the expiration of its nine local chapters.[92] The files also confirm that despite extensive and illegal surveillance the FBI uncovered no evidence implicating the Guild or its members in any violation of the law or of professional ethics. To the contrary, the FBI files highlight the political activism of Bureau officials—the criteria leading to the FBI's campaign against the NLG having been based solely on the conservative political philosophy of FBI Director Hoover and other high-level Bureau officials.

In part, the NLG was targeted because the lawyers' group had openly and persistently criticized important government policies—including the

Truman Doctrine, the Loyalty Program, and the Smith Act prosecutions of American Communists. For FBI officials, the Guild's other "subversive" offenses included not only the organization's refusal to purge Communists from its membership, but also its role as the professional association for dozens of lawyers who dared to appear as defense counsel for Communists when it was most hazardous to do so. Finally, and preeminently, FBI officials sought to discredit the National Lawyers Guild because in 1950, a quarter century before the Watergate revelations and the Church Committee investigation, NLG officials had attempted to insure an independent and searching inquiry into FBI illegality and violations of democratic processes.

Notes

1. McCarthy's sources for the charges appear to have been lower level Army intelligence agents and/or the FBI. See Frank Donner, *The Age of Surveillance: The Aims and Methods of America's Political Intelligence System* (New York, 1980), pp. 292, 504 n10. See also William Sullivan, *The Bureau: My Thirty Years in Hoover's FBI* (New York: 1979), pp. 45–46, 267.

2. The entire episode is described in Robert Griffith, *The Politics of Fear: Joseph R. McCarthy and the Senate* (Lexington, Ky., 1970), pp. 258–59, and in Eric P. Goldman, *The Crucial Decade—and After, 1945–60* (New York, 1960), pp. 274–79.

3. *New York Times*, June 10, 1954; Welch is quoted on p. 17. *Boston Globe*, June 10, 1954; Boston *Traveller*, June 10, 1954. See also Jerold Auerbach, *Unequal Justice: Lawyers and Social Change in Modern America* (New York, 1976), p. 237.

4. Proof of this microfilm appears in a memorandum from the files of the FBI's Boston Field Office (SAC [Special Agent in Charge], Boston, to SAC, New York, March 26, 1954) reporting that a roll of microfilm had been mailed from Boston to New York for processing, and was received back in Boston on April 15. This and all other FBI and Department of Justice documents cited hereafter have been released by the federal government in response to civil litigation filed on behalf of the National Lawyers Guild (NLG) by the National Emergency Civil Liberties Foundation, Inc., of New York. The Foundation has made these papers available to the public. Most newspaper citations in this paper, save those from the *New York Times* and the *Washington Post*, are from the

FBI's clipping files on the National Lawyers Guild.
    5. For the close relationship between the FBI, McCarthy, and other politicians, see Sanford J. Ungar, *FBI* (Boston, 1976), pp. 277–78, 354–68; Sullivan, *The Bureau*, pp. 45–46, 267; and Donner, *Age of Surveillance*, pp. 101–10, 173–74, 406, 409.
    6. "An Appeal to American Lawyers" (Dec. 1936) appears in Sugar MSS.
    7. For the origins of the NLG see Marc Bloom, "The National Lawyers Guild, 1936–38: The Formation and Early Years of a Liberal Bar Association" (M.A. thesis, Columbia University, 1973), pp. 2–21. See also Auerbach, *Unequal Justice*, pp. 191–210.
    8. For a brief account of Communist work in "mass" organizations, see Joseph Starobin, *American Communism in Crisis, 1943–1957* (Cambridge, Mass., 1972), pp. 29–38. See also Thomas A. Kreuger, *And Promises to Keep: The Southern Conference for Human Welfare, 1938–48* (Nashville, Tenn., 1967), pp. 72–92, 180. For the role of Communists in the NLG, I have relied on interviews with several of the Guild's radical founders, and on the testimony of a Communist who was its first national executive secretary, Mortimer Reimer. See U.S., House, Committee on Un-American Activities, *Hearings on Investigation of Communist Infiltration of Government*, P. 2, 84th Cong., 2d sess., 1955, pp. 3023–28.
    9. *New York Times*, Feb. 23, 1939; Feb. 24, 1939; Feb. 25, 1939. See also Auerbach, *Unequal Justice*, pp. 200–3.
    10. Thomas I. Emerson, *COHC*, pp. 774–77, 781–82; *New York Times*, May 29, 1940, and June 6, 1940. *Washington Post*, May 30, 1940 and May 31, 1940. A mimeographed membership report, dated June 30, 1940, appears in the Sugar MSS.
    11. *GL* 1 (Dec. 1942): 3; *GL* 4 (May 1954): 1; Emerson, *COHO*, 2201–4; E. R. Stettinius to Robert Krenny is reprinted in *LGR* 5 (March-April 1945): 58.
    12. *GL* 6 (Nov. 1947: 3; *GL* 8 (March 1949): 2; Clifford J. Durr to Thomas Emerson, Aug. 25, 1949, in possession of Emerson.
    13. For the FBI's persistent expansion of its domestic intelligence operations, see *SDSR*, pp. 392–421. See also Athan Theoharis, "The FBI's Stretching of Presidential Directives, 1936–53," *Political Science Quarterly* 91 (Winter 1976–77): 649–72; "The Truman Administration and the Decline of Civil Liberties: The FBI's Success in Securing Authorization for a Preventive Detention Program," *Journal of American History* 64 (March 1978): 1010–30; and *Spying on Americans: Political Surveillance from Hoover to the Huston Plan* (Philadelphia, 1978), pp. 65–93; and Donner, *Age of Surveillance*, pp. 52–78.

14. "Convention Resolutions," *LGR* 1 (June 1941), p. 67; and "Convention Resolutions and Statements of Policy," *LGR* 8 (Jan.-Feb. 1948), p. 320.

15. The documents cited here appear in the FBI's "main file" on the National Lawyers Guild, which is numbered consecutively from 1 to 15385. When citing documents from this file, I shall identify only their "main file" number. Hoover to L. M. C. Smith, Chief Neutrality Laws Unit, Dec. 20, 1940, 15; Smith to Hoover, January 13, 1941, 16; Report of SA (Special Agent) T. W. Dawsey, May 25, 1941, 26-805. Dawsey attributes his material, transcribed from microfilm, to "a highly confidential source"—a phrase the Bureau employed to designate various illegal investigative devices, including "black bag jobs." FBI regulations required the FBI director's (or an FBI assistant director's) explicit written authorization for black bag jobs. Such documents of authorization did not go into the Bureau's permanent files, and were destroyed as a matter of policy. FBI correspondents after 1946 employed the term "anonymous source" to denote a burglary. For the FBI's record destruction procedure for black bag jobs, see Theoharis, "Bureaucrats above the Law: Double-Entry Intelligence Files," *Nation* 225 (Oct. 22, 1977), pp. 394–95; see also SDSR, pp. 355–61. P. E. Foxworth to the Director, June 12, 1941, 886–87; Hoover to Assistant Attorney General Wendell Berge, Sept. 4, 1941, 925; Matthew F. McGuire to Hoover, Sept. 15, 1941, 928–29.

16. For the creation of the loyalty program see Eleanor Bontecou, *The Federal Loyalty-Security Program* (Ithaca, N.Y., 1953), pp. 23–30, 35–36, 168–79; and Theoharis, *Spying on Americans*, pp. 200–208. FBI use of the program is described in *SDSR*, pp. 432–35.

17. Director, FBI ("Director, FBI" is a Bureau designation for FBI headquarters in Washington, D.C., as distinguished from the FBI's Washington Field Office, or WFO), to SAC, New York, May 29, 1947, 1064; Report to SA Paul J. Tierney, Aug. 14, 1947, 1081–13; Director, FBI to the Attorney General, Nov. 28, 1947, 1355. The wiretap is first mentioned in D. M. Ladd to Director, Nov. 5, 1947, 1340, which refers to "the technical surveillance which is maintained on the office of Martin Popper, Vice President of the National Lawyers Guild." For FBI wiretapping practices, see Athan Theoharis, *Seeds of Repression: Harry S. Truman and the Origins of McCarthyism* (Chicago, 1971), pp. 124–32, and *SDSR*, pp. 277–83. The microfilmed NLG membership list appears in Report of SA Paul J. Tierney, April 2, 1948, 1372–456.

18. Clark's remark is quoted in Ladd to the Director, Aug. 2, 1948, 1463. See also Assistant Attorney General Peyton Ford to Hoover, Sept. 29, 1948, 1461–62; Associate Director Clyde Tolson to Hoover, Oct. 13, 1948, 1464. For the FBI's use of "thumbnail sketches" see *SDSR*, p. 435.

19. Guy Hottel (SAC, WFO) to Director, FBI, Jan. 27, 1948, 1358; Hottel to Director, FBI, Feb. 10, 1948, 1359–60; Hottel to Director, FBI, June 14, 1948, 1475; Director, FBI to SAC, New Haven, June 16, 1948, 1474; Director, FBI to SAC, New Haven, Oct. 25, 1948, 1480; Thomas I. Emerson and David M. Helfeld, "Loyalty among Government Employees," *Yale Law Journal* 58 (March 1949): 401–2, 416–25. In his reply, Hoover protested that "at no time did I have the opportunity, until after his article appeared in print, to answer his charges" (p. 425).

20. The *New York Times* extensively covered the Coplon arrest and trial; see especially *New York Times*, March 7, 1949; June 1, 1949; and June 4, 1949.

21. *New York Times*, June 9, 1949. See also Ungar, *FBI*, p. 110.

22. Velde's speech was reprinted in *Congressional Record*, Vol. 95, P. 6 (June 21, 1949), pp. 8080–81; Nixon was quoted in *New York Times*, June 15, 1949; Durr's request was published in *New York Times*, June 20, 1949.

23. Director, FBI (initialled "LBN") to Attorney General, June 20, 1949, 1670; *Washington Post*, June 20, 1949; Nichols to Tolson, June 28, 1949, 1669; Hoover to Lyle Wilson, June 28, 1949, 1668; *Washington Evening Star*, June 28, 1948. Nichols was the FBI's public relations specialist. Indeed, since 1941 and under order from Hoover, Nichols maintained an "official and confidential" file in his office. This file confirms the typicality of Nichols's passing of derogatory information about the Bureau's enemies to friendly reporters and politicians. For the FBI's extreme sensitivity to criticism, leaks to politicians such as Velde and Nixon, and manipulation of the media to maintain its public image, see Ungar, *FBI*, pp. 277–78, 368–90; and Donner, *Age of Surveillance*, pp. 209, 213, 233, 237–40, 477. For *FBI* media manipulation, see *IARA*, pp. 15–16. The Senate Select Committee on Intelligence does not provide much detail on the FBI's exploitation of media contacts, probably because the FBI has preserved little documentary evidence of such actions. Nichols's contact with Lyle Wilson on this occasion, for example, is reported in a memo (Nichols to Tolson, June 20, 1949, 1669) that is stamped at the bottom, "This memorandum is for administrative purposes—to be destroyed after action is taken and not sent to files." For reasons unknown, this particular document was sent to the FBI's regular files in August, 1958 (at the conclusion of one phase of the FBI investigation of the NLG); documentary accounts of other such media operations were conceivably destroyed as ordered. Moreover, as the Nichols memo makes clear, media contacts were sometimes made over the telephone, and may not have been recorded at all. There do exist, however, a host of FBI documents recording some of these contacts. These documents had originally been filed in Nichols's unserialized Official and Confidential file.

24. Ladd (initialled "HBF") to Director, June 24, 1949, 1708–9; Director, FBI ("HBF") to Attorney General, July 11, 1949, 1666.

25. WFO reports to headquarters based on the Guild wiretap appear in files 1660, 1661, 1662, 1700, 1701, 1702–3, 1706, 1707, 1711, 1712, 1713–14, 1755–56, and elsewhere. Ladd to Director, 1761–63; Director, FBI to SAC, WFO, Sept. 23, 1949, 1771.

26. Hottel to Director, FBI and SAC, NY, Oct. 5, 1959, 1745; Ladd to Director, Oct. 7, 1949, 1743–44. Hottel to Director, FBI, Oct. 17, 1949, 1750–52, refers to WFO letters dated Oct. 11, 1949, and Oct. 14, 1949, which the FBI has not released. Ladd to Director, Oct. 13, 1949, 1827–29. Ladd's recommendation resulted in the further refinement of the "June mail" reporting procedure, discussed in Athan Theoharis's essay "In-House Cover-up: Researching FBI Files" (Chapter 2).

27. Hottel to Director, Nov. 18, 1949, 1909–16; Ladd to Director, Nov. 25, 1949, 1870–08.

28. Director, FBI to Attorney General, Nov. 29, 1949, 1968–69. The letter from Attorney General Howard McGrath to Truman, Dec. 27, 1949, is reprinted in *HIA*, Vol. 6, Federal Bureau of Investigation, pp. 466–69. This letter, drafted by the FBI, is an excellent example of the manner in which the Bureau "stretched" its intelligence mandate by selectively quoting from previous presidential directives. However, some FBI wiretaps and surreptitious entries, such as those against the Guild, could not be rationalized under any directive, and were simply not mentioned in correspondence with the Justice Department or the White House. See *IARA*, pp. 24–46. See also Theoharis, "Bureaucrats above the Law," pp. 395–96. *Washington Daily News*, Dec. 5, 1949. Wilson wrote a similarly critical story on a proposed international peace conference in 1949. James Aronson, *The Press and the Cold War* (Indianapolis, 1970), p. 53. For the Bureau's use of friendly journalists as conduits for attacks on FBI adversaries, see Donner, *Age of Surveillance*, pp. 93, 110–13, 477; and *SDSR*, pp. 35–36, 75.

29. Hoover's handwritten note to Tolson and Ladd, undated, appears in 1839. Ladd to Director, Dec. 6, 1949, 1831–38; Hoover to Attorney General, Dec. 22, 1949, 1830. Hottel to Director, Dec. 22, 1949, 1860, mentions the appendices. The photographic copies of these are referred to in H. B. Fletcher to Ladd, Jan. 19, 1950, 2005. Hottel to Director, FBI, March 13, 1950, 2343–52, refers to "correspondence furnished by an anonymous source December 26, 1949," while Ladd to Director, May 29, 1950, 2593, refers to "the 3398 names of reported Guild members obtained from an anonymous source on December 26, 1949."

30. Ladd to Director, Dec. 6, 1949, 1831–38.

31. *New York Times*, Dec. 1, 1949; Dec. 6, 1949; Dec. 13, 1949; Dec. 14, 1949; Dec. 21, 1949; Dec. 22, 1949; and Dec. 28, 1949. The quoted passage is from *New York Times*, Jan. 15, 1950; the Fletcher memo is described in *New York Times*, Jan. 13, 1950.

32. Fly's letters were printed in *Washington Post*, Jan. 5, 1950, and *New York Times*, Jan. 17, 1950. McGrath's reply is cited in *New York Times*, Jan. 9, 1950. See also Theoharis, "Misleading the Presidents: Thirty Years of Wiretapping," *Nation* 212 (June 14, 1971): 745.

33. Hoover to Major General Harry Hawkins Vaughan, Military Aide to the President, Jan. 14, 1950, is printed in *HIA*, Vol. 6, Federal Bureau of Investigation, p. 469. Hottel to Director, FBI, Jan 18, 1950, 2087–88; Ladd to Director, Jan. 18, 1950, 1870. The account of Nixon's late-night calls to the wire services appears in Stone's column in *New York Daily Compass*, Jan. 29, 1950.

34. *Washington Evening Star*, Jan. 19, 1950; *Boston Traveller*, Jan. 19, 1950.

35. Hottel to Director, Jan. 19, 1950, 2102–03; *New York Daily Compass*, Jan. 20, 1950.

36. *New York Times*, Jan. 22, 1950.

37. *New York Times*, Jan. 23, 1950; *Washington Star*, Jan. 23, 1950; *Washington Post*, Jan. 23, 1950; *New York Daily Compass*, Jan. 23 and 25, 1950; *Washington Daily News*, Jan. 24, 1950.

38. "Report on Alleged Practices of the FBI," *LGR* 10 (Winter 1950), pp. 185–96.

39. SAC, NY to Director, March 16, 1950, 2397–98; Report of SA William W. Stickle, Jan. 24, 1950, 2092–101; Hottel to Director, Jan. 24, 1950, 2113; Hottel to Director, Jan. 25, 1950, 2126; Hottel to Director, Jan. 30, 1950, 2162; Ladd to Director, Jan. 31, 1950, 2227–28; L. L. Laughlin to H. B. Fletcher, Jan. 20, 1950, 2121; Nichols to Tolson, Feb. 20, 1950, 2223; SAC, Springfield, to Director, March 20, 1950, 2407–10; Ladd to Director, March 20, 1950, 2405; SAC, Chicago, to Director, May 26, 1950, 2413; SAC, Chicago, to Director, Sept. 13, 1950, 2937.

40. U.S. Senate, *Hearings before a Subcommittee of the Committee on Appropriations*, 81st Cong. 2d sess., Feb. 3 and 7, 1950, pp. 146–47, 158. These hearings were not made public until June. For Hoover's use of Appropriations Committee hearings for political purposes, see Ungar, *FBI*, pp. 259–68; and Donner, *Age of Surveillance*, pp. 103–4, 173–74, 173n. Nichols's speech is reported in *Washington Post*, Feb. 4, 1950.

41. E. H. Winterrow to Ladd, March 15, 1950, 2258.

42. V. P. Keay to A. H. Belmont, March 1, 1950, 2481; Keay to Belmont, March 21, 1950, 2450; Ladd to Director, May 29, 1950, 2593.

43. In another instance, NLG activist Reuben Lenske was subjected to an intensive Internal Revenue Service tax investigation, beginning in 1955 and extending to 1958. An IRS report recommending criminal prosecution of Lenske stated that the FBI and local police "have reason to believe Mr. Lenske is a Communist" and, with another attorney, had called a meeting for the purpose of forming a local NLG chapter. Donner, *Age of Surveillance*, p. 326.

44. Silberstein's account of the International Association of Democratic Lawyers (IADL) Convention appears in *GL* 7 (Dec. 1949), pp. 3, 6. The WFO memo is in 2584, but its dated first page is missing. F. W. Waikart to Nichols, April 19, 1950, 2458–59; *New York Post*, April 19, 1950. *New York Times*, May 8, 1950, reported that the NLG convention reversed Silberstein's vote to expel the Yugoslavs.

45. Director, to Attorney General, May 25, 1950, 2596; *New York Times*, June 9, 1950; *Washington Post*, June 21, 1950; Harrison to McGrath, June 13, 1950, 2580–81; Hottel to Director, June 16, 1950, 2579. The latter document refers to communications between a HUAC staff member and the WFO. In 1950, Hoover publicly conceded that congressional committees "have served a very useful purpose in exposing some of these activities which no federal agency is in a position to do, because the information which we obtain in the Bureau is either for intelligence purposes or for use in prosecutions, and committees of Congress have wider latitude in that respect." U.S., Senate, *Hearings before a Subcommittee of the Committee on Appropriations*, 81st Cong., 2d sess., Feb. 3 and 7, 1950, pp. 146–47, 158.

46. Walter Goodman, *The Committee* (New York: 1960), p. 417. Hottel to Director, Dec. 13, 1949, 1876; Nichols to Tolson, July 12, 1950, 2669; Nichols to Tolson, July 18, 1950, 2688. Hoover's comment appears in Nichols to Tolson, Aug. 29, 1950, 3068. An FBI "summary memorandum" dated Jan. 18, 1950, 2287–40, compares verbatim with passages in U.S. House, Committee on Un-American Activities, *Report on the National Lawyers Guild: Legal Bulwark of the Communist Party*, Sept. 17, 1950. For a thorough rebuttal of the HUAC report see Thomas I. Emerson, "The National Lawyers Guild: Legal Bulwark of Democracy," *LGR* 10 (Fall 1950), pp. 93–110.

47. *Washington Post*, Sept. 17, 1950; *New York Times*, Sept. 17, 1950; *Washington Sunday Star*, Sept. 17, 1950. Cedric Belfrage, *The American Inquisition* (Indianapolis, 1973), pp. 103–14, 117–27, 130–40; Richard M. Freeland, *The Truman Doctrine and the Origins of McCarthyism: Foreign Policy, Domestic Politics, and Internal Security, 1946–48* (New York, 1970),

pp. 346–60; Alonzo L. Hamby, *Beyond the New Deal: Harry S. Truman and American Liberalism* (New York, 1973), p. 409. SAC, Detroit to Director, FBI, Oct. 24, 1950, is one of several documents reporting resignations. Report of John J. Walsh, Feb. 2, 1951, 3642–48, concludes that the NLG lost one-third of its membership. Thomas Emerson, *COHC*, pp. 2180, 2191–92, corroborates this estimate.

48. *New York Times*, Jan. 27, 1950; Nichols to Tolson, Jan. 24, 1950, 3263–64; Hottel to Director, Dec. 4, 1950, 3293–94; *New York Journal-American*, Dec. 8, 1950. Director to Assistant Attorney General James L. McInerney, June 22, 1950, 2577, relays information clearly taken from the wiretap, which later became the basis of anti-NLG allegations in U.S. House, Committee on Un-American Activities, *Report on the National Committee to Defeat the Mundt Bill: A Communist Lobby*, Dec. 7, 1950. *Washington Star*, Dec. 12, 1950; Emerson, *COHC*, pp. 2209–10.

49. WFO to Director, and SAC, Boston, March 2, 1951, 2756; SAC, Boston to Director, March 5, 1951, 3757. Sears is quoted in *Boston Herald*, March 5, 1951; Griswold is quoted in *New York Times*, March 6, 1951; SAC, Boston to Director, March 10, 1951, 3745; SAC, Boston to Director, FBI, March 13, 1951, 3753. The existence of BOS-627 is first mentioned in SAC, Boston to Director, April 25, 1951, 3833. By 1953, BOS-627 had become president of the Harvard NLF Chapter. In March of that year, two chapter members, Jonathan and David Lubell, were subpoenaed before a Boston hearing of the Senate Internal Security Subcommittee. When they refused on Fifth Amendment grounds to discuss their political affiliations, Samuel Sears and the Boston newspapers demanded their expulsion from Harvard Law School. Although not expelled, the Lubells endured considerable hardship as a consequence of these attacks. Presumably BOS-627 had something to do with "tipping off" the Subcommittee. See Joel Seligman and Paul J. Rosenberg, "Jonathan Lubell and the *Law Review*: How Harvard Regained Its Nerve," *Nation* 226 (March 18, 1978): 297–300.

50. WFO to Director, FBI, July 6, 1951, 3913, reports the closing of the NLG Washington office. WFO to Director and SAC, Chicago, Oct. 4, 1951, 3936; SAC, Chicago to Director, Oct. 5, 1951, 3932. Several dozen references to BOS-627 appear over the next four years of the main file, between 3833 and 6821.

51. *GL* 8 (October 1950): 3. Auerbach, *Unequal Justice*, pp. 237–59 provides a useful survey of the harassment of radical lawyers from the late forties to the late fifties. Also see Belfrage, *American Inquisition*, pp. 151–52, 211, 221–23.

52. Auerbach, *Unequal Justice*, pp. 240–46. See also Michal Belknap, *Cold*

War Political Justice: The Smith Act, The Communist Party, and American Civil Liberties (Westport, Conn., 1977), pp. 112, 220. See also, n. 45.

53. "Independence of the Bar," *LGR* 13 (Winter 1953): 159–61.

54. "Report of the Board of Governors," *ABAJ* 34 (June 1948): 487; "Proceedings of the Assembly," *ABAJ* 34 (Oct. 1948): 899–901; "Proceedings of the House of Delegates," *ABAJ* 34 (Nov. 1948): 1070.

55. "Proceedings of the Assembly," *RABA* 75 (1950): 95–97; "The Proposed Anti-Communist Oath: Opposition Expressed to Association's Policy," *ABAJ* 37 (Feb. 1951): 123–25.

56. "The Lawyers' Loyalty Oath," *ABAJ* 37 (Feb. 1951): 128–29; "Proceedings of the House of Delegates, February 26–27, 1951," *RABA* 76 (1951):530–33. O'Conor is quoted in *The Washington Star*, March 5, 1951.

57. Belknap, *Cold War Political Justice*, pp. 136–40, 152–54, 220–23; Auerbach, *Unequal Justice*, pp. 248–49.

58. Seymour is quoted in *New York Times*, Jan. 26, 1952. Belknap, *Cold War Political Justice*, pp. 167–68, 222–23. Replying to Seymour in a letter to the *New York Times*, Feb. 4, 1952, Thomas Emerson insisted that he had encountered no political interference when serving as counsel for Communist Smith Act defendants in New York, despite having offered legal arguments "that differed sharply at important points from the Party's political position."

59. For defendants' accounts of the New York and California trials respectively, see George Charney, *A Long Journey* (Chicago, 1967), pp. 213–29, and Al Richmond, *A Long View from the Left* (Boston, 1972), pp. 298–308, 324–25.

60. Charney, *A Long Journey*, pp. 225–29; Richmond, *A Long View*, pp. 315, 323, 343–54.

61. SAC, San Francisco to Director, FBI, Nov. 26, 1951, 403–31; SAC, Los Angeles to Director, FBI, Nov. 27, 1951, 4032. U.S., House, Committee on Un-American Activities, *Hearings into Communist Activities Among Professional Groups in the Los Angeles Area*, P. 1, 32d Cong., 2d sess., Jan. 23–25, 1952, pp. 2501–629. Page 2606 reveals that HUAC investigators took a statement from one of the five, Milton Tyre, on December 14, 1951, but it is clear that others had been interviewed before Tyre.

62. Goodman, *The Committee*, pp. 312–14.

63. Report of Vincent T. K. Tracy, Dec. 6, 1950, 3296–358. Another example illustrates the point. The FBI had long regarded Yale law professor and NLG leader Thomas I. Emerson as a dangerous foe of the Bureau (see n. 19). In a 1953 memorandum, FBI Director Hoover confided to his chief assistants that "it had been impossible up to the present time to have Emerson called before any

Committee of Congress because of the intercession on his behalf of Senator Taft, who is on the Board of Trustees of Yale University. I indicated to the Attorney General that the House Committee on Un-American Activities had contemplated calling Emerson but had refrained from doing so because of the intercession of Senator Taft and that the same happened incident to the Jenner Committee of the Senate." Hoover to Tolson, Ladd, and Belmont, May 29, 1953, 4736–38. For other possible FBI attempts to influence the California trial, see Belknap, *Cold War Political Justice*, p. 171.

64. WFO to Director, Feb. 29, 1952, 4105, shows that on February 3, 1952, the Boston Field Office telegraphed an account of the Board meeting. The telegram itself, with the dated first page missing, appears at 4373–74. Reid's column appeared in the *New York Herald-Tribune*, Feb. 10, 1952.

65. *New York Times*, Feb. 26, 1952; "Report of the Special Committee to Study Communist Tactics, Strategy, and Objectives" (hereafter SCSCTSO), *RABA* 77 (1952): 574–77.

66. "Proceedings of the Assembly," Sept. 18–22, 1950, *RABA* 75 (1950): 92–93; "Report of the SCSCTSO," Sept. 17, 1951, *RABA* 76 (1951): 115–16, 349–51; "Report of the SCSCTSO," Feb. 25, 1952, *RABA* 77 (1952): 431–32; SCSCTSO, "Brief on Communism," (Notre Dame, Ind., 1952), pp. 32–52. Canfield is quoted in the *Washington Star*, Nov. 28, 1950. Shortly after the HUAC Report on the NLG appeared, American Bar Association (ABA) President Cody Fowler announced publicly that he would vote to exclude any Guild member from the ABA (*Los Angeles Times*, Oct. 4, 1950). An FBI memorandum dated April 9, 1951, cites Canfield as having contacted the FBI and received "blind" memoranda. This document was released to Los Angeles NLG member Benjamin Margolis in response to his Freedom of Information Act request.

67. Nichols to Tolson, Jan. 31, 1952, 4075; Nichols to Tolson, March 7, 1952, 4107–8.

68. U.S., House, Committee on Un-American Activities, *Hearings into Communist Activities Among Professional Groups in the Los Angeles Area*, P. 1, 82d Cong., 2d sess., 1952, pp. 2655–56, 2665–76.

69. U.S., House, Committee on Un-American Activities, *Hearings into Communist Activities*, P. 3, pp. 3899–4107.

70. "Report of the SCSCTSO," Feb. 23, 1953, *RABA* 78 (1953): 439.

71. "Proceedings of the House of Delegates, Feb. 23–24, 1953," *RABA* 78 (1953), pp. 388–89, *New York Times*, Aug. 26, 1953; "Report of SCSCTSO," Aug. 24, 1953, *RABA* 78 (1953): 291–92; "Proceedings of the House of Delegates, March 8–9, 1953," *RABA* 79 (1953): 454, 458.

72. *GL* 11 (Sept. 1953): 1.

73. Hoover to Legal Attache, Paris, France, April 18, 1951, 3886; Director to Assistant Attorney General James M. McInerney, April 18, 1951, 3885; Report of Thomas C. Ries, Feb. 21, 1952, 4099–102. Director to SAC, NY, Dec. 5, 1952, 4484–85. For the Bureau's use of the McCarran Act, see Ungar, *FBI*, p. 132. Hoover to Tolson, Ladd, and Belmont, May 29, 1953, 4736–38. Even when he learned of Brownell's agreement to include the NLG on the Attorney General's list, Hoover remained skeptical. Informed of the proposed date for Brownell's planned announcement, the FBI director commented: "I will believe it when I actually see its designation as subversive. The Dept. has hedged on this for years." The comment is written at the bottom of Belmont to Ladd, Aug. 19, 1953, 4989.

74. "Address by the Honorable Herbert Brownell, Jr.," Aug. 27, 1953, *RABA* 78 (1953): 339–40. Brownell's attack on the NLG before the ABA appeared on the front page of the *New York Times*, Aug. 28, 1953. His Veterans of Foreign Wars address is quoted from *New York Times*, Sept. 6, 1953.

75. *New York Times*, Sept. 22, 1953; *GL* 11 (Sept. 1953): 2. The only major paper to criticize Brownell's action was the *St. Louis Post-Dispatch*, Aug. 29, 1953, which editorialized that, if the Guild had really been subversive all along, "a lot of pretty intelligent people have attended its meetings and not caught on."

76. "National Executive Board Minutes, Sept. 12, 1953," NLG Minutebook, Meiklejohn Civil Liberties Institute, Berkeley, Calif. *New York Times*, Dec. 21, 1953; Emerson, *COHC*, pp. 2238–40. The ACLU publicly released a letter addressed to Brownell which, after assuring the Attorney General that the Union was "strongly opposed to Communist tyranny," suggested that the NLG should have been given a hearing *before* being declared subversive. *New York Times*, Sept. 3, 1953.

77. SAC, Boston to Director, Sept. 15, 1953, 4977–78; Director to Assistant Attorney General Warren Olney III, March 8, 1953, 5615; Hoover to SAC, Boston, March 23, 1954, 5641; Nichols to Tolson, Nov. 11, 1953, 5128; SAC, Boston to Director, Dec. 21, 1953, 5331–34.

78. Oran H. Waterman to David B. Irons, March 18, 1954; Irons to William E. Foley, March 24, 1954; Foley to Irons, March 29, 1954; these three documents appear among papers released by the Criminal Division of the Department of Justice to the NLG.

79. *New York Times*, Dec. 23, 1953, and July 15, 1955; *Washington Star*, March 24, 1953 and Nov. 2, 1955; *Washington Post*, May 5, 1954, and Nov. 5, 1954; Belmont to L. V. Boardman, Feb. 23, 1955, 6320–21; Emerson, *COHC*, pp. 2239–42.

174   Percival R. Baily

80. Black is quoted in Bontecou, *The Federal Loyalty-Security Program*, p. 202. Thomas Emerson stated that the NLG would have to dissolve if it were formally listed. Emerson, *COHC*, pp. 228–29, 2254. *Washington Post*, Aug. 28, 1953; *New York Times*, Oct. 24, 1953; *New York Herald-Tribune*, Aug. 28, 1953; *Washington Star*, Aug. 27, 1953; ACLU *Weekly Bulletin*, March 14, 1955. Wright is quoted in *GL* 12 (Oct. 1954), p. 4. The misunderstanding has persisted. Jessica Mitford, whose husband was a long-time NLG member in San Francisco, states in her memoirs that the NLG was "officially designated as subversive." See *A Fine Old Conflict* (New York, 1977), p. 213.

81. "Report of the SCSCTSO," March 8, 1954, *RABA* 79 (1954): 578–79; "Report of the SCSCTSO," August 16, 1954, *RABA* 79 (1954): 318–23.

82. "Proceedings of the House of Delegates, Feb. 21, 1955," *RABA* 80 (1955): 409, 461–62; *Miami Herald*, Feb. 8, 1955; "*Sheiner v. State of Florida*—Briefs Amici Curiae to the Supreme Court of Florida," *LGR* 15 (Spring 1955): 11–27.

83. Auerbach, *Unequal Justice*, p. 247; Belfrage, *American Inquisition*, pp. 221–23. Belfrage uses the pseudonym "Paul Newman" to protect Sheiner from further injury. By the time Sheiner was finally readmitted to the Bar in 1959, his law practice had evaporated and he had left Florida for New York. "Report of SCSCTSO," Aug. 22, 1955, *RABA* 80 (1955); 314–18; Nichols to Tolson, Sept. 19, 1955, 6796; "Report of SCSCTSO," Feb. 20, 1956, *RABA* 81 (1956); 469–74; "Report of SCSCTSO," Aug. 27, 1956, *RABA* 81 (1956): 320–25.

84. Belknap, *Cold War Political Justice*, pp. 224–28.

85. Belfrage, *American Inquisition*, p. 254; Belknap, *Cold War Political Justice*, pp. 228–321. Hoover is quoted in *New York Times*, March 20, 1956.

86. Sharp to Eisenhower, March 27, 1956, 7500–1; Director to Attorney General, March 27, 1956, 7498.

87. Hoover to Tolson, Boardman, Belmont, and Nichols, March 27, 1956, 7511; Belmont to Boardman, March 28, 1956, 7548–49; Belmont to Boardman, March 30, 1956, 9064; Nichols to Tolson, April 6, 1956, 7563; Nichols to Tolson, April 7, 1956, 7580–81; Hoover to Tolson, Boardman, Belmont, and Nichols, April 9, 1956, 7572–76.

88. Hoover to Sharp, April 9, 1956, 7609–610; *New York World-Telegram*, April 10, 1956; *New York Times*, April 11, 1956; *Los Angeles Times*, April 11, 1956; M. A. Jones to Nichols, April 10, 1956, 7587–88.

89. Belknap, *Cold War Political Justice*, pp. 236–40; Richmond, *A Long View*, pp. 355–63. *SDSR*, pp. 15–17, 27, 62–77. See also Theoharis, *Spying on Americans*, pp. 133–55; and Donner, *Age of Surveillance*, pp. 177–240.

90. Belknap, *Cold War Political Justice*, pp. 240–48; John T. McTernan, "Schware, Koenigsberg and the Independence of the Bar: The Return to Reason," *LGR* 17 (Summer 1957): 48–53; Belfrage, *American Inquisition*, pp. 211, 284.

91. *New York Times*, May 8, 1956, and Sept. 13, 1958; Department of Justice, Internal Security Division, Monthly Status Report for Sept. 1958, 9160; *Washington Post*, July 3, 1958; Hoover to Tolson et al., July 16, 1958, 9061; Osmond K. Fraenkel, *COHC*, p. 109.

92. The NLG membership list which the FBI photographed on December 26, 1949, included 3,398 names, according to Ladd to Director, May 29, 1950, 2593. An NLG Membership Report obtained by the FBI nine years later reveals 502 names in four chapters. SAC, Chicago to Director, Dec. 29, 1958, 9195. Thomas Emerson estimated NLG membership at 2,600 in May 1950, and 1,800 a year later. Emerson, *COHC*, pp. 2201–4.

5

The FBI, Congressman
Vito Marcantonio, and the
American Labor Party

Kenneth Waltzer

Apprehensive about the forthcoming presidential election in mid-1936, President Franklin D. Roosevelt approved Sidney Hillman's idea to establish a labor party in New York State. New York permitted candidates to run with multi-party endorsements, and provided relatively easy access for new parties to the ballot. Moreover, New York was pivotal in any presidential contest, and Hillman's idea for a labor party might win support from labor and leftist elements who otherwise would not vote for the Democratic candidate. Postmaster General James Farley was assigned to assure cooperation from Democratic Party county chairmen. As Bronx political boss Ed Flynn recalled, "President Roosevelt, with Jim Farley and myself, brought the American Labor Party into being. . . . Sidney Hillman and David Dubinsky [leaders of the needle trades unions in New York City, the Amalgamated Clothing Workers and the International Ladies Garment Workers] played a great part in it and we couldn't have formed the party without them."[1]

Thereafter, the American Labor Party (ALP) developed under the leadership of the needle trades unionists as the institutional form of the Popular Front in New York. It attracted a broad coalition of political elements, including laborites, Socialists, and Communists, and from 1937 to 1944 constituted the balance of power in New York state. Operating as a "satellite party," an independent pressure from the left on the New Deal, the ALP demanded the extension of economic and social demo-

The author acknowledges funding assistance under a Michigan State University Research Grant and also from the Michigan State University Library.

cray while helping reelect Herbert Lehman as governor, Fiorello La Guardia as New York City mayor, and Franklin Roosevelt as president. It also elected its own congressman, East Harlem's Vito Marcantonio, from 1938 to 1950, and won several state legislative and city council positions. Breaking with American Cold War foreign policy under the Truman Administration, the ALP later enlisted in Henry Wallace's Progressive Party crusade in 1948. Thereafter, under Marcantonio's leadership and Communist control until its demise in 1956, it opposed both major parties and the Cold War consensus.[2]

Concurrent with the development of the ALP during the late 1930s, the FBI began to investigate dissident political activities. During and immediately after World War I, the FBI had engaged in domestic intelligence operations that went beyond criminal law enforcement investigations. Pursuant to Attorney General Harlan Stone's ban in 1924, however, the FBI seemed to have ceased such investigations. Reasserting the FBI's domestic intelligence role in 1936, FBI Director J. Edgar Hoover ordered FBI field offices to seek information from all sources on "subversive activities" being conducted in the United States. In the years prior to American involvement in World War II, the FBI began to collect extensive information on left-liberal groups and activists, and compiled a Custodial Detention list of "dangerous" persons. These FBI investigations broadened further after World War II, ostensibly under authority of the Federal Employee Loyalty Program, or connected with the compilation of a Security Index of dangerous persons; the investigations then expanded sharply in the 1950s, coincident with passage of the McCarran Internal Security Act and the outbreak of war in Korea.[3]

This essay examines one dimension of the FBI's political intelligence activities: its investigations of radical Congressman Vito Marcantonio and the ALP. The FBI's targeting of Marcantonio and the ALP, its uses of special agents and confidential informants, and its apparent uses of more surreptitious methods—including wiretaps, bugs, and unlawful entries—adversely affected individual rights and, in the case of a legal political party, interfered with the electoral process.[4] In addition, the investigations were not authorized by statute, and were heavily predicated on, and shaped by, the FBI director's particular conception of disloyalty.

I

When the leaders of the needle trades unions formed the ALP, they intended to funnel the revived energies of American labor behind the New Deal and to lay the basis for an independent national labor party. The hope for a national labor party was implicit in the ALP's name and the content of its first campaign. The upsurge of mass labor militancy during 1936 and 1937, and the rise of the Committee for Industrial Organization (CIO) also lent credence to the hope. The ALP nonetheless remained a local party confined to New York state, and functioned largely by endorsing candidates of the major parties. Supported by the dominant needle trades unions, the ALP attracted a popular constituency rooted in the rising CIO unions and in specific New York City neighborhoods, and played an increasingly important role in state and city politics.

The ALP backed the New Deal ideologically, but pressed it from the left with demands for more vigorous action in the areas of employment and relief. As part of this pressure, the ALP endorsed a more just distribution of the national income and the right of all Americans to productive and socially useful work; the group also opposed Administration and congressional efforts to cut relief during the late 1930s. In New York state and local politics, the ALP fought to extend New Deal kinds of labor and social welfare policies, advocating government ownership of public utilities, slum clearance and public housing, state health insurance, and urban government in the interests of the masses. Yet, as former Socialist and ALP city council leader B. Charney Vladeck explained, ALP leaders and members also believed that a government that permitted unemployment and illness, and merely provided relief and hospitals was "not truly democratic."[5]

During 1937 and 1938, the ALP developed as a vital coalition of groups and movements ranging nearly the full left side of the political spectrum—with the exception of the Trotskyites. Socialists, Social Democrats, Communists, and "progressives" joined the ALP—including those who hoped for a labor party, who identified the sources of social change with labor, or who wanted merely to pressure the New Deal from the left. Still others joined because their unions were affiliated or because the ALP represented a means to support the New Deal nationally without endorsing the Democratic machine in New York. The bulk of the ALP constituency was mobilized in New York City, largely in East European Jewish neighborhoods. A focus of the practical politics and radical dreams of the New York left, the ALP also functioned as the political expression of a significant segment of the Jewish community.[6]

The ALP coalition, however, was internally unstable. Socialists and Social Democrats at first demanded an independent labor party and opposed a policy of supporting major party candidates. In contrast, Communists and their allies, at least momentarily, advocated a less radical course and backed the New Deal. In the mid-1930s, the Communists abandoned their earlier militant line of attacking the New Deal and labor leaders and supported "the broadest united front tactics of reformism." The growth of Communist-led CIO unions in 1937 and 1938—including the Transport Workers Union (TWU), National Maritime Union (NMU), and United Electrical Workers (UE)—increased Communist influence in the ALP. More important, however, Communists enrolled in large numbers as individuals in ALP clubs, many of which they controlled. It was a heady period for the Communists: their influence extended in ever-widening circles as they sought cooperation with their non-Communist allies in the ALP, and moderated their protest against the needle trades unionists' leadership and the absence of internal democracy.[7]

ALP unity ended in late 1939. In August, the Soviet Union signed a non-aggression pact with Nazi Germany, and in September, World War II began. Blindly defending the pact, the Communists denounced the war as a conflict of rival imperialisms. The needle trades unionists, who before 1939 had constrained the ALP from taking a stand on foreign policy, in contrast, moved both to put the ALP on record behind the Western democracies and to discipline the Communists. In October, the ALP adopted a statement labelling the Nazi-Soviet Pact a "treacherous blow to world civilization," and condemning the Communists as "betrayers of the labor movement" and "the blind servants of Russian International Policy." ALP energies then and thereafter for the next half-decade were absorbed in a bitter factional struggle: the needle trades unionists supporting Administration foreign policy and calling for aid to the Allies, while the Communists and others opposed American intervention and demanded renewed attention to domestic problems. To counter the needle trades unionists' control of the ALP hierarchy, the Communists organized the Progressive Committee to Rebuild the ALP and protested the Party's lack of internal democracy. The conflict was complicated by cross-currents in the CIO created by its leader John L. Lewis's isolationism, by a division among the needle trades unionists when the International Ladies Garment Workers Union (ILGWU) reaffiliated with the American Federation of Labor, and by the Communists' *volte-face* following the Nazi invasion of the Soviet Union.[8]

This factionalism continued through most of World War II. An uneasy truce prevailed during 1942, as the various groups united behind the Party's first independent gubernatorial candidate. The creation of the CIO Political Action Committee (PAC) and Sidney Hillman's ambition to make the ALP into the PAC arm in New York in 1943 and 1944 exacerbated the divisions again. Hillman introduced a plan in 1943 to reform the state committee, the ultimate objective of which was to introduce leaders from the left-wing CIO unions into ALP councils. Led by David Dubinsky of the ILGWU and Alex Rose of the Hat, Cap, and Millinery Workers, the ALP Old Guard opposed this effort. The result was a political conflict from which the Hillman-Communist alliance emerged victorious in the March 1944 primary. The Dubinsky-Rose forces then withdrew to create a new party, the Liberal Party. Exploiting their defection, Hillman became ALP state chairman and Hillman followers controlled the most important ALP offices; Hillman had also privately promised the President that he would contain the Communists.[9]

Immediately after the end of the war, the ALP operated as the instrument of national CIO politics in New York. Initially, it backed the Truman Administration, while serving as a persistent pressure from the left. The ALP advocated enactment of the Administration-proposed Full Employment Bill yet criticized the Administration's reconversion wage-price and labor policies and opposed new foreign policy initiatives. ALP leaders and members, who anticipated a New Deal revival at home and a stable world peace founded on the United Nations and American-Soviet friendship, however, grew increasingly disappointed by the Truman Administration's distinctly different priorities. The President retreated on price controls, called for punitive labor legislation, and embraced a new "get tough" policy with the Soviet Union. In response, the ALP condemned Administration proposals and efforts to weaken American-Soviet accord, and opposed economic and military aid outside the United Nations.[10]

Following Henry A. Wallace's famous speech at Madison Square Garden in September 1946, and his subsequent dismissal from the Truman Cabinet, the ALP moved toward independent political action. Wallace believed American-Soviet collaboration was crucial for a stable peace and an effective United Nations, and that Administration policy needlessly jeopardized such collaboration. Sharing Wallace's views, ALP leaders condemned his dismissal. The Communists, who in 1945 had changed their leadership to embrace a more militant line and already demanded independent action, now saw in Wallace the likely leader of a third-party movement. Similarly, ALP Congressman Vito Marcantonio, if reticent about international issues in 1945, grew voluble in 1946 about foreign policy, and became the most strident advocate of a new party. Marcantonio, the Communists, and other progressives pushed the ALP to serve as a spearhead in the national third party movement opposed both to the Truman Doctrine and the Marshall Plan. After Wallace announced his candidacy in early 1948, they enlisted the ALP in the Progressive Party, while the remaining needle trades unionists, wary of independent politics, dropped away. Mounting a vigorous campaign, the ALP mobilized a half million New Yorkers against the Administration. "We are giving birth to a new political movement," Marcantonio, the new ALP state chairman, naively announced early during the campaign.[11]

II

The FBI's initial investigative interest in Marcantonio began in 1930 when the young Republican was recommended for an appointment as Assistant United States Attorney in New York's Southern District. The FBI preappointment check revealed that Marcantonio had graduated from New York University Law School in 1925, had been admitted to the bar in 1926, and had developed a reputable civil practice both in the state and federal courts. Those whom the FBI interviewed reported his "exceptional ability" as a lawyer and orator. Although FBI officials were concerned about his liberal views on prohibition, the FBI investigation uncovered nothing derogatory about the East Harlemite. The FBI report detailed his close relationship with Congressman Fiorello La Guardia, whom he had served as campaign manager and assistant since 1924, but mentioned nothing about Marcantonio's earlier reputation for activist socialism.[12]

Marcantonio succeeded La Guardia as East Harlem's Republican Congressman in 1934, and, shortly thereafter, emerged as an outspoken radical. Supporting New Deal reforms, Marcantonio also demanded more far-reaching measures to aid the victims of "an unjust economic and social system which has failed." In addition, he favored neutrality legislation but vigorously opposed "militarism," "imperialism," and continued American hegemony over Puerto Rico. Finally, he joined congressional progressives and other radicals, including Socialists and Communists, in pushing for an independent farmer-labor party. "I believe," he observed in 1935, "that this country is in danger of falling into the hands of a dictatorship of reaction." Gradually, he was moving toward the Communists, increasingly sharing their association and perspective. Indeed, when George Blake Charney, Communist Party organizational secretary in Harlem, first made contact with Marcantonio, he believed Marcantonio "possessed a worldview almost identical with ours."[13] Nonetheless, Marcantonio never joined the Communist Party: throughout his career he remained an independent politician in symbiotic alliance with the Communists.

Defeated in the Democratic landslide in 1936, Marcantonio joined the ALP in 1937, and won reelection to Congress as an ALP and Republican candidate in 1938. He returned to Washington at a time when the New Deal was under attack and a considerably different Congress was in session. At first, he worked closely with the Administration and endorsed measures for collective security. The refusal of the Administration and Congress to confront the unemployment problem, and their willingness to abandon reform for military preparedness soon underscored his distinctive radicalism. After May 1940, and in line with Communist policy after the Nazi-Soviet Pact, Marcantonio denounced Administration domestic and foreign policy and characterized Roosevelt's purpose as an attempt to make the United States a "military reservoir" in defense of British imperialism. Opposing both appropriations and conscription measures in Congress, Marcantonio simultaneously became a leading figure in the Communist-run American Peace Mobilization (APM) and a rallying point for the ALP left wing.[14]

From about 1936 on, the FBI had kept a watchful eye on the radical Congressman, collecting campaign materials from the Non-Partisan Committee for the Reelection of Congressman Vito Marcantonio, and monitoring Marcantonio's activities as president of the International Labor Defense (ILD). In January 1938, the New York Field Office notified FBI headquarters that Marcantonio's name appeared on several pages of Elizabeth Dilling's *The Roosevelt Red Record and Its Background*; in October 1939, FBI officials recorded the testimony before the House Committee on Un-American Acitvities (HUAC) concerning his role as ILD president.[15] FBI interest in the East Harlemite, however, increased sharply after the outbreak of World War II.

In September 1939, President Roosevelt had approved an expanded FBI role to coordinate state and local counter-subversive intelligence information. FBI officials employed this limited authorization to enlarge the Bureau's domestic intelligence activities. FBI officials also initiated that month a program to detain "dangerous" dissidents in the case of war or national emergency. FBI headquarters compiled formal arrest lists, including on them those with "strong Nazi or Communist tendencies," "Communistic, Fascist, Nazi, or other nationalist background(s)," and members of "Communist organizations" or "front organizations." The Justice Department assumed supervisory authority over this effort in mid-1940, assigning responsibility for reviewing FBI listings to the Neutrality Laws Unit (later renamed the Special Defense Unit or Special War Policies Unit). Oddly enough, Hoover's January 1940 testimony before the House Appropriations Committee alerted Marcantonio to this detention program; he subsequently criticized the expansion of FBI activities as a threat to civil liberties and "a system of terror by index cards." Marcantonio perceptively noted the ill-defined and vague nature of the FBI's claimed right to investigate "subversive activities" and activities possibly "detrimental to the internal security."[16]

Bureau officials were already fully knowledgeable about Marcan-tonio's activities. Before 1939 and until 1941, the FBI may not have directly investigated Marcantonio. FBI agents, nonetheless, closely watched the united front organizations with which he was affiliated and reported on his speeches—including August 1940, and January 1941 speeches criticizing Hoover and the FBI, and two December 1940 speeches opposing lend-lease and conscription. Bureau agents also re-ported in early April 1941 that Marcantonio alone in the House had objected to a resolution to investigate strikes in defense industries, and had opposed convoys or other military cooperation with Great Britain during an April 5, 1941 APM rally.[17] In addition, the FBI received numerous citizen requests to investigate Marcantonio. Marcantonio's May 30, 1941 radio speech, in particular, excoriating President Roose-velt's proclamation of a national emergency, especially aroused one citizen, who wrote the White House: "Any man who thinks and talks like he did is bound to be a fifth-columnist and I hope you will have the G-men tap his wires and trail him twenty-four hours a day." The letter was duly forwarded to Hoover.[18] The FBI had already moved to take action.

Early in February 1941, the Office of Naval Intelligence submitted to the FBI a confidential report listing the names of suspected Communist sympathizers, including Marcantonio's, for purposes of custodial de-tention. Whether or not in response to this report, on February 17, 1941, Hoover sent a memorandum concerning Marcantonio to Attorney General Robert Jackson. Although the FBI has not released a copy of this memorandum, it indisputably raised the question of the need to list a member of Congress for "custodial detention" in case of a "national emergency." Whether or not Attorney General Jackson replied is also unknown. In any event, with or without the Attorney General's ap-proval, the FBI proceeded to prepare a Custodial Detention dossier on Marcantonio—perhaps as a contingency in case the President issued a proclamation authorizing the detention of "dangerous" citizens. FBI files show a flurry of excited activity during June and July involving an increasing number of FBI assistant directors and, by late July, Mar-cantonio's Custodial Detention dossier was completed.[19]

Sensitive to Marcantonio's status as a congressman, Hoover sent the completed dossier on July 28, 1941 to Assistant to the Attorney General Matthew F. McGuire—not, as was the normal procedure, to the Special Defense Unit. Hoover also requested advice as to whether a copy should be forwarded to the Special Defense Unit. Responding on August 7, McGuire advised Hoover that a copy "should not be furnished to the Special Defense Unit" since, as a citizen, "the Congressman naturally is not subject to internment as an alien enemy in the event of war," and since, if he violated any criminal statute, the matter could be considered for prosecutive action "at that time." Nonetheless, the FBI retained Marcantonio's name on its Custodial Detention list, continued to monitor his activities, and even looked for other means by which to secure his detention or prosecution. Although stopping short of authorizing a complete investigation, FBI officials opened a file marked "Vito Marcantonio: Internal Security–C" and maintained his name on the key figure list in the New York Field Office.[20]

The FBI's interest in the ALP began about the same time—following the Nazi-Soviet Pact and prior to American intervention in World War II. FBI officials closely followed the growing division within the ALP, carefully distinguishing between Communist activity in, and control over the party. Owing to the ALP's status as a legitimate political party, FBI officials approached their investigatory task very circumspectly.

Initially, FBI agents followed closely the activities of the Progressive Committee to Rebuild the ALP, and collected information on individual Communists in several upstate counties. Based on information from one disgruntled anti-Communist, in 1941 the Albany Field Office opened case files on those ALP members in Oneida County who had opposed an ALP state resolution condemning the Soviet invasion of Finland. Other FBI agents watched the activities of the Progressive Committee in New York City, ostensibly looking for violations of Selective Service Act provisions prohibiting interference with the draft. FBI investigations failed "to disclose Communist tendencies on the part of the American Labor Party" and were then relatively circumscribed, focusing primarily on monitoring the public record and observing the Progressive Committee.[21]

FBI interest in Communist infiltration of the ALP increased during World War II, especially in response to Progressive Committee second-front activities and perhaps to evidence that the ALP intended to run its own independent candidate for governor. In September 1942, P.E. Foxworth, an FBI assistant director in charge of the New York Field Office, transmitted a report to FBI headquarters on the history of the ALP and on Communist efforts to dominate it. Prepared by an ALP insider, the report described the bitter fight within the Party as a struggle for control between "Socialists" and "Communists," and emphasized Communist colonization of district clubs and Communist influence in the ALP. The Progressive Committee was characterized as having been formed to carry out Communist policies in the ALP, and important labor leaders were identified as concealed Communists on the Committee.[22] The FBI, in response, monitored the ALP state platform, regularly clipped newspaper articles on the ALP, and, for the first time, cultivated a list of confidential informants.

FBI interest in the factional struggle within the ALP during 1943 and 1944, primarily between social democratic needle trades unionists and the Hillman-Communist alignment, underscores Bureau investigative methods and biases. Based on information from public sources, confidential informants, and wiretaps on Communist Party organizations and Communist-led unions, including the NMU, FBI officials interpreted the struggle narrowly as a Communist Party attempt to take outright control. FBI leaders were insensitive to the internal rivalries in organized labor which also animated the conflict. Moreover, FBI leaders selectively reviewed evidence, like a report by Communist Party state legislative director Si Gerson, which stressed Communist anger at the ALP leaders' refusal to push for a second front and their attacks on the Soviet Union.[23] Yet, while obtuse about the full complexity of ALP politics, FBI officials were acutely aware of the political consequences of their own investigatory behavior. Responding in February 1944 to a request from the Albany Field Office for policy guidance, FBI leaders cautioned: "The Bureau is not investigating the activities of the American Labor Party as such, in view of the fact that it is a recognized political party."[24] FBI officials, however, approved opening a case file on the ALP and, to avert discovery of their interest, ordered that any information obtained be forwarded in "letter form" only to headquarters.

After the Hillman-Communist primary victory on March 28, 1944, the FBI grew less cautious. On March 30, FBI Assistant Director D. M.

Ladd hurriedly reported to Hoover the specific roles of Hillman, the CIO-PAC, and the Communists in the ALP, briefly noting Hillman's purposes, but emphasizing particularly a February 26 meeting of Communist Party leaders and pro-Communist ALP leaders. At this meeting, Communist Party general secretary Earl Browder stressed the significance of the ALP primary for the 1944 presidential election and ordered Communists to mobilize an effective campaign. Ladd also reported the allegations of the Dubinsky-Rose forces that "the American Labor Party is now completely controlled by the Communist element." The FBI immediately stepped up its surveillance of ALP meetings and, through its wiretap of Communist state headquarters, apparently confirmed the assessment of increased Communist strength. FBI electronic surveillance of a meeting of Communists and unionists in Buffalo further suggested that the Communists were concentrating on "building up the ALP as a mass party." Concerned that Communist strength had peaked in the ALP, FBI leaders and second-level officials in the Attorney General's office sought authorization for a full field investigation. Assistant Attorney General James J. McGranery, however, blocked a draft memorandum authorizing the FBI to investigate the ALP and ordered the FBI to take no action without prior consultation.[25] McGranery's action compelled the FBI to continue as before—clipping newspapers, enlisting confidential informants, and listening in on Marcantonio's and other ALP leaders' conversations through wiretaps on Communist state headquarters and the NMU.

During World War II the FBI actually watched Marcantonio more intensely than the ALP. Bureau officials accepted files of materials on the radical donated by superpatriot Walter Steel of the *National Republic* magazine and by someone at the Dies Committee (HUAC). FBI agents also checked out allegations from a confidential source that Marcantonio maintained a secret apartment as a meeting place for "inner circle" Communist gatherings and a hideaway for a mistress. Marcantonio's second-front activities, his speeches in Italian-American East Harlem after the Alled invasion of Italy, and his private meetings with ILD leaders were also closely followed. In addition, the FBI turned up considerable information on the congressman through its surveillance of Puerto Rican nationalist activities in New York. (An avid proponent of

Puerto Rican independence, Marcantonio was also legal counsel for Pedro Albizu Campos, president of the Puerto Rican Nationalist Party, who had been convicted in 1936 for conspiracy to overthrow the insular government.) In 1943, FBI agents monitored a Marcantonio speech at the Hotel Commodore commemorating the birth of a leftist newspaper, *Pueblos Hispanos*. Moreover, following Campos's mid-1943 release from prison for confinement in New York's Columbus Hospital, FBI agents bugged Campos's hospital room and intercepted his talks with Marcantonio. When Campos discovered the bug, Marcantonio summoned photographers and made obscene and insulting remarks into it.[26]

By late 1944, as the war neared an end, the FBI's steadily expanded investigations of Marcantonio and the ALP had slackened. In November 1944, FBI officials removed Marcantonio from the key figure list maintained at headquarters and in the field offices, and, in early 1945, the New York Field Office filed a 170-page memorandum summarizing its extensive attention to Marcantonio since 1940. For the record, this memorandum claimed that, due to Marcantonio's position as a congressman, the FBI had not directly investigated his activities, and that all information had been obtained from either outside or public sources or incidentally through other investigations. Nonetheless, FBI leaders continued an active file on Marcantonio, believing that, if not a Communist Party member, he was still the Party's spokesman in Congress and a dangerous radical. In contrast, although concerned about Communist domination of the ALP, Bureau officials were compelled to respect the limitations on FBI coverage imposed because the ALP was a "recognized political party" and by the oversight of Assistant Attorney General McGranery.[27]

III

FBI coverage of the ALP did not change appreciably during the immediate postwar period. In 1946, FBI officials kept special tabs on ALP delegations sent to Washington to lobby on housing and price control legislation, while FBI agents in New York watched over ALP meetings, conferences, and social gatherings. FBI leaders were particularly interested in the possibility that Wallace would endorse the ALP following his dismissal from Truman's Cabinet in October 1946. Apparently, Bureau officials also occasionally leaked file materials on the ALP to friendly reporters at several New York newspapers.[28] During the early Cold War years, however, the FBI refrained from interfering with ALP electoral activity, and Bureau coverage of the ALP continued nearly as much by clipping the record as by covert spying.

FBI restraint diminished, however, beginning in January 1948. Exploiting the newly ordered Federal Employee Loyalty Program's authorization to justify investigations of "subversive" and potentially subversive organizations, and spurred forward by the ALP's enlistment in the Progressive Party, FBI officials ordered a full report on Communist infiltration within the ALP. Consistent with past practice, FBI leaders requested no outside investigation but a review of all information in the New York files. At the same time, FBI leaders in executive conference directed that investigative reports under the Loyalty Program identify that an employee had "registered as a member of the ALP," linking this with HUAC's conclusion in March 1944 that the ALP was a "Communist front." Not submitted until September 1948, the New York Field Office report on Communist infiltration in the ALP recounted the ALP's history as a balance of power in the state, the alleged triumph of the Communist-dominated left wing in 1944, and the impressions of numerous confidential informants that the Communist Party controlled the ALP. The report also mentioned ALP support for Wallace and opposition to the Loyalty Program and the Marshall Plan. The New York Field Office followed this up with additional analyses of the Communist connections of numerous ALP officials.[29]

Thereafter, FBI surveillance intensified. In 1949, the New York Field Office reported extensively on ALP leadership plans, meetings, and demonstrations—particularly on an ALP-sponsored People's Lobby to Washington in June 1949 to oppose enactment of the North Atlantic Pact. FBI officials also followed ALP activities involving the Smith Act trial of Communist Party (CP) leaders, gathering copies of all letters and telegrams sent by the ALP to Judge Harold Medina. FBI agents collected lists of all ALP candidates for office and attended most ALP rallies, including the Madison Square Garden rally that capped Marcantonio's unsuccessful mayoralty campaign. And, when Edward Scheidt, Special Agent in Charge of the New York Field Office, suggested that the ALP and other Progressive Party state units might be designated as "the new rallying point for CP members in the event the CP should be outlawed," FBI leaders relayed this conclusion to Assistant Attorney General Alexander M. Campbell of the Criminal Division.[30]

FBI officials and agents now went considerably beyond past practice. In August 1949 and several times during 1950, the Albany Field Office sought permission to bug the ALP Club in Albany. Permission was denied, as headquarters noted that the FBI had already tapped and bugged Communist Party offices in the state capitol and that the ALP was still a recognized political party. In April 1949, FBI agents infiltrated the ALP Women's Conference in Albany; and, in November 1949, FBI agents pilfered a list of the state executive council members of the ALP Women's Division. In May 1949, FBI agents obtained copies of ALP Queens County executive committee minutes. Also in 1949, FBI officials were knowledgeable about internal rifts within the ALP in Brooklyn and may have discussed actions to exacerbate these divisions. (FBI files do not reveal whether FBI agents or informants acted on such discussions.)[31]

In contrast to the ALP, the FBI's expanded coverage of Marcantonio began before 1948. In the immediate postwar period, FBI officials were particularly interested in Marcantonio's relationship with the Communist Party, then in the midst of important ideological and leadership changes. In late May 1945, FBI agents observed a meeting between Marcantonio and deposed Communist leader Earl Browder in a taxi cab, and in September 1945, intercepted a telephone conversation between Gil Green, Communist state secretary, and Marcantonio. Based on information from a paid informant, FBI Assistant Director D. M. Ladd advised Hoover in late February 1946 that Marcantonio had been close to Browder and that, since Browder's expulsion, Marcantonio had drifted from Communist principles and the Party line. Nonetheless, efforts were being made to arrange a meeting between Browder's successor, William Z. Foster, and Marcantonio to establish an agreement. Early in August 1946, FBI agents reported on further friction between Marcantonio and the New York State Communist Party. From other sources, including wiretaps and bugs on Communist Party headquarters and conventions and confidential informants in Communist section meetings, the FBI learned that Marcantonio and the Communists continued to collaborate closely through the 1946 elections.[32]

FBI interest in Marcantonio also quickened in the wake of an election killing in November 1946. Joseph Scottorigio, a Republican district captain and a vigorous Marcantonio opponent, was beaten on election day and died several days later. A case still unsolved by the New York Police Department, the murder focused attention on the congressman and on East Harlem politics, and stimulated an inquiry into the election by a House special committee. FBI officials declined on the record a request from Robert Barker, assistant general counsel of the committee, for information from FBI files confirming Marcantonio's membership in the Communist Party in the event that House exclusion proceedings were instituted. As Hoover explained, the FBI could not release such information to Barker without the Attorney General's approval; more importantly, as Hoover admitted privately, the Bureau lacked any such evidence. Still, FBI leaders cultivated Barker and obtained the verbatim transcripts of the committee's interviews.[33]

Finally, the FBI increased its interest not merely in the extent but also in the nature of Marcantonio's links with the Communists. As before, Marcantonio's public positions and speeches were closely monitored, revealing his growing radicalism in 1947 and his support for a third party. The FBI now sought also to document Marcantonio's possible connection with espionage. Marcantonio, former *Daily Worker* editor Louis Budenz told the FBI early in 1947, was one of the "front line reliances" of the Communist Party; he added that, as a congressman, Marcantonio could wander around and associate "widely," and that "things have come out of Marcantonio's office." Budenz cited a "gray blond" who worked in Marcantonio's operation and frequently visited Communist headquarters. The FBI's increased coverage circumstantially linked Marcantonio at one point in early 1948 to Nathan Gregory Silvermaster, the accused head of a wartime Communist cell in Washington.[34] FBI leaders, however, turned down Congressman H. Carl Andersen's August 1948 offer to permit installation of a bug in Marcantonio's wall (Andersen had the office adjoining Marcantonio's), and refrained from any technical or physical surveillance specifically directed at Marcantonio—with a single exception. In October 1947, FBI agents, who had been instructed to track down another reported rift between Marcantonio and the Communists, had observed and filmed a meeting at Marcantonio's home between the Congressman and Communist Party general secretary Eugene Dennis.[35]

In September 1948, however, prompted by the FBI, Assistant Attorney General Peyton Ford, Attorney General Thomas C. Clark's top deputy, asked Hoover for "all information of a subversive nature" on Marcantonio. The FBI report, transmitted on October 8, listed the active Communist role in Marcantonio's electoral campaigns and Marcantonio's numerous contacts with Communist leaders, active association with more than a score of Communist-front organizations, and aid to Communists and to Puerto Rican nationalists in legal, immigration, and naturalization matters. FBI records reveal little about the purpose of this report; presumably it pertained to discussions about listing the congressman on the new Security Index.[36] The FBI's released files also do not reveal the outcome of these discussions, although it seems clear that Marcantonio was not listed owing to his continued position as an elected congressman and either the Attorney General's or the Bureau's wariness to investigate a congressman directly.

Expanded but still limited FBI coverage of the radical congressman continued in 1949 and 1950. FBI agents monitored Marcantonio's public positions, his activities on behalf of the Communist leaders on trial, and his reelection preparations. Following the outbreak of the Korean War and Marcantonio's lone opposition in Congress to an American troop commitment, FBI officials again proposed that Marcantonio be listed for detention. Asked why Marcantonio was not already included on the Security Index, FBI Assistant Director Alan Belmont informed D. M. Ladd in July 1950 that the Bureau had not instituted security investigations of members of Congress. Should Marcantonio be defeated in November 1950, Belmont observed, the FBI could then actively investigate him and consider putting his name on the Index. Hoover disagreed, scribbling on this memorandum: "I think [his] name should be in the Index. It will then be up to Dep't to finally decide if he should be picked up." Accordingly, in mid-August, and before Marcantonio's subsequent defeat, the New York Field Office was ordered to prepare an investigative report on Marcantonio and to file a Security Index recommendation. Due to the press of other investigations, however, the report was not completed until November 25, 1950. Marcantonio was then recommended for a "Detcom" (Detention-Communist) listing because he had been "a consistent supporter of the Communist Party line," had been under Communist Party "discipline" since the early 1940s, and, among other activities, had been state chairman of the ALP.[37]

Thereafter, FBI officials lifted most restraints on the surveillance and possible harassment of the ex-congressman, restored his key figure status, and subjected him to close scrutiny. When journalist Walter Winchell reported that Marcantonio would travel to the Soviet Union, FBI agents hastened to intervene with the State Department's Passport Division. When Marcantonio expanded his legal activities on behalf of the Communist Party and individual Communists, the New York Field Office forwarded "derogatory" information to Washington where he had opened a second law office. FBI agents carefully observed his activities as ALP state chairman, in the process intercepting information on the growing tensions between Marcantonio and the Communists. FBI officials also collected data on Communist disbursements to Marcantonio, probably for income tax purposes. Finally, the FBI also assisted Marcantonio's legal adversaries. When Kenneth Watson, an investigator for the Scripps-Howard chain, requested special information from the FBI on Marcantonio's links with gangsters and "Puerto Rican Reds" to be used to combat Marcantonio's libel action against the *New York World Telegram*, Hoover ordered "a check" and FBI officials prepared a report based upon public source materials "which might help Kenneth Watson in regard to the libel suit."[38]

With the outbreak of the Korean War, FBI scrutiny of the ALP also intensified—ironically, at a time when the ALP declined sharply in membership and influence. Former ALP upstate director Charles Campbell voluntarily approached the FBI in August to furnish information, identifying leading Communists in the ALP upstate, and claiming that "at the present time an individual could not be an official or on any important committee of the ALP unless that individual was first a member of the Communist Party." Another knowledgeable former ALP member told the FBI in October that "without question the dynamic force in the American Labor Party is the Communist Party," information which the FBI employed to update the "thumbnail sketch" on the ALP it submitted during loyalty proceedings. FBI officials gathered extensive information on ALP electoral candidates around the state and furnished it to Frederick Woltman of the *New York World Telegram*. Furthermore, FBI officials subsequently initiated an extensive investigation of the alleged failure of ALP congressional candidates to file with the clerk of the House of Representatives correct and itemized financial statements. Although this investigation was assigned to exerienced personnel who were to act discreetly, the FBI's interviewing of all ALP candidates ostensibly to build a case suggests tactics which were later formalized in the Bureau's now-infamous COINTELPROs (Counterintelligence programs).[39]

FBI activities, however, remained restrained. The New York Field Office did file a report in early 1950 labelling the ALP as a Communist front. The Attorney General, though, refused to include the ALP on the list of subversive organizations (the Attorney General's list pointedly omitted political and labor organizations), and the Bureau continued to be governed by the earlier limits on investigating a legitimate political party. As FBI Assistant Director Belmont informed Ladd in response to a December 1950 Army inquiry about the ALP, the FBI had conducted no investigation of the ALP because of its "political character."[40] The Bureau's tact and concern to be discreet, however, became increasingly more difficult during the early 1950s, given the conviction of FBI officials that the Communists were using the ALP to conduct their mass activities in New York.

IV

During the early 1950s, the disillusionment and anxiety that had built in the United States since the beginning of the Cold War burst forth into angry reaction. House and Senate committees hunted Soviet agents and Communist fellow-travelers, while the issue of internal subversion dominated mass media headlines. In September 1950, Congress passed the McCarran Internal Security Act, authorizing the registration and preventive detention of Communists and establishing a Subversive Activities Control Board empowered to order the registration of "Communist front" groups. In June 1951, the Supreme Court upheld the Smith Act convictions of Communist leaders, creating an unprecedented narrowing of First Amendment liberties. Not surprisingly, the ALP dwindled toward political insignificance: whereas ALP enrollment in New York City had been 199,947 in 1948, membership fell to 98,173 in 1950 after the dispatch of American troops to Korea, then to 52,734 in 1952. Thus, between presidential elections, ALP membership in New York City had dropped 73.6 percent.[41]

As earlier, FBI attention and resources devoted to following the ALP increased as the Party declined in size and importance. In part, this intensified coverage was a response to evidence of Communist control in the ALP, but it was also an outgrowth of the political priorities of FBI officials. Granted expanded responsibilities under the Loyalty Program, the Attorney General's detention plan, and the Internal Security Act, the FBI developed into a powerful intelligence agency having as one purpose ensuring political orthodoxy. FBI coverage of Communist control in the ALP shaded inexorably into coverage of the entire ALP and the activities of all ALP members. Paradoxically, the FBI coverage also contributed to intensifying Communist control. As the number of FBI agents and confidential informants in the ALP increased, so too did the pressure on non-Communist radicals to leave. (In their own commitment to orthodoxy, the Communists did even more to drive out the remnants of the Popular Front.)[42] FBI actions and the Communist response had a chilling effect on the expression of radical political ideas and activities in New York state.

When leading Communists went underground following the Supreme Court's upholding of the Smith Act convictions, FBI officials worried that Communists were meeting and conducting their activities in New York through the ALP. As a result, FBI surveillance of ALP state conferences, rallies, and dinners increased. The FBI now collected ALP materials sent by patriotic citizens and cooperative newsmen; FBI field offices perused ALP petitions and asked informants for background information on the signers. Continuing to draw the line at direct technical or microphone surveillance, Bureau officials formally refused several requests from upstate New York field offices to tap or bug ALP headquarters (there is evidence to suggest that at least in one instance this line may have been crossed). FBI field offices were nonetheless pressured to watch the ALP closely and to pay particular attention to ALP leadership plans to "broaden" the ALP as the center of a movement in 1952 against American involvement in Korea; FBI field offices strained to develop information satisfactory to Washington headquarters.[43]

FBI penetration into the ALP reached new dimensions—including coverage of the largest and smallest ALP meetings. Copies of ALP state conference reports and press releases were obtained or photographed and extensive reports were filed on ALP rallies. In 1953, the FBI began sharing its information with the armed forces intelligence agencies. FBI officials had carefully resisted requests from these agencies before 1950, responding that because the ALP was a legitimate political party the FBI had conducted no investigation.[44] Now, the FBI was clearly investigating the ALP and sharing its information with potentially competing agencies.

The FBI's surveillance of the ALP in the early 1950s probably proceeded furthest in the upstate counties, where the ALP was numerically miniscule, and where coverage focused on a single headquarters and a few individuals. "Confidential informants" reported extensively on ALP discussions and on the sources of ALP finances. ALP efforts to win support in black neighborhoods were closely monitored, files on ALP officers were opened, and all ALP electoral activities were charted. (FBI coverage sometimes reached absurd levels, including surveillance of a spaghetti supper in Gloversville and a Passover seder in Syracuse.) The FBI also gathered information on upstate ALP attempts to rally opposition to subcommittee hearings of the House Committee on Un-American Activities in Albany. FBI officials provided transcripts of the broadcasts the ALP was to make over radio stations in Albany to the Committee, and the Bureau probably provided the names of at least two former FBI informants who testified before the subcommittee.[45]

Such close surveillance enabled FBI officials to discover Marcantonio's intense conflict with the Communists in the ALP. While agreeing on programmatic matters—cease-fire in Korea, return to a peacetime economy, and an end to racial discrimination and to infringements on civil liberties—Marcantonio and the Communists disagreed strongly on organizational and tactical issues, specifically those concerning the ALP's future. After 1950, the Communists concluded that their earlier decisions to support Wallace and help create the Progressive Party had been mistaken. Increasingly, they advocated coalition politics, even reinfiltrating the major parties. Marcantonio and other radicals, notably those associated with the *National Guardian*, opposed this strategy and reaffirmed their belief in independent politics. Marcantonio was particularly adamant, concluding that Communist policy would sound the ALP's "death knell." Marcantonio reportedly even forbade ALP club officials from circulating petitions in the Rosenberg case for fear the such an action might blunt ALP hopes for a comeback. The conflict intensified, especially following Dwight D. Eisenhower's election in 1952 and the release of a Communist Party "Draft Resolution" declaring that the Progressive Party (and thus the ALP) was expendable.[46]

FBI officials closely followed this rift. When the ALP nominated a mayoral candidate in 1953 and the Communists hedged, refusing to endorse an independent campaign, the division sliced deeply into ALP unity. Confidential informants reported "bad blood" between Marcantonio and Si Gerson, commented extensively on Marcantonio's voluble anger at the Communist line, and noted that the Communists had boycotted the ALP rally to initiate the campaign. Others reported Marcantonio's insistent threat to resign and his charge of a Communist "double-cross" and "sell out." FBI leaders even knew about Marcantonio's "tongue-lashing" of William Z. Foster and his intended resignation from the ALP, publicly announced in November 1953. Indeed an October 30 FBI teletype advised FBI headquarters that Marcantonio would formally step out on November 4 or 5.[47]

Despite Marcantonio's resignation, the FBI's close surveillance of the ex-congressman and interest in his relationship with the Communists continued. FBI officials were particularly interested in his efforts during early 1954 to build a new local party in East Harlem, the Good Neighbor Party, and to make another try for Congress. Marcantonio died on August 9, however, felled by a heart attack on a lower Manhattan sidewalk. Consistent as ever in its coverage, the FBI checked the Department of Health records for the official cause of death and monitored the funeral procession, which wound through East Harlem past several thousand who gathered to pay Marcantonio tribute. FBI officials subsequently destroyed Marcantonio's Security Index card and perhaps his Custodial Detention file. In 1971, in response to charges by columnist Jack Anderson, an internal FBI report claimed that there existed "no information" in FBI files that Marcantonio "was ever subjected to [direct] electronic or physical surveillance despite his blatant communist sympathies."[48]

The FBI also watched the ALP, covering the party's attempts to rally anti-McCarthy sentiment in 1954, and to maintain its ballot position by running John McManus, editor of the *National Guardian*, for governor. A July 1954 FBI report suggested that "the CP . . . still is the leading force in the ALP" and that Marcantonio's departure had strengthened the CP's grip. When the ALP lost its ballot position by failing to poll fifty thousand votes in the election, FBI officials ordered the field offices to continue close surveillance, demanding special attention to whether the Communists intended to continue to control, or to abandon, the ALP as an electoral tool.[49]

FBI field offices were also pressed on another matter. Having long encouraged updating the ALP "thumbnail sketch" cited in investigative reports in applicant and security cases under the Loyalty Program, FBI officials demanded in 1954 that field offices provide increased data "regarding the domination and control of the organization . . . from its inception until approximately 1947 or 1948." In addition, FBI officials pressured the field offices to locate informants who could state when specific ALP county units became Communist-dominated. Because of earlier restraints against investigating a "recognized political party," the field offices confronted considerable difficulty in meeting this requirement. Urged to produce such information by other agencies—the Air Force Central Security Board, for instance, requested FBI assessment of the significance of ALP registration in New York since 1939—FBI officials harassed the field offices. Hoover eventually accepted the New

York Field Office's general conclusion that "by the early 1940s, the Communist Party emerged as the controlling force within the ALP in the major industrial areas in New York State." When Assistant Attorney General William F. Tompkins sought in December 1954 further information concerning Communist control or infiltration of the ALP from 1937 to 1939 for use in an employee security case, Hoover suggested that Tompkins interview an ex-Communist whom the Department employed as a consultant.[50]

We cannot presently ascertain what uses were made during loyalty proceedings of information that government employees had been enrolled ALP members. At minimum, such information was regularly cited and perhaps triggered FBI field investigations. During 1949, one former ALP member, who was then employed by the National Labor Relations Board, was cleared in loyalty proceedings; he did not remain in government service to discover whether he would again be cleared under the shifted burden of proof adopted in 1951.[51] William Vitarelli, a Columbia Ph.D. who served under the Department of Interior in the Pacific Islands, was suspended in 1954 and subsequently dismissed because of "sympathetic association" with Communists and having registered as an ALP member in 1945. Scientists and technicians employed by the Army Signal Corps at Fort Monmouth, New Jersey, were harassed in 1953 and 1954 for their own or their family members' enrollment in the ALP.[52]

The FBI continued in 1955 to follow the factionalism within the ALP between Communists and other radical Marxists. Hoover forwarded to Assistant Attorney General Tompkins of the Internal Security Division an ALP state executive committee report detailing the Communists' opposition to third-party action but continued commitment to the ALP— perhaps simply for information, or because the Attorney General was considering listing the ALP. Field office reports, in contrast, described the dormancy of the ALP and indicated that Communists were slipping back into the Democratic Party (the ALP's last effort was a modest peace petition to Eisenhower to ban nuclear weapons). There was soon no activity to cover. In July 1956, Assistant Attorney General Tompkins requested that the FBI determine whether the ALP still existed and was advised in October of the ALP's formal dissolution. FBI interest in Communist infiltration of the ALP and in the Party itself ceased; in 1957, the New York Field Office filed a closing report.[53]

V

The FBI's investigations of Marcantonio and the ALP raise important questions. Should the FBI have undertaken surveillance of a member of Congress and a recognized political party? If so, should the FBI have confined these investigations in duration, ending them when there was little evidence of illegal or treasonous activity? What political priorities governed FBI investigations of a radical congressman engaged wholly in lawful activities, and what objectives animated FBI coverage of a legitimate political party? Were FBI officials concerned only to ascertain Communist infiltration in and control of the ALP, or was their purpose to interfere with the electoral process? What factors contributed to the radical expansion of FBI activities during the early 1950s—absence of explicit constitutional and legal authority? Finally, do released FBI files reveal the full range of FBI activities and methods concerning the FBI's coverage of Marcantonio and the ALP?

In cooperation with the Attorney General's office, the FBI listed Marcantonio for custodial detention in 1941 on the basis of his speeches and associations, establishing special reporting procedures because Marcantonio was a member of Congress. FBI officials uncovered no evidence that Marcantonio was involved in espionage and certainly lacked any reason to prosecute the East Harlemite. Nonetheless, the FBI continued to investigate Marcantonio's public and private life during and after World War II. Bureau officials apparently tried to uncover derogatory personal information on the radical congressman when he embraced a leftist course with the Communists during the early Cold War period. In 1950 the FBI listed him again in its Detcom Index. Moreover, the Bureau harassed the ex-congressman during the early 1950s and provided information to his enemies. There were limits to FBI activities, however: Bureau officials, sensitive to Marcantonio's status as a congressman, carefully prepared reports affirming that Marcantonio had never been placed under direct physical surveillance, bugged, or wire-tapped.

FBI coverage of the ALP was more complex. Because the ALP was a recognized political party engaged in legitimate electoral activities, the FBI confined its surveillance through the mid-1940s (or was constrained by the Assistant Attorney General) to covering Communist infiltration of the ALP. FBI investigative activities ostensibly rose in correspondence with signs of Communist infiltration and control in the ALP (although FBI officials prematurely affirmed Communist control by several years), and FBI reports carefully established that FBI techniques and methods were limited, including no direct investigations of the ALP, wiretaps, bugs, or "black bag jobs."[54] Nonetheless, FBI coverage during the 1940s focused on ALP activities that had little to do with violations of federal law; in the 1950s, FBI scrutiny of the ALP centered on creating files containing derogatory and stereotyped information on individuals who were or had been members of the ALP, or who had signed ALP petitions. Finally, there is limited evidence that the FBI selectively released information to favored newsmen and cooperated with the House Committee on Un-American Activities, subtly crossing the line between intelligence coverage and political activism.[55]

Materials available to the historian sharply understate the range and character of FBI activities. Published reports by the Senate Select Committee on Intelligence Activities and by scholars have described the complex procedures employed by FBI officials to safeguard sensitive information; one such procedure was the sumbission of sensitive information to headquarters in memoranda not to be retained or filed (the Do Not File procedure).[56] Procedures of this kind and their intent to prevent knowledge adverse to the FBI's interests create serious difficulties for scholars who wish to interpret FBI actions. This is particularly the case concerning Marcantonio and the ALP because of the special care taken by the FBI when authorizing programs directed at the congressman; the Bureau specifically instructed the field offices to provide information about the ALP in "letter form" only (and not through retrievable [agent] investigative reports).[57]

While these research problems preclude the definitive resolution of the scope of the FBI's surveillance of the political activities of a radical congressman and a radical political party, the fact of this politically motivated surveillance is indisputable. And, this raises questions about the FBI's role as a political police.

Notes

1. Interview, Edward Flynn, *COHC*, pp. 20–21. On apprehension in the Roosevelt camp, see Harold L. Ickes, *The Secret Diary of Harold L. Ickes* (New York, 1953), I, 617; Eleanor Roosevelt to Franklin Roosevelt, July 16, 1936, in Elliot Roosevelt, ed., *F.D.R.: His Personal Letters* (New York, 1950), I, 600; and Arthur M. Schlesinger, Jr., *The Age of Roosevelt: The Politics of Upheaval* (Boston, 1960), p. 586. On the origins of the American Labor Party (ALP), see Warren Moscow, *Politics in the Empire State* (New York, 1948), pp. 104–5; Interview, Jacob Potofsky, pp. 275–77, *COHC*; and David Dubinsky and A. H. Raskin, *David Dubinsky: A Life With Labor* (New York, 1977), pp. 265–66.

2. On the history of the ALP, see Kenneth Waltzer, "The American Labor Party: Third Party Politics in New Deal–Cold War New York, 1936–54," (Ph.D. diss., Harvard University, 1977). After 1936, the ALP consistently polled more than four hundred thousand votes in national, state, and city elections. In national and state elections, it garnered from 6.7 percent to 10 percent of the statewide vote, in mayoral elections, from 19.2 percent to 21.6 percent. Between 1936 and 1940, the Democratic share of the presidential vote in New York State declined from 53.9 percent to 45 percent, while the Republican share rose from 39 percent to 48.2 percent. The Democratic share of the gubernatorial vote similarly fell—from 48.8 percent (1936) to 42 percent (1938) and 37 percent (1942)—while the GOP share rose—from 44.1 percent (1936) to 49.1 percent (1938) and 53 percent (1942). Given the trend toward Republican resurgence, the ALP, which drew heavily from Democratic voters, correctly claimed the balance of power during the period from 1937 to 1944. These statistics are based on the *New York State Red Book* (Albany, 1937–43).

3. On the history of FBI domestic intelligence operations from 1936 to the mid-1950s, see *IARA*, pp. 21–65; *SDSR*, pp. 391–452. See also Athan Theoharis, *Spying on Americans: Political Surveillance from Hoover to the Huston Plan* (Philadelphia, 1978). Other useful works include Don Whitehead, *The FBI Story* (New York, 1956); Vern Countryman, "The History of the FBI: Democracy's Development of a Secret Police," in Pat Watters and Stephen Gillers, eds., *Investigating the FBI* (Garden City, 1973), pp. 33–63; Sanford J.

Ungar, *FBI* (Boston, 1975); and Frank Donner, *The Age of Surveillance: The Aims and Methods of America's Political Intelligence System* (New York, 1980).

4. The late Alexander Meiklejohn argued that the intent of the First Amendment was to deny all agencies of government authority to abridge the freedom of "the electoral power of the people." See "The First Amendment is an Absolute," in Philip B. Kurland, ed., *Free Speech and Association: The Supreme Court and the First Amendment* (Chicago, 1975), pp. 9–10.

5. *New York Times*, Jan. 5, 1938, p. 2; *ALP News of the Week*, 5 (Jan. 8, 1938), p. 2. See also the ALP 1937 Municipal Platform and ALP 1938 Platform in ALP Papers, *OF* (1937, 1938).

6. On Socialists and the ALP, see Bernard K. Johnpoll, *Pacifist's Progress: Norman Thomas and the Decline of American Socialism* (Chicago, 1970), pp. 191–96; Frank Warren, *An Alternative Vision: The Socialist Party in the 1930s* (Bloomington, 1974), pp. 84–105. On the ALP's ethnic and labor base, see Waltzer, "American Labor Party," pp. 144–72; William Spinrad, "New Yorkers Cast Their Ballots" (Ph.D. diss., Columbia University, 1955), pp. 109–14. Ronald Bayor (*Neighbors in Conflict: The Irish, Germans, Jews, and Italians of New York City, 1929–41* [Baltimore, 1978], pp. 40–41), characterizes the ALP as "mainly a Jewish challenge to Irish Democratic control over politics."

7. See Earl Browder, "The American Communist Party in the Thirties," in Rita James Simon, ed., *As We Saw The Thirties* (Urbana, 1967), p. 237; James Weinstein, *Ambiguous Legacy* (New York, 1975), pp. 77–80. Communist policy in the ALP is treated superficially in David Saposs, *Communism in American Politics* (Washington, 1960), pp. 68–72, 109–11; and George Charney, *A Long Journey* (Chicago, 1968), pp. 94–95. The Communist role in the New York Committee for Industrial Organization (CIO) unions has yet to be treated adequately. The main protest over the lack of internal democracy came from Socialists and Social Democrats. See "Report of the Committee on the American Labor Party Situation," May 1939; "Minutes of the Social Democratic Federation (SDF), City Convention, May 13, 1939," SDF Papers; Louis Waldman, *Labor Lawyer* (New York, 1944), pp. 289–93.

8. *New York Times*, Oct. 5, 1939, pp. 1, 18; *Daily Worker*, Oct. 6, 1939, pp. 1, 6. On Communist defense of the Pact and its impact in the New York Jewish community, see Irving Howe and Lewis Coser, *The American Communist Party: A Critical History* (New York, 1962), pp. 387–95, 401–5; Melech Epstein, *The Jew and Communism* (New York, 1959), pp. 350–51. ALP policy during 1940 and 1941 can be followed in *ALP News of the Week* 6 (Oct. 16,

1939), p. 2; *ALP News of the Week* (Jan. 8, 1940), p. 1; *New York Times*, Sept. 29, 1940, p. 41; "ALP Statement on Lend-Lease, Feb. 3, 1941," Marcantonio Papers, box 25; and *American Laborite* 1 (July 15, 1941), p. 5. On the Communist *volte-face* in the ALP, see *New York Times*, July 11, 1941, p. 11.

9. On Hillman and the CIO Political Action Committee, see Matthew F. Josephson, *Sidney Hillman: Labor Statesman* (Garden City, 1956), pp. 600–606; Waltzer, "American Labor Party," pp. 278–298; and James C. Foster, *The Union Politic: The CIO Political Action Committee* (Columbia, Mo., 1975), pp. 29–32. The Hillman-Communist alliance carried 59.1 percent of the vote in the ALP primary, winning 60 of 62 New York City assembly districts and a majority of the 88 upstate; it also took 570 of the 750 ALP state committee seats. See *New York Times*, March 29, 1944, p. 1; Allen Goodwin to Hyman Blumberg, April 27, 1944, Blumberg Papers, *ALP* (1944). During the contest, Roosevelt met privately with Dubinsky and Hillman, and, unable to effect a truce, convinced Hillman to agree that no Communits would accede to important ALP office. Hillman carried out this promise with cooperation from the Communists. See John M. Blum, ed., *The Price of Vision: The Diary of Henry Wallace, 1942–46* (Boston, 1973), pp. 298, 304–5; "Minutes of the ALP State Committee, April 8, 1944," Blumberg Papers, *ALP* (1944); Kenneth Waltzer, interview with John Abt, Dec. 24, 1969.

10. On the ALP in the postwar period, see "ALP 1944 Platform," Blumberg Papers, *ALP* (1944); *Legislative Action*, ALP Papers; "ALP Statement on Foreign Policy, early 1946," in author's possession; Draft, "ALP 1946 State Platform," Blumberg Papers, *ALP* (1946); and "ALP 1946 State Platform," in author's possession. The ALP reached its peak enrollment in New York City in 1946: 252,313.

11. "Proceedings of the ALP State Executive Committee, Jan. 7, 1948," Marcantonio Papers, box 25. On Wallace, see Blum, ed., *The Price of Vision*, pp. 37–46; Norman Markowitz, *The Rise and Fall of the People's Century: Henry A. Wallace and American Liberalism* (New York, 1973). On Communist policy, see Joseph Starobin, *American Communism in Crisis, 1943–57* (Cambridge, Mass., 1972), pp. 71–141; David Shannon, *The Decline of American Communism* (New York, 1959), pp. 3–15, 113–22, 131–50. On Marcantonio, see Alan Schaffer, *Vito Marcantonio: Radical in Congress* (Syracuse, 1966), pp. 149–83; Waltzer, "American Labor Party," pp. 363–77. In 1948, the ALP polled its highest numerical tally (509,559) and its highest statewide percentage in a presidential election (8.3 percent).

12. The cited documents are from the FBI's "main file" 100-28126 on Marcantonio, which is numbered serially from 1 to 95. Other documents are

from the FBI's "main file" 100-25869 on the ALP, which is numbered serially from 1 to 240, from the FBI's "New York file" 100-53054 on Marcantonio, which is numbered 1 to 1192, and from the FBI's "New York file" 100-8522 on the ALP, which is numbered 1 to 3810. The serial number of a document appears in parentheses following the date; the file number appears after the serial number (or the final serial number of a group of documents). The Assistant Attorney General Charles P. Sissons, to Hoover, July 29, 1930 (1); C. Spears, Acting Agent in Charge, Telegram to FBI Director, Aug. 2, 1930 (2); Report by H. C. Leslie, Aug. 4, 1930 (3); and J. Edgar Hoover to Assistant Attorney General Sisson, Aug. 7, 1930 (4), 100-28126, *VM*. On Marcantonio's relationship with Congressman La Guardia and his reputation for activist socialism, see Leonard Covello, *The Heart is the Teacher* (New York, 1958); Arthur Mann, *Fiorello La Guardia: A Fighter Against His Times* (Chicago, 1959), pp. 175–76, 239–42; and Schaffer, *Marcantonio*, pp. 9–18.

13. Vito Marcantonio to Luigi Antonini, Aug. 14, 1935, Marcantonio Papers, box 4; Kenneth Waltzer, interview with George Charney, March 19, 1969. Marcantonio's turn to radicalism is traced in Schaffer, *Marcantonio*, pp. 28–46; see also Charney, *A Long Journey*, pp. 105–14. According to Charney, the Communist Party unsuccessfully attempted to recruit Marcantonio after his electoral victory in 1938. Charney told Donna Lieberman that Marcantonio never fully shared the Marxist view of the working class and preferred to remain independent of Communist Party discipline. Lieberman Interview, George Charney, Feb. 20, 1970.

14. Marcantonio's opposition to Roosevelt policy, which began only after the Progressive Committee took power in the Manhattan ALP, is discussed in Schaffer, *Marcantonio*, pp. 92–94; Norm Kaner, "Toward a Minority of One: Vito Marcantonio and American Foreign Policy," (Ph.D. diss., Rutgers University, 1967), pp. 91–100; and Waltzer, "American Labor Party," pp. 245–50.

15. Early coverage of Marcantonio can be traced in Morris Ernst to Matthews, Oct. 3, 1936, and in Memorandum, Anthony F. Ferentz, March 2, 1945 (26), pp. 2, 6–7, which summarizes information in the files of the New York Field Office. See SAC (Special Agent in Charge), New York to FBI Director, March 2, 1945 (26), 100-28126, *VM*. FBI officials have insisted that no materials exist in the Marcantonio file for the years 1936–40, but this 1945 memorandum clearly points to indirect FBI coverage of his activities with the International Labor Defense and the Workers Alliance and with Puerto Rican nationalists under the headings "Subversive Activities: General," "Communist Party of America and Affiliated Organizations: General Activities," and "Pedro Albizu Campos et. al., Nationalist Party of Puerto Rico." Elizabeth Dilling, *The

Roosevelt Red Record and Its Background (Kenilworth, Ill: 1936).

16. On FBI employment of Roosevelt's directive to expand its domestic intelligence activities, see Athan Theoharis, "The FBI's Stretching of Presidential Directives, 1936–53," *Political Science Quarterly* 91 (Winter 1976–77): 649–61. On the FBI's Custodial Detention program, see *SDSR*, pp. 413–14, 417–19; Athan Theoharis, "The Truman Administration and the Decline of Civil Liberties: The FBI's Success in Securing Authorization for a Preventive Detention Program," *Journal of American History* 64 (March 1978): 1011–14. According to the record, Hoover unilaterally initiated the emergency detention program and only reluctantly accepted oversight by the Justice Department unit. In his congressional testimony, Hoover reported the reestablishment of the FBI's General Intelligence Division and informed Congress that the FBI had initiated special investigations of persons active in "subversive activity" or in "movements detrimental to the internal security"; see Whitehead, *FBI Story*, pp. 170–71; Donner, *Age of Surveillance*, pp. 59–60. Marcantonio's response is in *Congressional Record*, 76th Cong., 2d sess., p. 292; see also Undated Typescript, Marcantonio Papers, box 2. In subsequent months, Marcantonio condemned the FBI raids on Spanish veterans organizations of February 1940, and joined in the call for an investigation of the FBI; see "Plot against Hoover," *Nation* 150 (March 9, 1940): 323–24.

17. Memorandum, Anthony F. Ferentz, March 2, 1945 (26), pp. 9–11, 15–17, 20–21, 23, 100-28126, *VM*.

18. [Name deleted] to Franklin Roosevelt, May 31, 1941 (4); [Name deleted] to J. Edgar Hoover, May 30, 1941 (4), 100-28126, *VM*. Marcantonio's national radio address is reprinted in *Congressional Record*, 77th Cong., 1st sess., A2654–A2656.

19. Memorandum, Anthony F. Ferentz, March 2, 1945 (26), p. 19; Hoover to Assistant to the Attorney General Matthew F. McGuire, Feb. 17, 1941 (4); and R. P. Kramer to P. E. Foxworth, July 21, 1945 (5), 100-28126, *VM*. The FBI has been unable to locate Hoover's memorandum to Attorney General Jackson or the Custodial Detention dossier.

20. Hoover to Assistant to the Attorney General Matthew F. McGuire, July 28, 1941 (4); Matthew F. McGuire to J. Edgar Hoover, Aug. 7, 1941 (7), 100-28126, *VM*. McGuire also informed Hoover that while Marcantonio's dossier included some "very reprehensible statements," they were made prior to passage of the Smith Act, which Hoover claimed made "the making of certain subversive statements a crime." On Marcantonio's Custodial Detention listing recommendation, see Hoover to Assistant to the Attorney General McGuire, Aug. 28, 1941 (8), 100-28126, *VM*. FBI documents also list the Hatch Act as authority

for investigating Marcantonio. See also John Bugas, SAC, Detroit to FBI Director, May 18, 1943 (16); Confidential Letter to FBI Director, June 14, 1943, cited in Memorandum, Anthony F. Ferentz, March 2, 1945 (26), pp. 83–84, 100-28126, *VM*.

21. Report on American Labor Party at Rome, N.Y., June 11, 1941 (1); Report on Communist Activities, American Labor Party, Rome, N.Y., Jan. 28, 1942 (3); Unrecorded Flyers of Progressive Committee to Rebuild the ALP; FBI Assistant Director P. E. Foxworth to FBI Director, Aug. 11, 1942 (7), 100-25869, *ALP*.

22. FBI Assistant Director P. E. Foxworth to FBI Director, Sept. 25, 1942 (12), 100-25869, *ALP*. See also Foxworth to FBI Director, Nov. 10, 1942 (13); E. E. Conroy, SAC, New York to FBI Director, May 21, 1943 (18); July 27, 1943 (24); and Aug. 9, 1943 (27), 100-25869, *ALP*.

23. S. W. Gerson, "The 1943 Primaries and General Elections," adopted by the New York State Committee, Communist Party, May 21, 1943 (32), 100-25869, *ALP*. The FBI had productive wiretaps on Communist Party national and state headquarters (NYT [New York Technical] 25), the West Side Workers' Center (NYT 111), and the National Maritime Union (NYT 52).

24. J. B. Wilcox, SAC, Albany to FBI Director, Feb. 14, 1944 (34); Hoover to SAC, Albany, Feb. 29, 1944 (34), 100-25869, *ALP*.

25. D. M. Ladd to Director, March 30, 1944 (38); Edw. A. Tamm to D. M. Ladd, July 11, 1944 (50), 100-25869, *ALP*. FBI agents either bugged or infiltrated the meeting of Communists and ALP leaders, which took place at the Cornish Arms Hotel; see SAC, New York to FBI Director, March 11, 1944 (49), *ALP*. See also SAC, New York to FBI Director, April 14, 1944 (42); E. E. Conroy, SAC, New York to FBI Director, April 6, 1944 (43); List of ALP State Committee (44); and John B. Little, SAC, Buffalo to FBI Director, May 5, 1944 (48), 100-25869, *ALP*. The bug was in the apartment of the secretary of the Buffalo CIO Industrial Union Council, and on April 27, 1944 it picked up Communist Party state secretary Gil Green's report. While Green indicated that the Communists were moving their best activists into the ALP, he also cautioned that they were "not out to capture" the ALP. "We must fight against any tendency . . . to feel that we are God's children. . . . Hillman said he wants . . . a united party, and it must be such, leading the fight for President Roosevelt." FBI officials focused on the Communist activity statements.

26. K. R. McIntyre to Mumford, Oct. 5, 1942 (12); Hoover to SAC, New York, June 23, 1943 (17), 100-28126, *VM*; see also E. E. Conroy, SAC, New York to FBI Director, Aug. 16, 1943 (35), 100-53054, *VM*. The first allegations about a secret apartment were made in April 1941; see Memorandum,

208   Kenneth Waltzer

Anthony F. Ferentz, March 2, 1945 (26), pp. 20, 22, 100-28126, *VM*. On FBI coverage of Marcantonio and Puerto Rican nationalist activities, see E. E. Conroy, SAC, New York to FBI Director, Feb. 22, 1943; Memorandum, Anthony F. Ferentz, March 2, 1945 (26), pp. 73–74, 79, 82–83, 110, 128; and A. H. Belmont to L. V. Boardman, March 2, 1954 (90), 100-28126, *VM*. A "confidential source" in the Peruvian Post Office also intercepted Marcantonio's mail to Mrs. Campos.

27. Hoover to SAC, New York, Nov. 29, 1944 (22); R. H. Cunningham to D. M. Ladd, Jan. 30, 1945 (25); Memorandum, Anthony F. Ferentz, March 2, 1945 (26), 100-28126, *VM*.

28. J. C. Strickland to D. M. Ladd, March 27, 1946 (58–59), 100-25869, *ALP*; Memorandas of Charles Heiner, July 8, 1946 (276); Nov. 5, 1946 (282), 100-8522, *ALP*; New York Teletype to FBI Director, Oct. 31, 1946 (60), 100-25869, *ALP*. See also Edward Scheidt, SAC, New York to FBI Director, Feb. 4, 1947 (61); Feb. 5, 1947 (62), 100-25869, *ALP*. The media assistance may have begun when FBI officials leaked information on the Communist meeting at the Cornish Arms Hotel in 1944 to the *New York World Telegram* and the *New York Herald-Tribune*. See SAC, New York to FBI Director, March 11, 1944 (49); Report, Herbert P. Carson, "Communist Infiltration into the ALP," Sept. 9, 1948 (79), p. 13, 100-25869, *ALP*.

29. Executive Order 9835 established the Loyalty Program, stipulating as one indication of disloyalty, membership in or association with groups designated on an Attorney General's list as "totalitarian, fascist, communist, or subversive." The FBI used this criterion to broaden the legal basis for its investigations of allegedly "subversive" organizations that might be included on the list and also to supply a body of data to be used in conducting name checks of federal employees and applicants. See *SDSR*, pp. 431–35. By early 1948, FBI field offices transmitted often outdated lists of ALP officers and club chairmen to headquarters for indexing: SAC, New York to FBI Director, Jan. 8, 1948 (66); Jan. 28, 1948 (67), 100-25869, *ALP*. FBI officials requested a full report on the ground "the Attorney General would be interested"; J. P. Coyne to D. M. Ladd, Jan. 31, 1948 (69); FBI Director to SAC, New York, Jan. 31, 1948 (66), 100-25869, *ALP*. On FBI designation of the ALP in investigative reports, see R. W. Wall to D. M. Ladd, April 26, 1948 (74); Executive Conference to the Director, May 5, 1948 (75), initialled "OK, H," 100-25869, *ALP*. Such information was set out even if the subject had severed all connection with the ALP. Report, Herbert P. Carson, "Communist Infiltration into the ALP," Sept. 9, 1948 (79); see also SAC, New York to FBI Director, Dec. 13, 1948 (80), 100-25869, *ALP*.

30. FBI officials ordered the New York and Washington Field Offices to report "all available information" on the People's Lobby. See FBI Director to SAC, New York, May 23, 1949 (94); SAC, New York to FBI Director, June 3, 1949 (94); FBI Director to Attorney General, June 3, 1949, (95); June 8, 1949 (107); Washington and New York Reports on People's Lobby, July 8, 1949 (104); July 20, 1949 (105), 100-25869, *ALP*. See also SAC, New York to FBI Director, Oct. 3, 1949 (108); Oct. 25, 1949 (109); Report on ALP, Jan. 25, 1950 (112); Edward Scheidt, Teletype to FBI Director, March 13, 1949 (87); FBI Director to Assistant Attorney General Alexander M. Campbell, March 29, 1949 (copy), 100-25869, *ALP*.

31. SAC, Albany to FBI Director, 5, 1949 (not recorded); FBI Director to SAC, Albany, Aug. 15, 1949 (not recorded); SAC, Albany to FBI Director, May 19, 1950 (114); FBI Director to SAC, Albany, June 1, 1950 (114), 100-25869, *ALP*. SAC, New York to FBI Director, April 15, 1949 (88); SAC, Albany to FBI Director, May 16, 1949 (90); SAC, New York to FBI Director, Nov. 21, 1949 (111), 100-25869, *ALP*. Minutes of the ALP Queens County Executive Committee, May 18, 1949 (779), 100-8522, *ALP*. SAC, New York to FBI Director, Jan. 11, 1950 (not recorded), 100-25869, *ALP*.

32. E. E. Conroy, SAC, New York to FBI Director, May 22, 1945 (122), 100-53054, *VM*; E. E. Conroy, SAC, New York to FBI Director, Sept. 11, 1947 (27); D. M. Ladd to FBI Director, Feb. 27, 1946 (30); J. C. Strickland to D. M. Ladd, Aug. 9, 1946 (30x1); FBI Director to Assistant Attorney General Peyton Ford, Memorandum on Vito Marcantonio, Oct. 8, 1948 (52), p. 304; Report by SA Clarence Porter, Nov. 25, 1950 (66), 100-28126, *VM*.

33. Hoover's refusal to release information on the Congressman does not mean, however, that the FBI did not provide Marcantonio's FBI file to Barker. FBI practice included hand-delivering declination letters to congressmen and congressional committees with the agent-messenger bringing along the requested file. Robert Barker to J. Edgar Hoover, Dec. 10, 1946 (37); Hoover to Barker, Dec. 13, 1946 (37); FBI Director to Attorney General, Dec. 13, 1946 (36); Report, Clarence Porter, Nov. 25, 1950 (66), 100-28126, *VM*.

34. FBI Director to SAC, New York, Feb. 7, 1947 (211), 100-53054, *VM*. Typescript, "Congressman Vito Marcantonio," Feb. 7, 1947 (40), 100-28126, *VM*. The FBI observed that early in 1948 Marcantonio had dinner one night with Silvermaster and his wife at the apartment of Elizabeth Sasuly; FBI Director to Assistant Attorney General Peyton Ford, Memorandum on Vito Marcantonio, Oct. 8, 1948 (52), p. 6; Report, Clarence Porter, Nov. 25, 1950 (66), p. 18, 100-28126, *VM*. On Silvermaster, see Earl Latham, *The Communist Controversy in Washington* (New York, 1966), p. 167; Allen Weinstein,

Perjury: The Hiss-Chambers Case (New York, 1978), pp. 9, 22–24.

35. D. M. Ladd to Fletcher, Aug. 2, 1948 (48); SAC, New York to FBI Director, Oct. 16, 1947 (45); FBI Director to SAC, New York, Oct. 28, 1947 (45); Report, Clarence Porter, Nov. 25, 1950 (66), pp. 17, 107; J. A. Sizoo, Memorandum on Surveillances of Senators and Congressmen, April 9, 1971 (not recorded), 100-28126, *VM*. See also Memorandum of A. H. Belmont, Oct. 25, 1947 (265); Edward Scheidt, SAC, New York to D. M. Ladd, Oct. 27, 1947 (266), 100-53054, *VM*.

36. Peyton Ford to J. Edgar Hoover, Sept. 3, 1948 (51); FBI Director to Assistant Attorney General Peyton Ford, Memorandum on Vito Marcantonio, Oct. 8, 1948 (52), 100-28126, *VM*. Indications are that similar information was requested and provided concerning Progressive Party vice-presidential candidate Senator Glen Taylor, Congressman Leo Isacson, elected by the ALP in a special by-election in February 1948, and Congressman Adam Clayton Powell, Jr. The FBI's Security Index and the Justice Department's Portfolio program are discussed in *SDSR*, pp. 436–42; Theoharis, "Truman Administration and the Decline of Civil Liberties," pp. 1016–20; and Theoharis, *Spying on Americans*, pp. 45–48. The FBI and Justice Department authorized far-reaching restrictions on civil liberties, anticipating *ex post facto* legislative approval in a national emergency.

37. *Congressional Record*, 81st Cong., 2d sess., 1950, pp. 9268–69; A. H. Belmont to D. M. Ladd, July 27, 1950 (58); FBI Director to SAC, New York, Aug. 18, 1950 (58); SAC, New York to FBI Director, FD-122, Nov. 25, 1950 (65); Report, Clarence Porter, Nov. 25, 1950 (66); 100-28126, *VM*. SAC, New York to FBI Director, April 16, 1951 (69) restored Marcantonio's key figure status.

38. SAC, Washington to FBI Director, May 21, 1951 (71); SAC, New York to FBI Director, May 17, 1951 (72); SAC, New York to FBI Director, June 6, 1951 (73); SAC, Washington to FBI Director, June 19, 1951 (74), 100-28126, *VM*. Actually, Winchell was wrong, and the FBI did not have to block Marcantonio's application for a passport. SAC, New York to FBI Director, March 5, 1951 (67); Report, Ralph Fishburn, Oct. 6, 1952 (83); L. B. Nichols to Tolson, Oct. 26, 1950, initialled "H," (not recorded); M. A. Jones to Nichols, Nov. 6, 1950 (64), Nov. 1, 1950 (64), 100-28126, *VM*. The *New York World Telegram* had charged that Marcantonio had met with unnamed persons in a midtown hotel to discuss a $100,000 offer to run for mayor in 1949. Marcantonio had filed suit, won, and been upheld on appeal. The case was headed for the Supreme Court. The FBI extensively reviewed its files but only set out limited public source materials. To do more, FBI officials concluded, would reveal confidential FBI sources.

39. SAC, New York to FBI Director, Aug. 1, 1950 (115), Aug. 15, 1950 (117), 100-25869, *ALP*; Report, Clarence Porter, Nov. 25, 1950 (66), 100-28126, *VM*; SAC, New York to FBI Director, June 8, 1951 (135); *New York World Telegram*, Sept. 6, 1950; Report on Communist Infiltration into the ALP, Jan. 22, 1952 (146), pp. 32–33, 100-25869, *ALP*. FBI agents interviewed twenty-four of twenty-six ALP congressional candidates, including Marcantonio. Most had filed reports showing no contributions or expenditures and most supported their statements. Joseph Martin, United States Assistant Attorney, declined to prosecute. See James McInerney, Assistant Attorney General to FBI Director, Aug. 14, 1951 (1); FBI to SAC, New York, Aug. 24, 1951 (1); Rosen to Ladd, Aug. 24, 1951 (2); FBI to SAC, New York, Aug. 31, 1951 (7); and Reports, Sept. 19, 1951 (9); Sept. 20, 1951 (8), 56-1033, *ALP*.

40. Survey Section, Intelligence Division to FBI Liaison Officer, Dec. 22, 1950 (123); A. H. Belmont to D. M. Ladd, Jan. 19, 1951 (127), 100-25869, *ALP*. Actually, the FBI disseminated information on the ALP in this case because the request came from "one of the best contacts of the Bureau at G-2." See V. P. Keay to A. H. Belmont, Jan. 26, 1951, 100-25869, *ALP*, initialled "H."

41. On the McCarran Act and the Supreme Court decision, see Robert Justin Goldstein, *Political Repression in Modern America* (Cambridge, Mass., 1978), pp. 322–24; Michal Belknap, *Cold War Political Justice* (Westport, 1977), pp. 136–43. ALP enrollment figures are in *Annual Reports of the New York City Board of Elections*. The ALP vote dropped even more sharply, from 509,559 (8.3 percent) statewide for Wallace in 1948 to 64,211 (0.9 percent) for Vincent Hallinan in 1952. See *New York State Red Book* (Albany, 1949, 1953).

42. On the scope of FBI Cominfil investigations, see *SDSR*, pp. 448–50. The Communists reacted to Cold War repression by purging Communist Party ranks and placing an added premium on the purity of Communist militancy. Their drive for self-purification spilled over into the ALP. See Starobin, *American Communism in Crisis*, pp. 195–203; Waltzer, "American Labor Party," pp. 434–35; and Charney, *A Long Journey*, pp. 110–11, 189–90.

43. In one instance, FBI agents attended an ALP affair, listened to Marcantonio attack the Supreme Court decision, and reported on a dinner skit concerning FBI surveillance. In another instance, Walter Winchell forwarded ALP material to Hoover. See Teletype, SAC, New York to FBI Director, June 5, 1951 (138); Winchell to FBI Director, May 21, 1951 (136), 100-25869, *ALP*. On FBI review of ALP nominating petitions, see Lee B. Wood to Morris Goldin, Sept. 15, 1954, ALP Papers, Series I (1954), C-Ed, Rutgers University. SAC, Buffalo to FBI Director, Jan. 27, 1951 (not recorded), a report on an ALP Upstate Conference in Albany, seems too detailed for a confidential informant report. On

FBI written refusal of authorization for a microphone surveillance on the ALP upstate office in Buffalo, see SAC, Buffalo to FBI Director, Feb. 24, 1951 (not recorded); FBI Director to SAC, Buffalo, March 2, 1951; SAC, Buffalo to FBI Director, March 31, 1951 (130); FBI Director to SAC, Buffalo, April 16, 1951 (130), 100-25869, *ALP*. Report on Communist Infiltration into the ALP, Jan. 22, 1952 (146), 100-25869, *ALP*. FBI reports regularly recorded the names of all ALP state and county officers, candidates, and club chairmen.

44. FBI Director to SAC, New York, Dec. 19, 1953 (152); Report on Communist Infiltration into the ALP, Feb. 20, 1953 (154), 100-25869, *ALP*. This latter report, a summary of FBI activities and confidential informant reports in 1952, was the first submitted to all armed forces intelligence agencies.

45. FBI activities upstate can be traced in the extensive Reports on Communist Infiltration into the ALP, Dec. 24, 1953 (164); Jan. 21, 1955 (202); June 20, 1955 (213); Oct. 15, 1955 (219); and June 28, 1956 (227), 100-25869, *ALP*. SAC, New York to FBI Director, Feb. 25, 1954 (166) indicates that FBI officials opened files on all ALP officers and activists. The spaghetti supper and seder are in (213) and (227). See also U.S., House of Representatives, Committee on Un-American Activities, *Hearings: Investigation of Communist Activities in the Albany, N.Y. Area*, 83rd Cong., 1st sess. (July 15–16, 1953), pp. 2488, 2501; 83rd Cong., 2d sess. (April 7–8, 1954), pp. 4300, 4320–21, 4356–57. John Patrick Charles and Emmanuel Ross Richardson were the two FBI informants.

46. Marcantonio and the *National Guardian's* conflict with the Communists began in 1950. See Report by SA Ralph Fishburn, Oct. 6, 1952 (83), pp. 4–9, 100-28126, *VM*. See also Cedric Belfrage and James Aronson, *Something to Guard* (New York, 1979), pp. 58–61. Report on Communist Infiltration into the ALP, Feb. 20, 1953 (154), p. 61, 100-25869, *ALP*; Report, Ralph Fishburn, June 4, 1953 (84), p. 4, 100-28126, *VM*; Report on Communist Infiltration into the ALP, Feb. 20, 1953 (154), pp. 67–70, 100-25869, *ALP*.

47. Report on Communist Infiltration into the ALP, Nov. 5, 1953 (159), pp. 7–8, 12–14, 100-25869, *ALP*; Report, Joseph Nally, May 6, 1954 (91), pp. 3–9, 100-28126, *VM*; Boardman, Air-Tel to Bureau, Oct. 30, 1953 (160), 100-25869, *ALP*.

48. New York, Teletype to Director, Nov. 4, 1953 (89); Report, Joseph Nally, May 6, 1954 (91), pp. 9–12; Report, James Fernan, Aug. 31, 1954 (92), 100-28126, *VM*; *New York Times*, Aug. 13, 1954, p. 36: SAC, New York to FBI Director, Aug. 31, 1954 (92); R. D. Cotter to C. D. Brennan, April 13, 1971 (not recorded), 100-28126, *VM*. See *Washington Post*, April 10, 1971.

49. SAC, New York to FBI Director, July 14, 1954 (172), p. 2; Report on

Communist Infiltration into the ALP, April 18, 1955 (210), 100-25869, *ALP*. By 1954, ALP enrollment statewide had fallen to 21, 885.

50. FBI Director to SAC, New York, Aug. 18, 1954 (177), 100-25869, *ALP*. See also FBI Director to SAC, New York, June 28, 1954 (169). Gilbert Levy, Chief, Counterintelligence Division to J. Edgar Hoover, July 21, 1954 (175); Hoover to Inspector General, Aug. 6, 1954 (175); SAC, New York to FBI Director, Sept. 10, 1954 (182); A. H. Belmont to L. V. Boardman, Sept. 30, 1954 (185), initialled "OK, H"; William F. Tompkins to FBI Director, Dec. 1, 1954 (197); FBI Director to Tompkins, Dec. 29, 1954 (197), 100-25869, *ALP*.

51. This individual, who shared information from his FBI file, has requested anonymity. On the shifted burden of proof under the Loyalty Program, see Athan Theoharis, "The Escalation of the Loyalty Program," in Barton J. Bernstein, *Politics and Policies of the Truman Administration* (Chicago, 1970), pp. 257–59.

52. David Caute, *The Great Fear: The Anti-Communist Purge under Truman and Eisenhower* (New York, 1978), p. 284; Ralph S. Brown, *Loyalty and Security* (New Haven, 1958), pp. 277–78.

53. See SAC, Albany to FBI Director, April 14, 1955 (not recorded); FBI Director to William F. Tompkins, Aug. 22, 1955 (214); SAC, Albany to FBI Director, Aug. 10, 1955 (214), 100 25869, *ALP*. Dennis Flinn, Director, Office of Security, Department of State, to Hoover, Aug. 1955 (215); SAC, New York to FBI Director, Sept. 1955 (217), 100-25869, *ALP*. Although ordered to index all names on the ALP petitions, the New York Field Office, in this instance, refused, arguing that it would place a heavy burden on manpower and that signatures on the petition would not establish membership in or affiliation with the ALP. William F. Tompkins to FBI Director, July 26, 1956 (229); SAC, New York to FBI Director, Oct. 8, 1956 (231); FBI Director to Tompkins, Oct. 23, 1956 (233); Report on Communist Infiltration into the ALP, Jan. 15, 1957 (237), 100-25869, *ALP*.

54. Given FBI record-keeping practices, this remains uncertain. Sanford Ungar (*FBI*, p. 198), observes that the field offices often undertook such surreptitious activities on their own, leaving behind no evidence. Released FBI files, though, suggest FBI leaders refrained from illegal methods.

55. FBI informants even gathered information on ALP members' legal strategies during appearances before the House Committee. See Report on Communist Infiltration into the ALP, June 20, 1955 (213), pp. 101–2, 100-25869, *ALP*.

56. See *IARA*, p. 148; Athan Theoharis, "Double-Entry Intelligence Files," *Nation* 22 (Oct. 22, 1977), pp. 393–94; and *HFBIO*, pp. 8–11, 14, 24. An FBI search of Hoover's Official and Confidential files failed to turn up anything on

Marcantonio. A congressional investigation, confirmed that Hoover had purged the files and that an unknown number of materials were destroyed in the year before and after his death.

57. J. P. Coyne to D. M. Ladd, Jan. 31, 1948 (69), 100-25869, *ALP*.

6

Weinstein, Hiss, and the Transformation of Historical Ambiguity into Cold War Verity

Victor Navasky

In the spring of 1978 the prestigious publishing house of Alfred E. Knopf published *Perjury: The Hiss-Chambers Case* by Allen Weinstein, a historian at Smith College. As *Time* magazine put it in a three-page feature article more than a month before the book's publication: "Weinstein turned up previously undisclosed evidence that inexorably led him to his unqualified verdict: 'The jurors made no mistake in finding Alger Hiss guilty as charged.' "[1]

Most reviewers in the popular press were persuaded. The conservative columnist George Will wrote in *Newsweek* that "the myth of Hiss's innocence suffers the death of a thousand cuts, delicate destruction by a scholar's scalpel." Alfred Kazin, the eminent literary critic, wrote in *Esquire*: "After this book, it is impossible to imagine anything new in this case except an admission by Alger Hiss that he has been lying for thirty years." Melvin Lasky, the editor of *Encounter*, wrote that "for now the guilt of Alger Hiss . . . may be taken as proven." ADA (Americans for Democratic Action) stalwarts Arthur Schlesinger, Jr., the liberal historian, and James Wechsler of the *New York Post*, and *National Review* editor William F. Buckley, Jr., all agreed. And Merle Miller wrote in the *Washington Post*: "I do not see how anybody can read Allen Weinstein's book and continue to believe in Alger's innocence, although a great many will."[2]

The book and its reception had significant political and cultural reverberations because of the nature of the Hiss case itself. As the philosopher Sidney Hook observed in *Encounter*, Hiss's partisans had "turned an issue of fact into one of symbolic allegiance."[3] Allen Weinstein made a variation of the same point himself in discussing what he called the "iconography" of the Cold War. In the public mind, Weinstein shrewdly suggested, Hiss was the retroactive beneficiary of Nixon's critical role in the case. "As anti-war sentiment converged with popular outrage over Watergate," he pointed out, "Hiss found himself transformed from a symbol of deception into one of injured innocence. Watergate and more responsive media brought Hiss, in short, a renewed measure of public acceptance. . . . Watergate helped create a new generation of believers in Hiss's innocence. The cultural verdict of the previous quarter century— indeed, the jury's verdict itself—was abruptly brought into question by Americans unfamiliar with the complex facts and history of the Case."[4] *Perjury*, presumably, would help reverse that process.

I think it is fair to say that not only Hiss's defenders but also many of his accusers have invested the dispute with ideological significance. And why not? At its origination there were reactionaries who wished to use the spy charges against Hiss to discredit the entire New Deal. And I would argue that there are still many center-liberal intellectuals whose base defense for their willingness to deny Communist Party members civil liberties during the Cold War years was the conviction of Hiss, which they viewed as establishing as fact that there indeed was an *internal* Communist espioinage menace; and that its existence mandated the incursion on civil liberties which some on the left denounce as Cold War repression. The whole affair had the effect of blurring the line between radical activism and involvement in espionage—at a time when both were believed to be subversive.

It is precisely because the Hiss case is fraught with such ideological baggage—the question of whether Hiss had lied when denying having engaged in espionage has contemporary implications far beyond the issue of his personal guilt or innocence—that the reception accorded *Perjury* makes such an ideal case study of the process I propose to discuss: the way in which historical ambiguities are converted by ideological dispute into political, even cultural, certainties. This process is more visible, and more dangerous, when it deals with issues related to national security, which so easily led themselves to an exaggerated and demonic image of the enemy—at least in part because information said to involve national security is routinely and systematically withheld by the state. Our need for certainty in periods of uncertainty such as the Cold War apparently feeds the popular culture's need to parade both the marginally guilty and the *arguably* innocent as "traitors," "spies," "agents of a foreign power." The matter is important since, more broadly framed, it has to do with the tension between our democratic commitment to openness and our national security need for partial secrecy.

My premise is that the accepted scholarly and journalistic conventions in the national security area, especially when the subject is espionage, are at war with the standards of evidence, precision, and disclosure that we insist on in virtually every other area of social policy. Our images of "spy rings," "Soviet agents," "the underground," are thus uniquely vulnerable to manipulation by those with hidden—or, for that matter, open—ideological agendas. My purpose here is simply to show how an account of even a thirty-year-old case lends itself to that process, and then to suggest some possible guidelines to help protect us against what George Orwell once called forged history.

Such an undertaking will require going over some territory covered elsewhere in this volume and of intrinsic interest only to close scholars of the case. I can think of no other way to make my point, however, and so with advance apologies I proceed.

Followers of the Hiss case have heard much about the Woodstock typewriter (Was it a forgery? Did Chambers have secret access to it? Was the machine at the trial the one that really typed the letters introduced in evidence?); the Bokhara rugs (What sort of secret agent would give four identical rugs as presents to his four most secret operatives?); the dispute over how well and for how long and under what names ("Carl," George Crosley," or "Karl") the Hisses knew Chambers, under what circumstances they met, and when and where, and whether Hiss gave Chambers an apartment, a car, and a loan—not to mention the State Department documents which would up on microfilm in a pumpkin on Chambers's farm? All of these matters came up at the two perjury trals and have been fought and refought in court appeals and in magazine articles and books which have been coming out sporadically for three decades.

But until *Perjury*, aside from cryptic and contradictory admissions from minor characters in the drama, we had heard nothing outside of Chambers's own memoir, *Witness*, to corroborate the basic outlines of his version of what he claimed were his six years in the Communist underground. Since Weinstein found no new witnesses who could directly implicate Hiss, he relied on the many people he tracked down and talked with and the many documents he consulted to corroborate Chambers's statements. Even though much of this mountain of research is only indirectly related to Hiss, a number of key interviews are the crux of his case. Weinstein's argument on the importance of these matters seems to be:

If Chambers told the truth about such matters as (1) J. Peters's and Colonel Boris Bykov's roles in the Communist underground, (2) how he was recruited into the Party by "Charles" (Sam) Krieger, (3) set up with literary agent Max Lieber an espionage front called the American Feature Writers Syndicate, and (4) how Paul Willert, an Oxford University Press editor, gave him translating work in *April 1938*, prior to the time he left the Party (the date is critical for reasons elaborated below)—if he was indeed telling the truth about all of these things, then it would be reasonable to assume that Chambers was telling the truth about Hiss.

As historian-detective, Weinstein appeared if not to have cracked the case, at least to have advanced it. He had tracked down and interviewed, among others, J. Peters (who had accepted voluntary deportation to Hungary in 1949); Sam Krieger (who according to Weinstein had returned to California after twenty years on the lam in the Soviet Union); Maxim Lieber (who had lived outside the United States for eighteen years before returning to Connecticut); and Paul Willert (now living in London, England, who "confirmed the essential elements in Chambers's account of their relationship,"[5] warning Chambers after his defection from the Party that a Comintern agent Willert had known in Berlin was after him).

Weinstein also was instrumental in forcing the release of two hundred thousand pages of background material on the case under the Freedom of Information Act, unearthing long-forgotten and apparently incriminating memoranda in the Hiss and other legal files, and interviewing in Munich, Germany, Karel Kaplan, a Czech historian and member of the 1968 Dubcek Commission which had investigated the political purge trials of the late Stalin era. Weinstein reported that Kaplan had read the long interrogations of Noel Field, and "according to Kaplan, Field named Alger Hiss as a fellow Communist underground agent in the State Department during the mid-Thirties."[6]

Nevertheless, I read *Perjury* with some skepticism and I should explain why.

In December of 1977 I had completed arrangements to start as editor of the *Nation* in February of 1978 and had retreated to upstate New York to work on a book that was tangentially related to the Hiss case—it focused on those who named names before congressional committees investigating Communist infiltration of the entertainment business. Because I was interested in the subject, because I had read Weinstein's previous writings on the case culminating in his *New York Review of Books* essay of April 1, 1976, which purported to catch Hiss in a lie, and because I believed that his book was going to be an important event in the political culture, I asked Elizabeth Pochoda, the *Nation*'s literary editor, if she could get me a set of advance galleys.

After a number of false starts (the publisher kept promising to ship them but they did not arrive), one day they appeared, and I quickly read *Perjury* with admiration for all of the new material Weinstein had brought to bear on the case, suspicion (because I did not believe the evidence he had compiled justified the conclusion he drew), and irritation. I set forth the causes of my irritation here in the interests of full disclosure and to reveal that I, too, did not approach the Hiss case without bias. (Indeed, in 1976 I had told a writer for *Harper's* that although I had never studied the case closely, it was my "impression" that Hiss was innocent.)[7]

First, the galleys had arrived without footnotes, making it impossible to tell where much of the new and critical data came from. (I immediately requested a copy of the chapter notes, but these did not arrive until quite close to publication date—too late for most reviewers to have done anything with them, but after much of the initial publicity had appeared.) Second, although the tone and posture of the narrative implied unbiased scholarship, the presentation of some of the most critical material in the case seemed slanted in such a way as to make it difficult for readers to draw their own conclusions.

An example is Weinstein's handling of the extremely important matter of the date on which Chambers quit the Communist Party (CP). As Weinstein himself pointed out in *The American Scholar* in 1971,[8] that date is critical because the papers Chambers produced in November of 1948, allegedly from Hiss, were all dated between January and April of 1938. If Chambers quit the Party in 1937, as he stated under oath on at least sixteen separate occasions, then his story is seriously compromised. It was only after he produced the apparently incriminating papers at least ten years after he allegedly received them, and then during his testimony during the Hiss trial in the summer of 1949, that he "remembered" leaving the Party in April 1938.

But Weinstein asserts in his introduction that Chambers was given some translating work "prior to [his] break with the CP in April 1938." The date is mentioned again, on page 5, when Weinstein describes Chambers in the House Un-American Activities Committee (HUAC) witness chair: "After defecting in 1938, Chambers asserted, he had 'lived in hiding, sleeping by day and watching through the night with gun and revolver. . . .' " But if he had not intruded as narrator, Weinstein would have had to cite Chambers as saying he left the Party in 1937, which was Chambers's story at the time, and which he repeated in numerous subsequent appearances the same month. Throughout the book we encounter similar entries: "When Chambers defected in April 1938 he took with him evidence. . . ." When Weinstein does mention the discrepancy in dates he says, "More than a decade had passed since his described friendship with the Hisses, and Chambers later admitted inaccuracies in his original August 3 testimony. . . . Thus . . . his defection from Communism came in 1938 rather than in '37."[9] But these were not "*admissions*" (emphasis added). They were adjustments, essential to the credibility of Chambers's tale, and it seemed to me Weinstein should have let the reader in on the grand dimensions of Chambers's conflicting court, HUAC, and FBI statements right at the outset.

Third, I had a more personal reason for irritation, which I hoped would not influence my judgment although it did (and properly, I would argue) raise my suspicion: Some years earlier I had been shown a copy of Professor Weinstein's letter to the Justice Department requesting access to materials on the Rosenberg case. In that letter he assured the Attorney General that, unlike some other writers whom he proceeded to name with quite reckless abandon, he believed the Rosenbergs guilty.[10] I say "reckless" because I was one of the writers he named (although his reference to me was syntactically ambiguous), despite the fact that at the time I had written nothing about my views on the Rosenbergs' innocence or guilt.

Finally, I confess to being irritated by the image Weinstein was presenting in advance publicity for the book as truth-seeking scholar who had traveled 125,000 miles, pored over hundreds of thousands of documents, studied hundreds of thousands of pages of hearings and trial records, gone through interview after interview and archive after archive, and had been forced by the weight of the evidence to reverse his initial belief in Hiss's innocence. I had read Weinstein's previous writings on the case: a paper delivered at the American Historical Association (1969), a book, and articles in *The American Scholar* (1971), *Commentary* (1970), *Esquire (1975), the New York Times* (1976), and the *New York Review of Books* (1976). And even though in 1978 he told the editor of the *Daily Hampshire Gazette* (Northhampton, Massachusetts) in a front-page interview that in 1974 he had co-authored a high-school textbook, *Freedom and Crisis, An American History*, "which concluded that Hiss was innocent,"[11] a close reading of the chapter on the case fails to reveal any such conclusion (although in fairness it should be pointed out that in a number of his early articles he raises real questions about Chambers's reliability).

I should add here that my suspicions were retrospectively strengthened when I received from the Hoover Institution, in response to a request for materials related to the papers of Herbert Solow (a minor figure in *Perjury* on whom Weinstein places considerable reliance), copies of correspondence from Weinstein to Solow's widow. In a letter dated July 30, 1975, in the course of explaining to Solow's widow why he was undertaking to write about the case in advance of publication of his book, Weinstein wrote: "The point of doing these articles, apart from a keen sense I have that they *should* be done even before the book comes out, was to deflect attention from the inevitable Hiss defense potboilers which will doubtless begin appearing this fall in the wake of Hiss's renewed efforts to prove his innocence."[12] On March 16, 1976 he again wrote Mrs. Solow, this time with a recommendation: "Not because I anticipate any problems but simply because there is the *possibility* that someone close to Hiss might ask to use this file (against your wishes, I assume), you might want to consider removing the folder marked Hiss-Chambers case or Hiss Case from Herbert's files."[13]

As a result of these various factors, and after consultation with colleagues in and around the *Nation*, I resolved to conduct an elementary source check with some of Weinstein's more spectacular interview-finds, to see whether they were quoted accurately and in context, and to examine some of the key documents he cited. With the help of the *Nation*'s staff and network[14] I located and wrote to seven of his key sources; in addition, I secured copies of documents from the State Department and the Hoover Institution, as well as Freedom of Information Act documents from the FBI and the Hiss archive maintained by the National Emergency Civil Liberties Committee. I also contacted Alger Hiss's brother Donald, since when one pre-publication interviewer asked, "Would you say you made any discovery that clinches the case against Hiss?" Weinstein zeroed in on the role of Donald Hiss "and what he called the real 'Woodstock coverup.' "[15] It was unclear from the text of *Perjury* just what Donald Hiss had and hadn't told Weinstein.

Six of the seven sources responded,[16] and each answered in a way which in my perhaps biased judgment cast serious doubt on the reliability of *Perjury*'s findings. Each of the six claimed he was misquoted or misunderstood, but it is not uncommon for a subject to disown even the most accurate verbatim reportage once he sees what he said in cold print, especially when it is used in a way which compromises or embarrasses a cause or a friend. Most revealing about the pattern of the six responses was that, with only one exception,[17] while each source freely conceded that part of what Weinstein reported was true, that which each denied having said, turned out on close inspection to have been contained in Whittaker Chambers's autobiography *Witness*, in Chambers's testimony, or in FBI interviews with Chambers. Thus I concluded that Weinstein had, in a number of instances, transposed *Witness* from the first to the third person and that much more of *Perjury* than one might deduce from the text or the footnotes drew on Chambers himself. (Frequently there is one footnote cited at the end of a paragraph which lists a half-dozen sources, leaving the reader in a quandary as to which fact or quote came from what source.) If I was right, I had identified a narrative method which gives us Chambers's version of events, sometimes in his own voice, sometimes in Weinstein's voice, and sometimes imputed to other characters in the drama, without one ever being quite sure which is which—and, lacking the sources, having no way of knowing. This, I argued, added up to a psychological structure that lent Chambers a perhaps undeserved credibility. Chambers, it seemed to me, was being used to corroborate Chambers—and in ways which were often invisible to the reader.

After I published the results of my mini-survey in the *Nation*, Weinstein told the press that if I had contacted him he would have invited me to examine the material in his archive proving he cited all six accurately. "Three of the six interviewees who have recanted their stories—Maxim Lieber, Karel Kaplan, and Sam Krieger—are on tape,"[18] he wrote. My view was that the 674-page *Perjury*, with all of its footnotes, should have been able to survive a minimal fact check without *ex parte* communications from the author, but perhaps he was right. In any event, when I later tried to examine his material, as I detail later in this essay, he retracted his offer. Here, however, let me illustrate the nature of the questions raised by discussing the three "recanters" who are on tape, so that when and if the tapes become available, there can be no dispute about where the truth lies.

Karel Kaplan: In a front-page review of *Perjury* in the *New York Times Book Review*, Irving Howe wrote that Weinstein adds "substantial material" regarding Hiss's involvement in the Communist underground. "And perhaps most striking," he added, is the material that comes from Weinstein's interview with the Czech historian Karel Kaplan concerning Hiss's relationship with Noel Field, "a confessed Soviet agent."[19] According to Weinstein, Kaplan had left Czechoslovakia in 1976 with a significant archive collected during his eight years as archivist from the Czech Communist Party's Central Committee, and had served on the 1968 Dubcek Commission that investigated the political purge trials of the late Stalin era in which Noel Field figured prominently. Kaplan said he had read the long interrogations of both Noel and Herta Field by Czech and Hungarian security officials, and he shared his findings with Weinstein in Munich, where "he described to me the material in those files that dealt with Alger Hiss."[20]

In *Perjury* Weinstein quotes Kaplan as having told him: " 'Field said that he had been involved [while at the State Department] and that Hiss was the other one involved' after he joined the Department. One major reason Field gave to his interrogators for not having returned to the United States in 1948 was to avoid testifying in the Hiss-Chambers case."[21]

Weinstein does not reprint the moving two-page private letter Field wrote Hiss after getting out of prison and reading Hiss's book *In the Court of Public Opinion*. In the letter (of whose existence Weinstein was aware, since he cites it[22]) Field offered to provide an affidavit attesting to the falseness of the evidence implicating Hiss (as it related to Field) and expresses his belief in Hiss's account.

I wrote to Kaplan, now employed with Radio Free Europe in Munich to ascertain whether he had cited evidence supporting Weinstein's claim that Hiss and Field had been engaged in espionage on behalf of the Soviet Union, In response, Kaplan wrote: "N. Field testimony, as far as I can remember, did not contain any facts or explicit statements which would indicate that A. Hiss was delivering U.S. documents to the Soviet Union."[23]

The gist of Weinstein's response to this revision of his claimed evidence was: At his key meeting with Kaplan in Munich in 1977 he was "accompanied by another American professor, an Italian journalist and a translator. All of those present heard Kaplan describe Czech and Hungarian secret police interrogations of Noel Fields [*sic*]," in which Field said Hiss was "the other one involved," and, says Weinstein, Kaplan even wrote it up in the Italian magazine *Panorama*.[24]

I discovered that David Kennedy was the other American historian present at this interview with Kaplan. (Kennedy is a specialist in twentieth-century history and is on the faculty of Stanford University.) What Weinstein neglected to mention and what Kennedy told me is that (a) Kaplan showed them no documentation to back up his claims; (b) in any event they had no way of authenticating Czech documents; (c) the Italian journalist, an editor of *Panorama*, ghost-wrote part of Kaplan's article; (d) it was unclear from the article when Kaplan was reporting what he remembered from Noel Field's interrogation and when he was simply citing Hede Massing's book *This Deception* as his authority; and

(e) "The whole encounter with Kaplan was troubling. I told Allen I was very surprised he used any of it in his book."[25]

Maxim Lieber: Lieber is the man Weinstein cites sixteen times "confirming" or "corroborating" or "participating in" underground work with Chambers, a "participant in Soviet intelligence work in the United States and Europe during the 1930s."[26] Lieber is Chambers's one-time friend, business associate, and literary agent, and currently resides in Connecticut after having spent the years 1950–68 first in Mexico and then in Poland, a refugee from the domestic Cold War who left the United States after Chambers's headlined charges before HUAC in 1948 and 1949 that he had been a Communist spy.

Weinstein calls Lieber a "sometime associate [of Chambers] in the underground," and says Lieber identified Peters as "the head of the whole Communist espionage apparatus in this country,"[27] and "worked with [Chambers] for a time on an underground project." Weinstein writes that "convincing corroboration of Peters' work as an agent during the 1930s came from . . . my interviews with Maxim Lieber, whom Peters assigned to occasional underground jobs." He describes Lieber's role in the American Feature Writers Syndicate as that of an "agent" engaged in "espionage abroad," a "front for Soviet espionage." Weinstein says Lieber gave Colonel Boris Bykov ("the chief agent for Russian military intelligence in the United States during the late 1930s") "low marks" as a spy-master. Weinstein credits Lieber with warning Chambers, who at the time believed the KGB was after him, about another client of Lieber's. He quotes Lieber as saying, "Some things are romanticized in *Witness*, but most of it—as I know of the incidents—is true."[28]

However, as I wrote in the *Nation* in April 1978, when I talked with Lieber, who freely admits to having been in the Communist party and who represented Party authors, among others, he told me: (a) "I never read *Witness*—Weinstein [who showed him a portion of the text and asked if it was accurate] is quoting me out of context" (Lieber asked if he could borrow the office copy); (b) "I was never a member of any underground and I never worked with Chambers on any underground project"; (c) Weinstein's "account of the American Feature Writers Syndicate (which was designed to sell the works of my clients such as Erskin Caldwell and Josephine Herbst overseas, and was not an underground project

Victor Navasky

at all), is an amalgam of a little truth and a lot of fiction—I don't know where Weinstein got that stuff unless it is in *Witness*—but it did not come from me, which is what he makes it sound like"; and (d) "I could not have identified Peters as the head of the underground because I knew nothing of the underground. I only met him once at the very end. . . . I never met or saw Priscilla or Alger Hiss or even knew about them until the trial. Weinstein's story is sheer poppycock. My son says I should consult a lawyer."

After I reported these remarks in the *Nation*, Weinstein speculated that Lieber, along with other recanters, might be claiming to have been misquoted because he disagreed with Weinstein's conclusions. After all, Lieber had told a reporter for the *Washington Post* on April 6: "I may have said things [to Weinstein] I wouldn't have said under different circumstances."[29] Perhaps Weinstein is right, although under normal circumstances one would assume that faced with such direct repudiations the cautious and maybe even the correct thing to do would be to reinterview his subjects, some of whom were born around the turn of the century, to make certain, whatever may be on tape, that one had not relied too heavily on or misinterpreted possibly unreliable sources.

Sam Krieger: Weinstein traveled to Rohnert Park, California, to interview the late Sam Krieger, the man who recruited Chambers into the Communist Party and, according to *Perjury*, "an important Communist organizer during the Gastonia textile strike of 1929," who "fled to the Soviet Union"[30] during the 1930s before returning to California where he now lived in retirement. *Perjury* also revealed that Krieger took Chambers to his first Communist Party meeting, whereupon he immediately signed up, and shortly thereafter joined the radical labor union, Industrial Workers of the World.

But when I sent Mr. Krieger copies of the pages in Weinstein's book concerning him, he replied, "No, Weinstein's account does *not* correspond with what I told him, nor did I tell Weinstein, in our interview, that I was the Clarence Miller of the Gastonia, N.C., Textile strike, who subsequently fled to the Soviet Union."[31]

All of this and more I published in the *Nation*, and not long after Weinstein responded in the *New Republic*. Here is Weinstein on Krieger:

He too is on tape, and his words are also quoted verbatim where they appear in *Perjury*, from two interviews in 1974. Krieger denies having told me that he posed as Clarence Miller during the Gastonia, North Carolina textile strike and later fled to the Soviet Union. I never say in the book that *he* told me that. I learned these crucial facts from FBI documents and from conversations with two people who had been contacted by an emigre Russian woman whose mother had lived with "Clarence Miller" in the Soviet Union during the 1930s. In 1975 this woman visited Krieger and identified him as Clarence Miller.[32]

Two things happened as a result of Weinstein's response. First, because he went beyond the evidence of his book in his identification of Miller, but also because on the "Today" show and on radio and television shows throughout the country he was inviting "Navasky and Alger Hiss and anyone else they want to bring along" to hear his tapes and inspect his files, I decided to take him up on his offer. And second, Krieger, who resented being mistaken for the fugitive from a murder rap in Gastonia, North Carolina, sued Weinstein, his publisher, and the *New Republic*.

Krieger won a settlement in his lawsuit of $17,500 and an apology, which appeared in the *New Republic*. In it Weinstein admitted that his statements about Krieger "were erroneous," that although Krieger did use the name "Clarence Miller" as a pseudonym in the Communist Party he was not in any way the Clarence Miller who was involved in Gastonia, nor did he later flee to the USSR, nor did the emigre Russian woman identify him. "I regret any distress caused Mr. Krieger by this misidentification," Weinstein wrote, "and by the mistakes in *The New Republic* article quoted above."[33] (The *New Republic* added that it "also regrets any distress caused Mr. Krieger by this misidentification.")

The chronology of my attempt to see Weinstein's files, excerpted from the *Nation*, speaks for itself and is included as an appendix to this essay. The bottom line is that Weinstein's invitation to inspect his files was withdrawn, and on April 30, 1978 I was informed that they would be deposited "later this year at [the] Truman Library."[34] (As of three and a half years later the relevant tapes and files still had not been deposited.)

Many reviewers were not persuaded by the doubts my own ad hoc research cast on Weinstein's monumental research. I myself still have questions about the full meaning of much that we uncovered. I think it worth noting, however, that many of the eminent older reviewers who hailed Weinstein's book as settling the case were already on record as believing in Hiss's guilt before *Perjury* was published, and to that extent the book may have confirmed previous opinion rather than changed minds.[35] (Since that may also be true of the reviewers initially more sympathetic to Hiss, such as myself, I'm not sure what it proves other than the need to improve the level of literary discourse and the difficulty men have in adjusting deeply held ideological and symbolically critical opinions.)

Weinstein's response to my research was to denounce the "recanters." Other critics, as diverse as William F. Buckley, Jr., Sidney Hook, and Murray Kempton, have claimed that even if I were right on all the particulars these facts didn't go to the essence, the center of the question.[36] The difficulty, of course, is that in matters of espionage, information is always released selectively, is frequently at three removes, and involves anonymous informants, double agents, the dead, the defected, the disappeared, the disinformed. In such circumstances there may *be* no single heart of the matter, certainly no discoverable heart, other than the credibility of the principals.

Nevertheless, by way of example, let me discuss an issue which a number of reviewers and commentators on the Hiss case and the Weinstein book have found to be central to the case and which the *New York Times* featured on its front page:[37] the charge that the Hisses knew where the missing typewriter was for two months, but kept this fact hidden from the FBI and a Hiss lawyer until the FBI was about to discover the typewriter on its own.[38]

The columnist Garry Wills, writing in the *New York Review of Books*, found Weinstein's "new" evidence on this point persuasive: "Weinstein's discovery is important not only or mainly because it destroys most popular theories of conspiracy against Hiss, but because it shows Hiss had reason to know those theories were flawed through all the years he has been promoting and espousing them."[39]

But my own reading was that Weinstein never adequately presented Donald Hiss's version of the episode. And when I wrote Donald Hiss to ask if Weinstein had accurately reported his own explanation for the "mysterious pause" of two months he replied:

Mr. Weinstein had exactly one interview with me. . . . Weinstein raised three subjects and only three during the interview. . . . He made no mention whatsoever of the typewriter or my search with Mike Catlett for it. [He] asked if I would be available to answer any further questions should they occur to him. To this I answered that I would be available at any time. He has never contacted me by mail or telephone since then. The interview was extremely brief and lasted no more than 10 to 15 minutes.[40]

Weinstein had responded in the *New Republic*: "I discussed Donald Hiss's version of the hunt for the Woodstock typewriter with him at great length." Weinstein further claimed to have covered the full story of the typewriter search in *Perjury*, adding "When I interviewed Donald Hiss in 1975, I still had not pieced together the full story of the cover-up, but it seems unlikely in any event, that he would then, or later, acknowledge his complicity. Apparently he has decided not to do so."[41]

Weinstein is not, of course, required to believe Alger Hiss's brother, but one would think he ought to have heard Donald's version before dismissing it, and in the absence of his having done so, I think it difficult to accept with equanimity the notion that this was the "lie" which "clinched" the case against Hiss.

Consider the related information—which the *New York Times* found sufficiently incriminating to feature on its front page—that memoranda in the Hiss defense files proved that "Alger Hiss lied."[42] According to Weinstein, "a defense lawyer, John F. Davis, on December 28, 1948, wrote the chief defense counsel that Alger Hiss asked him earlier that month to check on an old typewriter which he remembers he gave to Pat, the son of Claudia Catlett who used to do the washing."

This means, Mr. Weinstein asserts, that "Hiss deliberately misled the FBI, the Grand Jury and two trial juries about his knowledge of the Woodstock Typewriter's whereabouts." He adds that "Mr. Hiss three times between December 10 and 15 told the Grand Jury that he had no knowledge of how the typewriter had been disposed of."[43] This obviously impressed even the most knowledgeable of reviewers. Garry Wills, for example, refers to the fact that "Hiss called John F. Davis . . . and said he had given the Woodstock to Mrs. Catlett's son. Yet three days later he suffered another spell of forgetfulness, this time under oath, and told the grand jury that he had no idea where the typewriter was."[44]

A reading of the Davis memorandum, a search through the Hiss files, and a perusal of the correspondence that followed the Weinstein article in the *New York Review of Books*[45] reveals that Weinstein has reached a possible but surely not a necessary conclusion, and further that he did not share in an accessible way the available contrary evidence necessary for an independent judgment. First, the Davis document is, on its face, ambiguous. It refers to "an" old typewriter, not "the" old typewriter. Second, Weinstein doesn't mention in the text other evidence that suggests that it was not Hiss who recalled the machine at all but his stepson Timothy Hobson, and that Hiss merely relayed the message to counsel. In that context, asking counsel to "check on" something seems as much evidence of uncertainty as certainty. Finally, Weinstein doesn't clearly set forth the fact that other Hiss legal memoranda document four simultaneous typewriter searches for three typewriters. If Hiss really knew where the typewriter was all along, and if he knew which of his old typewriters the FBI was seeking, why would he waste his lawyers' and everybody else's time carrying on these simultaneous searches?

Thus the average intelligent reader or reviewer, not having been alerted in a systematic way to the key disputes in the already complicated case, is at something of a disadvantage in trying to decode, interpret, and understand the significant issues and evidence.

The specialist fares little better, given Weinstein's troublesome footnoting system. And in this insufficient citing of sources Weinstein is not alone. Sometimes, as in the bizarre case of J. Peters, Weinstein's footnotes lead one to secondary sources with even fewer adequate footnotes. For example, much was made on the book jacket and in advance publicity of Weinstein having tracked down and interviewed J. Peters, whom Weinstein describes, despite Peters' "pro forma denials," as "the head of the whole Communist espionage apparatus in this country," a "Soviet agent." Aside from the fact that there is only one substantive reference in *Perjury* to what he learned from Peters.[46]

Weinstein cited David Dallin's account in *Soviet Espionage* (New Haven, 1955) to help document his frightening description of Peters as:

Indefatigable . . . an outstanding leader, man of many aliases and a multitude of clandestine assignments, who remained at his American post from 1933 to 1941. His era was marked by great exploits. . . . [He was] the most active, energetic, and resourceful man in those obscure depths of the underground where Soviet espionage borders on American communism.

A nice definitive passage, but *it* was unfootnoted. When I finally located Dallin's papers—they were not deposited at Yale University, which is where he said in *Soviet Espionage* he was going to put them, but rather at the New York Public Library[47]—it turned out that no papers exist with reference to the page (412) in question. What papers are there make clear that Dallin's chief source for most of his unfootnoted passages was Whittaker Chambers. So once again, all roads appear to lead to Chambers corroborating Chambers.

To all my arguments it might be objected that I am merely restating why I disagree with Weinstein, that my points are mostly nitpicks and prove nothing. However, the fact that I wrote my critique and pointed to whatever defects there might be in *Perjury*'s presentation is what the business of the marketplace of ideas is all about; scholars can, as Weinstein himself has suggested, weigh my claims against his book and decide for themselves. So why all the fuss?

I was able to raise the questions I raised only because, as editor of the *Nation*, I had the luxury of a secretary, a Xerox machine, a staff, and a network of informed colleagues to help. Most reviewers lack such resources. And even with them I couldn't begin in two months to check out seven years' worth of research. Thus those who dismiss my preliminary probe on the grounds that it didn't deal with some mythical "heart of the matter" seem to me to miss the point, which has less to do with Weinstein than with the difficulty of pinning down any of the essential facts in cases like this, and the consequent danger that ideology rather than evidence will determine questions asked about facts.

Even an informed observer like Murray Kempton (who, although long on record as having believed Hiss guilty,[48] was also on record as respecting his character) seems to me not immune from the syndrome. "There *is* one central mystery in the Hiss case," wrote Kempton, which is almost never mentioned by either side.[49]

The mystery: the forgotten international incident of the Robinson-Rubens case. Kempton accepts Weinstein's summary, which he describes as brief but "exemplary": "Robinson was a Soviet agent in the United States who was recalled to Moscow during the 1938 purges. He took along his wife [Rubens] who was an American citizen." In Kempton-Weinstein's version, Robinson was arrested, and his wife went

to the American embassy and asked for its help. Our embassy sent some
cables to Washington asking how far it ought to go to help, and a copy of
one of the cables was among the handwritten documents that Chambers
produced as evidence against Hiss ten years later. Kempton notes:

> Hiss did not remember writing it or manage to think of any reason why he should
> have; it had no connection with any of his official duties in the State Depart-
> ment. What he wrote then came into the hands of Whittaker Chambers who by
> his account duly transmitted a copy of it to Moscow. I'm sorry, but I can't think of
> any way for Chambers to have gotten it except that Hiss gave it to him.

A few weeks later, Kempton—Weinstein's version continues, Robinson's wife was arrested in Moscow. The American embassy (the message suggested) was disinclined to intervene and

> since nothing except an American protest could remotely inconvenience the
> GPU in any plan to do away with her, it could only be a source of comfort to the
> Soviet police to know that America didn't much care.
> Again I'm sorry; but Alger Hiss ought to have thought a long while before de-
> ciding that he couldn't say how he happened to copy that telegram. No more than
> anyone in Washington had he given much evidence of deep sympathy for Stalin's
> victims. And absent such concern, and the slightest indication that the Robin-
> son-Rubens case had anything to do with his job, of what interest could the case
> be to him?
> I have to say, until there is some real effort to persuade me otherwise, that I
> cannot but believe that he helped and probably knew he helped assure the
> Russian police that they need not worry that a comparatively innocent woman in
> their custody might have friends to help her.

Never mind that Chambers gave scores of statements to the FBI over a
nine-year period (from 1939 to 1948) without once ever mentioning the
Robinson-Rubens case; never mind that the documents Weinstein obtained from the State Department indicate that Robinson himself was a
mystery man; never mind that his wife never asked the State Department for help.

The important fact, although one wouldn't know it from Weinstein's
telling (aptly summarized by Kempton), is that Hiss claimed that his
State Department duties and his practice of briefing his superior, Assistant Secretary of State Francis Sayre, accounted for the handwritten

note in question. All the reports at issue were distributed to Hiss in Sayre's office at State; in 1937 and 1938 the Robinson-Rubens case was a front-page sensation throughout the world and, as the first serious contretemps between the two nations since the 1933 signing of the Roosevelt-Litvinov agreements, was naturally of concern to every senior State Department official (Sayre was one of six). Moreover, Sayre, who was out of the country at the time of the first Hiss trial, testified at the second trial as a defense witness and fully corroborated Hiss's testimony about his practice of making handwritten summaries of material that came into their office in order to brief his superior on a day-to-day basis.

In other words, the Robinson-Rubens case, like all the other "central mysteries" of the Chambers-Hiss case, comes down to who-do-you-believe—Hiss or Chambers? The mystery of how Chambers got Hiss's handwritten note is no deeper than the mystery of how he got documents typed on Hiss's Woodstock typewriter. Did Hiss give it to him? Was it forged, leaked, stolen by someone else? Does it make a difference that security regulations at the State Department in 1938 were lax and that testimony in both Hiss trials established that Hiss's practice was to discard his briefing notes after they had served their purpose? Was it a coincidence that State cleared its non-vital files every ten years after the fact? Did Chambers come into possession of these documents in 1938, as he belatedly maintained, or in 1948, as the Hiss team originally maintained in their motion for a new trial?

If my assessment is accurate, then the image *Perjury* puts forth of Hiss as "traitor," as "Soviet agent," should at a minimum yield to the underlying reality of persistent ambiguity. But in the short run—and remember, when *Perjury* came out Hiss was seventy-three years old and had been preparing for three years a *coram nobis* petition, filed July 1978, to set aside the verdict in his case—that's not what happened. Many otherwise informed readers and reviewers accepted the Weinstein presentation as closing the issue. The late historian Fawn Brodie, for example, wrote her posthumously published meditation on Richard Nixon on the premise that the message of *Perjury* was definitive.[50]

Thus the picture of the obligatory Cold War enemy, the "agent of a foreign power," saturated the popular culture, virtually obliterating the more elusive possibility that the case was still in intellectual limbo.

But the Hiss-Chambers case is only one illustration of how the popular culture can opt against the unknown in favor of a sensationalized set of images of the enemy calculated to heat up the political atmosphere. We live in a time when front-page stories, headlines, docudramas, documentaries, novels, and movies, as well as allegations from the highest and best places about moles, spies, disinformation, secret wars, double and triple agents, and fourth and fifth men, seem to have mingled and escalated beyond calculation, with what consequences to our true national security we cannot begin to know. Such mystification of the "enemy" can only undermine our ability to understand and learn from the mistakes of past, no less to deal with the realities of the present. And since an open society by definition has a special obligation to audit not merely its suspects, but also its least open agencies and agents—its secret police and intelligence operations, lest they constitute as well as catch, the enemy within—it seems critical that we begin to consider ways to demystify the imagery of espionage, of dirty tricks, of codes and legends, and ultimately of national security itself. Only by demystifying the technology and personnel of national security can we hope to preserve it. And imbedded in the *Perjury* episode there seem to be a number of clues on how to go about it.

First, the trade publishing practice of circulating noteless galleys to reviewers where documentation is essential, if not "the heart of the matter," ought to be carefully scrutinized. Perhaps reviewers themselves could refuse to review, insist on proper notations and citations as a condition for proceeding, or punish the purveyors of such damaging goods in print. I do not contend that *many* reviewers would be ready, willing, and able to undertake the sort of fact check the *Nation* was able to launch with respect to *Perjury*, but the opportunity ought to be there. In its absence, an undocumented myth may be given too much benefit of the doubt, with unfortunate consequences for the political culture.

Second, we need a vocabulary of national security. Somebody ought to publish a lexicon, a dictionary of proper national security usage. One of the problems with *Perjury* is that "the underground" and "the secret underground," "secret work" and "party work," and "cell" and "espionage" appear to be used interchangeably and without definition. Confusion among and between the meanings of these various realms is, in my view, the most probable explanation for the Weinstein-Maxim Lieber misunderstanding. Whether or not I am right, such loose usage, by no means confined to Weinstein, is pervasive, permitting and perhaps even encouraging deception.

Third, although there is probably no less propitious moment than the present to propose adding to the budget of the administrators of the Freedom of Information Act, if the Act is to serve its purpose in the national security area, if scholars, researchers, and journalists are to learn from each other's work, a new system of accessibility has to be devised. Many of Weinstein's most critical citations were to "blind" or obscure FBI and other files whose whereabouts would be unknown and unavailable to most readers and reviewers. As it is, many books and studies that deal with the intelligence agencies are impenetrable because citations are to file numbers which refer to FBI or other files, available only in Washington or in esoteric field offices. There ought to be an amendment to the law, establishing a central national security data bank. Once this sort of vital information is made public under the Feedom of Information Act, it ought to go into a data bank which is accessible and available to all.

Fourth, it seemed to me to be a real methodological limitation of *Perjury* that its author failed to confront a single one of the principals with the evidence against them. Having concluded that Alger Hiss and Donald Hiss had lied, and having reported some malicious gossip suggesting that Priscilla Hiss said she was "sick of all the lies and cover-ups,"[51] a traditional investigative journalist would have confronted the accused with the evidence and elicited and evaluated the response. Investigative journalists and historians have something to teach each other. Academic and other institutions should bring them together in a skills exchange program. Interested historians could be trained in the methods of investigative journalism, and selected journalists could be taught the reasons for and conventions of scholarly research. Nowhere might the benefits be greater than in the coverage of national security affairs, where archives remain sealed and key documents are routinely not released until more than a generation after the fact.

Fifth, publishers ought seriously to consider submitting manuscripts of books like *Perjury* to specialists on either side of the fence from the author. I suggested in the *Nation* that Weinstein might have been better served had his publisher gotten someone like William A. Reuben or Fred Cook, both Hiss partisans but also each extremely knowledgeable about the case, to vet his manuscript prior to publication. Weinstein ridiculed this suggestion on the grounds that men such as these are not objective, but my point is not that they should have a voice in determining whether the manuscript should be published but rather that the publisher, having already made that determination, might improve the quality of the work by exposing the editor and author to what such critics have to say and then taking or leaving it.

Sixth, although many of the characters in the Hiss case are dead, some are still alive and have much to teach us. For example, in his original testimony about the "Ware group" Chambers named as members of this 1930s "spy ring" people like the economist Victor Perlo, the lawyers John Abt and Charles Kramer, and others who have never been convicted of anything, and who today deport themselves less like spies than like alumni of honest-to-goodness Marxist study groups. In the overheated political atmosphere of the Cold War they all had good reason to invoke the Fifth Amendment when asked for their testimony. But now that statutes of limitations have run, principals have died, and Cold War passions have cooled, historical truth must assert its claim. We will never know the true history of the Communist "underground" if people like these refuse to talk. It is, of course, presumptuous and on the edge of historical voyeurism to ask former or even unreconstructed Communists to describe what went on in the thirties, but if we don't do it now, no one ever will. The image of "spy ring" will linger and either distort our history or describe it in too hollow a way to instruct us. It is now nearly fifty years since the alleged spy rings were supposed to be in operation. Surely there is a non-defensive way those accused of "spying,"— whether or not they were guilty—can describe the past without betraying their friends or their values and thereby help us all to understand the present. I wish, for example, J. Peters had done more than smile for Weinstein.

Seventh, beyond a nation security lexicon there is need for a national security idiom. Perhaps the Library of Congress, the American Historical Association, or the Organization of American Historians is the right institution to bring together former and present agents, novelists, journalists, and historians to help us gain control of our discourse on these matters. George Orwell's warning against forging our history has a particular aptness, the more so since the new communications technology demonstrates its apparently limitless capacity to cosmeticize the counterfeit, present betrayal in the image of patriotism, give global circulation to the presumptions that entertainment counts for more than truth and that the claims for and against our heroes are not verifiable. There are no footnotes on television. The pressures of commerce mitigate against the qualifier, and readers have already learned to discount the "allegeds," that precede the identification of the accused, but surely all of this argues for the beginning of a dialogue on the specific meaning of national security.

Eighth, it probably makes sense to regard the critical response to Weinstein's book (or rather its for-the-most-part *uncritical* acceptance) as a particular instance of a more general class of situations in which political values override critical examination and intelligence. Scholarship-as-ideology is an underexamined phenomenon, but as the Weinstein-Hiss controversy suggests, there is must room here for empirical as well as analytical research. For example, given the fact that such commentators as Murray Kempton, Garry Wills, Merle Miller, Sidney Hook, Arthur Schlesinger, Jr., Irving Howe, and William F. Buckley, Jr. were already on record pre-Weinstein as having arrived at a Hiss-is-guilty conclusion—with no aspersions intended on any of those mentioned above—one might want to ask such questions as: Which review media, if any, took into account the reviewer's previous position before assigning the book for review? With what motive? What *are* the appropriate criteria for reviewer selection when dealing with symbolically significant cases in the national security/espionage area? How many minds— on either side of this particular dispute—were actually changed by the Weinstein book, and how did its critical reception affect that process? Under what conditions are intellectuals as a class likely to fulfill their critical function? Ought studies in this underdocumented but politically explosive area be evaluated by the same or different standards from conventional scholarship?

Ninth, and more politically, one wonders what relation, if any, the acceptance of Weinstein's thesis in certain academic quarters has to the more general context of the revival of Cold War attitudes and recent attacks on Cold War revisionists such as Alperovitz, Kolko, and Williams? Is it that new scholarship has discredited the revisionists (and that *Perjury* is simply additional discrediting evidence), or are we witness to a shift in ideological fashion and power, of which the reception to *Perjury* is but an additional instance?

Finally, one asks what there is to be learned from the Weinstein-Hiss episode about the critical media's ideological entrenchment—and how it relates to specific foundations, publishers, networks, and other organizations and institutitions. The nexus between funding sources and research is itself one of the great unexplored subjects. When both the subject and the funding source are enmeshed in a culture of secrecy, the possibility that the marketplace of ideas will fulfill its potential as truth-preserver is diminished.

Appendix: A Chronology

April 1 (issue date April 8): Navasky reviews Weinstein's *Perjury* in *The Nation.*

April 6: Weinstein tells *The Washington Post* that this summer he plans to write an essay responding to "legitimate criticism."

April 6 et seq.: Weinstein tells *The Washington Post, Newsweek,* the *Today* show, et al. that "Navasky, Hiss or anybody else" is invited to examine his thousands of documents, his tapes and notes, his original 1,600-page manuscript.

April 7: *The Nation* wires Weinstein offering him right of reply at his earliest convenience.

April 10: Weinstein tells a City University of New York audience that he intends to respond to *The Nation* in *The New Republic* because "a scholar has the right to choose his forum."

April 15: Weinstein publishes reply in *The New Republic*. It says "Navasky alleges that I misquoted six people whom I interviewed, misstated basic facts, and distorted evidence—grave accusations against a scholar. Had he contacted me—which he did not—I would have invited

Navasky to examine the material in my archive which proves that I have cited all six accurately. Three of the six interviewees who recanted their stories . . . are on tape."

April 21: Navasky calls Weinstein and takes him up on invitation to examine archives over weekend in time for response in *The New Republic*. Weinstein says he can't rearrange schedule to accommodate a weekend examination but says letter will follow.

April 25: A letter from Weinstein arrives, dated April 22:
Dear Sir: *Although I have declined requests from other journalists and scholars for access to my files prior to depositing them at the Truman Library, and despite your distortions and unprofessional attitude toward me—evidenced by your failure to fact-check your allegations with me before rushing into your first attack, and by your disparagement of the need to inspect my files in your most recent editorial—I have decided to allow you to examine the material in my records which you most urgently need to see. When you phoned yesterday, you stated that your purpose was to inspect this material prior to writing your response to my article in* The New Republic.

Please write me in advance, listing the items you wish to see as specifically as possible. I ask this for reasons of time and efficiency and, frankly, to prevent a time-consuming "fishing expedition" in my 50,000-page archive by you on behalf of third parties unconnected with your magazine. You are free to take notes of the material I show you, and you may bring with you your associates. . . .

The only occasion my schedule permits for such a visit over the next three weeks is Sunday, April 30, between 10 A.M. and 1 P.M. Since I cannot spend a great deal of time on this, I ask that you limit your requests to a reasonable number.

If the time and date are convenient for you, please write to confirm and include your list of requests.

Sincerely, Allen Weinstein

April 26: We send Weinstein a letter:
Dear Mr. Weinstein: *I have delayed my response to your article in* The New Republic *in order to take the opportunity to read your files, hear your tapes and otherwise inspect your records. Even though you have*

retreated from the recent offer you made on the Today *show and via the media to give us unrestricted access to your files at our convenience, I accept your offer to inspect them Sunday, April 30, at 10 A.M., though you must know, with your scholarly background, that three hours hardly permits a serious examination of complicated and extensive materials.*

I will be accompanied by my associate, Philip Pochoda and [one other]. . . .

The following materials are of particular interest to us in framing our reply to The New Republic:

The complete transcripts and tapes of the following interviews. (Dates for interviews are taken from Perjury.*):*

Prof. Karel Kaplan: March 27 and April 19, 1977

Sam Krieger: Aug. 16 and 18, 1974 (and any Krieger correspondence)

Maxim Lieber: May 10 and 13, 1975

Paul Willert: March 17, 1975 (and Willert correspondence)

Donald Hiss: Sept. 29, 1975

The complete transcripts of the following interviews (and any correspondence):

Nadya Ulanovskaya: Jan 3–6, 1977

Alden Whitman: eight 1974 interviews, (and all Whitman correspondence)

Dr. Viola Bernard: June 23, 1975

Rev. John Cronin: Nov. 26, 1975

Prof. Sidney Hook: April 30, 1975

Philip J. Jaffee: Sept. 17, 1975

Isaac Don Levine: Sept. 16, 1974: Oct. 18, 1974

T. S. Matthews: March 22, 1975

David Zablodowsky: Nov. 1, 1975

In addition we should like to inspect:

(1) The identification by the emigree Russian woman of Samuel Krieger as "Clarence Miller" who lived in the Soviet Union with her mother.

(2) The letter to Alden Whitman from Roberta Fansler describing the Chicago dinner party in which Priscilla Hiss [allegedly] said she was "sick and tired of all the lies and cover-ups."

(3)   The letter from Paul Willert's wife to Malcolm Cowley relating to Otto Katz.

(4)   The evidence from "pre-trial defense experts" to contradict Daniel Norman's post-trial affidavit that the envelope submitted by Chambers lacked the markings that would have been inevitable.

(5)   The copy of the Peters deportation hearing you secured under the Freedom of Information Act.

Unless we hear from you to the contrary, we will arrive at your house at 10 A.M. this coming Sunday.

Sincerely yours, Victor Navasky

April 27: Ashbel Green, Weinstein's editor at Alfred A. Knopf, Inc., calls and asks if we can send Weinstein a copy of the latest issue of *The Nation*, which includes an editorial commenting on Weinstein's reply in *The New Republic.* We agree and also tell Green we are sending Weinstein a telegram stating that Robert Sherrill will be the third *Nation* participant and that in addition to the materials already asked for we would like to see:

(1) Interviews with Meyer Schapiro, and the letters confirming *Chambers's departure from party.*

(2) Materials on Solow's interviews with Chambers.

(3) Materials on Weinstein interviews with all possessors of Hiss typewriter.

April 30: At 10 A.M., Sherrill, Pochoda and Navasky present themselves at the Weinstein home in Washington and are met by Mrs. Weinstein who tells them that Weinstein has sent a telegram the previous evening (Saturday night) withdrawing his offer. She hands them a copy of the telegram which reads: RETURNED TODAY. FOUND YOUR LETTERS, TELEGRAMS AND ARTICLE. SINCE THEY VIOLATE CONDITIONS I SET, MEETING CANCELLED. ALL MY FILES WILL BE DEPOSITED LATER THIS YEAR AT TRUMAN LIBRARY. ALLEN WEINSTEIN.

We offer to inspect only that which Mr. Weinstein cares to show and ask to speak with him, but Mrs. Weinstein declines on his behalf.

May 1: at 11 A.M. Weinstein's telegram (as quoted above) arrives at *The Nation* office.

Notes

1. *Time* (Feb. 13, 1978), p. 28.

2. *Newsweek* (March 20, 1978), p. 96; *Esquire* (March 28, 1978), p. 21; *Encounter* (August 1978, p. 48; see Schlesinger jacket copy blurb for *Perjury*; James Wechsler, *New York Post*, March 13, 1978, p. 31; William F. Buckley, Jr., *New York Post*, March 28, 1978; Merle Miller, "Alger Hiss: Truth and Consequences," *Washington Post Book World*, April 16, 1978.

3. Sidney Hook, "The Case of Alger Hiss," *Encounter* (August 1978), pp. 48–55.

4. *Perjury*, p. 551.

5. *Perjury*, p. 313.

6. *Perjury*, p. 205.

7. See Philip Nobile, "The State of the Art of Alger Hiss," *Harper's*, (April 19, 1976), p. 74.

8. See Allen Weinstein, "Reappraisals: The Alger Hiss Case Revisited," *The American Scholar* (Winter 1971); *Perjury*, pp. xix, 5, 237, 307–8, 314, 319, 418; Chambers's appearances were August 3, 7, 25, 27, and 30, 1948.

9. *Perjury*, p. 19.

10. See letter from Weinstein to Attorney General Elliott Richardson included as an exhibit in his 1973 Freedom of Information Act lawsuit, dated August 15, 1973.

11. See *Nation* files for undated story in the *Daily Hampshire Gazette*.

12. Allen Weinstein to Sylvia Salmi Solow, July 30, 1975; Weinstein-Mrs. Solow Correspondence, Herbert Solow, Collection, Hoover Institution Archives, Hoover Institution, Stanford, CA 94305.

13. Weinstein to Sylvia Salmi Solow, March 16, 1976. Emphasis in both letters is Weinstein's.

14. Special thanks should go to William A. Reuben, the late Carey McWilliams, Fred Cook, Donald Kirk, Phil Pochoda, and Karen Wilcox.

15. Philip Nobile interview with Allen Weinstein, *Politicks* (Feb. 28, 1978).

16. Nadia Ulanova, the seventh, didn't respond.

17. For replies of Paul Willert, Ella Winter, Sam Krieger, Karel Kaplan, Maxim Lieber, and Donald Hiss, see the *Nation* (April 8, 1978), pp. 395–97, and complete letters on file at the *Nation* offices.

18. Allen Weinstein, "Perjury! Take Three," the *New Republic* (April 15, 1978), p. 16 (hereafter cited as *TNR*).

19. Irving Howe, "Alger Hiss Retired," the *New York Times Book Review*, April 9, 1978, p. 1.

20. *Perjury*, p. xix.

21. *Perjury*, p. 205.

22. Noel Field, from Budapest, Hungary, to Alger Hiss, c/o Alfred A. Knopf, Inc., July 21, 1957, Hiss Archives, National Emergency Civil Liberties Committee, New York, NY. Field's 1957 letter to Hiss is cited by Weinstein in *Perjury* (p. 525).

23. Karel Kaplan to Victor Navasky, March 16, 1978, on file at *Nation* office.

24. *TNR*.

25. Weinstein then went to Kennedy and told him he had back-up material; if he had known that, Kennedy apparently told Weinstein, he certainly would not have spoken so frankly with me. See correspondence, *New Republic*, May 13, 1978, p. 5.

26. *Perjury*, see pp. 113, 126n, 127, 128, 129, 130, 148, 149, 196, 229, 308, 316, 317, 323, 324.

27. *Perjury*, p. 62.

28. *Perjury*, pp. 113, 126n, 129, 149, 196, 229, 308.

29. Michael Kernan, "A Literary Skirmish on Hiss," *Washington Post*, April 6, 1978.

30. *Perjury*, p. 100n.

31. *Nation* (April 8, 1978), p. 396.

32. *TNR*.

33. "Allen Weinstein Statement," *TNR* (June 7 and 14 1979), p. 11. For a total account of Weinstein's settlement of this lawsuit for $17,500, see Alexander Cockburn, "Press Clips," *Village Voice*, May 28, 1979; and Sam Krieger, "An Historian's Falsehoods," *Rights* (Sept. 1979).

34. Mailgram, Weinstein to Navasky, April 27, 1978, on file at *Nation* office.

35. *Perjury* reviewers previously on record as believing Hiss guilty included Richard Rovere, Merle Miller, Murray Kempton, Walter Goodman, Irving Howe, James Wechsler, and Arthur M. Schlesinger, Jr.

36. William F. Buckley, Jr., *New York Post*, March 28, 1978; Sidney Hook, *Encounter* (September 1978), pp. 53–54; and Murray Kempton, *New York Post*, April 22, 1978, p. 11.

37. Peter Khiss, "Professor Says Alger Hiss Lied about His Links with Chambers," *New York Times*, March 18, 1977, p. 1.

38. Actually, the typewriter became an issue only *after* Hiss sued Chambers for libel as a result of charges he made on "Meet the Press" in August 1948. Thereafter, Chambers was questioned by Hiss's lawyers in pre-trial examination, and on November 17, 1948, he produced sixty-five pages of typed copies of

ten-year-old State Department documents and four slips of paper in Hiss's hand-writing to back up his story. In his sworn statement Chambers said, "The method was for him [Hiss] to bring home documents in his briefcase, which Mrs. Hiss usually typed."

Because the statute of limitations had run out on espionage, Hiss was indicted for perjury. To convict one of perjury, moreover, the law requires either two witnesses (and the only witness to the alleged transaction was Chambers) or one witness plus independent corroborative evidence; therefore the typewriter was believed to be important as part of the complex of independent corroborative evidence.

39. Garry Wills, "The Honor of Alger Hiss," *New York Review of Books* (April 20, 1978), p. 29.

40. See Donald Hiss to Victor Navasky, March 7, 1978, on file at *Nation* office; see also Davis memorandum, Feb. 26, 1951, in Hiss defense files.

41. *TNR*. pp. 16–17.

42. See note 46.

43. Weinstein, *Perjury*, p. 74. See also his April 1, 1976 *New York Review of Books* article and his responses to his critics, cited in footnote 45.

44. Wills, "The Honor of Alger Hiss," p. 29.

45. "The Hiss Case: An Exchange," *New York Review of Books* 23 (May 27, 1976), pp. 32–48.

46. *Perjury*, pp. 62, 130. According to Weinstein: "My long talk with Peters in Budapest was his first with a non-communist western scholar since his 1949 deportation and included his first public comments on the Hiss-Chambers case. Peters smiled once during our talk when I suggested that his frequent use of the terms 'open' and 'secret' Communist parties, when describing the division in American CP ranks indicated an awareness of that second realm which most Party 'functionaries' would deny having possessed." *Perjury*. p. 597.

47. *Perjury*, p. 61. See Weinstein's reference to these papers in *TNR*, April 15, 1978, pp. 16–17.

48. See "The Sheltered Life," especially pp. 32–35, in Murray Kempton, *Part Of Our Time* (New York: Simon and Schuster, 1955).

49. Murray Kempton, *New York Post*, April 22, 1978, p. 11.

50. See chapters 15 and 16, "The Impact of Whittaker Chambers" and "The Destruction of Alger Hiss," in *Richard M. Nixon: The Shaping of His Character*, Fawn M. Brodie (New York: W. W. Norton and Co., 1981), pp. 197–231. Of the 109 source citations in these two chapters, 16 come from Chambers's *Witness*; all the rest bearing on questions in dispute or controversy are from Weinstein's *Perjury*.

51. *Perjury*, p. 546; see Priscilla Hiss's letter in *New York Times*, March 17, 1978, asserting that "at all times, and with my every fiber, I have believed in the innocence of Alger Hiss. I have never spoken a word to the contrary."

7

Unanswered Questions: Chambers, Nixon, the FBI, and the Hiss Case

Athan G. Theoharis

On January 21, 1950, in the second Alger Hiss trial, the jury returned a verdict of guilty, thereby closing one phase of the Hiss-Chambers case. The verdict, however, did not conclusively resolve whether Hiss was guilty or innocent of espionage, despite the preponderance of evidence that seemed to confirm that in 1938 he had given State Department documents to Whittaker Chambers, an admitted Communist. (See the Hiss-Chambers Chronology at the end of this chapter for a detailed outline of events bearing on the Hiss case.) Recent, more dispassionate raising of the evidence and research into formerly closed FBI files support a need for continued skepticism. At the heart of doubts over whether Hiss committed espionage (Hiss was formally indicted and convicted of perjury, the charges involving his denial of giving classified documents to Chambers) are questions about Whittaker Chambers's testimony that are as yet unanswered.

What are these questions? There are at least five: (1) Had Chambers left the Communist Party in late 1937 (or January-February 1938), as he repeatedly told interrogators from 1939 through November 1948? Or, had he left the Party in April 1938, as he testified during the two Hiss trials of 1949? If Chambers defected from the Communist Party in late 1937 or early 1938, how could he produce, in November 1948, State Department documents dated April 1, 1938 that he then claimed to have

I acknowledge the funding support of Marquette University—in particular, Dean John Oh—the Field Foundation, and Warsh-Mott Funds, which made possible my research into FBI files. I am also indebted to Kenneth O'Reilly for sharing his research findings; to Alger Hiss for permitting unrestricted access to his FBI files; to Robert Griffith for editorial assistance; and to Perry Raines and Janet Black for typing assistance.

received from Alger Hiss?[1] (2) Had Chambers and those he named—notably Henry Julian Wadleigh, Franklin (Vincent) Reno, Alger Hiss, and Harry Dexter White—been involved in espionage against the United States government during the 1930s? Chambers repeatedly maintained before November-December 1948 that neither he nor those he named as Communists had been involved in espionage—to the contrary, he then contended. Reversing this testimony after December 1948, Chambers described his own and Hiss's roles as participation in espionage. (3) Why did Hiss's role (and Hiss's participation alone) become the central component of Chambers's testimony of 1948–49? Was it simply fortuitous that Chambers possessed documentary evidence to convict Hiss alone of joint participation in espionage—and not any of the other individuals whom Chambers had also identified in 1939? (4) Had Chambers really left an envelope containing typed documents, handwritten notes, and microfilm with his nephew Nathan Levine in 1938? (5) Had Chambers received typed State Department documents from Hiss and a four-page memorandum written by Harry Dexter White from White?

Chambers did produce certain documents (on November 17, 1948, four notes written by Hiss and sixty-five pages of copied State Department documents allegedly typed on a typewriter once owned by the Hisses, and, on December 2, 1948 two strips of developed microfilm) that he then claimed Hiss had given to him as a Communist espionage agent. Neither then nor later did Chambers provide direct corroborative evidence that Hiss was involved in an espionage operation. By Chambers's admission, the documents in question were not transmitted to the Soviet Union. Nor is there evidence that Hiss gave Chambers other documents in 1937, or that Hiss lied when he said he had simply leaked information to a radical journalist (as he claimed to have done in 1935).

The testimony of others named by Chambers, notably Henry Julian Wadleigh and Franklin (Vincent) Reno, and a notarized November 28, 1938 memorandum of Chambers's friend Herbert Solow, confirm that Chambers was involved in Communist "underground" activities during the 1930s. These sources do not confirm that during the 1930s Chambers attempted to steal United States secrets—Chambers's particular characterization of his actions in testimony before the House Un-

American Activities Committee (HUAC) in December 1948 and during the two Hiss trials. The information that Wadleigh admitted providing to Chambers, as well as other testimony about Communist "underground" activities in the United States during the 1930s, pertained to German policy and intentions—indeed, Wadleigh characterized his own role as anti-fascist.

This essay cannot conclusively answer the many questions because the available evidence itself is inconclusive. Additional research is needed before answers will arise. Historical research, moreover, must move beyond the question of Hiss's innocence or guilt, to address what can be characterized as abuse of power issues, particularly the relationship between HUAC and the FBI.

Questions about Chambers's Credibility

The persistence of doubts about Hiss's guilt stems principally from doubts about Chambers's credibility. Central to these doubts is Chambers's revised dating of his own break from the Communist Party. Until producing the microfilmed State Department documents in December 1948, Chambers consistently claimed to have broken from the Communist Party in late 1937 (although during his HUAC testimony he claimed at times to have left the Party in late 1937 and at other times to have left in January-February 1938). The occasions for Chambers's varying testimony included: a 1939 interview with Assistant Secretary of State Adolf Berle; a 1940 meeting with the writer Malcolm Cowley; a 1942 FBI interview; a 1945 interview with State Department security official Raymond Murphy; August 1948 HUAC testimony; the recollection of *Time* magazine publisher James Linen; and Chambers's November 5, 1948 deposition in pre-trial proceedings involving a libel suit brought by Alger Hiss.[2] Chambers's impressive recollections during the HUAC hearings, for example, of details about Hiss's various residences during the 1930s and Hiss's disposition of a Ford automobile in 1936 (Hiss erred in his HUAC testimony dating his disposition of this automobile in 1935) make suspect Chambers's later revised dating of his own break from the Communist Party. The wrenching nature of

Chambers's break from what had been his active Communist political career would suggest that his initial and consistent recollection of a 1937 break-date was accurate.

A pre-April 1938 break-date is corrobrated, moreover, by the other testimony of Whittaker Chambers and his wife Esther in 1948; by the termination date of Chambers's employment with the National Research Project; and by the date of a translation assignment Chambers obtained from Oxford University Press.

Interrogated by Hiss's attorneys on November 5, 1948, Chambers testified to breaking from the Communist Party and ceasing Communist "duties" in February 1938:

Q: Now, how long did you stay at Mt. Royal Terrace?
A: I should think we stayed there until February or March of 1938.
Q: February or March of '38. And what then?
A: Then we moved to the Old Court Road . . .
Q: In other words, as I now understand it, on the day that you moved from Mt. Royal Terrace, you ceased to go to Washington and perform the duties you previously had been performing in connection with the Party?
A: That is correct.

Chambers accurately recalled the time of his move from Mt. Royal Terrace. Advertising the Mt. Royal Terrace apartment for sublet in the February 27, 1938 *Baltimore Sun*, he subsequently rented it as of March 14.

When responding earlier to Congressman Richard Nixon's questions during August 30, 1948 HUAC hearings, Chambers reaffirmed a February break-date:

MR. NIXON: After you left the job [with the National Research Project on January 31, 1938], what happened then? Did you leave the party immediately?
MR. CHAMBERS: I think there may have been 2 or 3 weeks in between. I have no longer a recollection, but I left shortly thereafter.
MR. NIXON: In other words, you severed your relationship with the party a few weeks afterward?
MR. CHAMBERS: I disappeared.

Esther Chambers corroborated her husband's February 1938 break-date version. In her deposition of November 17, 1948, Mrs. Chambers recalled having remained in hiding at their Old Court Road residence for several months ("no longer than three months") after their break and before going to Florida with her husband, a trip which took place in early April 1938. (Henry Wadleigh indirectly corroborates this break-date, recalling his inability to contact Chambers in late February-early March 1938. At the time, Wadleigh was attempting to apprise Chambers of his imminent departure on March 11, 1938, for Turkey.)[3]

A late 1937 or February 1938 break-date is of crucial significance. All the State Department documents that Chambers produced in November and December 1948 were dated in 1938, the last one, April 1, 1938. Had he broken from the Party in late 1937 or, at the latest, February 1938, Chambers could not have received all of them from Hiss. The dates of the various types of documents is equally significant. The documents reprinted in the two strips of developed microfilm bore the State Department's receipt stamp of January 14, 1938. In contrast, the four notes in Hiss's handwriting were dated January 28, March 2, 3, and 11, 1938, and the sixty-five pages of typewritten documents varied in date from January 5 to April 1, 1938. Chambers could only have received the microfilm documents had he defected from the Communist Party in January-February 1938.

Chambers's State Department source for the microfilm documents, moreover, could have been Henry Julian Wadleigh. A variety of sources support this conclusion. These include: Chambers's original testimony before HUAC on December 6, 1948; Chambers's December 28, 1948 attempt to explain away this earlier testimony; the January 14, 1938 receipt stamp on these State Department documents (predating Wadleigh's March 11, 1938 departure for Turkey); microfilmed documents that were of copies of State Department documents, which would have gone to the Trade Division where Wadleigh was employed, whereas Hiss's office had received the originals; and, the microfilming process for these documents, which conforms to Wadleigh's and photographer Felix Inslerman's account of how Inslerman photographed State Department documents temporarily removed by Wadleigh.[4]

Confronted by the striking discrepancy during the 1949 trials, Chambers and his wife abruptly changed their testimony, Chambers maintaining that he had broken with the Party on April 15, 1938. This precise dating was not unimportant. After accusing Hiss of collaborating in Communist espionage, Chambers claimed to have regularly visited Hiss at his house on a weekly or ten-day basis. Because Hiss might not have had immediate access to the April 1, 1938, document, an April 15 break-date permitted the necessary leeway to convince jurors that, prior to breaking from the Communist Party, Chambers could have secured a copy of the document from Hiss. Chambers further revised the interval between the termination of his employment with the National Research Project (NRP) and his defection from the Communist Party—in his HUAC testimony Chambers had maintained that he left the Party "2 or 3 weeks" after leaving the NRP, whereas during the Hiss trials the period became "at least" two months.[5]

Because Chambers's revisions could not withstand critical scrutiny, during the trials Chambers offered another explanation for the timing of his break. Chambers then correlated his break with his success in obtaining another source of income, one month after he had left the Party, a translating job through Paul Willert, a New York literary agent. To devote full and uninterrupted time to this project, Chambers further testified, he and his family had traveled to Florida.

Willert obtained two translation assignments for Chambers. The first involved Martin Gumpert's *Dunant: The Story of the Red Cross*, which Oxford University Press published in English, and which (according to Willert's 1952 deposition) Chambers had received "at the end of 1937 or at the very beginning of 1938." Documents in the files of Oxford University Press confirm Willert's recollection. These include a March 18, 1938 shipping form addressed to "David Chambers, 2124 Mt. Royal Terrace," and specifying "Rush—Must Reach Baltimore Saturday [March 19] Express." On May 1, 1938, Chambers also wrote to advise Willert that he had traveled to Florida, and could be reached through "General Delivery, St. Augustine, Florida." Chambers then sent to Willert the first hundred pages of completed translation, and requested a two-week extension. (Willert had written Chambers on April 12, 1938, forwarding a check for $250 and reminding him of a May 1 completion deadline.) In another letter of May 3, 1938, Chambers informed Willert that he had "not been at Mt. Royal Terrace for more than a month."

Given Chambers's trial testimony of having secured a translation job one month after formally breaking with the Communist Party, this would place his break in January, at the latest, Februrary 1938.

The second translation assignment Chambers secured through Willert (for the publisher Longman-Green) was Gustav Regler's *The Great Crusade*. Although Chambers testified during the trials to having travelled to Florida in May to work on the Regler translation, correspondence between Chambers and the publisher confirm that the translation was not commissioned until June 1938, after Chambers returned from Florida.[6]

Allen Weinstein claims to have uncovered evidence confirming an April 1938 break-date. Chambers did not break abruptly from the Party, Weinstein argues, but began to "prepare" for the break as early as December 1937. This argument apparently resolves the problem of Chambers's earlier citation of a 1937 break-date. What, then, is the supporting evidence?

In both the mimeographed letter, "A Response to Robert Sherrill," and in *Perjury*, Weinstein identifies the evidence as certain *undated* letters between Chambers and his friend, Meyer Schapiro. In a brief back-to-the-book note to *Perjury*, Weinstein explains why he concluded that these undated letters had been written in January, February, March, July, September, October, and mid-November 1938: "Not only did Prof. Schapiro prove helpful in dating this correspondence, but Chambers's [undated] letters to Herbert Solow *from fall 1938 to spring 1939* contained sufficient references to Schapiro's letters (and vice versa) to allow more precise dating. *Solow*, moreover, retained the postmarked envelopes *in most cases* [emphasis added]."[7]

Weinstein, however, details neither the supporting evidence nor the "sufficient references" that he relied on when dating the letters, particularly those of January, February, and March 1938. He also fails to describe how undated Chambers-Solow letters from "fall 1938 to spring 1939" confirm that undated Chambers-Schapiro letters had been written in January, February, and March 1938, rather than January, February, and March 1939.

Weinstein could not provide the needed elaboration because the undated Chambers-Shapiro letters were written in 1939. In April 1979,

I wrote Meyer Schapiro to request permission to review the correspondence. He refused my request. Three months later, in July 1979, I discovered that five of the Chambers-Shapiro letters were otherwise accessible—the three that were not were those Weinstein dates as written in January, March, and July 1938. On December 5, 1949, Schapiro gave copies of five letters he had received from Chambers to FBI agent L. H. Bracken; these copies were included among the FBI's released Hiss case files. Two of the five Chambers-Schapiro letters were not written in February 1938 (as Weinstein claims), but in February 1939, and therefore contradict Weinstein's contentions about Chambers's mid-April 1938 break-date. Weinstein has no evidence either that Chambers began preparing to break from the Communist underground in December 1937 or that he formally broke in April 1938.

On page 264 of *Perjury* (note 83, page 624), and again on page 327 (although the letter is not cited in note 46, page 626), Weinstein dates a Chambers-Schapiro letter as having been written "ca. Feb. 1938." In this letter, Chambers stated that "the moment when the last base where the union of workers and peasantry was effective has just been wiped out: Spain, of course." The reference to Spain, insofar as Republican Spain finally collapsed in January 1939, combined with Chambers's citation of February in the letter, confirm that the letter had been written sometime in February 1939. Continuing, Chambers acknowledged Schapiro's help enabling him to secure a "new translation" assignment, and mentioned the possibility that he might obtain another "Einstein popularization" translation from another publisher (possibly Modern Age Books). Then, on page 327 (note 45, page 626), and again on page 313 (note 14, page 625), Weinstein dates another Chambers-Schapiro letter as also having been written in February 1938. In this letter, Chambers again acknowledged Schapiro's assistance in securing the aforementioned translations, and further commented on the death of a mutual friend, Hideo Noda. Noda died in January 1939, which Chambers's letter cited: "Ned [Hideo Noda] died 1939." From a review of the other three letters Schapiro provided to the FBI in 1949, it is impossible to ascertain why Weinstein dates one as having been written in September 1938 (page 319; note 28, page 625) and the others in October 1938 (page 323; note 37, page 626; and pages 319–20; note 29, pages 625–

26). The letters contain no internal references to contemporary datable events. Weinstein's dating system, furthermore, appears to be extremely capricious: for example, on page 323 (note 27, page 625), and earlier on page 243 (note 31, page 617), he quotes from the same letter, but in his notes gives two different dates—October 1938 for the page 323 reference, and mid-November 1938 for the page 243 reference.

In 1949, Schapiro had not yet turned over to the FBI the three Chambers-Schapiro letters that Weinstein claims had been written in January 1938 (page 313; note 14, page 625), March 1938 (pages 313-14; note 15, page 625), and July 1938 (page 317; note 24, page 625). In November 1980, I was able to review a copy of the Chambers-Schapiro letter that Weinstein dates as March 1938. (Meyer Schapiro had sent a copy of this letter to Professor James Hamilton of the Medical College of Wisconsin. Schapiro advised Hamilton that he had been unable to locate the other two [Weinstein-dated] January and July 1938 letters. Hamilton kindly allowed me to review the copy.)

In this letter, Chambers advised Schapiro that Willert "gave me the book on which to do a couple of chapters as an advance," and that were Willert satisfied Chambers could go ahead, but that "eight have failed before me." Chambers claimed to have begun work on this translation, and requested, "Before I show it to [Willert], though, I should much appreciate if you will look over my results." Weinstein concluded, from this reference to a translation obtained through Willert, that Chambers was discussing the *Dunant* translation; furthermore, having erroneously dated the earlier Chambers-Schapiro letters as having been written in February 1938, he dates this letter March 1938. The reference to a translation does apparently correlate with the references to Schapiro's assistance, which enabled Chambers to land this "new translation" assignment mentioned in the February 1939 letters, suggesting that the letter had been written in March 1939. The letter could not have been written in March 1938, in any event, since the Chambers-Willert correspondence of March-May 1938 confirms that Chambers could not have consulted with Schapiro on the translation before submitting it to Willert. It is conceivable, however, that the referenced translation was to Regler's *The Great Crusade*; therefore, the letter could have been written sometime after June 1938.

I have also reviewed the Chambers-Solow correspondence—these letters are included in the Solow Papers deposited at the Hoover Institution. This correspondence lacks references to contemporary events, references essential to dating the letters confidently (excepting one that refers to the imminent fall of Republican Spain). The letters confirm, however, that when drafting a manuscript recounting his knowledge of the Communist underground, Chambers was not preparing a "life preserver," but instead was seeking to sell a story through the "arbiter" (Isaac Don Levine) and "Meg" (although this might refer to the same person). In one of his letters to Solow, Chambers commented that "naturally" Solow "must take an agent's fee should there be a sale of the material."[8]

In a 1952 petition for a new trial, Alger Hiss pointedly challenged Chambers's trial testimony. Hiss specifically cited documents he had recently obtained confirming that Chambers had secured a translating assignment from Oxford University Press in February 1938 (pre-dating Chambers's claimed April 15, 1938 break-date, and further trial testimony about having received a translation assignment one month after leaving the Party). Confronted by this evidence, FBI agents interviewed Chambers. After first reviewing Hiss's court motion and attendant exhibits, Chambers revised his previous claim to having obtained the translation after he had defected. An FBI report of February 12, 1952 recounts Chambers's corrections of his earlier "mistakes":

CHAMBERS *now believes* that he must have contacted WILLERT through SCHAPIRO *prior to his break* with the Communist Party and *in preparation for such break*. Although CHAMBERS does not have any clear recollection in this regard, he believes that he contacted WILLERT regarding the translation job at least once and possibly twice before the trip to Florida. Again, although CHAMBERS cannot recall it clearly, he believes that he must have gone to New York and contacted WILLERT while the CHAMBERS family was still residing at 2124 Mount Royal Terrace, Baltimore, and possible a second time while the CHAMBERS family was living at the Old Court Road address [emphasis added].

Seeking corroboration for Chambers's revised account, on February 18, 1952, FBI agent Edward Scheidt interviewed Meyer Schapiro. Scheidt's "urgent" teletype report to Hoover on this interview recounts that Schapiro "could offer no documentary proof relative to date of Chambers break with CP." More important, Schapiro's 1952 testimony contradicts both Chambers's revised testimony of February 1952 and Schapiro's later dating of these Chambers-Schapiro letters. Thus Scheidt reports:

[Schapiro] did not see Chambers again until the spring of nineteen thirty-eight, exact time of which he could not recall, when Chambers came to his home in NYC [New York City] and told him he *had broken* from the Party and requested some assistance in securing a translating job. At this time Shapiro [*sic*] contacted Willet [*sic*] of Oxford University Press [*sic*] and secured a translating job for Chambers. *After reviewing all correspondence that he has from Chambers during this pertinent period Shapiro [*sic*] stated that since Chambers never dated his letters he could not document the time of Chambers break.* However, he believes that he, himself, wrote Chambers during this time and it is quite possible Chambers would have retained some of these which, according to Shapiro [*sic*], would be dated. Accordingly, Baltimore [field office] is requested to ask Chambers for such documentation at next interview [emphasis added].[9]

Chambers never produced Schapiro's letters, allegedly because he had already destroyed all his correspondence.

A second, equally important change in Chambers's testimony involves his initial allegations about the Communist activities of Alger Hiss and other federal employees—whether to Assistant Secretary of State Berle in 1939, to FBI officials in 1942, 1945, 1946, and 1948, to HUAC in August 1948, or to the federal grand jury as late as October 1948. Hiss and the others, Chambers consistently claimed, had not been involved in espionage, but had only sought to promote Communist infiltration of, and thereby its influence in, the New Deal. Abruptly changing his testimony, again after November 1948, Chambers accused Hiss and others of espionage, describing Hiss as the "most zealous" Communist espionage agent with whom he had contact.

In a sworn deposition of November 5, 1948, Chambers admitted to having read State Department documents at Hiss's home during the 1930s. Chambers then insisted that he had never "obtained" any documents from Hiss or transmitted them to the Communist Party. In every single one of his FBI interviews dating from 1942, Chambers's sole allegation had been that Hiss was a member of a Communist Party cell. A

November 13, 1953 memorandum of FBI Assistant Director D. Milton Ladd recommending against disseminating an enclosed memorandum (reprinting FBI summary memoranda on Alger Hiss) to "a Congressional committee" (the Senate Internal Security Subcommittee then investigating alleged subversive activities of federal employees) directly confirms this. As one reason for this recommendation, Ladd emphasized:

Up to the time Hiss left the Government in January 1947, the Bureau had no evidence to prove a case against Hiss. We had Whittaker Chambers' story given by him in 1942 and 1945 naming Hiss as a member of the Harold Ware underground group of the Communist Party in Washington, D.C., during the middle 1930's. (No espionage allegations were received from Chambers regarding Hiss until November 1948, when Chambers produced documentary evidence in the form of the "Baltimore documents," which resulted in Hiss's conviction for perjury.)

In addition, FBI agent Thomas Spencer's March 28, 1946 report of an interview that day with Chambers further highlights the limited thrust of Chambers's original charges against Hiss, and his further admission to *not* having documentary evidence to support these accusations:

[Chambers] related that his actual knowledge of HISS' activities concerned the period *shortly preceding 1937* and he was unable to elaborate on any information concerning HISS' connection with the Communist Party or Communist Front organizations [other than that Hiss was a member of a Communist cell when an employee of the Agricultural Adjustment Administration]. . . . [Chambers] stated that as a matter of fact he has absolutely no information that would conclusively prove that HISS held a membership card in the Communist Party or that he was an actual dues paying member of the Communist Party *even while he was active prior to 1937*. He volunteered that he knew that in 1937 HISS was favorably impressed with the Communist movement and was of the present opinion that HISS still was of the same beliefs. He indicated that he did not have any documentary or other proof to substantiate this belief and based it solely upon comments made by various Washington and New York newspaper writers. . . . CHAMBERS was again asked if in any of his past activities he had any documentary evidence or any independent recollection that HISS was a dues paying member of the Communist Party. He again stated that he had no such information and that if he did have this information he would be more than glad to supply it to this Bureau. *He further remarked in previous interviews with Agents of this office that he had never purposefully held out any information and had always been forthright in relaying any information that he had in which the Bureau had shown an interest* [emphasis added].[10]

Chamber's forthright denial that Hiss had engaged in espionage assumes greater significance in the light of other omissions in his earlier testimony. In neither his 1942 FBI interview nor his public testimony before HUAC in 1948 had Chambers specifically named Henry Julian Wadleigh, Franklin Reno, or Harry Dexter White. During the September 1939 meeting with Assistant Secretary of State Berle, Chambers identified eighteen individuals as members of the Communist "underground" (the phrasing being Berle's characterization of Chambers's accusations). Chambers offered no evidence to support these contentions; Berle understood that "underground" activities did not encompass espionage, but rather the promotion of Communist influence in the New Deal. Among those whom Chambers had specifically named in 1939 were Alger Hiss, Henry Julian Wadleigh, and Franklin Vincent Reno.

Berle did not forward to the FBI his notes on Chambers's interview until June 1943. Berle's reason(s) for not forwarding the notes earlier remains unclear, since the State Department security official had numerous opportunities to do so. After at least March 20, 1940, Berle met frequently with FBI Director Hoover and other FBI officials to discuss espionage and counter-espionage work. In addition, Berle was the State Department's representative on the Joint Committee on Intelligence Services, which met infrequently in Hoover's office throughout 1940 to coordinate intelligence and domestic surveillance activities.

On learning of the death of Walter Krivitzky (a former Soviet intelligence official who had defected to the West) on February 10, 1941, Berle recorded in his diary: "This is an OGPU [Soviet intelligence agency] job. It means that the murder squad which operated so handily in Paris and in Berlin is now operating in New York and Washington." Following a March 12, 1941 meeting with Soviet consular official Constantine Oumansky to protest Soviet propaganda activities, Berle recorded in his diary: "We know, of course, that all of this agitation against defense, against the Lend-Lease Bill, and so forth, was inspried by the Communists—probably by agreement with the Germans."

Because of concern about Krivitzky's death or about Soviet propaganda activities, Berle requested FBI officials to "contact him to obtain the information on Whittaker Chambers" in March 1941. In response, FBI officials advised Berle that they were not "conducting any investigation" of Chambers. Berle expressed grave concern that "the Russian agencies were looking for" Chambers. The FBI memoranda on these contacts with Berle raise a host of questions: Why did the FBI not follow up on Berle's contention? What was the basis for Berle's fears? Why had FBI officials decided not to investigate Chambers in 1941? (At the time, the FBI had considered listing Chambers on its Custodial Detention index of individuals to be apprehended in the event of war.) The FBI, however, did interview Chambers on May 13, 1942—in response to allegations of another ex-Communist, Ludwig Lore. On May 9, 1941, Lore informed FBI agent George Starr that he knew an "OGPU agent" (whom he did not directly identify) who had been "in contact with two girls who were private secretaries to Assistant Secretaries of State and was also in touch with a girl who was employed in a secretarial capacity with one of the high officials of the Department of Commerce; that the OGPU agent obtained from the latter girl all necessary statistical data." Starr reinterviewed Lore on August 3, 1941, at which time Lore identified Whittaker Chambers as this OGPU agent, and reaffirmed that "until fairly recently Chambers had held an important position in the OGPU; that he definitely handled arrangements for placing agents in the Government service at Washington or for making contacts through which the OGPU agents could obtain information at Washington." If assured of immunity from prosecution, Lore continued, Chambers would furnish this information to the FBI and had already unsuccessfully sought such immunity from the FBI director. In response to this information, the FBI's New York Field Office interviewed Chambers, and reviewed the FBI file on Chambers.

During the resultant FBI interview in 1942, and in another May 10, 1945, FBI interview, Chambers reaffirmed his allegations about Communist efforts to influence New Deal policy. He did not charge that these efforts involved espionage (thereby refuting Lore's contentions while at the same time highlighting his later, March 28, 1946, claim to FBI agent Spencer of having cooperated fully with the FBI). During the 1942 interview, Chambers cited but did not name all twenty individuals whom he claimed had been involved in Communist underground activities. Among those named by Chambers were Alger Hiss, Lee Pressman, Donald Hiss, and Charles Kramer. Significantly, Chambers did not name Henry Julian Wadleigh, but instead referred obliquely to an unnamed individual employed in the Trade Division of the Department of State. (Chambers also did not then, or in 1945, identify Harry Dexter White to the FBI.) Furthermore, in March 1945 and August 1946 interviews with State Department security official Raymond Murphy, Chambers identified Alger Hiss, Donald Hiss, Harold Ware, Harry Dexter White, Charles Coe, Frank Coe, and Henry Collins—but again, not Henry Julian Wadleigh (who had been a State Department employee) or William Ward Pigman (who had been employed in the Bureau of Standards).

In his August 1948 HUAC public testimony, moreover, Chambers named but eight individuals (Nathan Witt, John Abt, Lee Pressman, Alger Hiss, Donald Hiss, Victor Perlo, Charles Kramer, Henry Collins, and Harold Ware).[11] Chambers did not at this time publicly name Henry Julian Wadleigh, Franklin Reno, or William Ward Pigman either as fellow-travelers or members of a Communist cell.

Chambers first identified Henry Julian Wadleigh to the FBI during a December 3, 1948 interview. At this time Chambers claimed to have received State Department documents from Alger Hiss during 1937 and 1938, and said that other State Department documents were turned over to him "possibly by [Henry] JULIAN WADLEIGH."[12]

Why had Chambers not given Wadleigh's name to the FBI earlier, and why had he not publicly identified Wadleigh during his August 1948 HUAC testimony? When Chambers on his own volition decided to name only eight individuals before HUAC, was he intentionally restricting his public testimony to those who had engaged merely in Popular Front political activities? Did he intentionally refrain from naming those who had participated in "espionage?" In contrast to Hiss, who made consistent public denials to having given classified documents to Chambers, in December 1948 and again in 1949 Wadleigh admitted to the FBI to having done so (as did Reno, another former associate not publicly named during Chamber's August 1948 HUAC testimony).

Chamber's reluctance to name Wadleigh was not due to a faulty memory. Chambers might very well have decided not to name Wadleigh, whether to the FBI in 1942 or HUAC in August 1948, for reasons of self-preservation. A very reluctant witness before HUAC, after 1940 (as indirectly highlighted by the FBI report on Ludwig Lore's testimony and Chambers's May 13, 1942 and March 28, 1946 FBI interviews) Chambers carefully avoided implicating himself, and thereby adversely affecting his recently obtained respectability and position with *Time* magazine. Had Chambers publicly identified Wadleigh before HUAC, for example, accusing him of having belonged to a Communist cell and having sought to promote Communist influence in the New Deal, Chambers ran the risk that Wadleigh might not take the Fifth Amendment. Had Wadleigh instead admitted giving State Department documents to Soviet espionage agent Whittaker Chambers during the 1930s, his testimony in August 1948 would have been devastating to Chambers's reputation and credibility. At the time, Chambers was representing himself as a savior of Western Civilization, willing to sacrifice his career to publicize the insidious nature of the Communist threat to American society. By not publicly naming Wadleigh in August 1948, then, Chambers reduced his own vulnerability. Was, then, his decision to name Alger Hiss reflective of Chambers's confidence that he was not similarly vulnerable should Hiss respond—because Hiss either had not been involved in espionage (as had Wadleigh) or could not risk admitting this fact (owing to his position with the Carnegie Endowment)?

Questions Involving the So-called Life Preserver

After breaking with the Communist Party, did Chambers deposit a "life preserver" packet with his nephew, Nathan Levine, consisting of two developed microfilm strips, three undeveloped rolls of microfilm, a four-page memorandum handwritten by Harry Dexter White, sixty-five typed pages of copied State Department documents, and four notes handwritten by Alger Hiss? Chambers turned over these documents in 1948, the typed and handwritten documents to his attorneys on November 15, and the microfilm to HUAC staff members on December

2. Alternatively, did this "life preserver" contain instead a "statement" that Chambers had prepared in late 1938 and/or the developed and undeveloped microfilm? Recently released FBI files and other sources support the latter conclusion.

First, when retrieving the packet in November 1948, Chambers did not disclose its contents to his nephew, Nathan Levine. Thus, there is no independent corroboration that the documents Chambers turned over either to his attorney or to HUAC counsel had been deposited in the envelope. Documents examiner Daniel Norman, hired by the Hiss defense, concluded that the sixty-five typewritten pages of State Department documents had not all aged in the same way and lacked the markings and chemical stains that would invariably accompany ten-year storage; he further testified that the stains on the typed pages did not match the stains on the inside of the envelope. When responding to Norman's conclusions, government analysts significantly claimed *only* that the paint stains on the *envelope* matched those taken from inside the dumb-waiter, where it was supposed to have been hidden while in Levine's care. Second, Herbert Solow's notarized memorandum recording a November 1938 conversation with Chambers and Chamber's undated letters to Schapiro and Solow provide a far different characterization of the possible contents of the envelope.

In late 1938, Solow first attempted to convince Chambers to issue a public statement, and when Chambers demurred to persuade him to prepare and privately distribute a "statement" detailing his activities as a Communist. Chambers concurred with the latter suggestion, adding that he "had, in fact, written the statement [preparing three copies] and would soon inform the CP [Communist Party]." In an undated letter to Schapiro, moreover, Chambers admitted to having sent "some photographic copies of handwritten matters [to former Communist associates], the appearance of which would seriously embarrass them." In December 1938, Chambers also gave Solow a fifteen-thousand-word manuscript "describing in general terms the methods of Soviet passport racketeers in the U.S." Finally, in an unpublished article (apparently the same one he had given Solow in December 1938), Chambers recounted his knowledge of Soviet espionage activities. Significantly, Chambers did not then claim to have secured classified documents from federal bureaucrats—

he described the activities of Communist federal employees as intended to "influence Government decisions." Chambers's article also unqualifiedly asserted that "the Soviet's spy organization was at its peak" in 1934.[13]

In none of the contemporary accounts did Chambers report having received classified information from Government employees. The Communist activities he then described were limited to securing false passports or attempting to "influence" government policy. This characterization, as well as his further contention that the most significant "underground" activities occurred prior to 1935—the period of the so-called Ware Group—strikingly parallel his original August 1948 HUAC testimony. There is also the matter of the three copies of the "statement" that Chambers admitted having compiled. To date, apparently, none of these three statements has surfaced. Chambers gave one of the three copies to Ludwig Lore. Was the second copy the unpublished article Chambers gave to Solow in the attempt to have rightwing journalist Isaac Don Levine arrange for its publication? Did Chambers deposit the third in the "life preserver" packet he left with his nephew, Nathan Levine?

Precisely when, moreover, did Chambers retrieve the packet from Nathan Levine? In his book *Witness*, and during his December 3, 1948 FBI interview, Chambers claimed to having left an envelope with his nephew in 1938 that contained the microfilm, the Hiss notes, the White memorandum, and the sixty-five typewritten pages, which he retrieved on November 14, 1948. In his FBI interview, Chambers did not precisely chronicle the methods he later claimed to have employed to retrieve this envelope (underlined below): (1) *phoning his nephew on November 12, 1948* that he would be coming to New York in a day or two "to obtain the envelope"; (2) *telegraphing his nephew on November 14 from Baltimore about his pending arrival that afternoon*; (3) traveling to New York on November 14; and (4) recovering the envelope from Levine's mother's house in Brooklyn—"They [the documents] were hidden in a dumb-waiter shaft in his mother's house."[14]

The date when Chambers retrieved this envelope from Nathan Levine is crucial, since on November 15, 1948, the ex-Communist gave his attorney the four handwritten Hiss notes, the sixty-five pages of typed documents, and the four-page White memorandum, which he later claimed had been stored in this envelope. Chambers did not deliver the microfilm until December 2, 1948, and then to HUAC counsel.

Chambers's delivery of the microfilm to HUAC counsel, moreover, was elaborately staged to ensure maximum publicity. Having hidden the microfilm in his farm house after retrieving it from Levine's hiding place, on the morning of December 2, 1948, Chambers wrapped it carefully and placed it in a hollowed-out pumpkin. Chambers left Westminster that morning for Washington to testify at a scheduled State Department loyalty hearing. Before attending this hearing Chambers happened to stop by HUAC's office whereupon HUAC counsel Robert Stripling presented him with the Committee's subpoena. Stripling unconvincingly claims learning only that morning that Chambers possessed additional documents. Yet, the evening before, on December 1, 1948, Congressman Richard Nixon and Stripling had visited Chambers at his farm, at which time Chambers informed them of his possession of additional documents. More than likely, they then concerted on a strategy whereby, to insure maximum publicity, Chambers transferred the microfilm to a pumpkin—with the attendant melodrama of having used such a receptacle to stymie any lurking Soviet espionage operative who, to protect Alger Hiss, might attempt to pilfer the sensitive material.[15]

Had Chambers recovered the envelope from his nephew on November 14, 1948? In interviews with the FBI on December 4 and 5 Nathan Levine contradicted Chambers on this crucial date. At the time of his first FBI interview, and to a lesser degree at his second, Levine had not had the opportunity to make his testimony agree with Chambers's—in striking contrast to his later testimony before HUAC on December 9, the grand jury on December 8, and in the Hiss trials of 1949. A December 6, 1948 FBI teletype specifically reported Levine's testimony:

Nathan L. Levine . . . denied Dec. fourth that Chambers had ever left with him for safekeeping any personal property, specifically any documents or other written material. Levine stated Chambers had visited him in NYC [New York City] about two weeks ago [November 21, 1948] and when Levine was driving Chambers to Penna. RR Station for return to Wash, Chambers requested they stop at residence of Levine's parents at 260 Rochester Avenue, Brooklyn, that Chambers *looked over some material in storage in basement of premises and removed therefrom a folder or envelope.* Levine claimed not to know nature thereof. . . . On evening of December fifth Levine was again questioned re Chambers allegations and was informed agents desired to inspect basement area where he said Chambers secured material. *Levine then admitted material not taken from basement, but rather from dumb waiter shaft in parents home,* that he placed it there *nine years ago* after Chambers had asked him to hold material, and that he had given it back to Chambers when latter visited NYC *about two weeks ago [November 21, 1948].* Levine claimed *envelope sealed* when Chambers gave it to him, that he never touched it until day he returned it to Chambers, that he did not know its contents, *and that Chambers never knew precisely where Levine had hidden it* [emphasis added].

Another lengthy FBI summary report, of March 30, 1949, described Levine's intended trial testimony: that the envelope had been "sealed," that Chambers had carefully instructed Levine to safeguard the material and had specified what to do should "anything happen" to Chambers or his wife, and that the envelope had been secreted in an abandoned dumbwaiter shaft in the second-floor bathroom of Levine's parents' house. The report continued:

He [Levine] will testify that this envelope was sealed when he received it from CHAMBERS and remained sealed until he turned it back to CHAMBERS *on November 21, 1948,* when he and CHAMBERS were at [Levine's parents'] residence. (It is to be noted that LEVINE is undoubtedly mistaken as to this date, inasmuch as the documents were produced by CHAMBERS at the pre-trial examination on November 17, 1948, and CHAMBERS fixes date he received same as November 14, 1948.) He [Levine] will testify that . . . his only knowledge of the contents thereof came from watching CHAMBERS open the envelope in the kitchen of [his parents'] residence immediately after he had handed the envelope back to CHAMBERS. He will testify that he paid no attention to CHAMBERS as the latter was extracting material from the envelope, *except that he did know there were some documents among the material,* and he remembered that CHAMBERS *made some exclamation of surprise as he was removing the material* [emphasis added].[16]

Levine's December 4, 1948 FBI interview had been decidedly unhelpful to Chambers. On December 5, Levine continued to hold to the November 21, 1948 delivery date—thus the March 30, 1949, FBI observation of the need to rectify this "mistake." By December 5, however, Levine had radically revised his original testimony as to where the documents had been stored and what the "sealed" envelope contained. Storage of the envelope in the basement with other materials as opposed to an "abandoned dumb-waiter shaft" scarcely supported a "life preserver" claim. Levine's further revision that the "sealed" envelope contained "some documents" was far more helpful than his original testimony that Chambers had "looked over some material" which had been stored in an unsealed "folder or envelope."

By the time of his December 9 HUAC testimony, Levine exactly followed Chambers's account. Levine then claimed: first, that Chambers had retrieved the envelope "three weeks ago" (November 14); second, that Chambers had contacted him on either Thursday or Friday (November 11 or 12); and third, that Chambers telegraphed him on Sunday (November 14) to advise him of his arrival that same day at 1:00 P.M.. There still remained one striking discrepancy between Levine's revised account of a "sealed" envelope and Chambers's December 28, 1948 executive session HUAC testimony. Queried by HUAC counsel Stripling whether this envelope had been "sealed," Chambers responded "No, it was not sealed. *As I recall*, it had rubber bands around it [emphasis added]."[17] Chambers's evasive December 28 response suggests that by this time, at least, Chambers and Levine had not yet agreed how to characterize this retrieved envelope.

In 1949, however, the FBI claimed to have discovered a copy of Chambers's November 14, 1948 telegram to Levine. In a May 27, 1949 report, FBI agent M. W. McFarlin advised FBI Director Hoover and the special agent in charge of the New York field office that:

Chambers had advised [on May 24, 1949] he telephoned Levine from Westminster or Baltimore on or about Nov. 12, [1948], telling Levine he was coming up to Brooklyn in a day or so *to obtain envelope* stored with Levine years before. Chambers was not sure Levine knew what Chambers was talking about. On Sunday, Nov. 14, last, Chambers came from Westminster to Baltimore enroute to Brooklyn to contact Levine. At Pa. RR Station in Baltimore Chambers sent Levine a telegram via WU [Western Union] telling Levine he was coming up and to have Chambers's things ready. *Chambers states he did not sign own name to telegram but hoped Levine would guess its author* and locate the envelope before Chambers arrival. Following message, *believed to be the telegram in question*, located in files of Western Union at Baltimore. Message, handwritten in pencil throughout, was filed at Pa. RR station in Baltimore at 9:34 AM, Nov. 14, 1948, *addressed to Nathan Levine*, 960 Sterling Place, Brooklyn, NY, and *signed "Whit."* Message read "Arriving around one. Please have my things ready." Filed message reflects sender's name and address as "W. Simpson, 27 Oak Street, Greenmount, MD." US Postal Guide lists a Greenmount in Carroll County, Md., same county in which Westminster is located but name and street address probably fictitious . . . [Western Union] will produce original of above message in court under subpoena duces tecum. . . . Efforts to obtain original of delivered message from Levine being left to discretion of NY office [emphasis added].[18]

McFarlin's discovery of this telegraph message does not, however, conclusively confirm a November 14, 1948 arrival date. The FBI agent could not conclusively state that Chambers had sent the telegram, insofar as another (seemingly fictitious name) had been used. Neither Levine nor Chambers had earlier told FBI agents (Levine on December 5, 1948, and Chambers on December 3, 1948 and during March 1949—the latter at a time of FBI concern about Levine's testimony citing a November 21, 1948 retrieval date) that Chambers had sent Levine a telegram under the fictitious name of "W. Simpson, 27 Oak Street, Greenmount, MD." Only on May 24, 1949 did Chambers admit sending the telegram under another name. Since presumably he was telegraphing to advise Levine of the time and date of his arrival, would Chambers have used a fictitious name? Why had Levine not already produced the original telegram? By December 9 (the date of his HUAC testimony), Levine knew of the problems posed by his earlier assertions of a November 21 retrieval date. More significant when telegraphing Levine, Chambers had thereby created a written record of a November 14, 1948 arrival. Chambers's telephone call on November 12 had presumably advised Levine of his imminent arrival to retrieve the envelope. No record, however, would have been created of the participants in or the specifics of a telephone conversation (that is, if the conversation was not tapped). In contrast, a telegram creates such a written record—clearly essential in this case given Levine's at first unhelpful statements to the FBI.

If Chambers retrieved an envelope from Nathan Levine on November 21 then this envelope could not have contained the four handwritten Hiss notes, the sixty-five pages of State Department documents allegedly typed on the Hiss's old Woodstock typewriter, and the White memorandum. This explains Chambers's failure to turn the microfilm over to his attorneys on November 15, and thus the two transmission dates.

Questions Involving the HUAC-FBI Relationship

If the Hiss notes and typed documents were not stored in the envelope Chambers deposited with Nathan Levine in 1938 or 1939, how did Chambers come to possess them in November 1948? One explanation relates to the nature of the relationship between the FBI and HUAC (specifically Congressman Richard Nixon) throughout the year 1948. This relationship had its origins in an FBI "educational" program initiated in February 1946.

Former Communist Elizabeth Bentley's allegations during a November 1945 FBI interview, and former Soviet consular official Igor Gouzenko's October 1945 allegations to Canadian security officials had provided the catalyst for this "educational" program. Bentley and Gouzenko had claimed that a number of (United States and Canadian) government officials were involved in espionage on behalf of the Soviet Union. While Gouzenko's testimony pertained to Canadian officials, he claimed to have learned from "Lieutenant Kulakov in the office of the Soviet military attache that the Soviets had an agent in the United States in May 1945 who was an assistant to then Secretary of State Edward R. Stettinius." From this hearsay statement and Whittaker Chambers's listing of members of a Communist cell, FBI Director Hoover concluded that the reference was to Alger Hiss, "though there was no direct evidence to sustain this suspicion." Bentley concurrently identified a number of predominantly Treasury and State Department employees. She named Treasury employees Harry Dexter White, Irving Kaplan, William Henry Taylor, Harold Glasser, Nathan Gregory Silvermaster, Sonia Steinman Gold, Solomon Adler, William Ludwig Ullmann, Virginius Frank Coe, and Victor Perlo. The State Department officials she identified were Alger Hiss, Maurice Halperin, Donald Niven Wheeler, Robert Talbot Miller III, Michael Greenberg, Joseph Gregg, and Peter Christopher Rhodes. Rounding out Bentley's list of names were William Walter Remington, John Hazard Reynolds, Norman Chandler Bursler, Harry Samuel Magdoff, Duncan Chaplin Lee, Edward Joseph Fitzgerald, Helen B. Tenney, Bela Gold, Bernard Sidney Redmont, and Alan Robert Rosenberg.

Gouzenko's and Bentley's charges were undocumented. Nonetheless, convinced that a serious espionage problem existed, FBI Director Hoover bombarded the Administration with reports detailing Bentley's allegations—reports that also incorporated Whittaker Chambers's allegations. Hoover not only submitted reports; he also urged Administration officials to fire Alger Hiss and Harry Dexter White, the two most prominent individuals of those cited by the Bureau's informers. At the least, Hoover convinced White House aide George Allen that Hiss should be fired. On June 3, 1946, Allen advised FBI agent Ralph Roach of his own and President Truman's appreciation of the information that the FBI had been supplying on Soviet matters. On the basis of these reports, Allen continued, they "had been able to disapprove numerous appointments that come up to the President for a decision." Allen had concluded that Hiss, Dean Acheson, Gustave Duran, and Robert T. Miller should be "summarily dismissed" and furthermore that Acheson was the principal problem—Acheson's removal would result in a "different atmosphere" at State. The White House aide informed Roach that he intended to "again take the matter up with the President at a convenient opportunity and was hopeful that some action would be taken."

Truman did not fire Acheson or Hiss. Nevertheless, although lacking evidence to justify Hiss's dismissal (at the time Hiss was director of the State Department's Office of Special Political Affairs), Hoover obtained Attorney General Tom Clark's authorization to wiretap the State Department official. On Hoover's exclusive authority, FBI agents also began following Hiss, a surveillance that included intercepting and reading his mail. This intensive surveillance uncovered no evidence of disloyalty. (This is confirmed by an internal FBI memorandum. See Memo, Ladd to FBI Director, Nov. 13, 1953, FBI 101-2668-52, *AH*.)

Hoover also sought to impugn White's loyalty. At the time, White was under final consideration for appointment as executive director of the International Monetary Fund. To submarine White's appointment Hoover persistently sent the unsubstantiated allegations of "a highly confidential source" (Bentley was not identified, nor was the credibility of her allegations assessed) to President Truman, Attorney General Clark, Secretary of State James Byrnes, Secretary of the Navy James Forrestal, Secretary of the Treasury Fred Vinson, Assistant Secretary of State Spruille Braden, White House aide Admiral William Leahy, Lt. General Hoyt Vandenberg, Secretary of State Byrnes's aide Frederick Lyon, and Special Assistant to the Attorney General A. Devitt Vanech.

Although failing to stymie White's appointment, Hoover urged Attorney General Clark and Secretary of State Byrnes to remove Hiss from his sensitive postion. Hoover, however, opposed a security dismissal hearing because the information the FBI had acquired about Hiss was "confidential" (obtained through a wiretap, mail intercept, and informants). Such a hearing would compromise the Bureau by revealing its sources and investigative techniques. Instead, in March 1946, the FBI Director recommended that, to force Hiss's resignation, Byrnes transfer Hiss to an "innocuous position." Hoover concurrently urged Byrnes to leak unsubstantiated derogatory information about Hiss to congressional leaders "like [Senator] Tom Connally, [Senator] Arthur Vandenburg [sic], [Congressman] John McCormack or [House Speaker] Sam Rayburn." Byrnes was unable to implement this strategy because he was concentrating on preparing for a United Nations Security Council meeting the next week. Byrnes did contact Rayburn "who advised [Byrnes] that he could do nothing with [conservative Democratic Congressman John] Rankin." (At the time, Rankin was publicly criticizing State Department loyalty procedures.) Not having time to "contact anyone on the hill as the [FBI] Director had suggested," Byrnes decided to confront Hiss directly. In this meeting, Hiss denied the allegations about his loyalty and agreed to repeat these denials during a formal FBI interview.[19]

Hoover's March 1946 recommendation to Byrnes comported with a more general program that FBI officials had authorized the previous month. On February 22, 1946, FBI Assistant Director D. M. Ladd recommended that "an effort should be made now to prepare educational material which can be released through available channels." To brief all

FBI field office "Communist supervisors," a two-day training conference should be convened. Communist support could thereby be undermined in the labor unions, among prominent religious personalities, and "liberal elements." This "educational" effort, Ladd concluded, should particularly emphasize "the basically Russian nature of the Communist Party in this country." Ladd's recommendations were approved that month by the FBI executive conference (composed of all high-level FBI officials).[20]

The executive conference decision of 1946 formalized what had been an ongoing informal practice whereby FBI officials leaked information to conservative reporters and congressmen. The Bureau's Crime Records Division and FBI Assistant Director Louis Nichols (and his successor Cartha DeLoach) assumed responsibility for cultivating "friendly" reporters, congressmen, and public opinion leaders. In time FBI officials developed a so-called Mass Media Program to leak to the news media— for example, derogatory information on prominent radicals—while the Crime Records Division helped draft speeches and/or letters for members of Congress. To further this effort to influence key congressmen, FBI agents began in 1950 to collect personal background information on congressional candidates—particularly on their attitudes toward the FBI.[21]

The program had not been refined by the spring of 1946. Nonetheless, supplementing the pressures on the Truman Administration, FBI officials leaked derogatory information on Hiss and other federal employees to selected conservative congressmen. Although he had not read Hoover's December 4, 1945 report on Hiss and other State Department officials, Secretary of State Byrnes learned of the allegations from Mississippi Senator James Eastland and Georgia Congressman Edward Cox. Eastland advised Byrnes that "the FBI had information indicating that ALGER HISS was a Communist" while Cox reported his intent "to make a speech on the House floor to that effect, naming HISS and others in Government service who were suspected of being Communists."

Cox did not name Hiss publicly, apparently convinced of Byrnes's commitment to purging Communists from the State Department. Nonetheless, in a May 2, 1946 speech, Cox did lament that there were "too many undesirable people holding important places in the State Department and too many of like character occupying positions of less importance." Maintaining that hundreds of State Department employees had been fired in a "purge of leftist elements," Cox commended the recent efforts of State Department officials who "for weeks now" were "screen[ing] out" all "undersirable" personnel. Suggesting that "congressional agitation" had caused the needed purge, the Georgia congressman claimed that "the State Department many weeks ago . . . set about to clean out the Department from top to bottom. The FBI was called in and was given a free hand in the screening of personnel. . . . The FBI has been at work."

Cox and others (Senators Pat McCarran, Kenneth Wherry, and Kenneth McKellar; Congressmen Carl Curtis, George Dondero, Richard Wigglesworth, Howard Smith, Frederick Bradley, Louis Rabaut, Andrew May, John Rankin, and John Taber; and Congresswoman Edith Rogers) publicly demanded the purging of Communists from the State Department. Apart from Curtis, none of the congressman identified the "undesirables." In an April 10, 1946 speech, Taber threatened to do so: "I am not going to read the names here. I am not going to get into that question today. On the other hand it is a situation that calls for a house cleaning. These people are presently on the roll and they ought not to be on the roll." Senator McCarran, moreover, demanded FBI Director Hoover's appearance before the Senate Committee on Appropriations to respond to questions about the "Communist tendencies of certain persons" and to bring "the files on [name deleted], Hiss, and on an additional person who is not connected with the Government." Informed of this request, Attorney General Clark interceded with McCarran, later advising Hoover that there was no need for further action on this matter.

If conservative Democrats demanded only the purging of Communists, conservative Republicans accused the Truman Administration of shackling the FBI. "It has come to my attention," Congressman Dondero charged, "that in some instances the efforts of the FBI have been almost completely frustrated in attempting to deal with this condition within our own country." Moreover, Congressman Bradley claimed that a Bureau of Budget official, who had sought Hoover's replacement as FBI director, had destroyed and continued to destroy records documenting Communist influence in key government agencies. With FBI files purged, Bradley warned, "we would never have a record of any of the Communists who now seek employment with the Government."[22]

Privileged knowledge about the "Communist problem" extended beyond the Congress. Radio commentators Walter Winchell and Drew Pearson, and *New York Journal-American* reporter Howard Rushmore somehow acquired access to FBI reports on Hiss. In a March 24, 1946 speech before a group of Catholic journalists, Catholic Bishop Fulton J. Sheen maintained that an unidentified congressional committee had uncovered the fact that a "full-fledged Soviet agent was picked up." Pressed for additional details on the identity either of the agent or the committee, Sheen responded that the agent was male, from Chicago, and not an elected official. Calling upon the press to report more on "the undermining of government by alien and foreign interests," Sheen claimed that his purpose was not "to give information, but to stimulate members of the press." A *New York Times* reporter pursued this lead but discovered that neither the FBI nor HUAC knew anything about the "arrest" of the "spy."[23]

How had Taber secured a list of "disloyal" Government employees? How had Cox become aware of the FBI's involvement in purging the State Department? How had Dondero learned that the FBI had been "shackled"? How had Eastland, McCarran, McKellar, Rushmore, Winchell, and Pearson learned of the FBI's file on Alger Hiss? Apparently, their source was the FBI.

Beginning at least in August 1948, in their efforts to intensify public concern about threats to the internal security, FBI officials covertly collaborated with Congressman Richard Nixon. To insure that this collaboration, which ran counter to the political interests of the incumbent Democratic Administration, could not be discovered, FBI officials devised tight security procedures.

In early 1948, HUAC had attempted to create the impression that the Truman Administration was insensitive to the seriousness of the internal security threat. On March 13, 1948, responding to a HUAC request for the loyalty file of Bureau of Standards Director Edward Condon, President Truman issued a far-reaching executive order. Under the order, heads of federal agencies and departments were specifically directed not to comply with congressional requests for loyalty files, even if subpoenaed, but to forward such requests for the President's approval. Congressman Nixon successfully circumvented this restriction. "Because of Truman's executive order," Nixon writes in his recently published memoirs, "we [HUAC] were not able to get any direct help from J. Edgar Hoover or the FBI. However, we had some informal contacts with a lower-level agent that proved helpful in our investigations." In his introductory comments preceding the testimony of Elizabeth Bentley, HUAC chairman J. Parnell Thomas also confirmed that "the closest relationship exists between this committee [HUAC] and the FBI. . . . I think there is a very good understanding between us. It is something, however, that we cannot talk too much about."

Catholic priest John Cronin describes one means by which this was done. "Ed Hummer was one of the FBI agents I had worked with," Cronin told interviewer Garry Wills. "He could have got in serious trouble for what he did, since the Justice Department [in 1948] was sitting on the results of the Bureau's investigation into Hiss—the car, the typewriter, etc. But Ed would call me every day, and tell me what they had turned up; and I told Dick [Nixon], who then knew just where to look for things, and what he could find." During a November 26, 1975 interview with Allen Weinstein, Cronin further elaborated (in Weinstein's summarization) "that he phoned Nixon's private line frequently *between August and December 1948*, supplying these F.B.I. tidbits [emphasis added]."[24]

Inexplicably, in *Perjury*, Weinstein totally avoids Cronin's account of his own and the FBI's helpful assistance to Nixon during this period. Cronin's admission raises serious questions about why and when the FBI began to investigate Hiss's "car, typewriter, etc." Apparently, the FBI began its investigation of Hiss's disposition of the car and typewriter before the HUAC hearings were convened in August 1948, and furthermore, before the grand jury proceedings leading to Hiss's indictment in December 1948. Cronin's role as an intermediary in forwarding information from these FBI investigations to Nixon helps explain Chambers's impressive testimony of August 1948 before HUAC and Nixon's devastating interrogation of Hiss during these hearings as to how Hiss had disposed of the automobile.[25] More important, since Cronin failed to date precisely when the FBI began to investigate the typewriter, we are left with the possibility—as Hiss has alleged—of "forgery by typewriter"; that is, if the FBI investigation of the Hiss typewriter predated November 1948.

The dating of FBI leaks to Cronin is crucial: if they occurred after December 1948, the FBI was simply following up on the development precipitated by Chambers's dramatic presentation of documents he claimed to have received from Hiss. Had the FBI begun to investigate Hiss's disposition of the car and typewriter as early as July-August 1948, we need to understand why the investigations were initiated and when. Because documents recording the investigations as well as the attendant leaks to Nixon would have been extremely sensitive, conceivably they may have been created under a Do Not File procedure. The allegation is not merely speculative. From other FBI files, we know of a close relationship between Nixon and FBI Assistant Director Louis Nichols during 1948. Released FBI files do not recount the nature of that relationship, suggesting either that no record was created or that Nichols's memoranda and reports were prepared under a Do Not File procedure.[26]

Thus, an FBI memorandum of December 9, 1948, on Congressman Nixon's conversation the previous day with former FBI agents Patrick Coyne and Robert King, records Nixon as having "voluntarily stated during the course of the evening that he had worked very close with the Bureau and with [FBI Assistant Director Louis] Nichols *during the past year* on this matter [emphasis added]." Another, December 2, 1948 FBI memorandum confirms the closeness of the Nichols-Nixon relationship "during the past year." In this memorandum to FBI Associate Director Clyde Tolson, Nichols reported that "late last night on a strictly personal and highly confidential basis" Nixon had called Nichols to report on his December 1 meeting with Whittaker Chambers in Westminster, Maryland. Chambers told him, Nixon briefed Nichols, he had already produced (on November 17 in the Baltimore pre-trial hearings) "highly incriminating" State Department documents that Mrs. Hiss had typed and that Hiss had given him for transmission to the Russians. Chambers "did not *tell the FBI* everything he knew and as a matter of fact *still has other documents and material* that substantiate and vindicate his position which have up to this time not become publicly known [emphasis

added]." (Either Nixon erred, since Chambers had not yet been interviewed by the FBI about the Baltimore documents, or this interview was
not recorded.) Nixon detailed his proposed strategy for handling the new
development:

> to subpoena these documents at [HUAC-scheduled] hearings on December 18
> [1948, following Nixon's planned return on December 15 from a vacation to
> the Caribbean on the cruise ship *Panama*] and the purpose of this call, which
> he reiterated was strictly personal and highly confidential, was merely to apprise
> the Bureau so that the FBI would not be caught off base. He stated that they
> [HUAC] were handling the matter so that there will be no criticism to the FBI
> and he particularly urged that we do nothing about the information which he has
> just furnished as he feels the statute of limitations has run.
>
> Nixon specifically urged that we not tell the Attorney General that we were
> told of this information as the Attorney General would try to make it impossible
> for the Committee to get at the documents. He also asked that the Bureau not
> look for the documents thermselves.[27]

The closeness of this relationship explains the audacity of a freshman
congressman calling in the middle of the night to suggest that the Bureau:
(1) not look for incriminating documents until the Committee publicly
released them sixteen days later; and (2) purposefully mislead the
Attorney General. Given the "closeness" of the Nixon-Nichols relationship "during the past year," FBI Director Hoover not surprisingly
ordered, "Do so and let me know result."

Nichols was not a "lower level" FBI agent but a powerful FBI official
who served as the FBI's liaison with conservative congressmen and reporters. To expedite this mission, in October 1941, FBI Director
Hoover had apprised other FBI officials of his decision to maintain
an "Official and Confidential" file in Nichols's office. (Hoover had maintained an Official and Confidential file in his own office since the 1920s.)
Having direct access to this file, Nichols could, and did leak highly sensitive information to conservative congressmen and reporters. Nichols
worked closely with Nixon in 1948, and continued in 1949 and 1950;
he also kept in close contact with, among others, syndicated Hearst
columnist Fulton Lewis, Jr., UPI Washington bureau chief Lyle Wilson,
and *New York Herald-Tribune* Washington bureau chief Don Whitehead.[28]

Nixon, however, was not entirely candid with Nichols that evening of December 1, 1948. His deception involved the date HUAC planned to release the Pumpkin Papers—not December 18 but December 6. The earlier release date was stage-managed to convey the impression of a dedicated congressman returning from vacation because of the press of congressional responsibilities.

Despite having kept the microfilm in his home since retrieving it from New York (either on November 14 or 21), Chambers secreted the microfilm in a hollowed-out pumpkin in the patch adjoining his Westminster home before departing for Washington on the morning of December 2. Former House doorkeeper William "Fishbait" Miller writes of a conversation he had "about one or two o'clock" the morning of December 2 with Congressman Nixon, following Nixon's late-night return from the meeting with Chambers. The congressman was in "high spirits," Miller writes, and was in a hurry. Nonetheless, Miller continues, Nixon

was so delighted with something that he had to share it. He said, "I'm going to get on a steamship and you will be reading about it. I am going out to sea and they are going to send for me. You will understand when I get back, Fishbait!" He looked very elated and keyed up, as if he were dancing on wires. Even his eyes were dancing.

Two other sources confirm that Nixon's dramatic December 6, 1948 return to Washington was prearranged. (On December 3, Nixon had left New York on the *S.S. Panama* on a Carribbean vacation cruise.) At around 5:00 P.M. on December 5, Nixon's administrative assistant contacted Secretary of Defense James Forrestal (and not Secretary of the Treasury John Snyder) to secure authorization to dispatch a Coast Guard helicopter to pick up Nixon from the *S.S. Panama*. Forrestal's authorization was *pro forma* since the helicopter carrying Nixon from the *Panama* had already returned to Biscayne Bay, Florida, at approximately 2:10 P.M., some three hours before Forrestal's authorization had been sought. (The helicopter had taken off at approximately 6:20 A.M. from the St. Petersburg, Florida, Coast Guard station.) The absence of any flight orders in the Coast Guard's communications or operations logs of December 4 or 5, further suggests that the planning for the pick-up predated the *S.S. Panama's* December 3 departure.

Following his and Stripling's December 1 meeting with Chambers, moreover, Nixon also telephoned *New York Herald-Tribune* reporter Bert Andrews, who rushed over to Nixon's office. Nixon briefed Andrews about the Westminster trip and Chambers's claims to having already handed over documents (on November 17) and to possess additional documents. Nixon maintains that he telephoned Stripling the night of December 1 directing him to be at HUAC's office the next morning at 8:00 A.M. to subpoena the documents from Chambers that day. (This seems to be a cover story since Stripling had accompanied Nixon on the trip to Chambers's Westminster, Maryland, farm.) In response to the subpoena, and after completing his testimony during the State Department loyalty proceeding, Chambers left Washington at around 5:00 P.M., arriving at his Westminster farm at 10:00 P.M. accompanied by HUAC investigators Donald Appell and William Wheeler. Leading the HUAC investigators to his pumpkin patch, Chambers produced the microfilm. Appell and Wheeler thereupon returned to Washington, arriving around 1:00 A.M., December 3.

Before the HUAC investigators returned to Washington with the microfilm, Andrews had already telegraphed Nixon (the evening of *December 2*): "Information here is that Hiss-Chambers case has produced new bombshell. Indications are that Chambers has offered new evidence. All concerned silent. However, Justice Department particularly confirms by saying 'it is too hot for comment.' " Since Nixon had already briefed Andrews about this material and the HUAC investigators had not yet returned to Washington, Andrews's telegram contained no new information. Allegedly after reviewing the microfilmed documents, HUAC counsel Stripling also telegraphed Nixon: "Second bombshell obtained by subpoena 1 A.M. Friday. Case clinched. Information amazing. *Heat is on from the press and other places.* Immediate action appears necessary. Can you possibly get back?" (The claim about press interest is intriguing since presumably the press and "other places" [the FBI?] did not know about the microfilm until the Committee publicized the dramatic development the following day.) Whether or not he was aware that Nixon had phoned Nichols the night of December 1, Stripling telephoned Nichols on December 3. The HUAC counsel either was acting independently because he knew about the close relationship between Nixon and Nichols, or was phoning by prearrangement with

Nixon for the purpose of revising the congressman's misleading report that HUAC hearings were to resume on December 18.[29] (The hearings began instead on December 6.)

The close FBI-HUAC relationship dated from HUAC's August 1948 decision to subpoena Chambers. The catalyst to the hearings had been the hope of the Republican congressional leadership to undercut the impact of President Truman's dramatic recall of the Republican-controlled Eightieth Congress for a special session. Even then, HUAC had no specific witness list. Writing as late as July 26, 1948 to Committee member Karl Mundt, HUAC chairman J. Parnell Thomas observed that "since the Federal Grand Jury which has been sitting in New York has returned its indictments, I feel we are now free to proceed with the taking of open testimony *from various witnesses* who were subjects of this Grand Jury investigation (emphasis added)."

HUAC first subpoenaed Elizabeth Bentley. In early July 1948, the *New York World Telegram* had published a series of stories by Frederick Woltman luridly highlighting Bentley's grand jury testimony about a World War II Communist spy ring.[30] Bentley's July 31, 1948 HUAC testimony failed to have major effect. Her personal background and unsubstantiated charges combined to undermine her credibility. As an August 2 FBI memorandum confided, HUAC subpoenaed Chambers to testify on August 3 "to furnish background information which would substantiate the information already furnished by ELIZABETH T. BENTLEY."

Unlike Bentley, Chambers had *not* testified before the grand jury. As early as March 1948, Justice Department officials had considered subpoenaing Chambers to testify before the grand jury, but first sought the FBI's clearance, since Chambers would then become publicly exposed as an FBI informer. United States Attorney D. J. Donegan eventually decided not to subpoena Chambers. Appraising the information Chambers had given during a Treasury Department loyalty proceeding as "negative," Donegan concluded that "Chambers' testimony before the Grand Jury would not be helpful and decided against any attempt to have Chambers appear." The FBI learned of Donegan's decision on August 2—coincidentally, the very day HUAC subpoenaed Chambers to testify before the Committee.

Later that month, on August 13, 1948, *Washington Star* columnist

David Lawrence attributed HUAC's decision to convene hearings to the discovery that the "FBI was not advised as to what evidence was presented to the special grand jury in New York." Lawrence continued: "Just why the FBI has been deprived of knowledge of what evidence was presented to the grand jury has not been explained." On August 16, 1948, commenting on the grand jury's failure to issue indictments, Lawrence further charged that the "recent presentation of evidence before the grand jury was made contrary to the wishes of the Federal Bureau of Investigation, which did not believe the case was sufficiently constructed to assure convictions."

Clearly, Lawrence had excellent sources. Whether Lawrence's information came directly or indirectly (via HUAC) from the FBI,[31] his columns suggest HUAC's future useful role. Hearsay allegations could be highlighted in widely publicized hearings, thereby undercutting the impact of the grand jury's failure to issue indictments and the resultant impression that there was no evidence of a Communist espionage ring operating during the New Deal years.

Lawrence was not the sole recipient of leaked information concerning the grand jury's confidential proceedings. In the December 1947 issue of *Plain Talk*, conservative journalist Isaac Don Levine detailed with uncanny accuracy the thrust of the allegations about Communist espionage being presented to the grand jury. How Levine became privy to this confidential information raises interesting questions. More important, however, was the specificity of one of Levine's revelations: "Certain high and trusted officials in the State Department, including one who had played a leading role at Yalta and in organizing the United Nations, delivered confidential papers to Communist agents who microfilmed them for dispatch to Moscow."

This reference to a "high and trusted" official who attended Yalta and helped organize the United Nations was to Alger Hiss. At the time, neither in testimony before the grand jury nor in confidential FBI interviews had any witness so accused Hiss. The principal government witness before the grand jury, Elizabeth Bentley, had had no connection with Hiss; she had neither received from nor known whether Hiss might have stolen State Department documents. Justice Department officials having concluded that he could offer no convincing testimony, Whittaker

Chambers did not testify before the grand jury. Until December 1948, moreover, Chambers had not accused Hiss of espionage.

In an October 1948 article in *Plain Talk*, Levine seemed to describe the source of his information about Hiss: Levine's attendance at Chambers's September 2, 1939 meeting with State Department security official Adolf Berle. Levine claimed that in this 1939 meeting Chambers had described two Soviet underground rings, both of which "were gathering and supplying confidential data to Moscow." Levine's account, however, conflicts with Berle's notes on the meeting and Berle's August 1948 account before HUAC. In his HUAC testimony, Berle characterized Chambers's testimony about the Communist underground as simply repeating the standard right-wing charge of Communist efforts to infiltrate the New Deal.

Berle's differing characterization of Chambers's testimony was not a case, as Allen Weinstein has recently written, of Berle's New Deal partisanship; the frequent references in Berle's notes to "underground" activities do not confirm that Chambers had testified about espionage. Berle's notes on the 1939 meeting were eventually transmitted to the FBI in 1943. Thus, if the notes had recorded testimony about espionage, then during subsequent interviews FBI agents were in a position to elicit further elaboration from Chambers or to challenge him on his seemingly changed contentions about Communist underground activities. FBI officials would have been particularly sensitive to information about espionage in March 1946, since at the time, they were seeking confirmation from Chambers in order to force Hiss's dismissal from the State Department.

By the time Levine's October 1948 *Plain Talk* article was published, moreover, Chambers had not accused Hiss of espionage, explicitly denying in testimony under oath (before HUAC in August and a federal grand jury in October) that Hiss had been involved in espionage. What, then, was the basis for Levine's December 1947 and October 1948 allegations? Had Chambers told Levine privately what he hesitated to tell the FBI until December 1948? The available documentary evidence—notably Solow's notarized memorandum of November 1938, and the manuscript that Chambers had prepared in 1938 on Communist underground activities hoping that Levine could secure its publication—suggests that Chambers did not identify Hiss as a participant in espionage.

What were the sources for Levine's allegations? Levine's information could have come from FBI officials who either orally briefed him or showed him classified FBI documents. This speculation can only be resolved once we are assured access to the FBI files concerning the relationship between FBI officials and Levine in 1947 and 1948, and dating from 1939. Levine's December 1947 article does confirm his privileged knowledge of the confidential conversations of Canadian Prime Minister Mackenzie King and President Truman on October 2, 1945, and of the hearsay allegations of Soviet defector Igor Gouzenko about "an assistant to the Secretary of State, Edward R. Stettinius." Unserialized and separately filed documents in FBI Director Hoover's Official and Confidential files record Hoover's immediate reaction to this report suspecting that Hiss was the individual. FBI officials conceivably shared their suspicions with Levine in late 1947, also permitting him to review relevant FBI documents. If the FBI was Levine's source, this explains why the Bureau failed to interview Levine and reinterview Chambers once apprised of Levine's startling public "revelations" of December 1947 and October 1948.[32]

The FBI was clearly not a disinterested party, For example, responding to Chambers's production on November 17, 1948 of the typed State Department documents, the Justice Department considered instituting perjury charges against Chambers, given his October 1948 grand jury denial to having any such documents. Apprised of this departmental policy, FBI Director Hoover commented: "Interesting but I wonder why they don't move against Hiss also." "Careful and meticulous" effort should be made to establish Hiss's access to these State Department documents, Hoover ordered, adding again, "Collaterally I can't understand why such effort is being made to indict Chambers to exclusion of Hiss."

As part of their "careful and meticulous" effort, FBI officials sought the original copies of the State Department documents (either the sixty-five typed pages on the four handwritten Hiss notes). They were obtained, FBI agent Kenneth Delevaigne soon reported, through a State Department source (released FBI documents delete the source's name). The source allegedly contacted an FBI agent because he was fearful that the State Department might "freeze" all the relevant documents, and "wanted the Bureau to have copies of these documents just in case a 'freeze' was put on the material." The source asked that the FBI photostat and return the copies to him "before the close of business" that day, and further advised Delavaigne that in 1938 the State Department had no "system of classification" for the documents. The FBI's source could not identify the individuals responsible for routing the received documents. (The FBI Director did not apprise the Attorney General of this arrangement. In a December 16, 1948 memorandum to Clark, Hoover innocently reported that Donald Nicholson [Chief of the State Department's Division of Security] had "made available" to the FBI's Washington Field Office a "list of the original State Department documents" from which the Chambers-produced documents had been made. Pursuant to the Attorney General's request, Nicholson was making copies of the documents, Hoover continued, and would provide them "in the near future.")[33]

Questions about the Harry Dexter White Memorandum

The specific nature of the FBI-HUAC relationship becomes more intriguing when we examine Chamber's presentation in November 1948 of "handwriting specimens" of both Alger Hiss and Harry Dexter White. It is suspicious that Chambers possessed notes written during 1938 by Hiss and White, and only these two men. Hiss and White had not figured prominently in Chambers's pre-August 1948 testimony; they alone among the twenty individuals Chambers named to the FBI in 1942 rose to positions of influence within the Roosevelt and Truman Administrations. Why could Chambers produce documents in *November 1948* written by the former executive director of the International Monetary Fund (White) and the former director the State Department's Office of Special Political Affairs (Hiss), but not notes in the handwriting of say, Henry Julian Wadleigh, William Ward Pigman, or Franklin Vincent Reno?

Until August 1948, Chambers had not even given White's name to the FBI, let alone accused him of membership in the "Communist underground." These occasions included Chambers's September 1939 interview with Berle, May 13, 1942 FBI interview, and May 10 and 11, 1945, FBI interviews. The FBI first learned of White's "subversive" activities in November 1945, but then because of Elizabeth Bentley's testimony. In October 1947, FBI Assistant Director Nichols first learned that Chambers had known White; his source was not Chambers but two conservative reporters, James Walter and Ed Nellor. Walter had given Nichols a copy of State Department security official Raymond Murphy's memorandum on an interview with Chambers. In the interview, Chambers did not directly name White but, when describing his own attempt to convince Hiss to break with the Communist Party, claimed: "Went to eminent money theorist Harry White. . . . White is a great coward. Thought he [Chambers] scared him [White] into breaking with Party. Hiss is not a coward."

Chambers had also not volunteered White's name during his August 3, 1948 HUAC testimony. White's name came up only because HUAC counsel Stripling specifically asked Chambers about White. (Stripling was seeking corroboration for Elizabeth Bentley's July 31, 1948 testimony.) White was not a Communist Party member, Chambers replied, but "certainly was a fellow traveller, so far within the fold that his not being a Communist would be a mistake on both sides."[34]

During the pre-trial Baltimore hearing on November 17, 1948, however, Chambers slightly changed his testimony about White. After producing the Hiss notes and sixty-five pages of typed State Department documents, Chambers volunteered that Colonel Boris Bykov—his Communist superior and, after 1936, the head of Soviet military intelligence in the United States—had been particularly interested in White. White had also supplied information for Bykov, "a piece of which in [White's] handwriting is in my possession." When Hiss's attorney queried whether White had given him "secret papers," Chambers replied, "No, I don't believe he did, but he used to write out reports of interesting things he had heard in the Treasury [Department]." Further pressed as to whether these were secret papers, Chambers confusedly replied: "No—well, sometimes, yes. Well, secret papers—he would give me his written report. He sometimes gave them to George Silverman to give to me."[35]

Allegedly the White "handwriting" had been included in the "life preserver" packet Chambers had left with Nathan Levine in 1938.
Chambers later claimed to have given this memorandum to his attorney
on November 15, 1948, along with the Hiss material. Because it was not
relevant to the Hiss libel suit, Chambers's attorney did not produce the
memorandum during the November 17 pre-trial hearing. Chambers's
pre-trial deposition, however, alerted the FBI to the existence of the
memorandum. Interviewing Chambers on December 3, FBI agents
asked Chambers for the document. Chambers then claimed that White's
handwritten notes were "examples of material that HARRY WHITE made
available to me from the Treasury Department for delivery to Colonel
BYKOV. I met HARRY WHITE always in Washington and he insisted
upon having the meetings near his home." In subsequent FBI interviews, Chambers characterized his relations with White as "touchy,"
and said that White's "transmissions were irregular and in small quantities."[36]

Apart from Chambers's radically changed testimony and his ability to
produce the four-page memorandum in White's handwriting, there are
intriguing questions about when the FBI received the document and
about Chambers's relations with the FBI. On December 3, 1948,
Chambers's attorney, Richard Cleveland, turned the White memorandum
over to FBI agents, having kept it in his safe since receiving it from his
client. Yet a January 3, 1949 FBI report specifically claims that the
White memorandum was *"delivered to Bureau agents by WHITTAKER
CHAMBERS in early November 1948* [emphasis added]."[37] The
"early November" date reference suggests a covert relationship between
Chambers and the FBI, and that this relationship predated the FBI's
formal involvement in the investigation. The FBI's authentication of
White's handwriting on the memorandum, in turn, raises additional, intriguing questions.

After comparing the "handwriting on these pieces of paper with the
known handwriting of Harry Dexter White," the FBI laboratory determined that White had written the memorandum; FBI Director Hoover
apprised Assistant Attorney General Campbell of his finding on
December 8, 1948. To reach their conclusion, FBI experts compared
the handwriting of the Chambers-produced memorandum with "three

letters written by Harry Dexter White to his wife, which were obtained through Washington Field Office Informant Z."

FBI documents of December 9 and 23, 1948, confirm the sensitivity of "Washington Field Office Informant Z." On December 9, FBI Director Hoover ordered the special agent in charge (SAC) of the Washington Field Office to "attempt to obtain additional handwriting specimens of Harry Dexter White through *available sources* such as public records, et cetera, for additional comparison with the Chambers' material since the original identification was made by comparing the Chambers' material with specimens obtained through Washington Field Office's Confidential Informant Z [emphasis added]." Another FBI memorandum of December 23 more directly acknowledged the legal problem: "By teletype dated December 16, 1948, the Washington Field Office advised that the Bureau desired adequate *legally admissible* specimens of the handwriting of HARRY DEXTER WHITE for comparison with the alleged writings of HARRY DEXTER WHITE supplied originally to the Baltimore office by CHAMBERS and his attorney, RICHARD F. CLEVELAND [emphasis added]." The FBI eventually succeeded in obtaining other handwriting samples. An FBI report of January 3, 1949 describes this source:

At the office of [deleted phrase and name of individual] of HARRY D. WHITE was examined for specimens of handwriting to compare with the handwritten documents delivered to Bureau Agents by WHITTAKER CHAMBERS in early November 1948. From this file five documents [White's letters to another Treasury official, a personal statement, and letter of resignation] were obtained and the originals forwarded to the Bureau for comparison purposes.[38]

Was "Confidential Informant Z" a Bureau euphemism for a break-in? Alternatively, does "Confidential Informant Z" refer to a separate file the FBI had maintained on White, one that contained copies of illegally opened letters? Since White died on August 16, 1948, the FBI could not have intercepted White's letters to his wife in December 1948. Either FBI agents broke into Mrs. White's residence that month to pilfer dated correspondence, or the FBI had earlier intercepted White's letters and maintained copies of them in a separate file. It appears more likely that the FBI had maintained a separate file on White, dating from 1936,

1938, or 1945. In November 1945, the FBI began to investigate White intensively in response to Elizabeth Bentley's allegations that month and, concurrently, at the time of Truman's proposed appointment of White to the International Monetary Fund. FBI surveillance of White could have begun as early as 1936 or 1938 as part of a far-reaching FBI program, intitiated in September 1936, that focused, among other categories, on federal employees.[39] Documents confirming FBI investigations of the political activities of prominent New Dealers, including the opening of their mail, would have been sufficiently sensitive to have been nonserialized and filed separately from the Bureau's central records system.

The FBI's interest in Hiss conceivably dates from the 1930s, as well, perhaps stemming from Hiss's association with radical attorneys in the Legal Division of the Agricultural Adjustment Administration and later service as counsel to the Nye Committee. In his book on FBI Director Hoover, based in part on privileged access to FBI files and oral information, Ralph deToledano alleges that since *1938* the FBI maintained files on Communist cells in the Treasury and State departments.[40] The earliest dated document in released FBI files on Hiss, however, is from 1941, when the FBI initiated a Hatch Act investigation of the then-State Department employee. The 1941 investigation, in contrast to those from 1936 to 1940, had legislative authority. Did the FBI, then, maintain a separate file on Alger Hiss that included documents dating from 1938?

Released FBI documents confirm that FBI investigations of Hiss's activities included the use of highly sensitive, and often illegal, investigative techniques. These included: intercepting Hiss's mail, telegrams, and telephone conversations; and use of an informant employed at the bank patronized by the Hisses. Not all FBI records for the investigations have been retained—the New York Field Office's subfiles A through D, and the New York SAC's "personal" file, Hiss's main file, 101–141, and Whittaker Chambers's main file, 65–6766, having been destroyed at some unknown date.[41]

The possibility that the FBI maintained separate files on White and Hiss, the FBI's contacts in the State and Treasury departments, and the FBI's reliance on Confidential Informant Z to authenticate White's handwriting demonstrate only that the FBI could have framed Hiss (not that it had done so). The records and contacts do confirm FBI officials' partisan interest in preserving Chambers's credibility. It is therefore conceivable that, in November 1948, when Chambers produced documents in Hiss's and White's handwriting and copies of State Department documents typed on a machine reproducing the same characteristics as the Hisses' discarded Woodstock typewriter, he had received them from the FBI. While unavoidably raising the possibility of a conspiracy, this hypothesis has the merit of explaining Chambers's inconsistent testimony about his Communist activities and the date of his break with the Party.

Why would FBI officials have attempted to frame Hiss? And if FBI officials supplied documents to Chambers, why did they not do so in August—at the time of Chambers's initial testimony before HUAC? FBI officials had no personal commitment to Chambers—they had little respect for the ex-Communist informer—but they may have had a desire to preserve HUAC.[42] HUAC had served as a useful conduit for sensitive information in FBI files that, when publicly released, could educate public opinion to the seriousness of the internal security threat. By November 1948, however, HUAC's continuation was in jeopardy.

President Truman initially dismissed HUAC's August hearings into the Chambers-Hiss case as a "red herring" to divert public attention from the "reactionary" record of the Eightieth Congress. Thereafter during the fall presidential campaign, Truman denounced the Committee's investigations as partisan publicity-seeking. Following his November victory, the President publicly disparaged the "defunct" Committee, and privately directed Attorney General Tom Clark to prepare for the use of the Democratic House leadership during the organizational session of the Eighty-first Congress a resolution to amend House rules to terminate HUAC.[43] Whether fortuitous or not, Chambers's production of documentary evidence submarined Truman's termination strategy and gave the Committee a new, and more powerful, lease on life.

The FBI might not have sought to frame Hiss in order to preserve HUAC. Nonetheless, the legal problems posed by the Bureau's authentication of the White memorandum and surreptitious acquisition of the White memorandum from Chambers in early November 1948 help explain FBI Director Hoover's vague and elliptical November 17, 1953 testimony before the Senate Internal Security Subcommittee.

Attorney General Herbert Brownell's November 6, 1953, Chicago speech provided the catalyst for Hoover's appearance before the Senate Subcommittee. In the Chicago speech, Brownell pointedly condemned the Truman Administration's response in 1945 and 1946 to FBI reports on White. Received at a time when Truman was considering appointing White executive director of the International Monetary Fund, these reports, Brownell charged, had confirmed White's disloyalty. Former President Truman responded by challenging the accuracy of Brownell's charge claiming further that he had not ignored the FBI reports on White, and then accusing the Eisenhower Administration of McCarthyism. To help rebut Truman and to document his serious charge, FBI Director Hoover accompanied Brownell later that month to testify before the Internal Security Subcommittee.

In his testimony, Brownell repeated his earlier contention, condemning Truman this time for bad judgment not treason. The 1945 and 1946 FBI reports, Brownell conceded, had not cited hard evidence of White's earlier involvement in espionage. However, incontrovertible evidence was subsequently provided: the presence of White's memorandum among the Pumpkin Papers (the documents retrieved on December 2, 1948 from Chambers's pumpkin patch). Brownell continued:

Of course, no one could with any validity, suggest today that there is any doubt that White was in this espionage ring. Some of White's original espionage reports, written by him in his own handwriting for delivery to agents of the Red Army Intelligence, were recovered and are now in the possession of the Department of Justice. I have photostatic copies of them here and I offer the copies as part of the record of my testimony.

Hoover was not any more precise as to the date when the White memorandum was "recovered." The FBI director, however, did not repeat Brownell's error that the White memorandum had been part of the so-called Pumpkin Papers. Instead, Hoover elliptically testified:

Miss Bentley's account of White's activities were later corroborated by Whittaker Chambers, and documents in White's own handwriting concerning which there can be no dispute, lend credibility to the information previously reported on

White. Subsequent to White's death on August 16, 1948 events transpired which produced facts of an uncontradictable nature which clearly established the reliability of the information furnished in 1945 and 1946.[44]

Brownell publicly released the White memorandum in November 1953. HUAC members, however, already had a copy. Under HUAC's subpoena of December 2, 1948, Chambers was ordered to produce all documents in his possession relating to Alger Hiss, John Abt, Lee Pressman, Harold Ware, Alexander Stephens, Victor Perlo, Elizabeth Bentley, Harry Dexter White, George Silverman, Irving Kaplan, Nathan Witt, Henry Collins, Priscilla Hiss, Donald Hiss "and all other material in documentary form which has to do with the investigation of espionage in the Federal Government." Nonetheless, on the night of December 2 Chambers only gave HUAC investigators Donald Appell and William Wheeler three aluminum containers holding developed and undeveloped microfilm. Chambers did *not* give them the White memorandum, and yet had technically complied with the subpoena, since his attorney held the White memorandum—and Cleveland gave it to the FBI the next day.[45]

Although Chambers did not give the White memorandum to HUAC, since December 1948 Congressman Nixon had photostatic copies of it. Nixon publicly admitted this in a January 26, 1950, House speech, at which time he had the full text of the White memorandum reprinted in the *Congressional Record*. Questioning Chambers during an executive session hearing of a HUAC subcommittee on December 28, 1948, Nixon then stated; "I now show you what are photostatic copies of documents which are alleged to be in the handwriting of Harry Dexter White and which were testified to have been in the package which you received from Mr. Levine."[46]

How, then, did Congressman Nixon obtain a copy of the White memorandum? There is indirect evidence that he may have obtained the copy from the FBI.

FBI officials reaped no tangible benefits from their possession of the White memorandum. First, White had died on August 16, 1948, and thus could not be indicted for perjury—for denying, as had Hiss, having given this memorandum to Chambers in 1938. Second, despite the FBI's haste to authenticate White's handwriting and report to Justice Department officials directing the grand jury inquiry, the White memorandum was not used during the Hiss trial to substantiate Chambers's revised charges. To use the memorandum entailed major risks: if interrogated by Hiss's attorneys, FBI officials who would be testifying under oath might have to disclose the FBI's use of illegal methods to authenticate White's handwriting.[47] HUAC provided a safer outlet—and one the FBI regularly exploited to "launder" unusable information, either because the information was merely derogatory and did not confirm a federal statutory violation or because the information had been illegally obtained and thus could not be used for prosecutive purposes.

Former HUAC member Karl Mundt inadvertently confirmed a covert relationship. Speaking to the Bonneville (Utah) Knife and Fork Club in November 1953, then-Senator Karl Mundt extolled the valuable work of congressional committees in identifying Communist agents who were "still" actively engaged in espionage. A *Salt Lake Tribune* editorial writer, who was a member of the social club and attending the meeting, subsequently wrote an editorial endorsing Mundt's position. The editorialist summarized Mundt's remarks:

One point he [Mundt] made in justification of continued congressional investigation was that these probes are a valuable supplement to the investigative work of the F.B.I. The F.B.I. may compile much evidence on Communist infiltration, but not enough to justify indictment. *Often in such cases, said the senator, the F.B.I. will tip off a congressional committee as to a situation when it is convinced American security is endangered. The committee's inquiry makes it possible to bring the case into the open and, with the suspected Communist spy usually taking refuge in the fifth amendment's protection against incriminating himself, it is possible to eliminate that particular threat.*
Just that, the senator said, had happened in a number of cases, and he implied it would and should continue to happen [emphasis added].[48]

In conclusion, let me stress that the most important questions relating to the Hiss-Chambers case remain unanswered, and perhaps can never be resolved. Scholars in the future will, I hope, secure access to the fuller record essential to resolving questions about Hiss's innocence or guilt, and about the nature of the roles of the FBI and HUAC in effecting

Hiss's indictment and conviction. The latter questions, however, are of more transcendent importance to an understanding of the politics of Cold War America.

Hiss-Chambers Chronology

1925—Whittaker Chambers joins the United States Communist Party and soon devotes full time to Party work, notably on staff of *Daily Worker.*

1929—Chambers drifts away from Communist Party over internal factional dispute leading to the expulsion of Jay Lovestone.

1931—Chambers returns to assume an active role in Communist Party; assumes editorship of *New Masses*, the Party's intellectual journal.

July 1932—Chambers terminates his editorial duties to recruit for Communist Party in the New York City area.

April 1933—Alger Hiss accepts appointment to the Legal Division of the Agricultural Adjustment Administration; moves to Washington.

July 1934—Hiss is assigned to legal staff of the Nye Committee, remains on the payroll of the Agricultural Department.

August 1934—Chambers moves to Baltimore-Washington, D.C., area to continue role as Communist Party functionary; after 1936 he shifts to role as Communist espionage operative.

Fall 1934-January 1935—First meeting between Hiss and Chambers; Hiss claims that he met Chambers as a free-lance reporter covering the Nye Committee hearings, while Chambers claims that he met Hiss as a member of a Communist cell, the so-called Ware Group. Hiss sublets apartment to Chambers in spring 1935.

August 1935—Hiss terminates duties with Nye Committee and as employee of Agriculture Department and accepts appointment in Solicitor General's office of the Department of Justice; he helps prepare brief for *United States v. Butler* case.

July 23, 1936—Hiss disposes of a Ford automobile; title is assigned to Cherner Motor Company.

September 1936—Hiss accepts appointment to Trade Division of the Department of State.

late 1937-early 1938—Chambers defects from Communist Party and ceases underground activities.

January 31, 1938—Chambers terminates employment with National Research Project (a New Deal-funded program).

February 1938—Chambers obtains a translation assignment (through literary agent Paul Willert) from Oxford University Press for Martin Gumpert's book *Dunant: The Story of the Red Cross*. Chambers moves from Mt. Royal Terrace apartment to apartment on Old Court Road.

March 1938—Chambers travels to Florida to complete translation assignment.

March 11, 1938—Henry Julian Wadleigh leaves United States for consular assignment to Turkey.

April 12, 1938—First public hearing convened by House Special Committee on Un-American Activities.

June 1938—Chamber receives second translation assignment (again through Willert) from Longman-Green for Gustav Regler's book *The Great Crusade*.

November 1938—Chambers is interviewed by Herbert Solow, an anti-Communist radical, about his Communist Party activities; Chambers seeks his assistance in an effort to publish a manuscript on the subject. Chambers also gives his nephew, Nathan Levine, an envelope for safe keeping.

December 1938—Chambers gives Solow the promised manuscript, which was never published.

April 1939—Chambers obtains employment with *Time* magazine.

September 2, 1939—Chambers, accompanied by conservative journalist Isaac Don Levine, is interviewed by Assistant Secretary of State Adolf Berle; he gives Berle the names of eighteen individuals whom he claims were members of a Communist "underground" group—the list includes Alger Hiss's name. The interview was arranged by Levine who, after the Molotov-Ribbentrop Pact of August 23, 1939, pressured Chambers to advise Administration officials about his knowledge of Communist activities. Levine had learned about Chambers's allegations from the manuscript that Chambers had given to Solow—Levine having earlier secured the serialization of the memoirs of a Soviet defector, Walter Krivitzky, in the *Saturday Evening Post.*

May 13, 1942—Chambers is interviewed for the first time by FBI agents, who had learned about his former Communist activities from another ex-Communist, Ludwig Lore. Chambers lists, but does not name, twenty individuals who he claims were members of a Communist cell.

May 1944—Hiss is appointed special assistant to the director of the newly created Office of Special Political Affairs, Department of State; his major responsibility is planning for postwar collective security organization.

February 1945—Hiss attends the Yalta Conference as a member of the United States delegation.

April 1945—Hiss is appointed a member of the United States delegation to the San Francisco Conference at which United Nations Charter is drafted; appointed temporary Secretary-General at the Conference.

July 1945—Hiss is appointed Director of the Office of Special Political Affairs. He retained this post until February 1947 when he accepted appointment as president of the Carnegie Endowment for International Peace and moved to New York City.

October 1945—President Truman is briefed by Canadian Prime Minister Mackenzie King about allegations of a Soviet defector, Igor Gouzenko, concerning Soviet espionage activities in Canada and the United States.

November 25, 1945—FBI interviews Elizabeth Bentley who claims to have acted as a courier for a Communist espionage ring in wartime Washington. FBI officials obtain Attorney General Tom Clark's approval for a wiretap of Hiss. From November 1945 through March 1946, the FBI submits a series of memoranda to various Truman Administration officials based on Bentley's allegations. The two most prominent officials named in these FBI reports are Alger Hiss and Treasury Department official Harry Dexter White.

February 1946—FBI officials approve an "educational campaign" to leak "educational materials" through "available channels" about the seriousness of the Communist threat. The FBI also convenes a two-day conference to brief all FBI field office "Communist supervisors" of this planned program.

March 1946—FBI Director Hoover attempts to convince Attorney General Clark to leak information about Hiss to key members of Congress as one means to force Hiss's resignation. This strategy is aborted by Secretary of State James Byrnes's decision to confront Hiss and Hiss's willingness to submit to an FBI interview.

March 25, 1946—Hiss is interviewed by the FBI; he denies charges of Communist activities.

March 28, 1946—The FBI interviews Chambers again to seek corroboration or any evidence linking Hiss with Communist activities. Chambers provides no evidence.

March-April-May 1946—A number of news stories are published about Communist influence in federal agencies; charges are reiterated by key conservative congressmen.

June 1946—Former FBI agents join the staff of a new journal to be edited by Isaac Don Levine and financed by Arthur Kohlberg, *Plain Talk*. They soon leave to form their own newsletter service, *Counterattack*.

December 1947—Isaac Don Levine publishes an article in *Plain Talk* alleging Communist infiltration of the State Department.

July 1948—*New York World Telegram* publishes series of articles by reporter Frederick Woltman on the charges of the "Red Spy Queen," Elizabeth Bentley.

July 31, 1948—Elizabeth Bentley testifies publicly before the House Committee on Un-American Activities (HUAC) about Communist espionage activities.

July-August 1948 (if not earlier)—Close contacts are established between FBI officials and staff members and congressmen on HUAC, notably Congressman Richard Nixon.

August 3, 1948—Chambers testifies publicly before HUAC for the first time; he names nine individuals as members of a Communist cell whose purpose was to promote Communist infiltration of the New Deal, including Alger Hiss and Harry Dexter White but not Henry Julian Wadleigh.

August 3, 1948—Hiss sends HUAC a telegram requesting the opportunity to testify on August 5 in order to deny Chambers's charges that he had been a member of a Communist cell in the 1930s.

August 5, 1948—Hiss appears before HUAC; he denies Communist membership and knowing anyone "by the name of Whittaker Chambers."

August 5, 1948—HUAC convenes an executive session and debates whether to abandon investigation into Chambers's charges. Nixon convinces the Committee to focus investigation on whether Chambers and Hiss knew each other during the 1930s and assumes responsibility for this inquiry.

August 7, 1948—HUAC Subcommittee, headed by Nixon, interviews Chambers in New York City hearing; Chambers details Hiss's personal activities during the mid-1930s and claims close friendship.

August 13, 1948—HUAC hearings in Washington focus on testimony of Harry Dexter White. White denies Bentley's and Chambers's allegations of his involvement in Communist activities.

August 16, 1948—White dies of a heart attack.

August 16, 1948—HUAC interviews Hiss in executive session, focusing on his personal activities during the mid-1930s.

August 17, 1948—A confrontation between Hiss and Chambers occurs during executive session HUAC hearing; Hiss, after feigning doubt, affirms knowing Chambers as a free-lance reporter under the name of George Crosley.

August 19, 1948—During press conference, President Truman dismisses HUAC hearings as a "red herring."

August 25, 1948—HUAC convenes highly publicized and televised hearings in Washington on Hiss-Chambers relationship; one of more damaging issues to Hiss in this hearing is his testimony as to when and how he disposed of an old Ford automobile in the mid-1930s. Hiss challenges Chambers to repeat charges outside Committee hearings where he would be open to libel suit.

August 27, 1948—HUAC publishes interim report on its August 1948 hearings based on Bentley's and Chambers's allegations, titled *Hearings Regarding Communist Espionage in the United States Government.*

August 27, 1948—Chambers repeats charge that Hiss had been a member of a Communist cell during the 1930s on the "Meet the Press" radio program; he denies that this involved actual espionage but rather sought to influence Government policy.

September 27, 1948—Hiss files libel suit against Chambers.

October 14, 1948—Chambers testifies before grand jury in New York City; he denies any knowledge of espionage activities.

November 4, 1948—Pre-trial hearings on Hiss's libel suit are initiated in Baltimore. Hiss's attorneys interview Chambers and press him to produce any written communications he had received from Hiss during the 1930s in view of his claim of a close friendship. During November 5, 1948 deposition, Hiss's attorneys again press this matter of written communications.

November 14 or 21, 1948—Chambers travels to New York City to retrieve an envelope he had left in 1938 with his nephew, Nathan Levine, for safe keeping.

November 15, 1948—Chambers turns over to his attorneys four handwritten notes and sixty-five pages of typed State Department documents which he claims to have received from Hiss during the 1930s. The handwritten notes and typed pages are dated variously January 5 through April 1, 1938.

November 17, 1948—Chambers turns over copies of these notes and typed documents to Hiss's attorneys during pre-trial hearings. Hiss's attorneys turn over these documents to the Department of Justice on November 19, 1948.

December 1, 1948—*Washington Daily News* runs UPI story, headlined "Hiss and Chambers Perjury Probe Hits Dead End," in which it reports that the Department of Justice intends to drop any perjury prosecution involving Hiss's testimony before HUAC.

December 1, 1948—Nixon and HUAC Counsel Robert Stripling visit Chambers at his Westminster, Maryland, farm and allegedly learn that he possesses additional documents involving Hiss.

December 1-2, 1948—Upon returning to Washington after this trip to Chambers's farm, Nixon telephones FBI Assistant Director Louis Nichols and *New York Herald-Tribune* reporter Bert Andrews to brief them on Chambers's contention.

December 2, 1948—HUAC subpoenas Chambers to produce any documents in his possession pertaining to Hiss and other individuals (notably Harry Dexter White) identified during the Committee's hearings. That night HUAC investigators accompany Chambers on his trip back to his farm, whereupon Chambers leads them to a pumpkin patch and extracts from a pumpkin fifty-eight frames of developed microfilm (of State Department documents stamped received January 14, 1938) and three rolls of undeveloped microfilm.

December 3, 1948—The FBI interviews Chambers about Communist espionage activities. Chambers for the first time accuses Hiss, Harry Dexter White, and Henry Julian Wadleigh of having engaged in espionage activities. Chambers gives FBI agents a four-page memorandum written by White that he claims to have received from White during the 1930s.

December 3, 1948—Nixon departs from New York on a long-planned vacation to the Caribbean on the cruise ship *Panama*.

December 5, 1948—Nixon cuts short his vacation trip and flies back to Washington on a helicopter dispatched to the *Panama*.

December 6–9, 1948—HUAC convenes dramatic, highly publicized hearings on the microfilm documents and the change in Chambers's charges, now claiming that Hiss had been engaged in espionage during the 1930s.

December 6, 1948—HUAC asks Kodak to authenticate the date of the microfilm produced by Chambers. Kodak's first response is that the microfilm could not have been manufactured before 1945. After further checking, Kodak claims that the microfilm was discontinued during the World War II period and thus could have been manufactured in the 1930s. In the interim between these phone calls, Nixon berates Chambers and then apprises him of the change in assessing the date of the microfilm.

December 6, 1948—In the evening Chambers unsuccessfully attempts to commit suicide.

December 15, 1948—Federal grand jury in New York indicts Hiss on two counts of perjury. (This indictment and Hiss's resultant conviction effectively forecloses the libel suit that Hiss had filed in September 1948, which had precipitated the production by Chambers of the handwritten notes, typed pages, and microfilm documents.)

December 28, 1948—A HUAC Subcommittee, chaired by Congressman Karl Mundt, interviews Chambers during an executive session; during these hearings Nixon queries Chambers about the White memorandum, a copy of which he has in his possession.

May 31, 1949—The first trial of Hiss on the perjury counts begins.

July 7, 1949—The first trial ends; jury is unable to reach a unanimous verdict, voting 8-4 for conviction.

November 17, 1949—Start of the second trial of Hiss on the perjury counts.

December 5, 1949—FBI agents interview Chambers's friend Meyer Schapiro about Chambers's activities during 1930s; Schapiro gives these agents copies of undated correspondence he had received from Chambers in the late 1930s.

January 21, 1950—Jury in second trial convicts Hiss of both perjury counts.

Notes

1. This question raises other questions about the relationship between the FBI and the House Un-American Activities Committee (HUAC) in 1948: (1) the timing and focus of HUAC's hearings of August and December 1948; (2) the relationship between members of the Committee and the FBI; (3) the FBI's role both in effecting Hiss's indictment and in the Committee's earlier efforts to discredit Hiss; and (4) the confusing chronology of Chambers's production (and the FBI's and HUAC's acquisition) of a four-page memorandum written by former Treasury Department official Harry Dexter White.

2. Allen Weinstein, "Reappraisals: The Alger Hiss Case Revisited," *The American Scholar* (Winter 1971–1972), p. 129; Allen Weinstein, "The Alger Hiss Case: An Assessment" (Paper delivered at the December 1969 meetings of the American Historical Association New York City), pp. 20–25, nn. 31, 33; *HRCE*, pp. 19, 44, 51, 564–66, 1287–89, 1293; Letter, James Linen to Edmund Soule, Aug. 26, 1948, Hiss Defense File, *AH. Baltimore Depositions*, Nov. 5, 1948, Vol. 3, p. 402. Fred Cook, *The Unfinished Story of Alger Hiss* (New York: Morrow, 1958), pp. 82–106. FBI documents consistently cite Chambers's 1937 break-date testimony, one stating that Chambers was a Party member "until the Spring of 1937." See Memo, A. H. Belmont to D. M. Ladd, Dec. 22, 1953, FBI 74-1333; Memo, L. B. Nichols to Tolson, re: Chapter 29, June 26, 1956, FBI 62–116606–1; Memo D. M. Ladd to FBI Director, Aug. 3, 1948, FBI 65–56402–356236; Letter, E. E. Conroy to FBI Director, March 28, 1946, FBI 65–6766; all in *AH*. See also *HISG*, pp. 1181–82.

3. Weinstein, "Reappraisals," p. 130. Weinstein, "The Alger Hiss Case," pp. 21–24. Allen Weinstein, *Perjury: The Hiss-Chambers Case* (New York: Knopf, 1978), p. 314. *Baltimore Depositions*, Nov. 5, 1948. Vol. 3, pp. 412, 434–36; Nov. 17, 1948, vol. 4, pp. 685–94. *HRCE*, pp. 1287–89. Henry Julian Wadleigh, "Why I Spied for the Communists," *New York Post*, July 12–24, 1949.

4. Weinstein, *Perjury*, pp. 231, 233–36. U.S., House, Committee on Un-American Activities (HUAC), Subcommittee on Espionage, *Executive Session Hearings*, Dec. 28, 1948, pp. 68–69, *KM* (copy). Report, Frank Johnstone, Dec., 4, 1948, FBI 418; Memo, H. B. Fletcher to D. M. Ladd, Dec., 6, 1948, FBI 110; Memo, H. B. Fletcher to D. M. Ladd, Dec. 4, 1948, FBI 46; all in *AH*. In addition, Chambers had not received the two rolls of undeveloped microfilm from Hiss. These rolls reproduced Navy Bureau of Aeronautics documents. Chambers later claimed to have received these documents from William Ward Pigman, a Bureau of Standards employee.

5. *Baltimore Depositions*, Feb. 17, 1949, vol. 7, pp. 939–41, 1007.

6. Weinstein, "Reappraisals," pp. 130–31. Weinstein, "The Alger Hiss Case," pp. 23–24. Cook, *The Unfinished Story*, pp. 82–106. Meyer Zeligs, *Friendship and Fratricide* (New York: Viking, 1967), pp. 287–307. William Reuben, *The Honorable Mr. Nixon and the Alger Hiss Case* (New York: Action Books, 1958), app. 40–51. *Baltimore Depositions*, Nov. 17, 1948, Vol. 4 (B), pp. 783–84. U.S. District Court, Southern District of New York, *U.S. v. Alger Hiss*, Motion for a new trial based on the ground of newly discovered evidence, Jan. 24, 1952. See Supplemental affidavits in support of motion for a new trial. See Federal Supplement 1952, Vol. 107. See also, Report, Thomas Spencer, May 11, 1949, FBI 3220; Memo, SAC, New York to FBI Director, March 7, 1949, FBI 65–14920; both in *AH*. Edith Tiger, ed., *In Re Alger Hiss* (New York: Hill and Wang, 1979), pp. 56–64, 251–52, 274, 277.

7. Allen Weinstein, "A Response to Robert Sherrill," mimeographed, pp. 12, 13; Weinstein, *Perjury*, p. 625 n28. For other note citations in *Perjury* where Weinstein dates Chamber's undated correspondence by comparing it with the correspondence of Schapiro and Solow, see p. 625 nn. 14, 15, 24, 29; p. 626, nn. 33, 34, 37, 38, 42, 46.

8. In a December 5, 1949 interview with FBI agent L. H. Bracken, Chambers indentified the new translation as Gustav Regler's *The Great Crusade*. Chambers's February 1939 letter to Schapiro, however, reported that "the publisher expects to bring the book out this April." Since Chambers began work on the Regler translation in June 1938, Chambers's 1949 recollection is in error. My hunch is that this was a third translation assignment, commissioned in

the spring of 1939. The letter was apparently written after another February 1939 letter in which Chambers acknowledged Noda's death, and thanked Schapiro for "the tip about the translating." Memo, L. H. Bracken, Dec. 6, 1949, and accompanying five undated Chambers-Schapiro letters, FBI 65–14920–4966, *AH*. Letters, W., Wh., or Henricus II [Whittaker Chambers] to Herb or Herbert [Solow], all undated, Herbert Solow Papers, Hoover Institution, Stanford, Calif. Letter, Athan Theoharis to Meyer Schapiro and replies, April 30, 1979 and May 8, 14, and 18, 1979. Letter, unsigned [Whittaker Chambers] to Mike [Meyer Schapiro], undated. Weinstein, *Perjury*, pp. 314–15, 320; Weinstein, "The Alger Hiss Case," n. 36, pp. 13–14 n.

    9. Memo, SAC, Baltimore to FBI Director, Feb. 12, 1952, FBI 5009; Teletype, Edward Scheidt to FBI Director and SAC [deleted, but Baltimore], Feb. 18, 1952, *AH*.

    10. Hiss's attorneys could have used this March 28, 1946 report on the FBI's interviews with Chambers during the trial to impugn Chambers's credibility with the jury. This explains why the FBI and the prosecuting attorneys did not honor a court order to provide the defense with all FBI interviews with Chambers. Other FBI interviews with Chambers, but not this report, were given to the defense. See John Chabot Smith, *Alger Hiss: The True Story* (New York: Penguin, 1977), pp. 239–40, Memo, unsigned and unaddressed but identified as LW: DS, March 25, 1946, FBI 101–2668–20X; Letter, E. E. Conroy to FBI Director, March 28, 1946, FBI 65–6766; Memos, Ladd to FBI Director, July 26, 1948, FBI 65–56402–3561; H. B. Fletcher to Ladd, Aug. 2, 1948, FBI Whittaker Chambers 46; Ladd to FBI Director, Aug. 3, 1948, FBI 65–56402–356236; Fletcher to Ladd, Aug. 6, 1948, FBI 65–56402–3344; Nichols to FBI Director, Sept. 1, 1948, FBI Whittaker Chambers 52; Ladd to FBI Director, Sept. 9, 1948, Whittaker Chambers 53; Ladd to FBI Director, Dec. 10, 1948, FBI 1478; Teletype, Mason (FBI, Savannah) to FBI Director and SAC, New York, June 26, 1949, FBI 3455; Report, Wilmer Thompson, Aug. 29, 1949, FBI 3860; Memo, Ladd to FBI Director, Nov. 13, 1953, FBI 101–2668–52; Memo, Nichols to Tolson, re: Chap. 29, June 21, 1956, FBI 62–116606–1; all in *AH*. See also Memo, V. C. Wilson to Amshey, March 9, 1949, State Department 2, *AH*.

    11. Chambers had not named Alger Hiss when recounting to Herbert Solow in November 1938 his Communist activities, duly recorded by Solow in a contemporary notarized statement. Chambers had then identified, among others, John Abt, Larry Duggan, and Noel Field as "people involved in his work either as agents, sources or what not." Memos, V. C. Wilson to Amshey, March 9, 1949, State Department 2; FBI Director to Assistant Attorney General Warren Olney III, Nov. 16, 1953, FBI 100-25824; A. H. Belmont to D. M. Ladd, Nov.

14, 1953 (not recorded, but FBI 100–25824); Ladd to FBI Director, Aug. 3, 1948, FBI 65–56402–356236; Nichols to FBI Director, Sept. 1, 1948, FBI Whittaker Chambers 52; Nichols to Tolson, re: Chap. 29, June 21, 1956, FBI 62–116606–1; Nichols to Tolson, June 26, 1956, FBI 62–116606–1; H. B. Fletcher to Ladd, Aug. 6, 1948, FBI 65–56402–3344; all in *AH*. See *HRCE*, pp. 565–66, 574, 576–77, 1180. Weinstein, *Perjury*, pp. 62–66, 157, 220, 236n, 238, 324, 324n, 329–30, 340–41. Beatrice B. Berle and Travis Jacobs, eds., *Navigating the Rapids, 1918–71: From the Papers of Adolf A. Berle* (New York: Harcourt Brace Jovanovich, 1973), pp. 231, 297, 298, 320, 321, 337, 346, 363, and 583.

12. Report, Frank Johnstone, Dec. 4, 1948, FBI 418; Memo, D. M. Ladd to FBI Director, Dec. 7, 1948, *AH*. Tiger ed., *In Re Alger Hiss*, II, 208–09.

13. Weinstein, *Perjury*, pp. 232–33, 317–19, 323, 325.

14. Whittaker Chambers, *Witness* (New York: Random House, 1952), pp. 737–39. Weinstein, *Perjury*, pp. 172, 191–93. Report, Frank Johnstone, Dec. 4, 1948, FBI 418, *AH*. During a December 28, 1948 executive session hearing of a HUAC subcommittee, Chambers also claimed to have received some of the microfilm from Wadleigh. By then, however, Chambers had responded to suggestions from HUAC staff to adopt the position that he had received all the microfilmed State Department documents from Hiss. Thus, when HUAC investigator Donald Appell asked if the "trade documents dealing with trade matters" had been received from Wadleigh, Chambers replied, "I am not clear about that." Appell then asked whether it was Chambers's "assumption" that he "probably did"; Chambers responded, "Yes." Abruptly interrupting Appell's line of inquiry, HUAC chief counsel Robert Stripling interjected, "I don't think it is his assumption that it did." Appell then recalled Chambers's testimony earlier that month that he had received "the trade papers, papers dealing with trade, that he got from Wadleigh." Catching Stripling's cue, Chambers quickly asserted, "You are right about that, but not necessarily in this instance [referring to the microfilm documents]." U.S., House, Committee on Un-American Activities, Subcommittee on Espionage, *Executive Session Hearings*, Dec. 28, 1948, pp. 68–69, *KM* copy.

15. Weinstein, *Perjury* pp. 172, 191–93. Chambers had shown the microfilm to Meyer and Lillian Schapiro before delivering it to HUAC counsel on December 2, 1984. In an interview with Allen Weinstein, Schapiro asserted that Chambers had shown him the microfilm—and only the microfilm—around Thanksgiving 1938. Schapiro's admission indirectly suggests that Chambers had retrieved the envelope on November 21, 1938. In short, after retrieving the envelope from his nephew and before returning to his home in Westminster, Maryland, Chambers showed its contents to Schapiro.

16. Teletype, Edward Scheidt to FBI Director and SACs, Washington Field Office and Baltimore, Dec. 6, 1948, FBI 53; Memo, D. M. Ladd to FBI Director, Dec. 7, 1948; and FBI Report, March 30, 1949, FBI 3221, all in *AH*. See also Memo, F. L. Jones to H. B. Fletcher, Dec. 5, 1948, FBI 20, *AH*.

17. *HRCE*, II, p. 1454. U. S., House, Committee on Un-American Activities, Subcommittee on Espionage, *Executive Session Hearings*, Dec. 28, 1948, pp. 73–74, *KM* (copy).

18. Teletype, Special Agent M. W. McFarlin to FBI Director and SAC New York, May 27, 1949, FBI 3188, *AH*.

19. HISG. Weinstein, *Perjury*, pp. 356–57. Routing Slip, FBI Director Hoover, Elizabeth Bentley, Testimony Nov. 20, 1953, and accompanying twenty-eight charts, *O&C*. Memos, D. M. Ladd to FBI Director, Nov. 13, 1953, FBI Alger Hiss 48; E. A. Tamm to FBI Director, Oct. 8, 1945, FBI 62–116606–1; Hoover to Tolson, Tamm, Ladd, and Carson, March 19, 1946, FBI 62–116606–1; D. M. Ladd to E. A. Tamm, March 20, 1946, FBI 62–116606–1; Hoover to Tolson, Tamm, Ladd, and Clegg, March 19, 1946, FBI 62–116606–1; Hoover to Tolson, Tamm, and Ladd, March 20, 1946, FBI 62–116606–1; Conversation between FBI Director, Secretary of State Byrnes, and Attorney General, March 21, 1946, FBI 101–2668–52; Hoover to Tolson, Tamm, and Ladd, March 21, 1946, FBI 62–116606–1; Conversation between Ralph Roach and George Allen, June 3, 1946, FBI 101–2668–52; Unidentified, to Hoover, Nov. 13, 1953, FBI Alger Hiss 52; FBI Director to Attorney General, Jan. 17, 1949, FBI 1921; D. M. Ladd to FBI Director, Dec. 10, 1948, FBI 1478; D. M. Ladd to FBI Director, Aug. 3, 1948, FBI 65–56402–356236; H. B. Fletcher to D. M. Ladd, Aug. 6, 1948, FBI 3344; Letter, Edward Scheidt to FBI Director, Sept. 15, 1949, FBI 3850; FBI Memo, March 25, 1946, FBI 101–2668–20X; Report, Thomas Spencer, Oct. 3, 1949, FBI 4007; Report, Wilmer Thompson, Aug. 29, 1949, FBI 3927; Memo, Bannerman to Russell, March 22, 1946; all in *AH*.

20. *SDSR*, pp. 16, 429–30. *IARA*, pp. 66, 211 n1.

21. The Official and Confidential files maintained by FBI Assistant Director Louis Nichols confirm that this leaking activity dated at least from 1941. See also Garry Wills, *Nixon Agonistes* (New York: New American Library, 1971), pp. 36–37; Peter Irons, "American Business and the Origins of McCarthyism: The Cold War Crusade of the United States Chamber of Commerce," in Robert Griffith and Athan Theoharis, eds., *The Specter: Original Essays on the Cold War and the Origins of McCarthyism* (New York: New Viewpoints, 1974), pp. 79–82. For examples of post-1946 FBI leaks and the more formal procedures, see Sanford J. Ungar, *FBI* (Boston: Atlantic Monthly/Little, Brown, 1975), pp. 277–78, 283–88, 355–58, 373–86; *HIA*, Vol. 6, Federal Bureau of Investi-

gation, pp. 88–89; Robert Wall, "Special Agent for the FBI," *New York Review of Books* (Jan. 27, 1972), pp. 140–67; Robert Friedman, "FBI: Manipulating the Media," *Rights* (May–June 1977), pp. 13–14; *IARA*, pp. 242–43, 242 nn105, 106, 109; and Memo, Data re: Raymond Murphy, Nov. 13, 1953, *AH*; Frank Donner, *The Age of Surveillance: The Aims and Methods of America's Political Intelligence System* (New York: Knopf, 1980) pp. 93, 100, 102–3, 112, 116–17, 173–74, 493 n54.

22. James F. Byrnes, *All in One Lifetime* (New York: Harper & Row 1958), pp. 322–23. Teletype, Mason to FBI Director and SAC, New York, June 29, 1949, FBI 3455; Report, Wilmer Thompson, Aug. 29, 1949, FBI 3927; Report, Thomas Spencer, Oct. 3, 1949, FBI 4007; all in *AH*. U.S., *Congressional Record*, 79th Cong., 1st sess., 1945, Vol. 91, P. 13, p. A5159; 79th Cong., 2d sess., 1946, Vol. 92, Ps. 2, 3, 4, 7, 8, 10, and 12, pp. 2092–93, 2330–31, 2683–84, 3180, 3360, 3467, 3625–26, 4007–8, 4349–51, 4366–67, 4413, 9389–90, 10531, A2447, A4891–92. See *New York Times*, Feb. 15, 1946, p. 27; April 10, 1946, p. 21; April 19, 1946, p. 20; April 29, 1946, pp. 1, 7; April 30, 1946, pp. 1, 7; May 3, 1946, p. 23. See Memo, Hoover to Tolson, Tamm, and Ladd, May 27, 1946, FBI 101–2668–27; Memo, Hoover to Attorney General, May 31, 1946, FBI 101–2668–23; Letter, TCC [Tom Clark] to Edgar [Hoover], June 3, 1946, FBI 101–2668–24; all in *AH*. See also R. Harris Smith, *OSS* (New York: Dell, 1977), p. 364; *Time*, 48 (Aug. 26, 1946): 16.

23. *New York Times*, March 25, 1946, p. 6. Donald Crosby, "The Politics of Religion: American Catholics and the Origins of McCarthyism," in Griffith and Theoharis, eds., *The Specter*, pp. 30–31. See Weinstein, *Perjury*, p. 366; Jack Anderson and James Boyd, *Confessions of a Muckraker: The Inside Story of Life in Washington during the Truman, Eisenhower, Kennedy, and Johnson Years* (New York: Random House, 1978), pp. 6, 181, 191, 231. See also Letter, E. E. Conroy to FBI Director, March 28, 1946, FBI 65–766, *AH*.

24. *Public Papers of the Presidents of the United States, Harry S. Truman: 1948* (Washington, D.C.: G.P.O. 1964), pp. 181–82. Wills, *Nixon Agonistes*, pp. 36–37; Richard Nixon, *RN: The Memoirs of Richard Nixon* (New York: Grosset and Dunlap, 1978), p. 58; Allen Weinstein, "Nixon vs. Hiss: The Story Nixon Tells, and the Other Story," *Esquire* (Nov. 1975), p. 77; Weinstein, *Perjury*, pp. 7–8, 16, 347, 645; I. F. Stone, *The Haunted Fifties* (New York: Vintage, 1969), p. 26.

25. I have unsuccessfully requested the release of all FBI documents pertaining to Cronin, and have been advised that the Bureau has no index listing such reports. Cronin's role during the period 1945–48 and his relationship with the FBI warrant further study. It might have been simply coincidental that in early

1946—at the very time of the initiation of the FBI's "educational" program—Cronin arranged a meeting to which he invited a group of former FBI agents, HUAC staff member Benjamin Mandel, and the wealthy importer Arthur Kohlberg. At this meeting, Kohlberg agreed to fund a new anti-Communist journal, *Plain Talk*, and, in Kohlberg's words, "a sort of FBI file system for use of magazines and for others interested." The group decided to approach Isaac Don Levine to serve as editor—Levine accepted at a June 1946 meeting—and the former FBI agents were to run the file service. (They eventually split from *Plain Talk* to start their own newsletter service, *Counterattack*.) See Joseph Keeley, *The China Lobby Man: The Story of Alfred Kohlberg* (New Rochelle: Arlington House, 1969), pp. 196–97.

26. In addition to FBI files pertaining to Cronin, I also unsuccessfully requested the release of Hummer's reports. I was again advised that the Bureau has no index listing these reports.

27. Memo, Ladd to FBI Director, Dec. 9, 1948, FBI 157; Memo, Nichols to Tolson, Dec. 2, 1948, FBI 101; Memo, M. A. Jones to Nichols, Dec. 28, 1948, FBI 055; all in *AH*.

28. These facts are confirmed both by documents in Nichols's unserialized "Official and Confidential" file and in other released FBI files—for example, the William Remington, Julius and Ethel Rosenberg, American Civil Liberties Union, and Alger Hiss files. See also the papers of Bishop G. Bromley Oxnam and Karl Mundt cited in note 48. *HIDFBI*, pp. 154–55. See memos, Nichols to Tolson, Dec. 9, 1948, FBI 181; L. Whitson to H. B. Fletcher, Dec. 9, 1948, FBI 150; Nichols to Tolson, Dec. 10, 1948, FBI 213; Ladd to FBI Director, Dec. 17, 1948, FBI 352; Nichols to Tolson, Jan. 14, 1949, FBI 1002; Guy Hottel, SAC, Washington, D.C. to FBI Director, March 31, 1949, FBI 2728; Nichols to Tolson, June 28, 1949, FBI 3470; Nichols to Tolson, July 11, 1949, FBI 3651; Nichols to Tolson, Jan. 11, 1950, FBI 4478; Ladd to FBI Director, Oct. 9, 1952; FBI 5403; all in *AH*. See also Memo, Nichols to Tolson, June 28, 1949, FBI 1669; Letter, Hoover to Lyle Wilson, June 28, 1949, FBI 1668; Memo, Nichols to Tolson, July 18, 1950; all in *NLG*. See Ungar, *FBI*, pp. 373–75. See also Nixon's Jan. 26, 1950 speech, U.S., *Congressional Record*, Vol. 96, P. 1, 81st Cong., 2d sess., 1950, pp. 999–1007.

29. Weinstein, *Perjury*, pp. 189–91. U. S., House, Committee on Un-American Activities, Subcommittee on Espionage, *Executive Session Hearings*, Dec. 28, 1948, pp. 97–98, *KM*. Kenneth O'Reilly called these subcommittee hearings to my attention. William Miller, *Fishbait—The Memoirs of the Congressional Doorkeeper William "Fishbait" Miller as Told to Frances Spatz Leighton* (Englewood Cliffs: Prentice-Hall, 1977), p. 45. Smith, *Alger Hiss*, pp.

256–57. Bert Andrews and Peter Andrews, *A Tragedy of History* (Washington: Robert B. Luce, 1962), pp. 175–76. See Letter, Harlan Vinnedge to Alger Hiss, Aug. 3, 1974; Memo, Nichols to Tolson, Dec. 3, 1948, FBI 74–1333–647; both in *AH*. Apparently a series of visits to HUAC offices by Nicholas Vazzana were the catalysts to Nixon's decision to visit Chambers on Dec. 1, 1948. An investigator, Vazzana was hired by Chambers's attorneys to assist during the Hiss libel suit proceedings. See Memo, Guy Hottel, SAC, Washington Field Office to FBI Director, Dec. 21, 1948, FBI 617, *AH*.

30. Letter, J. Parnell Thomas to Karl Mundt, July 26, 1948, *KM*. I thank Kenneth O'Reilly for calling this letter to my attention. Apparently, Woltman learned about Bentley's confidential grand jury testimony from the FBI. The FBI's released Marcantonio files confirm a close relationship between FBI officials (especially Nichols) and Woltman in which the leaking of information was commonplace. Syndicated columnist Drew Pearson, moreover, claims that Senator Homer Ferguson, the chairman of the Senate subcommittee that first initiated hearings focusing on Bentley's charges in July 1948, had previously been provided with a copy of the FBI's Bentley file. See Drew Pearson, *Diaries, 1949–1959* (New York: Holt, Rinehart and Winston, 1974), pp. 58–60; see also Drew Pearson folder, LN.

31. Memos, H. B. Fletcher to D. M. Ladd, Aug. 2, 1948, Whittaker Chambers 46; H. B. Fletcher to D. M. Ladd, Aug. 6, 1948, FBI 65–56402–3344; Ladd to FBI Director, Aug. 3, 1948, FBI 65–56402–3562; all in *AH*. *Washington Star*, Aug. 13 and 16, 1948. That the FBI might have been the source of Lawrence's information is indirectly confirmed by a series of FBI memoranda detailing a very close relationship between Lawrence and FBI Assistant Director Louis Nichols. These memoranda recount the conservative journalist's interest in the possibility that defense attorneys might subpoena Bernard Redmont to testify during the William Remington trial. See Memos, Nichols to Tolson, Oct. 21, 1950, FBI 74–1379–?; Oct. 31, 1950, FBI 74–1379–435; Nov. 6, 1950, FBI 74–1379–532; and Dec. 2, 1950, FBI 34–1379–621; all in FBI Files, William Remington, J. Edgar Hoover Building.

32. Levine's December 1947 and October 1948 articles are reprinted in Isaac Don Levine, ed., *Plain Talk: An Anthology from the Leading Anti-Communist Magazine of the 40s* (New Rochelle: Arlington, 1976), pp. 197–98, 202–7. See also Berle, *Navigating the Rapids*, pp. 249–50, 582–85; and Weinstein, *Perjury*, pp. 59, 62–66, 232–33, 317–19, 323, 325.

33. Memos, D. M. Ladd to FBI Director, Nov. 23, 1948; FBI Director to SAC, Washington Field Office, Dec. 1, 1948, FBI 18; H. B. Fletcher to D. M. Ladd, Dec. 2, 1948, FBI 98; L. L. Laughlin to H. B. Fletcher, Dec. 2, 1949, FBI

99; H. B. Fletcher to D. M. Ladd, Dec. 3, 1948, FBI 30; H. B. Flectcher to D. M. Ladd, Dec. 8, 1948, FBI 137; SAC, Washington Field Office to FBI Director, Dec. 13, 1948, FBI 930; FBI Director to Attorney General, Dec. 16, 1948, FBI 90; all in *AH*.

34. Memos, A. H. Belmont to D. M. Ladd, Nov. 14, 1953, FBI 100–25824; Warren Olney III to FBI Director, Nov. 14, 1953, FBI 5565; FBI Director to Olney, Nov. 16, 1953, FBI 100–25824; A. H. Belmont to D. M. Ladd, Dec. 22, 1953, FBI 74–1333; A. H. Belmont to D. M. Ladd, Dec. 22, 1953, FBI 74–1333; Nichols to Tolson re: Chapter 29, June 26, 1956, FBI 62–116606–1; all in *AH*. See also *HRCE*, pp. 565–66, 574, 576–77, 580, 1180, 1265.

35. *Baltimore Depositions*, Nov. 17, 1948, Vol. 4 (B), pp. 766–68.

36. Letter, M. W. McFarlin to FBI Director, Nov. 23, 1948, FBI 319; Memo, FBI Director to Assistant Attorney General Alexander Campbell, Nov. 30, 1948, FBI 96; Memo, H. B. Fletcher to D. M. Ladd, Dec. 3, 1948, FBI 21; Letter, M. W. McFarlin to FBI Director, Dec. 4, 1948, FBI 107; Memos, H. B. Fletcher to D. M. Ladd, Dec. 3, 1948, FBI 103; H. B. Fletcher to D. M. Ladd, Dec. 4, 1948, FBI 46; H. B. Fletcher to D. M. Ladd, Dec. 3, 1948, FBI 104; Report, Frank Johnstone, Dec. 4, 1948, FBI 418; Memos, J. H. Randolph to H. B. Fletcher, Dec. 5, 1948, FBI 34; H. B. Fletcher to D. M. Ladd, Dec. 6, 1948, FBI 110; F. L. Jones to H. B. Fletcher, Dec. 5, 1948, FBI 20; FBI Director to Assistant Attorney General Alexander Campbell, Dec. 6, 1948, FBI 112; Report, Thomas Spencer, May 11, 1949, FBI 3220; Memo, SAC, New York to FBI Director, Marcy 23, 1949, FBI 2618; Memo, D. M. Ladd to FBI Director, July 22, 1949, FBI 3680; all in *AH*.

37. Report, Washington Field Office, Jan. 3, 1949, FBI 940, *AH*.

38. Memos, FBI Director to Assistant Attorney General Alexander Campbell, Dec. 6, 1948, FBI 112; Sizoo to Harbo, Dec. 7, 1948, FBI 109; FBI Director to Campbell, Dec. 8, 1948, FBI 109; L. Whitson to H. B. Fletcher, Dec. 6, 1948, FBI 108; FBI Director to SAC, Washington Field Office, Dec. 9, 1948, FBI 80; [names of sender and recipient deleted], re: Obtaining Handwriting Specimen of Harry Dexter White, Dec. 23, 1948, FBI 857; and Washington Field Office Report, Jan. 3, 1949, FBI 940; all in *AH*.

39. *HIA*, Vol. 6, Federal Bureau of Investigation, pp. 563–64.

40. Ralph deToledano, *J. Edgar Hoover: The Man in His Time* (New Rochelle: Arlington House, 1973), p. 206.

41. Tiger, *In Re Alger Hiss*, II, 118–24, 129, 131–36, 246, 247, 249–53, 257, 259–60, 262–63, 268, 272–73, 275, 280–85, 288, 295, 299–310, 357–58, 367, 374–76.

42. The striking parallel between the Hiss and William Remington cases

warrants further research. Accused publicly by Elizabeth Bentley in July and August 1948 of having provided her with classified government documents, Remington denied Bentley's characterization of his actions as espionage. When Bentley (like Chambers) repeated these charges publicly, Remington sued for libel. In 1949, Remington seemed to have impugned Bentley's credibility—receiving both an out-of-court settlement in his libel suit and a loyalty clearance. HUAC, however, resumed public hearings in April 1950 into Remington's past political activities—the upshot of which was that Remington was indicted (and eventually convicted) of perjury. The background to HUAC's 1950 interest in Remington, public hearings, and investigation warrants further study.

43. *Public Papers of the Presidents*, pp. 432–34, 460–61, 844–45, 882–88, 925–30, 959–60, 963–66. See memo, Attorney General Tom Clark to President Truman, Dec. 21, 1948, Tom Clark Papers, Harry S. Truman Library, Independence, Mo.

44. *HISG*, pp. 1120, 1139–40, 1145. See David Rees, *Harry Dexter White: A Study in Paradox* (New York: Coward, McCann and Geoghegan, 1973), pp. 420–23, 439–41.

45. *HRCE*, II, pp. 1381–82.

46. U.S. *Congressional Record*, Vol. 96, P. 1, 81st Cong., 2d sess., 1950, p. 1003. U.S., House, Committee on Un-American Activities, Subcommittee on Espionage, *Executive Session Hearings,* Dec. 28, 1948, p. 75, *KM*. Chambers had not testified to this either in the December 28, or earlier, HUAC hearings. He had so testified, however, during his December 3, 1948 FBI interview.

47. When Nixon wished to authenticate White's handwriting on the memorandum in February 1949, he sought the assistance of Harold Gesell, a handwriting expert in the Veterans Administration.

48. *Salt Lake Tribune*, Nov. 22, 1953, p. A12. See also Letter, J. D. Williams to Karl Mundt, May 20, 1954; and reply, May 29, 1954; Letter, Edgar (Hoover) to Karl (Mundt), June 14, 1954; and reply, June 16, 1954; Letter, Karl Mundt to William J. [sic] Fulbright, June 16, 1954; and reply, June 21, 1954; all in *KM*. I thank Kenneth O'Reilly for sharing this research discovery. This was not the only known instance when FBI officials created a paper record indicating that they had *not* (when in fact they had) leaked FBI reports to favored individuals. See also, Letters, Bishop G. Bromley Oxnam to FBI Assistant Director Nichols, March 10, 1949; Feb. 16, 1950; Oct. 14, 1955; Letter, Nichols to Oxnam, Oct. 19, 1955; Memo, G. B. O. [G. Bromley Oxnam] Oct. 20, 1955; G. Bromley Oxnam Papers, MS Division, Library of Congress.

8

Liberal Values, the Cold War, and American Intellectuals: The Trauma of the Alger Hiss Case, 1950–1978

Kenneth O'Reilly

Contrary to one widely accepted myth, few liberals, at the time of Alger Hiss's conviction, questioned a federal jury's verdict that Hiss had committed perjury and, by implication, espionage. This response to Hiss's conviction reflected the emergence of an anti-Communist consensus among liberals and conservatives. As late as 1948 many liberals might have assailed anti-Communist charges as masking reactionary politics (succinctly captured in President Truman's August 1948 "red herring" remark). The liberals' position had so shifted by 1950, however, as to be virtually indistinguishable from the conviction of Cold War conservatives that the United States had confronted and continued to confront a serious internal security threat. Liberal intellectuals argued among themselves over just how anti-Communist one should be and just how dangerous or naive were those few civil libertarians who claimed American Communists were entitled to constitutional protections.[1]

The Alger Hiss case graphically symbolizes the altered perspective of American liberal intellectuals in the fifties. After 1950, many liberals increasingly employed Hiss's conviction to indict the "popular front mentality," and reinforce the new realism of the "vital center." Conservatives also exploited the Hiss affair. For them, Hiss's conviction confirmed New Deal disloyalty, and the subversive character of President Roosevelt's diplomacy at Yalta, and the Truman Administration's foreign and domestic policies.

The author expresses his appreciation to Susan Cooney, Barton Bernstein, and Athan Theoharis for their editorial criticisms.

Acceptance of Hiss's guilt, moreover, had become a necessary step for many liberals in their transition from what Arthur M. Schlesinger, Jr., called the "tender-mindedness" of the popular front, to a "tough-minded" liberalism, free from any delusions about the intent of American Communists.[2] Identifying with the "responsible" anti-Communism of the Truman Administration, the new liberals, by 1950, had rejected traditional liberal tenets (a belief in progress, popular democracy, and man's inherent goodness and perfectibility) in favor of a creed that stressed man's corruptibility, the inevitability of conflict among nations, and the dangers of democratic rule.[3]

The Hiss case played a salient role in the formation of this intellectual climate—a climate wherein mainstream liberalism abandoned a set of tolerant beliefs for an ideology that denied traditional First Amendment rights to Communists and, to a lesser degree, "fellow travellers." The merging of liberal and conservative thought on the issue of Hiss's guilt, furthermore, has proven resilient despite a series of challenges to the tenets of Cold War anti-Communism in the decades following Hiss's conviction.

The liberal reaction to Allen Weinstein's *Perjury* underscores this continuity of opinion, and further highlights the Cold War's impact on the priorities of many liberal intellectuals.[4] Cold War liberals attempted to disassociate the Hiss case first, during the 1950s, from the abuses of the McCarthy era, and later, during the 1970s, from Richard Nixon's disgrace. Unreconstructed Cold War liberals have clung to the Hiss affair as an example of a prudent anti-Communism, free from the abuses caused by an irrational public and the rantings of the junior senator from Wisconsin.[5]

I

As John Kenneth Galbraith observed in 1978, Alger Hiss confirmed the Cold War's impact on traditional liberal values when he agreed with Whittaker Chambers "that the behavior of which he was accused was terrible, unforgiving."[6] After 1950, few liberals defended the anti-fascist concerns and tolerance of American Communists common in the popular-front era. The vast majority, instead, chose an alternative response; their anti-Communism helped shape the political phenomenon known as McCarthyism. Cold War liberals castigated fellow liberals for often, if unwittingly, aiding the Communist "conspiracy."

"In the United States," *Reporter* editor Max Ascoli warned, "the enemy does not need a particularly large Communist Party, for some of the work in his behalf is done by thoroughly respectable, and undoubtedly anti-Communist, fuzzy-minded Americans." "A strong American Party," former Party member Murray Kempton argued, would actually hinder the Communists: "Men like Alger Hiss do not have to become Communists, at least in the West; it is an act of will." Ex-Communist Granville Hicks (a self-proclaimed "critical liberal") even argued that "neutrality is . . . impossible: if you aren't for [Stalinism], you have to be against it." Communism, announced former Marxist Sidney Hook, "is especially formidable in drawing to itself politically innocent men and women . . . whose minds are unfortified with relevant information."[7]

Conservatives did not substantially differ from the tenets applied by Cold War liberals to condemn the popular front. If liberals claimed that "fuzzy-minded" anti-Communists furthered Soviet objectives, conservatives pointed to Hiss's service in the Roosevelt Administration as evidence that President Roosevelt and the New Dealers abetted the Communist conspiracy. Was not the government obliged to purge not only Communists from sensitive positions but those "whose minds are unfortified with relevant information"? If one were not anti-Communist, was that not an indication of Stalinist tendencies?

Troubled by conservative attempts to exploit Hiss's service in the Roosevelt Administration, many Cold War liberals walked an impossible tightrope, attempting in the process to defend the New Deal, but not Alger Hiss or the "popular front mentality" he allegedly represented. "[T]he Hiss case was a red herring," said Richard Rovere, "though Hiss himself was a red agent." Only naive intellectuals, James Wechsler averred, could believe that the Hiss case symbolized a generation on trial. Wechsler found equally ludicrous "those conservatives who want to believe the New Deal was merely another phase of the Communist world conspiracy," as did David Riesman, Arthur Schlesinger, Jr., and Philip Rahv. Riesman concluded that "it was not a generation on trial but a fringe." Schlesinger implied that Alger Hiss and "the Popular Front mind" were fair game, but labeled efforts to identify Hiss with New Deal personnel in general a "vulgar anti-Communism." At worst, the New Deal could be charged with "neglect."[8]

The red-baiting of radicals and maverick liberals was not a tactic peculiar to a conservative politicians and intellectuals. Liberals might have objected to the more indiscriminate demands of conservatives, notably the House Committee on Un-American Activities (HUAC), to purge Communists and Communist ideas. Nonetheless, Cold War liberals also red-baited, and, although opposed to the compulsory registration provisions of the Mundt-Nixon and McCarran bills, advocated a repressive emergency detention bill (S. 4130).[9]

In addition, such Cold War liberals as Schlesinger and Hook were already alerting the public to the dangers of Communism, actively promoting exposure as the most efficient means to combat internal subversion. Schlesinger may not have spoken "the language of McCarthy with a Harvard accent," as Carey McWilliams lamented, but he did provide tips for identifying "Communists and fellow travellers who pose as ordinary liberals." The liberals' commendation of exposing Communist sympathizers further highlights the Cold War's impact: liberals objected not to red-baiting but indiscriminate and irresponsible red-baiting—that is, confusing liberals with Communists.[10]

Liberals objected to conservative attempts "to dishonor Adlai Stevenson with the stigma of Alger Hiss," but employed similar red-baiting tactics against some progressives. The *Nation*, the only liberal periodical to take a consistent pro-Hiss position throughout the 1950s, was a frequent target of the anti-Communist liberals. "The *Nation*," former *Nation* art critic Clement Greenburg wrote to the magazine's editors in March 1951, has a moral obligation "to side with the Stalin regime when it holds itself compelled to by principle (though it does it so often that that constitutes another, if lesser scandal), but not to put its pages at the regular disposal of [Julio Alvarez del Vayo] whose words consistently echo the interests of that regime; nor has it the right to make [del Vayo] its foreign editor." The *Nation* declined to publish Greenburg's letter, and, after the *New Leader* published it, sued for libel. Reinhold Niebuhr and Robert Bendiner promptly resigned from the *Nation*'s staff reportedly "in protest against its fellow-travelling policies."[11]

An avowedly independent socialist periodical, the *New Leader* relished the challenge raised by the *Nation*'s suit, and enlisted the support of Norman Thomas and such Cold War liberals as Schlesinger, Hook, Rovere, and William L. White. Writing to *Nation* editor Freda Kirchwey, Schlesinger complained that the *Nation* "prints, week after week, . . . *wretched apologies for Soviet depotism.*" Schlesinger reiterated his earlier complaints of 1949 that "sentimentality has softened up the progressive for Communist . . . conquest," and that the "devotional essays of Señor Del Vayo and pious genuflections by Miss Kirchwey herself" confirm devotion to "the Soviet mystique." Lamenting "that not all Americans are as wise in the ways of Communists as the editors of the *New Leader*," Rovere contributed an article condemning "doughface anti-McCarthyism," McCarthyism, and Soviet power as threats to U.S. security.[12]

Hook also indicted "ritualistic liberals" for adhering to "the Kirchwey-del Vayo line." The *Nation*'s pages did not simply contain "Communist ideas," which are "heresies," but supported the "Communist movement," which Hook defined as a "conspiracy." Another liberal, Diana Trilling, expressed the same view: "The espionage to which Hiss's Communist commitment led him is the awful evidence that ideas are not the innocent little things we think them, that they have a commanding life of their own, that they can look both ideal and legal but turn out to be neither."[13]

For the *New Leader*, Alger Hiss became a symbol to be employed to discredit the *Nation* and other "tender-minded" progressives. In a September 1950 article, entitled "Lattimore: Dreyfus or Hiss," Eugene Lyons urged concerned citizens not to assume Owen Lattimore innocent lest they "be as embarrassed as they were when the Hiss case was clarified." Shortly after Hiss's conviction, the *New Leader* proclaimed that "pro- versus -anti-Communism is a dead issue among American liberals." A new split had arisen "*within*" the anti-Communist liberal camp." The "Softs" or pro-Hiss liberals were either "blind to the political realities exposed by the [Hiss] case" or "emotional . . . innocents . . . [who] can't look the cold war in the face." More important, "the Softs though staunchly anti-Communist, lend respectable cover to Communist propaganda, and hinder sensible and thorough investigation of Communist machinations by their incessant harping about 'persecution' and 'hysteria.' " In contrast, the "Hards" were by this analysis "sophisticates."[14]

Former Trotskyite Irving Kristol, then managing editor of *Commentary* and now a leading neoconservative ideologue, also questioned the effectiveness of such cautious anti-Communists as Henry Steele Commager, Zechariah Chafee, Francis Biddle, and Alan Barth. These liberals "are sincerely anti-Communist," Kristol conceded in 1952, but nonetheless excessively tolerant and naive. Kristol buttressed his argument by a brief survey of the recent past: "Roosevelt certainly didn't see in Stalin any symptoms of blood lust. Hermann Goering in jail struck one as a clever clown. And there are still plenty of people who can't believe that Alger Hiss ever did any such thing."

Naive liberals, Kristol continued, refused to concentrate on the Communist threat, preferring to gaze at Communism "out of the left corner of the eye." Kristol was particularly upset because Barth had questioned "the guilt of Alger Hiss," "the utility of exposing it and punishing it a decade later," and Chambers's veracity. Although alienated by Kristol's tolerance of Senator McCarthy, many liberals, such as Americans for Democratic Action (ADA) leader Joseph L. Rauh, Jr., cited their own anti-Communist credentials before attacking Kristol's extreme position.[15]

Liberals condemned McCarthy for his tactics not his avowed purposes. Dwight Macdonald, for instance, longed for "that idyllic era of the Hiss case when tangible evidence was frequently produced," while lamenting that McCarthy's charges popped like pricked balloons. A few liberals tentatively supported McCarthy and searched for a "sober" definition of the concept of guilt by association. (Kristol suggested as such a test membership in three or more organizations declared subversive by a federal authority.) "The wrong people are looking for Soviet agents" and investigating "such important matters" as the Hiss-Chambers espionage cell, Diana Trilling complained; liberals could do a better job. Being a realist, she did not dismiss "the possibility that a McCarthy, too, may turn up someone who is as guilty as Hiss." Not inconsistently, the Cold War liberals vacillated on controversial civil liberties issues. Morris Ernst of the American Civil Liberties Union, Senator Hubert H. Humphrey, and Congressmen Emanuel Celler and Jacob Javits, for example, commended the 1949 Foley Square Smith Act convictions of American Communist Party leaders; liberal opposition to HUAC declined strikingly following the second Hiss trial.[16]

Extending the analysis, Merle Miller argued that Hiss "along with Whittaker Chambers, [contributed] to the uncontrollable and menacing hysteria in this country." Hiss was "guilty of enacting the Big Lie," and was "as responsible as any man now living for the un-nerving success of the Junior Senator from Wisconsin." "Hiss, in his arrogant treatment of Chambers and [HUAC]," David Riesman believed, "was doing the country a far more serious disservice than in his earlier, very likely inconsequential espionage and other efforts to influence foreign policy." Marquis Childs also personally blamed Hiss for McCarthy's success, the prevailing anti-intellectualism, and failures in American foreign policy.[17]

Although blaming Hiss for McCarthy's and HUAC's abuses, the same liberal intellectuals cited the Hiss case as proof that not all of the McCarthyites' victims were innocents. Reflecting on her years as an anti-Communist activist, Diana Trilling found McCarthy "opportunistic" and "the greatest gift the United States could have given the Soviet Union," and HUAC "poorly equipped to make the difficult necessary discriminations between protecting democracy and weakening it." She nonetheless argued that there was a real need to expose Communist influence within American politics and culture, and characterized Senator McCarthy and "doughface progressives" as unwitting allies of the Soviet Union. Richard Rovere faulted HUAC's procedures and personnel, but concluded that "with few exceptions, the investigators and the investigated have seemed richly to deserve each other." And the *New Leader* starkly contended that "McCarthyism need never have been born had the main body of liberalism purged the Hisses and Lattimores from its ranks."

Such logic found cautious support from other liberals—including Granville Hicks, Mary McCarthy, Irwin Ross, and Daniel Bell. Bell articulated the standard Cold War liberal position when condemning McCarthy's "reckless methods disproportionate to the problem," particularly "the violent clubbing of the Voice of America (which under the sensible leadership of anti-Communists, such as Bertram D. Wolfe, had conducted intelligent propaganda in Europe)."[18]

By the 1950s, many liberals had also abandoned their traditional commitment to defend unpopular ideas—a commitment labeled archaic, an example of "know-nothing or Bourbon liberalism" defensible only in the "pre-Hiss era." Writing in *Commentary* in 1951, Robert Bendiner objected to the McCarthyites' "crass attempts to exploit the justified hostility toward Communists for their own political purposes." At the same time, Bendiner urged liberals not to object "every time a Communist is exposed, on the ground that his political beliefs are private." Some liberals even commended the McCarthyites' restraint. Comparing McCarthyism with post–World War I anti-radicalism, Irwin Ross concluded that the present day "authorities . . . comport themselves with far greater decorum." Bendiner concurred: "Our anti-Communism is vastly different from the reactionary drive led by [Attorney General] A. Mitchell Palmer in the early 1920s. . . . The resort to undemocratic methods today is, by contrast, the reaction to a very real and grave threat from abroad."[19]

Reflecting in 1978 on liberal anti-Communism, Arthur Schlesinger defensively concluded that in the late 1940s and early 1950s the "real liberals" had faced a perplexing dilemma:

The fact that the American reaction in those years was largely hysterical and contemptible does not mean the problem was non-existent. . . . Did we really have anything in common with Stalinists with regard either to means or to ends? And, if not, what were we supposed to do about it? [Did not] a democratic society [have a responsibility to ferret out] Stalinists (or Nazis or whatever) in government, trade unions or other positions of influence?[20]

After 1950, Cold War liberals consistently defended Whittaker Chambers's efforts to expose Stalinists and upheld the integrity of the Hiss trial, as if Hiss's conviction legitimized the liberal role in the subsequent purge of radicals. Irving Howe found it "highly probable" that Chambers had told the truth during both trials, and asked rhetorically whether the Hiss-Chambers confrontation threatened only "those popular-front liberals who had persisted in treating Stalinism as an accepted part of 'the Left?' " "Some day," wrote *Commonweal* editor John Cogley, "perhaps Alger Hiss will write a book, an honest book, and it will fill out this history of the times to which Mr. Chambers has brought such burning, eloquent witness." Schlesinger considered Chambers's memoir *Witness* "one of the really significant American autobiographies," and characterized as "convincing" Ralph de Toledano's and Victor Lasky's description of Chambers "as a man of inquiring and sensitive mind." Walter Goodman judged Chambers a "truthful man, who on certain subjects could not quite separate the real from the fantastic"; Philip Rahv appraised *Witness* as "a fully convincing account of the role its author played in the Hiss case"; while Murray Kempton opined that "the little stories [Chambers] told do not appear to have been untruths."[21]

Most Cold War liberals concluded that Chambers had accurately described Alger Hiss's role in a Soviet espionage cell. They took issue only with Chambers's emphasis on Communist infiltration of the New Deal. One "must distinguish," Sidney Hook admonished, "between the facts to which [Chambers] bears witness and the interpretations he places upon them." Conceding the seriousness of the internal security threat, liberals rejected Chambers's contentions that Communists had had a strong influence in the liberal administrations of Franklin D. Roosevelt and Harry S. Truman, and, as Hannah Arendt put it, that liberalism was the "inconsistent, inconsequential ally of Communism." Liberal intellectuals sharply questioned Chambers's apocalyptic vision and self-appointed status as unqualified expert on Communist infiltration.[22]

Schlesinger found *Witness* too dogmatic and Chambers too tenderminded. Chambers had rejected Communist discipline in favor of a new "fellowship of the righteous," claiming Christianity represented the only hope for Western civilization in a world spinning toward a final Armageddon between Communists and ex-Communists, revolutionaries and counter-revolutionaries. Schlesinger also deemed simplistic Chambers's prescribed choice for the West: either God or Stalin. Elmer Davis, although convinced of Hiss's guilt, considered Chambers's new absolutism little different from Soviet totalitarianism. The ex-Communists, wrote Davis, "have clung to this certainty of their superiority to the unsaved—and to their concomitant certainty that their dogmas . . . are complete, perfect, and infallible."

Cold War liberals preferred the "tough-mindedness of pragmatism" to the "tender-mindedness of absolutism," whether advanced by Stalin (and his American "sympathizers") or Chambers. They believed themselves to be better anti-Communists than the zealous ex-Communists who made such spectacular headlines. "Chambers has no understanding of or sympathy for," Merle Miller complained, "those twentieth century democrats who never have and never could become agents of the

Kremlin, members of the Communist Party, or defenders of the tyranny of the Soviet Union." Irving Howe "remind[ed] Chambers that a good many 'left-wing intellectuals' . . . fought a minority battle against Stalinism at a time when both he and Hiss were at the service of Mssrs. Yagoda and Yezhov."[23]

Because they identified with Chambers's militant anti-Communism, some Cold War liberals shared or—like Arthur Schlesinger Jr.—championed Chambers's sense of guilt. Schlesinger tempered his condemnation of the McCarthyites' style by noting that "liberals . . . often contribute as much to hysteria as reactionaries. When they denounce the Un-American Activities Committee for failing to distinguish between liberals and Communists, they should remember how long it took them before they started making that distinction themselves." For the new realists, the Hiss affair was the consequence of the naiveté of the 1930s, but not of the new liberalism of the post-1948 period, which tolerated neither radical critiques of, nor alternatives to, official American foreign and internal security policies. The writings of these intellectuals abounded with symbolic interpretations and psychological sketches; an entire generation was indicted. Conservative poet Peter Viereck described the period as "the whole guilty 1930s."[24]

Asserting that Chambers's "only real sin is his maudlin prose-style," Viereck lamented that many genuine "anti-communazis" had been compelled by the forces of "reaction and philistia" to support Hiss. Viereck then provided a standard by which to identify unrepentant "lumpen-intellectuals of the Thirties": "belittling the importance or influence of Hiss's high posts; . . . finding excuses or doubts on his behalf; . . . spreading scandalous rumors against Mr. Chambers and his act of public service and moral atonement." David Riesman, Leslie Fiedler, and other Cold War liberals shared these views, hoping Hiss would confess—a necessary step for all former radicals in their progression "from a liberalism of innocence to a liberalism of responsibility." "The failure of Hiss to confess," Fiedler asserted, "far from casting doubt on his guilt, merely helps to define its nature."

Fiedler's "age of innocence" ended in stages: the Moscow show trials of 1937–38, the Nazi-Soviet pact of August 1939, and, finally, the Hiss-Chambers confrontation before HUAC in August 1948. For Fiedler, Hiss symbolized "the Popular Front mind at bay, incapable of honesty even when there is no hope in anything else." Philip Rahv concluded that "the Popular Front mind . . . fought to save Hiss in order to safeguard its own illusions and to escape the knowledge of its gullibility and chronic refusal of reality." Robert F. Drinan discerned in Hiss "no expression of moral aversion to communism," while Murray Kempton attributed Hiss's guilt to "status anxiety" caused by the social degeneration of Baltimore's "shabby gentility."[25]

A belief in Alger Hiss's guilt had become a litmus test of the Cold War liberals' new realism. The Hiss case, as Diana Trilling stated, symbolized the need to "separate . . . liberalism from tolerance of Communism." The leadership of America's anti-Communist intelligentsia, from Arthur Schlesinger, Jr., to Sidney Hook, and from Lionel Trilling to Irving Howe, were convinced that Alger Hiss was the just victim of, to use Howe's phrase, a "principled . . . anti-Communism." Richard Rovere's comments succinctly capture how Cold War liberals considered the Hiss affair:

The conviction of Alger Hiss was a triumph of due process, . . . his exposure . . . a triumph of the House Committee on Un-American Activities—its one significant triumph in fourteen years. Of the Hiss case . . . it can be said that if the Committee regularly conducted itself as it did then, no one could raise any reasonable objection to it. It subjected Whittaker Chambers to rigorous tests of credibility and gave Hiss a full, fair, prompt hearing and the opportunity to confront his accuser. It was solicitous in the extreme of Hiss's rights, allowing his to become almost the classic example of a man hoist by his own petard.[26]

With Hiss's conviction, many liberals had abandonned traditional liberal principles in favor of a new political creed whose central tenet was a rationalistic anti-Communism. The United States Constitution, these anti-Communist liberals implied, was ill-equipped to face the unique challenges presented by the Soviet Union abroad and internal subversion at home.

II

Cold War liberalism remained philosophically intact up to, and during the decade of the 1970s.[27] Although no longer indiscriminately red-baiting their left-liberal and radical adversaries, Cold War liberals (and conservatives) were more likely to characterize critics of Allen Weinstein's *Perjury* as partisan zealots. These critics of Weinstein's conclusion of Hiss's guilt could not accept the "facts" of the case.

Cold War liberals, however, continued to commend respectable anti-Communism. For example, writing in *Commentary*, now the leading neoconservative organ of Cold War anti-Communism, Michael Ledeen opined that "we may at long last be emerging from the shadow of Joseph McCarthy" with anti-Communism regaining its proper respectability. Weinstein's *Perjury* had provided the occasion for Ledeen's expressed hope for an anti-Communist resurgence.[28]

More than a historical monograph, *Perjury* reinforced the convictions of Cold War liberals and conservatives hardened nearly thirty years earlier, and upheld the correctness of their earlier critique of "naive," "treasonous" popular-front liberals. Indeed, Weinstein's ambitious monograph attempts to reestablish the tenets of Cold War liberalism. Using Hiss as a straw man, *Encounter* editor Melvin J. Lasky contended that to have believed in Hiss's guilt a liberal had to fight a "lonely battle," and that Weinstein's reaffirmation of the jury's verdict was an "unpolular position."[29]

Lasky's comments are misleading—establishment liberals have consistently favored Whittaker Chambers since the 1950s. For example, Meyer Zeligs's psychoanalytic study *Friendship and Fratricide*, when published in 1967, was dismissed as a partisan diatribe aimed at discrediting Chambers. Zeligs's book was scathingly reviewed by a host of anti-Communist intellectuals: Walter Goodman in *Commentary*, Sidney Hook in the *New York Times Book Review*, and Meyer Schapiro in the *New York Review of Books*. Claiming that the book "reeks of partisanship," Goodman chastised Zeligs for not sorting out "the cold facts of [Chambers's] conspiratorial existence . . . from among his fiery imaginings."[30]

Yet, *Perjury* is as vulnerable to the charge of partisanship as Zeligs's *Friendship and Fratricide*.[31] A book much heralded by the media (including front-page news stories in the *New York Times* and *Washington Post* in 1976, and a cover blurb in *Time* magazine in 1978) *Perjury* was not subjected initially to rigorous review. Most reviewers, especially those writing before *Nation* editor Victor Navasky's celebrated critique, were uncritically eulogistic.[32] Others dismissed Navasky's critical review as ephemeral and the proponent as an ideologue. "Icons and symbols," University of Wisconsin historian Stanley Kutler mused, "are not easily demolished: witness the few but strident critics of Weinstein's book."[33]

Because they reinforced previously held Cold War beliefs, *Perjury*'s conclusions about popular-front complicity in Soviet espionage and Chambers's veracity were extolled by Cold War liberals and conservatives alike. *Perjury* offered "the most objective and convincing account we have" of the case, Schlesinger affirmed; for John Kenneth Galbraith, Weinstein's book was "definitive." An "unemotional blockbuster of fact, . . . a revelation of how politicized, partisan and hallucinated most of the pro-Hiss (and even a little of the anti-Hiss) literature has been," Alfred Kazin opined. Irving Howe praised Weinstein's "balanced account . . . lucidly written, impressively researched closely argued," which proved that "Chambers was indeed what he said he had been." "Allen Weinstein's bestseller," William F. Buckley, Jr., concluded, "will convince everyone who is not a member of the Flat Earth Society that Alger Hiss was guilty." For George Will, *Perjury* was "a monument to the intellectual ideal of truth stalked to its hiding place. . . . The myth of Alger Hiss's innocence suffers the death of a thousand cuts, delicate destruction by a scholar's scalpel."[34]

Newsweek's liberal reviewer, Peter Prescott, unintentionally confirmed how radically liberalism had been transformed during the Cold War years. *Perjury*, Prescott lamented, "should finally lay the case to rest but it won't. Too many people have invested too much ego, energy and ideology in proclaiming Hiss's innocence to let the controversy lapse simply because Allen Weinstein has come up with the facts." Prescott then acclaimed the political value of Weinstein's study: liberals could keep their villains—Nixon, HUAC, J. Edgar Hoover, McCarthy, a Cold War mentality—while condemning Alger Hiss.[35] Prescott neglected to mention that *Perjury* allowed Cold War liberals to retain their most significant villains—American radicals, anti–anti-Communists, and those who had remained consistent adherents of traditional libertarian and constitutional values.

III

"If Alger Hiss has been telling the truth for thirty years, as many American liberals believe," Alfred Kazin has written, "then he is a victim of the most outrageous injustice and, in particular, of the fanatical anti-Communism of ex-Communist Whittaker Chambers and of the always unscrupulous Richard Nixon." Kazin failed to observe that Hiss's guilt or innocence is far less important than understanding the methods that the FBI, HUAC, and the Justice Department employed to impeach Hiss's integrity and secure his conviction. Kazin and other Cold War liberals have ignored this dimension, focusing exclusively on Hiss's behavior and the popular-front days of the 1930s.

In his autobiographical *New York Jew*, Kazin characterized the popular-front mind as "stuck in the habits of a lifetime" and "Alger Hiss [as] . . . a proven liar . . . an obvious case of what was wrong with liberals." "The central issue [of the Hiss case]," Irving Howe concurred when discussing Weinstein's *Perjury*, "had to do with the culture of Stalinism and its multiple peripheries passing themselves off as 'progressive'—the culture that had formed Chambers and, at the least, touched Hiss. It was a political culture combining purity of intent and corruption of deed, one in which idealism and nihilism came to be almost indistinguishable." "Hiss and the government bureaucrats near him," Howe further asserted, were elitists who, like Chambers, were susceptible to "the lure of authoritarianism" and "the brutal realities of Communism." "In the long run, historically," Howe concluded, their vision of a new world and its accompanying naiveté "will seem far more important than the guilt of Chambers or Hiss or both."[36]

Establishment liberals, moreover, did not consider Hiss to have been Richard Nixon's victim. Hiss was not a "real New Dealer," John Kenneth Galbraith argued. According to Galbraith, Hiss had more in common with the Nixon White House "plumbers" than with Nixon's real victims—the Berrigan brothers and Daniel Ellsberg. "Both Alger Hiss and Richard Nixon," Galbraith concluded, "succumbed to the ruthless geometry of covering up the cover-up of a cover-up." Hiss, Sidney Hook maintained, was "a victim of the facts," not of Nixon. Richard Rovere accused Hiss's attorneys of having "conducted a Mc-

Carthyite defense before Senator Joe McCarthy surfaced," and Lionel Trilling disassociated Chambers "morally" from Nixon. Moreover, Cornell Law Professor Irving Younger rehashed the old records—trial transcripts, exhibits, and briefs—finding no evidence of prosecutorial impropriety, and reaffirming Hiss's guilt.[37]

Most of *Perjury*'s liberal reviewers praised Weinstein's effort to counter Hiss's recent gains resulting from Richard Nixon's disgrace. These reviewers hoped that *Perjury* would reverse the Watergate atmosphere of distrust and suspicion—an accomplishment, conservative columnist George Will noted approvingly, that would rank as a "substantial public service." Will particularly hoped that *Perjury* would counter the prevailing "anti–anti-Communism." For T. S. Matthews, *Perjury* was "not so much a book . . . [but] a massive document . . . placed in evidence."[38]

A central tenet of Cold War liberals has been that the abuses of power common to other political trials of the McCarthy era were fostered by a hysterical McCarthyism rather than a rational anti-Communism. For them, the Cold War assault on civil liberties was the inevitable consequence of the naiveté of the 1930s, and, as Arthur Schlesinger, Jr., asserted, "the Stalin administration" but not of the Truman Administration's or the liberals' own anti–Communist politics.[39] Cold War liberals have further dismissed as irresponsible and partisan scapegoating, attempts to raise serious questions about the past. Writing in the "Op-Ed" section of the *New York Times*, for example, Walter Goodman lamented that "Watergate may have created a new and receptive audience for conspiracy theories." "The controversy over 'Perjury,'" Goodman continued, "has given fresh work to the cottage industry dedicated to manufacturing theories of conspiracy for the convenience of Alger Hiss." Conspiracy buffs will seize "any rumor, hint, supposition" and "any *possibility* becomes raw material for construction of an overarching conspiracy."[40]

The initial reaction of liberal intellectuals to Weinstein's *Perjury* suggested that this problem had been solved—Alfred Kazin and Richard Rovere concluding that no new revelations would be forthcoming in the Hiss case.[41] Weinstein's conclusions, touted as based upon a careful analysis of declassified FBI files, indeed, reveal no substantive transgressions by either HUAC, the FBI, or the Justice Department. In contrast, Alger Hiss's *coram nobis* petition (based on these same FBI documents) claims that the government committed "a multitude of improprieties" of "constitutional dimensions" in the attempt to secure a conviction. According to Hiss's petition,

> The prosecution maintained an informer in the legal councils of the defense for several critical months before the trial; pre-trial statements, given by Chambers to the FBI and prosecution, were concealed and the very existence of these statements was falsely denied; critical facts concerning the typewriter . . . were kept from the defense, the court and the jury; and the prosecution suffered perjury to be committed by its witnesses without protest.[42]

Yet Weinstein is no dispassionate chronicler. Reviewing four studies of McCarthyism in March 1971, Weinstein argued that McCarthyism "will lose its force only when Americans have rejected those spurious devil theories . . . which purport to explain the dilemmas of the cold war." Weinstein's critical remarks are revealing because the "devil theories" were allegedly propounded principally by "cold war revisionists"—not the McCarthyites of whom they wrote. In his review, Weinstein lamented that Alan Harper's sympathetic pro-Truman study, *The Politics of Loyalty*, "provides unwitting support for the [revisionist] argument that no major threat to America's internal security existed that might have justified the [Truman Administration's] loyalty program." Two years before the publication of *Perjury* and before he could have carefully studied the majority of the yet-unreleased FBI documents on the Hiss case, Weinstein announced in a *New Republic* article that FBI files revealed no documentary "smoking guns."[43]

Anti-Communist commentators have also commended Weinstein for shredding "into absurdity" the conspiracy theories proposed by Alger Hiss's advocates. Indeed, Sidney Hook has argued that the federal government's institutional structure precluded any plot to frame Hiss. According to his reasoning, because administratively subordinate to President Truman, the Justice Department and the FBI were therefore "acting in concert" with the President, who would have been embarrassed had Hiss been indicted. By this logic, the FBI should have attempted to exonerate Hiss because that was Truman's wish. Despite the

President's partisan intent, Hook suggests, the FBI and the Justice Department were forced by the facts to pursue Hiss.

Hook misunderstands the actual lines of authority between the President and the FBI. Recent congressional investigations and scholarly studies, based on access to heretofore classified FBI files, fully document the FBI's insubordination. FBI officials often acted on the basis of their own priorities, even when those contravened the political interests of the administration. Thus, during the 1948 campaign, FBI officials covertly assisted Truman's Republican opponent, Thomas E. Dewey—drafting position papers, issued as Republican campaign pamphlets, condemning the Truman Administration's internal security policies.[44]

Cold War liberals have further identified conspiracies allegedly undertaken by Hiss "partisans" or *Perjury*'s critics. When reviewing Meyer Zeligs's *Friendship and Fratricide*, for instance, Walter Goodman reflected on "Zeligs's ulterior motive in his need to destroy Whittaker Chambers." During an interview with Philip Nobile, Weinstein declared that "Alger Hiss has had the enormous benefit of extremely protective friends, family, and associates for three decades now, and a whole variety of people who could have hurt his cause voluntarily keeping silent." "No sooner had Weinstein's book appeared," Sidney Hook opined, "than a corps of researchers coordinated by Victor Navasky of the *Nation* checked out its every line." Hiss's continued assertions of innocence, Hook observed, were those of a " 'true believer' . . . a species of fanatical Communist (even if formally not a member), case-hardened by his experience, sustained by the hope, and sometimes by the conviction, that someday he will be honoured as a hero of the New Order when it spreads throughout the world."[45]

Another characteristic of the favorable reviewers of *Perjury* has been a willingness to extend Weinstein's indictment of Hiss. Richard Rovere considered Hiss "a victim of his own moral arrogance and that of his high-minded friends in high position." "Hiss's stonewalling," wrote Congressman Robert F. Drinan, "resulted from an unfathomable personal idiosyncracy rather than any ideological conviction. . . . Alger Hiss stood for no moral or intellectual values, but was obsessed by an overwhelming ambition." Murray Kempton summarily dismissed Hiss as "a truly great con." Kempton further commended Weinstein's failure to resolve the troubling question of the date of Chambers's defection from the Communist Party as "one mystery that Weinstein was wise to give up trying to solve." Rather than making a clean break, Sidney Hook instead argued, Chambers had gradually weaned himself from the party.[46]

For these "partisans," Chambers's contradictory testimony was easily explained. Kempton emphasized Meyer Schapiro's and Lionel Trilling's character references for Chambers, while T. S. Matthews described "the witness" as a "man of honor." When appraising John Chabot Smith's *The True Story* in April 1976, *New Republic* editor John Osborne complained of a "cult of Hiss defenders." "I was convinced then [1949–50] and am convinced now," Osborne continued, "that Smith [who had covered the Hiss trials for the *New York Herald Tribune*] simply did not comprehend Whittaker Chambers and didn't know how to distinguish [Chambers's] truth from his lies—or . . . his misjudgments."[47]

In contrast to the reviewers' judgement of Chambers was their view of Hiss. Alfred Kazin "was struck . . . by the number of well-known Communists [Hiss] seemed to be in touch with." Irving Howe lumped Hiss and Chambers together as two authoritarian souls: "Not to have a 'position' [as Chambers once asserted], or to bear ambiguity [Hiss once claimed he had never been ambiguous in his life], would have landed them in those shaded areas of complexity and doubt in which most thoughtful people find themselves." Merle Miller's review disparagingly characterized Hiss as a man capable of "lying to his son" and a "somewhat shabby . . . cult figure" while commending *Perjury*'s arguments as "superb and detailed."[48]

During the 1970s, Cold War liberals again emphasized Hiss's responsibility for the McCarthy era. Michael Ledeen concluded that "the unwillingness . . . to accept the evidence about Hiss (and about others like him) made McCarthyism possible. Had the FBI done its job in the 40's, and had the government been willing to admit that it had been infiltrated, demagogues like the late Senator from Wisconsin would have been undercut." Weinstein's case against Hiss is "irrefutable," Ledeen concluded. *Perjury*'s "enduring value" is its "extensive documentation of Soviet espionage," which should counter "the discrediting of any concern over Communist espionage and subversion in the United States."

"McCarthyism of the 50s has its mirror image today in the war against the CIA and the FBI," Ledeen complained. "FBI and CIA men" have sadly come to be viewed as the "real subversives," not those, like Hiss, who were "convicted . . . KGB agents." Echoing Whittaker Chambers's earlier concern, Ledeen protested that "one of the most durable and most damaging legacies of McCarthyism has been the besmirching of the good name of anti-Communism." Ledeen further opined that a "reluctance to act against Soviet espionage was characteristic even of the notoriously anti-Communist J. Edgar Hoover and Allen Dulles, and even in instances [such as the Hiss case] where the information was abundant."[49]

Most reviewers, moreover, have focused narrowly on the question of Hiss's guilt. Sidney Hook, a self-described "unreconstructed 'cold warrior,' " attacked Zeligs's *Friendship and Fratricide* in the *New York Times Book Review* and Smith's *The True Story* in the *Wall Street Journal* long before the publication of *Perjury*. Indeed, for thirty years Hook had denounced Hiss's claims to innocence while defending Chambers's account of Soviet espionage. "After Judge [Felix] Frankfurter appeared as a character witness for Hiss at the first trial," Hook recalled in 1976, "I sent a message to him . . . [asserting] that I had very good reasons to believe that Chambers was telling the truth in the light of which it would be unwise to go out on a limb for Hiss. . . . Frankfurter's failure to appear as a character witness for Hiss at the second trial may have had nothing to do with my message." The note to Frankfurter "was based not only on a close study of the evidence but on experiences that involved Chambers and his friends more than a decade earlier."[50]

With the publication of *Perjury*, Hook commended Weinstein for establishing "firmly and exhaustively the credibility of Chambers' own story of his involvement in the Communist underground assigned to collect information from strategic sources in the US government of possible use to the Soviet regime." To Hook, Weinstein's second important achievement was to destroy "the credibility of Alger Hiss by showing that he lied persistently and consistently about one of the key pieces of evidence . . . the Woodstock typewriter." The typewriter question, however, remains a complex and troublesome issue. Hiss's *coram nobis* petition indirectly confirms this: one of its central issues involves evidence concerning the typewriter. For those harboring preconceived notions of Hiss's guilt, however, there are no unresolved questions. "Although we cannot now determine the extent or degree of Hiss' guilt," Hook concluded in his review of *Perjury*, "the fact of his guilt can no longer be contested on any rational grounds."[51]

IV

Since leading liberals still averred that the United States had confronted a serious espionage problem during the 1930s and 1940s, it is hardly surprising that they unabashedly heralded Weinstein's *Perjury*. In the 1950s, recognition of Alger Hiss's guilt had become a central tenet of a case-hardened liberalism and of a rational anti-Communism. It remained so in the 1970s. The Cold War had propelled America's liberal intellectuals from disillusionment with radicalism to militant anti-Communist politics. By the late 1940s, the crusade against fascism that had dominated American intellectual concerns in the 1930s had been replaced by a war against Communism. Reactive anti-Communism shaped the responses of Cold War liberals toward Alger Hiss, McCarthy, Vietnam, and, more recently, even the Watergate and Church Committee investigations.[52] With few exceptions, anti-Communist liberals have failed to reassess their earlier role in legitimating the indiscriminate anti-radicalism that characterized American society following the collapse of the fragile World War II alliance with the Soviet Union.

And did the FBI contribute to the evisceration of traditional liberal values during the Cold War? The fact that FBI officials were committed to securing Alger Hiss's conviction and, further, specifically targeted the liberal community's values can no longer be dismissed as the rantings of conspiratorialists. In February 1946, the very month FBI officials began to leak derogatory information about Hiss to their congressional and media allies, the Bureau launched a sweeping program intended to undermine Communist support among "labor unions," "persons prominent in religious circles," and "the Liberal elements." The Bureau's underlying purpose—to create an "informed public opinion" about "the basically Russian nature of the Communist Party in this country"—was to be carried out by disseminating "educational materials" through "available channels" (what the FBI later described, under its series of harassment programs code-named COINTELPRO, as "friendly and reliable media contacts").[53] The extent to which this FBI campaign affected liberal values cannot be determined precisely. The response of mainstream liberals to the Hiss case suggests that the impact of the FBI's "educational" activities may have been substantive. Whether or not influenced by the Bureau, by 1950 liberal values had indeed changed.[54] Although many Cold War liberals remained bona fide Bureau critics, FBI officials must have been pleased.

Notes

1. In the early 1950s, anti-Communist liberals—including Arthur Schlesinger, Jr., Sidney Hook, Irving Kristol, Daniel Bell, Elmer Rice, David Riesman, and Richard Rovere—found common ground with such conservatives as Whittaker Chambers, James Burnham, John Dos Passos, James T. Farrell, Ralph de Toledano, and John Chamberlain in the American Committee for Cultural Freedom (ACCF). Ironically, the ACCF dissolved its formal ties with the CIA-financed international Congress for Cultural Freedom, deeming the Congress insufficiently anti-Communist. Apparently, the ACCF also received limited CIA funding. See Mary S. McAuliffe, *Crisis on the Left: Cold War Politics and American Liberals, 1947–54* (Amherst: University of Massachusetts Press, 1978), pp. 115–29; Diana Trilling, *We Must March My Darlings* (New York: Harcourt Brace Jovanovich, 1977), p. 61.

2. Rejecting traditional distinctions between right and left, the proponents of the new liberalism argued that fascism and communism were both totalitarian, and, therefore, not diametrically opposed. See Reinhold Niebuhr, *The Irony of American History* (New York: Charles Scribner's Sons, 1952) and *Christian Realism and Political Problems* (New York: Charles Scribner, 1953); Sidney Hook, *Political Power and Personal Freedom* (New York: Criterion, 1959) and *Heresy, Yes—Conspiracy, No* (New York: John Day, 1953); Arthur M. Schlesinger, Jr., *The Vital Center* (Boston: Houghton Mifflin, 1949); and Lionel Trilling's novel, *The Middle of the Journey* (Garden City, N.Y.: Doubleday, 1957). See also Les K. Adler and Thomas G. Paterson, "Red Fascism: The Merger of Nazi Germany and Soviet Russia in the American Image of Totalitarianism, 1930's–50's," *American Historical Review* 75 (April 1970): 1046–64. For the emergence of the new liberalism, see McAuliffe, *Crisis on the Left*; and James

A. Nuechterlein's more sympathetic "Arthur M. Schlesinger, Jr., and the Discontents of Postwar Liberalism," *Review of Politics* 39 (Jan. 1977): 3–40.

3. Elitists who endorsed the center, the new liberals distrusted mass politics and characterized McCarthyism as a product of status anxiety, mass hysteria, and the social irresponsibility of a populistic culture. See Daniel Bell, ed., *The New American Right* (New York: Criterion, 1955), reissued as *The Radical Right* (Garden City, N.Y.: Doubleday, 1963).

4. Allen Weinstein, *Perjury: The Hiss-Chambers Case* (New York: Knopf, 1978). Important books on the case include Whittaker Chambers, *Witness* (New York: Random House, 1952); Morton Levitt and Michael Levitt, *A Tissue of Lies: Nixon vs. Hiss* (New York: McGraw-Hill, 1979); Fred J. Cook, *The Unfinished Story of Alger Hiss* (New York: Morrow, 1958); Alistair Cooke, *A Generation on Trial* (Baltimore: Penguin, 1952); Ralph de Toledano and Victor Lasky, *Seeds of Treason* (New York: Funk and Wagnalls, 1950); Alger Hiss, *In the Court of Public Opinion* (New York: Knopf, 1957); William A. Jowitt, *The Strange Case of Alger Hiss* (Garden City, N.Y.: Doubleday, 1953); Richard M. Nixon, *Six Crises* (New York: Pocket Books, 1962); John Chabot Smith, *Alger Hiss: The True Story* (New York: Holt, Rinehart and Winston, 1976); and Meyer A. Zeligs, *Friendship and Fratricide* (New York: Viking, 1967).

5. For example, see Michael Ledeen, "Hiss, Oswald, the KGB, and Us," *Commentary* (May 1978), pp. 30–36.

6. John Kenneth Galbraith, "Alger Hiss and Liberal Anxiety," *Atlantic* (May 1978), p. 47.

7. Max Ascoli, "The Great Hoover Debate," *Reporter* (Jan. 23, 1951), p. 4; Granville Hicks, *Where We Came Out* (New York: Viking, 1954), pp. 178–79; Sidney Hook, "Communism and the Intellectuals," *American Mercury* (Feb. 1949), p. 136; and Murray Kempton, *Part of Our Time: Some Monuments and Ruins of the Thirties* (New York: Simon and Schuster, 1955), p. 32 See also, Arthur Schlesinger, "Whittaker Chambers and His 'Witness,'" *Saturday Review* (May 24, 1952), pp. 10, 39.

8. Letter, Richard Rovere to Arthur Schlesinger, Sept. 30, 1952, Richard Rovere Papers, box 32, Wisconsin State Historical Society, Madison; Schlesinger, "Whittaker Chambers," pp. 39–40; letter, Schlesinger to editor, *Commentary* (July 1952), p. 84; Schlesinger, "Espionage or Frame-Up?," *Saturday Review* (April 15, 1950), pp. 21–23; James Wechsler, "The Trial of Our Times," *Progressive* (Feb. 1949), pp. 10–12; Philip Rahv, "The Sense and Nonsense of Whittaker Chambers," *Partisan Review* 19 (July–Aug. 1952): 478–79; and David Riesman, *Individualism Reconsidered and Other Essays* (Glencoe, Ill.: Free Press, 1954), p. 129, n5.

9. William R. Tanner and Robert Griffith, "Legislative Politics and Mc-Carthyism: The Internal Security Act of 1950," in Robert Griffith and Athan Theoharis, eds., *The Specter: Original Essays on the Cold War and the Origins of McCarthyism* (New York: New Viewpoints, 1974), pp. 172–89. For the liberal role in securing enactment of another repressive legislative measure, see Mary S. McAuliffe, "Liberals and the Communist Control Act of 1954," *Journal of American History* 63 (Sept. 1976): 351–67.

10. Carey McWilliams, "The Witch Hunt's New Phase," *New Statesman and Nation* (Oct 27, 1951), p. 455; Arthur Schlesinger, *What about Communism?* (New York: Public Affairs Committee, 1950), pp. 23–24. As articulated by ACCF officers Sidney Hook and Sol Stein, the ACCF's purpose was similar to the McCarthyites'. In 1952, Hook urged the organization "to expose Stalinism and Stalinist liberals wherever you may find them." In 1954, Stein considered it a duty to inform "non-Communists of Communist-dominated organizations with which they seem to get involved" (quoted in McAuliffe, *Crisis on the Left*, p. 116).

11. Jean Begeman, "Hiss and Stevenson—the Truth," *New Republic* (Aug. 25, 1952), p. 10; "The *Nation* Censors a Letter of Criticism," *New Leader* (March 19, 1951), pp. 16–18; "The *Nation* Sues Us," *New Leader* (April 2, 1951), p. 2; "By J. Alvarez del Vayo," *New Leader*, p. 3; Louis Jay Herman, "The *Nation*: The Ideology of Surrender," *New Leader* (Oct. 25, 1954), pp. 15–16; Carey McWilliams, "The War among the Liberals," *Nation* (March 4, 1978), p. 248; McAuliffe, *Crisis on the Left*, pp. 113–15; and Alonzo L. Hamby, *Beyond the New Deal: Harry S. Truman and American Liberalism* (New York: Columbia University Press, 1973), pp. 471–73. The two publications agreed to end the litigation in 1955 without cost to either party.

12. McAuliffe, *Crisis on the Left*, pp. 113–15; Hamby, *Beyond the New Deal*, pp. 471–73; letter, Arthur Schlesinger to Freda Kirchwey, March 26, 1951, reprinted in Peter Viereck, *Shame and Glory of the Intellectuals* (Boston: Beacon, 1953), p. 179; Schlesinger, *Vital Center*, pp. 37, 37n; Richard Rovere, "How Free is the *Nation*?" *New Leader* (July 14, 1952), pp. 12–14; and Rovere, "Communists in a Free Society," *Partisan Review* 19 (May–June 1952): 343.

13. Hook, *Heresy, Yes*, pp. 22, 56; Hook, *Political Power*, p. 267; and Diana Trilling, "A Memorandum on the Hiss Case," *Partisan Review* 17 (May–June 1950): 499. Conservatives are perhaps more susceptible to conspiracy theories. A *National Review* symposium analyzed Alger Hiss's *In the Court of Public Opinion* "from the standpoint of Bolshevik tactical methods." Commenting on the proposed symposium in a letter to William F. Buckley, Jr., Whittaker

Chambers wrote: "Whether or not Alger is still useful to the [Soviet] Apparatus is not the point—useful that is, as pilferer. His chief value was never this, but as shaper of policy and mover of personnel." See "The Hiss Maneuver," *National Review* (May 25, 1957), pp. 496–97; Buckley, ed., *Odyssey of a Friend: Whittaker Chambers's Letters to William F. Buckley, Jr., 1954–1961* (New York: Putnam's Sons, 1969), p. 179.

14. Eugene Lyons, "Lattimore: Dreyfus or Hiss?," *New Leader* (Sept. 2, 1950), p. 19; "Communist Organ Hails the 'Nation,' " *New Leader* (Aug. 25, 1952), p. 8; and "The Hards and the Softs," *New Leader* (May 20, 1950), pp. 30–31. See also Norbert Muhlen, "The Hysteria of the Hisslings," *New Leader* (May 13, 1950), pp. 16–18. Considering a belief in Alger Hiss's innocence a sign of "Retarded Liberalism," Granville Hicks accordingly attempted to discredit Kirchwey, Julio Alvarez del Vayo, Matthew Josephson, Carey McWilliams, and Corliss Lamont. (Ironically, however, for all his hard-headed realism, ex-Communist Hicks was himself labeled a Stalinist by Whittaker Chambers.) See Hicks, "Liberals: Fake and Retarded," *New Leader* (March 22, 1954), pp. 16–19; Buckley, *Odyssey*, p. 59.

15. Irving Kristol, " 'Civil Liberties,' 1952—A Study in Confusion," *Commentary* (March 1952), pp. 229, 231, 233, 235; letter, Rauh to editor, *Commentary* (May 1952), pp. 493–94. "But what of the record of the Americans for Democratic Action," Rauh wrote, "which, having repeatedly excluded Communists from its own ranks, led the successful drive to expose and deflate the Progressive party as an arm of Soviet foreign policy? What of the anti-Communist records of the American Civil Liberties Union . . . the American Veterans Committee . . . the CIO's action in ridding itself of all vestiges of the Communist influence? Who is this hypothetical liberal Mr. Kristol finds too soft towards Communism? It certainly is no spokesman of organized liberalism in America today." Imitating HUAC tactics, the ADA "exposed" the Progressive Party by publicizing the communist associations of Henry Wallace's financial supporters. HUAC member Karl E. Mundt then read into the *Congressional Record* the list of names compiled by the ADA together with their HUAC dossiers. Karl M. Schmidt, *Henry Wallace: Quixotic Crusade 1948* (Syracuse: Syracuse University Press, 1960), p. 159.

16. Dwight Macdonald, "McCarthy and His Apologists," *Partisan Review* 21 (July–Aug. 1954): 423; Kristol, " 'Civil Liberties,' " p. 236; Diana Trilling, "A Memorandum on the Hiss Case," p. 500; Michal R. Belknap, *Cold War Political Justice: The Smith Act, the Communist Party, and American Civil Liberties* (Westport, Conn.: Greenwood, 1977), p. 113; and McAuliffe, *Crisis on the Left*, pp. 50–51, 75–88, 130–31, 157 n5–n6. For different reasons, Whit-

taker Chambers shared the liberals' aversion to McCarthy's "irresponsible" McCarthyism. Writing to William F. Buckley, Jr, in 1954, Chambers worried that "all of us . . . have slowly come to question [McCarthy's] judgment and to fear acutely that his flair for the sensational, his inaccuracies and distortions . . . will lead him and us into trouble. In fact . . . we live in terror that Senator McCarthy will one day make some irreparable blunder which will . . . discredit the whole anti-Communist effort for a long while to come" (Buckley, *Odyssey*, pp. 49–50, 52). Though—like Chambers—reluctant to cooperate with or support McCarthy, some Cold War liberals covertly assisted the FBI's red hunting activities. ACLU officials Irving Ferman and Morris Ernst, for instance, both requested from and provided to FBI officials information about the political activities and affiliations of ACLU activists. See the FBI's recently declassified files on the ACLU in the J. Edgar Hoover FBI Building, Washington, D.C.

17. Merle Miller, "The Unfinished Tragedy of Alger Hiss," *New Republic* (Sept. 25, 1950), p. 25; Miller, "Memoirs from Sanctuary," ibid., May 26, 1952, p. 19; Miller, "The Trial of the Age," ibid., Aug. 3, 1953, p. 17; Riesman, *Individualism Reconsidered*, p. 129 n5; and Marquis Childs, "The Hiss Case and the American Intellectual," *Reporter* (Sept. 26, 1950), pp. 24–27. The notion that Alger Hiss spawned McCarthyism has persisted. Writing in 1970 John Kenneth Galbraith blamed Hiss "in degree . . . for Joe McCarthy," while Allen Weinstein concluded in 1976: "Had Hiss told the truth from the start, we cannot know what the consequences would have been both for him and for national politics; but they could hardly have been worse." See Galbraith, "A Revisionist View," *New Republic* (March 28, 1970), p. 17; Allen Weinstein, "Was Alger Hiss Framed?," *New York Review of Books*, April 1, 1976, p. 19.

18. Diana Trilling, *We Must March*, pp. 51, 56–57, 46n; Walter Goodman, *The Committee: The Extraordinary Career of the House Committee on Un-American Activities* (New York: Farrar, Straus and Giroux, 1968), foreward by Richard Rovere, p. vii; "How to Beat McCarthy," *New Leader* (Sept. 22, 1952), p. 30; Daniel James, "The Debate on Cultural Freedom," *New Leader* (April 7, 1952), p. 4; Hicks, *Where We Came Out*, p. 189; and Daniel Bell, *The End of Ideology: On the Exhaustion of Political Ideas in the Fifties* (Glencoe, Ill.: Free Press, 1960), p. 110.

19. Robert Bendiner, "Has Anti-Communism Wrecked Our Liberties?" *Commentary* (July 1951), p. 16 and Irwin Ross, "Is it Hysteria?," *New Leader* (Feb. 11, 1952), pp. 16–17 See also, David Caute, *The Fellow-Travellers: A Postscript to the Enlightenment* (New York: Macmillan, 1973), p. 327 and Viereck, *Shame and Glory*, pp. 116, 289.

20. Arthur Schlesinger, "A Shameful Story," *New York Times Book Review*, March 19, 1978, pp. 44–45.

21. Irving Howe, "God, Man, and Stalin," *Nation* (May 24, 1952), p. 502; John Cogley, "Witness: Whittaker Chambers," *Commonweal* (May 23, 1952), p. 177; Arthur Schlesinger, "Espionage or Frame-Up?," pp. 21–23; Schlesinger, "Whittaker Chambers," pp. 8–10; Goodman, *The Committee*, p. 261; Rahv, "The Sense and Nonsense of Whittaker Chambers," pp. 472–77; and Kempton, *Part of Our Time*, p. 27. In striking contrast, Charles Alan Wright, a conservative attorney who later became Richard Nixon's chief defense counselor during the Watergate episode, characterized *Witness* as "A Long Work of Fiction." See *Saturday Review* (May 24, 1952), pp. 11–12.

22. Sidney Hook, "The Faiths of Whittaker Chambers," *New York Times Book Review*, May 25, 1952, p. 1; Hannah Arendt, "The Ex-Communists," *Commonweal* (March 20, 1953), p. 596. Some conservatives are currently promoting Chambers as an American Solzhenitsyn. See Gerhart Niemeyer, "Rewitness," *National Review* (Aug. 4, 1978), pp. 964–67. Other conservative anti-Communists, however, lamented that Chambers cultivated a "personality cult," and became "the idol of a circle or worshipers who regarded him as a seer and holy crusader." See Isaac Don Levine, *Eyewitness to History* (New York: Hawthorn Books, 1973), pp. 181–82, 210–11. For the impact of the Hiss Case on American conservatism, see George Van Dusen, "The Continuing Hiss: Whittaker Chambers, Alger Hiss and *National Review* Conservatism," *Cithara* 11 (Nov. 1971): 67–89.

23. Schlesinger, "Whittaker Chambers," pp. 10, 39–41; Miller, "Memoirs from Sanctuary," p. 20; Irving Howe, "Madness, Vision, Stupidity," *New Republic* (Nov. 28, 1964), pp. 22–24; and Howe, "God, Man, and Stalin," pp. 502–3. Other liberals were more tolerant of Chambers. Dismayed that many Americans still deemed Hiss innocent in December 1948, *Partisan Review* editor William Phillips even offered Chambers a chance to write an article on the case. For *Partisan Review*'s "hard anti-communism," see James B. Gilbert, *Writers and Partisans: A History of Literary Radicalism in America* (New York: John Wiley, 1968), pp. 253–82.

24. Schlesinger, *Vital Center*, p. 217; Peter Viereck, "Symbols: Hiss and Pound," *Commonweal* (March 28, 1952), pp. 607–8. Many liberals did not subscribe to what Morris Ernst called "the susceptible generation theory," the contention that Hiss symbolized the sordid past of American liberalism. Historian Harry Barnard agreed that Hiss and the neo-fascist poet Ezra Pound "may have been ['symbols of liberalism'] in certain areas of Manhattan island, but . . . not in

the great homeland of indigenous American progressiveness . . . that stretches west of the Hudson River" (letter, Barnard to editor, *Commonweal* (May 30, 1952), pp. 198–99).

25. Leslie Fiedler, *An End to Innocence* (New York: Stein and Day, 1972), pp. 6, 8, 23–24; Fiedler, "McCarthy," *Encounter* 3 (Aug. 1954): 18; Rahv, "The Sense and Nonsense of Whittaker Chambers," p. 478; and Robert Drinan, "The Enigma of Alger Hiss," *America* (June 1, 1957), p. 288. See also, Riesman, *Individualism Reconsidered*, p. 129, n5.

26. Diana Trilling, "A Memorandum on the Hiss Case," p. 498; Irving Howe et al., "Liberal Anti-Communism Revisited: A Symposium," *Commentary* (Sept. 1967), p. 51; and Rovere, "Communists in a Free Society," p. 344. "Not even men as critical as I of the old House Committee," Norman Thomas similarly conceded, "could challenge its procedures in uncovering the Hiss case." See *The Test of Freedom* (New York: Norton, 1954), p. 124.

27. Many Cold War liberals—and particularly the triumvirate of writers for *Commentary*, the *New Leader*, and *Partisan Review*—have more recently defected to "neoconservatism." See Peter Steinfels, *The Neoconservatives: The Men Who Are Changing America's Politics* (New York: Simon and Schuster, 1979).

28. Ledeen, "Hiss, Oswald, the KGB," p. 36. Ledeen also reviewed Edward Jay Epstein's *Legend: The Secret World of Lee Harvey Oswald* (New York: Reader's Digest / McGraw Hill, 1978).

29. Written as introductory remarks to Sidney Hook's review of *Perjury* ("A Historian's Verdict," *Encounter* 51 [Aug. 1978]: 48–55), Melvin Lasky's comments reflect the thrust of Hook's review. During the 1950s, however, the *Chicago Sun-Times* and the *St. Louis Post-Dispatch* were two of the few liberal newspapers to question Hiss's guilt and the methods employed by the government to secure his conviction. Among liberal periodicals, the *Nation* was perhaps the only one arguing that one day Alger Hiss might be proved innocent. Nonetheless, Diana Trilling contended in 1976 that "we still live with the cultural detritus of Communist fellow-travelling, and highly volatile it is, whatever the form it now takes. Especially in the advanced literary community, and despite certain notable exceptions, liberal anti-Communism was not, and still is not, the recommended path to professional success." See *We Must March*, pp. 46–47n. Others, as the unrepentant anti–anti-Communist Studs Terkel, saw things differently. "Had I brains," Terkel wrote when recalling his radical past, "I might have grown up to be Daniel Patrick Moynihan. Dare I dream the dream of Dr. Kissinger? I might have become a respected contributor to *Commentary*.

Hell, I might have written a scholarly treatise proving Alger Hiss indubitably guilty." See *Talking to Myself: A Memoir of My Times* (New York: Pantheon, 1977), p. 125.

30. Meyer Schapiro, "Dangerous Acquaintances," *New York Review of Books* (Feb. 23, 1967), pp. 5-9; Walter Goodman, "Ulterior Motives," *Commentary* (April 1967), pp. 91-92; and Sidney Hook, "On the Couch," *New York Times Book Review*, Feb. 5, 1967, pp. 4, 40-41.

31. For critical reviews and comments on *Perjury*, see Robert Griffith, "Perjury?" *Civil Liberties Review* 5 (July-Aug. 1978): 64-71; Eric Jacobs, "Open Letter to an 'Historian,'" *Events*, Sept. 8, 1978, p. 53; David Levin, "Perjury, History, and Unreliable Witnesses," *Virginia Quarterly Review* 54 (Autumn 1978): 725-32; Lee E. Lowenfish, "The Odd Couple Revisited and Other Reevaluations of American Communism and anti-Communism," *Minnesota Review* 11 (Fall 1978): 117-25; Victor Navasky, "Allen Weinstein's 'Perjury': The Case Not Proved Against Alger Hiss," *Nation* (April 8, 1978), pp. 393-401; John Chabot Smith, "The Debate of the Century (Con't.)," *Harper's* (June 1978), pp. 81-85; Philippa Strum, "Guilt by Innuendo," *Commonweal* (July 7, 1978), pp. 441-43; Athan Theoharis, "Unanswered Questions," *Inquiry* (June 12, 1978), pp. 21-24; and Sidney Zion, "The Hiss Case: A Mystery Ignored," *New York Magazine* (April 24, 1978), pp. 10-12. See also Rhodri Jeffreys-Jones, "Weinstein on Hiss," *Journal of American Studies* 13 (April 1979): 115-26; David A. Hollinger, "The Confidence Man," *Reviews in American History* 7 (March 1979): 134-41; and Eric Jacobs et al., "Arguments (New and Old) About the Hiss Case," *Encounter* 52 (March 1979): 80-90.

32. For the effect of Navasky's criticisms, see the dramatic change in tone of the last paragraph of Christopher Lehmann-Haupt's review in the *New York Times*, April 7, 1978, p. C-25.

33. Stanely Kutler, "A Retrial of Alger Hiss," *Progressive* (Sept. 1978), p. 39. Other uncritical reviews and comments include William F. Buckley, Jr., "Goodbye Hiss," *National Review* (April 28, 1978), p. 548; D. Keith Mano, "The Last Traitor," *National Review* (May 26, 1978), pp. 658-70; Robert F. Drinan, "Perjury, Piety, Politics," *America* (Aug. 5, 1978), p. 65; Roscoe Drummond, "Historian's Verdict on Hiss Case," *Christian Science Monitor*, April 19, 1978, p. 22; Galbraith, "Alger Hiss and Liberal Anxiety," pp. 44-47; Walter Goodman, "The Conspirators," *New York Times*, April 25, 1978, p. 36; Hook, "A Historian's Verdict," pp. 48-55; Irving Howe, "Alger Hiss Retired," *New York Times Book Review*, April 9, 1978, p. 1; Alfred Kazin, "Why Hiss Can't Confess," *Esquire* (March 28, 1978), pp. 21-22; Murray Kempton, "Alger Hiss—An Argument for a Good Con," *New York Post*, April 22, 1978;

Robert Kirsch, "Hiss-Chambers: Pre-Watergate Stonewalling," *Los Angeles Times Book Review*, May 7, 1978, p. 1; Ledeen, "Hiss, Oswald, the KGB," pp. 30–36; T. S. Matthews, "Perjury: The Hiss-Chambers Case," *New Republic* (April 18, 1978), pp. 27–29; Merle Miller, "Alger Hiss: Truth and Consequences," *Washington Post*, April 17, 1978, pp. E-1, E-6; Chalmers M. Roberts, "The Lessons from Chambers and Hiss," *Washington Post*, July 21, 1978, p. A-13; Philip Nobile, "Allen Weinstein: Who is He and What Has He Got on Alger Hiss?," *Politicks* (Feb. 28, 1978), pp. 4–5, 26–30; Peter S. Prescott, "The Guilt of Alger Hiss," *Newsweek* (April 3, 1978), pp. 79–82; Leonard Reed, "Perjury: The Hiss-Chambers Case," *Washington Monthly* (April 1978), pp. 66–67; Richard Rovere, "The Case," *New Yorker* (May 22, 1978), pp. 133–37; Vermont Royster, "The Hiss Case Exhumed," *Wall Street Journal*, May 3, 1978, p. 22; "Hiss: A New Book Finds Hiss Guilty as Charged," *Time* (Feb. 13, 1978), pp. 28–30; Edmund S. Wehrle, "Perjury: The Hiss-Chambers Case," *Critic* (Aug. 1978), pp. 5–6, 8; George F. Will, "The Myth of Alger Hiss," *Newsweek* (March 20, 1978), p. 96; and Garry Wills, "The Honor of Alger Hiss," *New York Review of Books*, April 20, 1978, pp. 29–30.

34. Galbraith, "Alger Hiss and Liberal Anxiety," p. 44; Kazin, "Why Hiss Can't Confess," p. 21; Howe, "Alger Hiss Retired," p. 1; William F. Buckley, Jr., "Beyond the Hiss Case," *National Review* (Aug. 4, 1978), p. 978; and Will, "The Myth of Alger Hiss," p. 96. Arthur Schlesinger's comments appear on the book jacket.

35. Prescott, "The Guilt of Alger Hiss," pp. 79–80.

36. Kazin, "Why Hiss Can't Confess," p. 21 and *New York Jew* (New York: Knopf, 1978), pp. 190, 194; Howe, "Alger Hiss Retired," p. 25.

37. Galbraith, "Alger Hiss and Liberal Anxiety," pp. 44–47; Hook, "A Historian's Verdict," p. 49; Rovere, "The Case," p. 133; Lionel Trilling, "Whittaker Chambers and 'The Middle of the Journey,' " *New York Review of Books*, April 17, 1975, pp. 18–24; and Irving Younger, "Was Alger Hiss Guilty?," *Commentary* (Aug. 1975), pp. 23–37. See also the critical response to Younger's article *Commentary* (Dec. 1975), pp. 4–18. When David Levin criticized Younger's piece, the Cornell law professor noted that "we come to the case from different sides, [Levin] from Hiss's and I from mine." Trilling's novel, *The Middle of the Journey*, wherein the character "Gifford Maxim" was based on his personal acquaintance with Chambers, was reissued in cloth (Scribner's) and paper (Avon) in 1976. See Irving Howe's favorable note "On 'The Middle of the Journey,' " *New York Times Book Review*, Aug. 22, 1976, p. 21.

38. Will, "The Myth of Alger Hiss," p. 96 and T. S. Matthews, "Perjury," p. 28. See also, Wehrle, "Perjury," pp. 5–6, 8.

39. Schlesinger, "A Shameful Story," p. 44.

40. Goodman, "The Conspirators," p. 36. For an alternative view, see Frank Donner, "The Assasination Circus: Conspiracies Unlimited," *Nation* (Dec. 22, 1979), pp. 641, 654–58.

41. Rovere, "The Case," pp. 134–37; Kazin, "Why Hiss Can't Confess," p. 21.

42. For the petition and exhibits (which formed the basis for John Lowenthal's film, *The Trials of Alger Hiss*), see Edith Tiger, ed., *In Re Alger Hiss: Petition for a Writ of Coram Nobis* (New York: Hill and Wang, 1979). These alleged "abuses of power," Weinstein counters, can be dismissed because Hiss's defense team also committed "abuses." See the introduction to the paper edition of *Perjury* (New York: Vintage, 1979).

43. Allen Weinstein, "Point of Order!," *New York Times Book Review*, March 7, 1971, pp. 36, 38; and Weinstein, "On the Search for Smoking Guns: The Hiss and Rosenberg Files," *New Republic* (Feb. 14, 1976), pp. 16–21. In addition to Alan Harper's *The Politics of Loyalty: The White House and the Communist Issue, 1946–1952* (Westport, Conn.: Greenwood, 1969), Weinstein reviewed James Aronson, *The Press and the Cold War* (New York: Bobbs-Merrill, 1970), Robert Griffith, *The Politics of Fear: Joseph R. McCarthy and the Senate* (Lexington: University of Kentucky Press, 1970), and Theoharis, *The Yalta Myths*.

44. Hook, "A Historian's Verdict," pp. 52–53; William C. Sullivan and Bill Brown, *The Bureau: My Thirty Years in Hoover's FBI* (New York: Norton, 1979), pp. 41, 44. For the FBI's abuses and insubordination, see Frank J. Donner, *The Age of Surveillance: The Aims and Methods of America's Political Intelligence System* (New York: Knopf, 1980); Sanford J. Ungar, *FBI* (Boston: Little, Brown, 1975); David Wise, *The American Police State* (New York: Random House, 1976); Morton Halperin et al., *The Lawless State* (New York: Penguin, 1976); Athan Theoharis, *Spying on Americans: Political Surveillance from Hoover to the Huston Plan* (Philadelphia: Temple University Press, 1978); Pat Watters and Stephen Gillers, eds., *Investigating the FBI* (Garden City, N.Y.: Doubleday, 1973); and John T. Elliff, *The Reform of FBI Intelligence Operations* (Princeton: Princeton University Press, 1979).

45. Goodman, "Ulterior Motives," p. 92; Nobile, "Allen Weinstein," p. 27; and Hook, "A Historian's Verdict," p. 50.

46. Rovere, "The Case," pp. 134–37; Drinan, "Perjury, Piety, Politics," p. 65; Kempton, "An Argument for a Good Con;" and Hook, "A Historian's Verdict," p. 54.

47. Kempton, "An Argument for A Good Con;" T. S. Matthews, "Perjury,"

p. 29; and John Osborne, "Alger Hiss: The True Story," *New Republic*, April 17, 1976, pp. 28–29. See also, editor, " 'Perjury,' Take Three," *New Republic*, April 15, 1978, pp. 16–17.

48. Kazin, "Why Hiss Can't Confess," p. 22; Howe, "Alger Hiss Retired," p. 25; and Miller, "Truth and Consequences," pp. E-1, E-6. Other reviewers, such as Garry Wills, if less tolerant of liberal anti-communism, also concluded that the Hiss affair confirmed the reality of the internal security problem during the Cold War years. "So far as any one book can dispel a large historical mystery," Wills wrote, *Perjury* "does it, magnificently." Speculating on why Hiss did not flee to the Soviet Union as Great Britain's confessed espionage agent Kim Philby did, Wills concluded that Hiss might have been "urged [by the Soviets] to undertake the line he did." In addition, Wills revived the "status anxiety" theory, once central to the Cold War liberals' explanation of the ascendancy of the vulgar anti-Communism espoused by McCarthyites: "Only later did [Hiss] come to see that innocence is an affront to the narrow-minded. Nixon did not like Hiss's earned air of superiority any more than Hiss liked Chambers's teeth. The mob abhors a gentleman—even a political gentleman's gentleman like the impeccable Jeeves of Yalta, the New Deal's first civil martyr." See "The Honor of Alger Hiss," pp. 29–30.

49. Ledeen, "Hiss, Oswald, the KGB," pp. 30–31, 35–36. Compare Ledeen's review of *Perjury* with the caustic reviews of David Caute's *The Great Fear: The Anti-Communist Purge under Truman and Eisenhower* (New York: Simon and Schuster, 1978), by Herman Belz in *Commentary* ([June 1978], pp. 70–76), Sidney Hook in *Encounter* (52 [Jan. 1979]: 56–64), and John P. Roche in *Political Science Quarterly* (94 [Summer 1979]: 361–62).

50. Sidney Hook, "What the Cold War Was About," *Encounter* 44 (March 1975): 66; Hook, "On the Couch," p. 4; Hook, "Alger Hiss: The Continuing Whitewash," *Wall Street Journal*, March 22, 1976, p. 14; Hook, "An Autobiographical Fragment: The Strange Case of Whittaker Chambers," *Encounter* 46 (Jan. 1976): 78, 79 n2, 80–87.

51. Hook, "A Historian's Verdict," pp. 49–55. Hook's response to *Perjury* paralleled his 1952 reaction to Chambers's memoirs: "The internal evidence of [Witness] is so overwhelmingly detailed and cumulative, it rings with such authenticity, that it is extremely unlikely that any reasonable person will remain unconvinced by it." See "The Faiths of Whittaker Chambers," p. 1.

52. Reviewing Arthur Schlesinger's *The Bitter Heritage: Vietnam and American Democracy, 1941–66* (Boston: Houghton Mifflin, 1967), Irving Howe conceded the liberals' responsibility for Vietnam, but then qualified this critique: "American liberalism in helping to prepare the ground for our Vietnam

policy . . . allowed the valid principle of anti-Communism to be twisted and exploited for crude reactionary ends." See "A New Turn at Arthur's, *New York Review of Books*, Feb. 23, 1967, p. 13.

53. *IARA*, p. 66; *SDSRIARA*, p. 430.

54. The extent to which Cold War liberals were cultivated as "available channels" alongside HUAC, Senator Joseph R. McCarthy, and right-wing journalists is another question crucial to understanding Cold War liberalism. At least one Cold War liberal, ACLU official Morris Ernst, worked closely with FBI Assistant Director Louis Nichols to discredit those who criticized the anti-Communist ethos. A prolific writer on civil liberties issues during the Cold War, Ernst had obtained regular access to the FBI's confidential files and editorial and research assistance from FBI officials. For Nichols's special relationship with Ernst and the FBI's so-called Ernst projects, see Morris Ernst folder, *LN*. Nichols's relationship with Ernst, apparently was not an aberration. He also leaked derogatory information on dissidents to another prominent Cold War liberal, Methodist Bishop G. Bromley Oxnam. See G. Bromley Oxnam Papers, Louis B. Nichols folder, Library of Congress.

9

The Arrangement: The FBI and Harvard University in the McCarthy Period

Sigmund Diamond

On June 9, 1949, the *New York Times* reported the recommendation of the National Education Association's (NEA) educational policies commission that Communists "should be excluded from employment as teachers." The exclusion of Communists from the teaching profession, the commission had concluded, far from being an "abridgement of academic freedom, would serve a contrary purpose": "Such [Communist] membership involves adherence to doctrines and disciplines completely incon sistent with the principles of freedom on which American education depends. Such membership, and the accompanying surrender of intellectual integrity, render an individual unfit to discharge the duties of a teacher in this country."

The report warned that teachers should not be called Communists "carelessly and unjustly." Such charges, "with their usual accompaniment of investigations, book burning, and efforts at intimidation," could seriously impair the efficiency of the school system if they became "too violent, frequent, and widespread": "The whole spirit of free American education will be subverted unless teachers are free to think for themselves. It is because members of the Communist party are required to surrender this right, as a consequence of becoming part of a movement characterized by conspiracy and calculated deceit, that they should be excluded as teachers."[1]

On that same day, the undergraduate editors of the *Harvard Crimson* dissented from the commission's argument. How could Communists be barred from teaching without encouraging "too violent, frequent, and widespread" charges and thereby impairing the efficiency of higher education? And how could Communists be barred as teachers without investigating faculties? There was no "just and fair method" of investigating faculties for Communists, the *Crimson* concluded: "Competence alone should be the standard."[2]

On campuses throughout the country the investigation of faculty members—by congressional committees or otherwise—had already become a divisive issue. At some public universities the issue was not merely being debated; such investigations had already been instituted. Nor were private universities wholly immune from similar public pressures. At Harvard, for example, Frank B. Ober, an alumnus of the law school who as a Maryland state legislator had sponsored the Maryland Subversive Activities Act of 1949, was urging alumni to stop contributing financially to Harvard until the University ceased being a refuge for "reds" and "pinks." The distinguished attorney and Harvard Corporation member Grenville Clark responded to Ober's call by affirming that no threat of financial sanctions would deter the University from its traditional defense of academic freedom.

Clark's response seemed to suggest that Harvard had adopted a policy of rejecting any review of its faculty's political activities. But had it? In a June 22, 1949 talk before the Harvard Fund for Advanced Study and Research, Harvard President James B. Conant sought to reassure *both* his faculty, who in an opinion poll had supported his NEA position, and his students, who had rejected it. He reaffirmed the position he had taken as a member of the NEA commission that Communists should not be permitted to teach, but then added that "as long as I am president of the University I can assure you there will be no policy of inquiring into the political views of members of the staff and no watching over their activities as citizens."[3] How, then, did Conant propose to detect Communist teachers without investigating the political activities of faculty members?

I

On the basis of research into FBI documents made available through the Freedom of Information Act, I have already described the relationship, existing in 1949, between the FBI and the administration of Yale University concerning investigations of alleged Communists.[4] Did a similar arrangement exist at Harvard, involving understandings between university officials and the FBI? FBI agents and informers were active in Harvard Yard, yet this does not confirm that a relationship existed in the sense in which I am using the word. The FBI's activities might have been carried on without the knowledge—indeed, in the face of opposition—of university authorities. When reporting on the political activities of Harvard faculty members to the FBI, university personnel might not have been acting on the basis of official policy. Their cooperation might have been personally motivated: whether to curry favor, to forestall an investigation of oneself, or to do one's patriotic duty.

Recently released FBI documents confirm that the FBI's Boston Field Office—and other federal investigative agencies (for example, military intelligence)—closely followed the activities of the Harvard faculty and, in the process, developed sources of information on the Harvard faculty and staff. Whatever the basis for this cooperation, FBI officials were concerned that it be discreet. Paragraph 5A, Section 87, of the *FBI Manual for the Conduct of Investigations* specified the restrictions governing interviews "with individuals connected with institutions of learning." Before "initiat[ing] a security investigation of a faculty member," FBI agents had to obtain prior authorization from FBI headquarters. Prior authorization was not normally required in the case of students or non-academic employees "providing no unusual circumstances exist which would require advice from the Bureau prior to initiating the investigation."

When requesting Bureau authority to conduct a security investigation of an individual connected with an institution of learning, the letter should set forth the identity of the subject, his position, and the reason for which the investigation is desired. Information concerning the individual's identity should be obtained from the Registrar's office unless some specific reason exists which would make it undesirable to contact the Registrar's office.

Once Bureau authority had been granted to conduct a "security" investigation, the FBI agent could "contact all established reliable sources including those connected with the institution of learning." A principal source was the university registrar: "If the Registrar is reliable and can be depended upon not to divulge the Bureau's identity, Bureau authority is not needed in these cases to contact the Registrar's office to obtain background data useful for identification purposes, to develop other proper investigative leads or to verify connection with the institution of learning." If it became necessary to "interview a student, faculty member, or other employee of an institution of learning who is not an established reliable source," prior Bureau authorization was needed. In that event, "a positive statement concerning [the person's] discretion and reliability" had to be provided.[5]

The use of various types of informants involved the FBI in a very broad spectrum of activities in Harvard Yard, making it all the more important to determine whether the cooperation of the informants had been based on personal idiosyncrasy or official university policy. A few examples of informant cooperation and the FBI's investigative interest follow:

(1) On December 31, 1948 the Boston SAC (Special Agent in Charge) wrote: It is believed desirable that contact be established with a responsible person or persons within the [Russian] Research Center in order to have an indication of the programs being developed and perhaps have available for review purposes, results of these programs. . . . Accordingly, the Bureau is requested to advise what information they [sic] may have in its possession relating to the background of the above-named individual [name deleted] and authorization is requested to establish contact with him which contact can be commenced on a pretext basis, developed and expanded providing the circumstances warrant and justify such expansion in the light of his interest and availability of information relating to this project.

The "responsible person" had earlier "stated he would be pleased to be of assistance or cooperation with the Bureau whenever his services might be desired."[6] The Boston SAC later requested approval to recruit this potential informant in the Russian Research Center.[7]

(2) On February 25, 1949, the Boston SAC forwarded a "confidential informant's" report that the "two members" of the Russian Research Center "faculty who disturb him more than all the rest" were

Isaiah Berlin and Harold J. Berman. The latter person has been the subject of separate correspondence between the Bureau and Boston. Berlin arrived in the

United States in January, 1949 from England. He is a native of the latter country. [Berlin is a native of Riga, Latvia.] He is giving a course entitled 'The Development of Revolutionary Ideas in Russia.' A photostatic copy of the outline of this course and the required reading therein are enclosed herewith.

We may know the identity of this "confidential informant." On May 5, 1949, the Boston SAC reported on the Russian Research Center and cited the February 25, 1949 report "wherein the Boston Field [Office] stated that it would check its indices against the 'list of staff members' provided by confidential informant [name deleted] and the names of the project workers in that program, entitled 'Programs and Census of Current Projects—January 1949' also provided by confidential informant Charles Baroch." Baroch was a member of the staff of the Russian Research Center.[8]

(3) On May 1, 1951, the Richmond (Virginia) SAC reported on Robert Lee Wolff's recent public address and private discussion in Richmond. Formerly Director of the Balkan Section of the Research and Analysis Branch of the wartime Office of Strategic Services, Wolff at the time was an associate professor of history at Harvard and a director of the Russian Research Center:

Graduates of this Russian study school either go into Russian Research Center or are individually placed by Wolff . . . in government positions in Washington, D.C. . . . Wolff states that Harvard University feels that this is a contribution to good government and they endeavor thereby to fill the vital and overwhelming need for government personnel with knowledge of the U.S.S.R. Dr. Wolff appeared to me to be a very stable and unusual individual who, I feel, would be of immeasurable value to the Bureau as at least a SAC contact for the Boston Office. He was very friendly to me and highly complimentary to the Bureau.

The Richmond SAC reported Wolff's explanation of

. . . the internal security problem in the United States as to the handling of Communists in an entirely accurate and commendatory point of view as to the Bureau's very heavy responsibilities in this regard. . . .

It is suggested for the benefit of the Bureau, if it has not already been done, that Dr. Wolff and Professor Kluckhoehn [sic] be contacted by the Boston Office in order that those studies and published results be made available to us; and further, that the New York Office similarly ascertain the situation at Columbia University.[9]

The FBI was interested in Wolff, as later correspondence shows. Whether it succeeded in making him a regular informant we do not yet know. We do know that on occasion he provided information to the FBI. On May 24, 1951, the Boston SAC notified Washington headquarters that as early as April 16, 1947, Wolff had "turned over to the FBI" a letter he had received from a government employee requesting sources of information bearing on the question "of the guilt or innocence of Mihailovitch," a subject on which Wolff had just published an article in the *Atlantic Monthly*.[10]

On June 11, 1951, Hoover instructed the Boston SAC:

The purpose of this authorization is to enable you to establish and maintain the coverage needed in order that your office will be promptly advised of the identity of individuals whose activities may constitute a real or potential danger to the internal security of the United States. Please advise the Bureau promptly concerning the results of your preliminary contact. Make certain that Wolff does not receive the erroneous impression that the Russian Research Center is under investigation.

On June 20, 1952, Hoover sent the Boston SAC a memorandum which throws light on two paragraphs of a May 29, 1952 memorandum which the FBI has deleted on release for "security" reasons:

Reurlet May 29, 1952.
The Bureau has no objection to a contact with Robert Lee Wolff. For your information, the LGE [Loyalty of Government Employee] investigation concerning Wolff failed to develop any information which would preclude his use in a confidential capacity. The Bureau agrees with your suggestion concerning the method of contacting Dr. Wolff in order to determine his attitude toward cooperation.[11]

(4) On August 17, 1951, the Boston SAC submitted an extensive report on the Russian Research Center, based largely on interviews with informants. The first half of the first sentence of page 2, paragraph 3 of that report has again been deleted; the rest of the paragraph reads:

while the intention of the Carnegie Foundation was to set up a strictly private research institute, they also wanted a more personal contact with United States government agencies. One of the jobs of [Clyde] Kluckhohn [Director of the Russian Research Center] is to obtain pertinent information requested by government departments and, within limits, shape the research program of the Center to the needs of the United States. He cited as an instance of this application [sic] the State Department would communicate with him to suggest they were short in certain aspect of Soviet activity. Kluckhohn would then suggest to a graduate student at the School that he might do a thesis on this particular problem, making no mention to him of the fact that the State Department was also interested. Subsequently the results of the individual research could be brought to the attention of the State Department.

That Kluckhohn may have felt under pressure to cooperate with the FBI is suggested by an October 27, 1952 FBI memorandum "Re: Russian Research Center, Harvard University" and marked "Secret," in which the FBI claimed to have information that, if leaked, could have subjected Kluckhohn to humiliation.[12]

(5) On March 12, 1953, in a memorandum to the FBI Director captioned "Harvard College Observatory/Information Concerning," the Boston SAC reported an earlier telephone call from a Harvard official, whose name and title have been deleted, requesting that an FBI agent visit him at his Harvard office the following day so that he could provide "information of interest to the Bureau." SA [name deleted] "who acts as liaison agent at Harvard, was designated to interview [name deleted]." At that interview, the informant gave the FBI agent a copy of Professor Donald H. Menzel's (Acting Director of the Observatory) letter to Harvard provost Herman Buck. A copy of Menzel's letter was attached to the agent's report; it stated that "Some one in the Observatory is distributing or attempting to distribute sizable quantities of Communist literature, real red propaganda an investigating committee would love to pick up." "For the moment we have decided to keep quiet, holding the documents as they come in," Menzel wrote Buck:

although my first reaction was to destroy them and send a note around to the Observatory personnel that nothing was to be placed in the box but pure science. I should appreciate having your advice.

The Harvard official who provided the FBI with a copy of Menzel's letter stated that Menzel had:

stated such activities, if made known to an investigating committee, would add to the woes of Harvard University officials especially in the light of the projected

HCUA [House Committee on Un-American Activities] investigation among members of the Harvard University faculty. He added he "well realized Harvard was on the spot" and requested SA [name deleted] to discuss the matter with Dr. Menzel, the original complainant, who was greatly concerned about the matter.

The FBI agent did interview Menzel, who told him "he had been advised by [name deleted] that he, Menzel, would be visited by a representative of the FBI" and that he had provided information to Buck about the matter. Menzel was urged to provide "anything which he thought would be of interest to this Bureau."[13]

(6) On December 29, 1954, FBI Assistant Director Louis Nichols reported on his recent conversation with William C. Brady, "representative of the Harvard Conservative Society." Brady had dropped in to invite FBI Director Hoover to address the Society

in order to dispel ignorance among the students, many of whom believed erroneously that the FBI is rapidly approaching a police state type of agency while others are of the opinion that the . . . FBI sponsored the program of having all ROTC students throughout the United States sign loyalty oaths. . . . Mr. Brady appeared to be deeply appreciative of the time spent with him and stated that the discussion certainly opened his mind as to the real role of the FBI. He indicated that he would return to Harvard to spread the true gospel as to our activities."

At the bottom of this memorandum appeared the statement: "No record identifiable with Brady in Bureau files."[14]

II

The FBI clearly sought to obtain information concerning the activities of the Harvard faculty in unobstrusive ways. It is equally clear that the FBI obtained this information from individuals employed by or associated with the University. Let me again cite a few examples.

On January 7, 1954, the Boston Field Office, in a security report on the author, notified FBI headquarters that

[name deleted], Corporation office, Harvard University, advised her records indicate [Diamond is] currently residing at 2 University Road. . . . These same records indicate that on September 15, 1953, Diamond received a Corporation appointment as Advisor to Faculty Fellows. . . . On July 1, 1953 . . . Diamond had been appointed Research Fellow in Entrepreneurial History. . . . According to information in her files [name deleted] stated Diamond was interviewed by McGeorge Bundy, Dean of Harvard College, prior to his appointment. . . . [name deleted] stated she could provide no information concerning the Fund for Advancement of Education which is underwriting one half of Diamond's salary.[15]

The FBI has justified the deletions as necessary to "protect the name of an individual" or "the name and position of an individual" interviewed by the FBI "during the course of an investigation." The FBI source in this case was a relatively low-level Harvard employee, but some information was provided to the FBI by high-level Harvard employees. In a report dated July 28, 1954, the Boston SAC wrote:

From information provided the Boston Division by other individuals having Harvard Corporation appointments, it appears that Dean Bundy is insisting that former Communist Party members, who now have Harvard Corporation appointments shall provide the Federal Bureau of Investigation a full and complete account of their activities in the Communist Party and shall at the same time identify all individuals known to them as participating in activities of the Communist Party and its related front organizations.[16]

A ten-page FBI report on the Russian Research Center, dated April 12, 1949, contained numerous deletions made by the FBI "to protect the name and information concerning the activities pertaining to a confidential source *reporting information to the FBI on a regular basis*, the release of which would lead to the source's indentification [emphasis added]." This claim confirms that the informant had been of a different kind, one who had provided information to the FBI "on a regular basis."[17]

Another FBI memorandum of February 16, 1949, concerns Harvard Professor of Social Relations Talcott Parsons and his wife, "Secretary in the office of Professor Clyde Kluckhohn, who is Director of the Russian Research Center." In this memorandum, FBI agent Thomas McLaughlin reported that "[name deleted] believes that Mrs. Parsons holds liberal views with respect to political and social matters and would possibly not be a desirable contact in connection with any information desired relating to the Russian Research Center. Informant has no information relating to the loyalty or responsibility of Mrs. Parsons but provided this information as indication of the attitude Mrs. Parsons might take in the event direct contact were made through her for information relating to the Russian Research Center and its program."[18] The name of this informant and other identifying material have again been deleted to maintain the confidentiality of the source and the information he/she was regularly providing to the FBI.

On April 12, 1949, FBI agent Brenton S. Gordon reported on an April 1, 1949 telephone conversation with an informant. The informant "felt this Bureau would be interested in a man whom he had seen touring the Harvard Research Center on that day. He identified this individual as Owen Lattimore." On April 4, 1949, the informant reported Lattimore's earlier appearance at Harvard as the guest of Professor John K. Fairbank. He gave a full account of Lattimore's lecture at Harvard on that occasion and "further reported that Fairbank, while not explicitly endorsing everything Lattimore had said, gave every indication to the audience that he supported Lattimore in spirit."[19]

As a result of a recent court order, the FBI has made available a second copy of this memorandum, restoring three words that had been deleted in the first released copy. Those three words, the very last in the memorandum, are: "cc Michael Karpovich."

The reference to Karpovich, the distinguished professor of Russian history at Harvard, is tantalizing. It could mean that Karpovich had been sent a copy of Gordon's memorandum. But why should an internal FBI memorandum have been sent to Karpovich unless he had an extraordinarily close relationship with the Boston FBI? Or does it mean that a copy of Gordon's memorandum had been placed in Karpovich's file? But why should the FBI have maintained a file on Karpovich?

One possible answer is suggested by another Gordon memorandum to the Boston SAC also dated April 21, 1949.; After two long paragraphs that have been totally deleted to protect the identity of "an informant reporting on a regular basis," Gordon reports that his informant had at an earlier date provided information that Karpovich was not in the good graces of the authorities at the Russian Research Center: he was so much a supporter of "the fallen Kerensky regime" as to be unable to conceive of other possibilities for a Russian government. The mutual dislike between the authorities of the Russian Research Center and Karpovich, the informant advised Gordon, created an opportunity for the FBI: "in the opinion of Karpovich the men operating this institution were exceedingly pro-Communist and he was, therefore, exceedingly unwelcome. . . . [name deleted] stated he feels certain if the Bureau desires to interview Mr. Karpovich it will probably be able to obtain additional facts upon which the former [the informant] predicated his opinions and conclusions."[20]

The FBI was interested in a broad range of activities and persons at Harvard and had a variety of campus informants. Was the FBI's relationship with Harvard, then, in any way similar to the Yale relationship, that is, a covert institutional arrangement? If so, we would have a possible explanation for Conant's apparently contradictory statements that Communists were unfit to teach but that Harvard would not investigate its faculty.

III

A series of eight memoranda exchanged between the Boston SAC and FBI headquarters, beginning in June 1950, shed light on this question and further suggest that some understanding between the FBI and Harvard antedated even the first of these reports.

The FBI has refused to release the first document of this series, and I have filed suit to obtain it. It is a two-page memorandum, dated June 16, 1950, and captioned "Harvard University/Cambridge, Massachusetts/ Confidential National Defense Informant [CNDI]."

The second document of the series, dated June 19, 1950 and marked "Personal and Confidential," is also a memorandum from the Boston field office to the FBI Director. It is captioned "Bernard A. DeVoto/Information Concerning." On January 7, 1982, in response to the order of United States District Judge Robert L. Carter (U.S.D.C., S.D.N.Y., Ca 79-Civ-3770), the FBI released a second version of this document, one which does not delete, as the first version did, the caption of the document and the whole of paragraph four. Some deletions still remain, but the document deserves being quoted *in extenso* because of what it reveals and the tone in which it is written:

[Three lines deleted] asserted that while the Harvard University authorities were desirous of cooperating with the Bureau, and while the Bureau's interests and those of the university were identical, there was a constant fear that some independent agency of the government might assert itself in connection with the Bureau's records and thus cause embarrassment to the University in its cooperation with the Bureau.

It is noted that as a result of [half line deleted] on this date, arrangements have been completed for a most cooperative and understanding association between the Bureau and Harvard University.

[name deleted] stated that it was his judgement that many of the conditions existing today, referring to internal security problems, were most distasteful and obviously some action was necessary in order to correct them, but he felt that in most instances the methods utilized in order to effect the correction, were not in good taste, and tended in some instances to destroy the real effectiveness of the work done. He asserted that information came to his attention some time ago with respect to a condition involving immorality and homosexuality among State Department employees and he felt that some action should have been taken by the State Department some time ago, with respect to this matter. He asserted, however, that he did not believe that a Senate Investigating Committee was the proper method to be used in order to bring about a correction of this condition. He did not offer any suggestion as to what methods might be utilized in this respect.

[one and one-half lines deleted] article by Bernard DeVoto, appearing in the October 1949 issue of Harper's Magazine under the general caption "Easy Chair" [few words deleted] gave the definite impression that he felt if DeVoto had some complaint with respect to the Bureau, and its activities, that the method he used, namely an open statement in a national magazine, was obviously not the fair and judicious method of bringing such matter to the attention of proper authorities. [few words deleted] did not specifically condemn DeVoto, but gave the agent who was present with him, the definite impression that he was displeased with the method which DeVoto utilized in that connection and was using that as a further illustration of the fear which may exist in the minds of some university authorities who desire to cooperate with the Bureau in its work but are conscious of the possibility that a Congressional inquiry or directive might usurp the confidential character of the Bureau's files.

As indicated previously, [name deleted] has been most cooperative in his contacts with the Boston Office and this information is provided the Bureau for information purposes with the request that no dissemination be made under any circumstances.[21]

Even allowing for some hyperbole on the part of the Boston SAC, overstating the magnitude of the coup in establishing a relationship with Harvard, it seems clear that, as we have already seen in the documents relating to the Observatory, there were those at Harvard who had more confidence in the FBI than in congressional committees; some kind of "arrangement" existed between the University and the FBI for sharing information; the FBI was pleased by this cooperation; the relationship was sufficiently cordial as to allow the topics discussed to range, as the report on DeVoto illustrates, into the areas of political belief and political activity; Harvard officials would be embarrassed if some "blundering independent agency of the government"—a congressional committee, perhaps—would reveal the University's cooperation with the Bureau.[22]

That FBI Director Hoover understood Harvard's need for discretion is shown in a memorandum he wrote on July 31, 1950:

It is noted from your letter of June 16, 1950, [withheld in its entirety] that arrangements have been perfected whereby information of interest will be made available to the Bureau on a confidential basis [several words deleted]. This arrangement will be effective in connection with Harvard College and the Graduate School of Arts and Sciences.

[Three paragraphs deleted.]

[One line deleted] should, of course, not be contacted at any time without specific Bureau authorization.

In contacting [name and title deleted] who is approved for contacts by the Bureau, prior Bureau instructions must be followed regarding investigations on campuses of colleges and universities.[23]

At this point in the file, a two-page letter from the Boston Field Office to FBI headquarters, dated August 28, 1950, has been withheld in its entirety. The series resumes with another letter, also dated August 28, 1950, captioned "Harvard University/Cambridge, Massachusetts/Potential CNDI's." Heavily expurgated, this letter reported:

The [July 31, 1950] letter in authorizing continued contact [one line deleted] should not be contacted without specific Bureau authority.

[Paragraph deleted.]

[Five lines deleted] it would appear that contact with him on applicant and other matters will be of frequent occurrence. The Bureau is requested to advise whether in each specific instance, authorization must be obtained. [Two lines deleted.]
[Paragraph deleted.]
[Entire page withheld.][24]

The FBI director replied on October 5, 1950, in a letter also captioned "Harvard University/Cambridge, Massachusetts/Potential CNDI's":

Reurlet [regarding your letter of] August 28, 1950.

Provided the files of your office show no reason to the contrary, there is no objection to your office contacting [one line deleted] with Harvard University in accordance with arrangements [five lines deleted].

With respect to [name and title deleted] the Bureau feels that this person should be contacted only if there is no other manner or means of obtaining the desired information. You are, therefore, requested to advise whether there is a more prudential method of procuring information [several words deleted] rather than contact [name and title deleted].

[Paragraph deleted.][25]

Exactly what FBI Director Hoover meant by "a more prudential method of procuring information" is not clear. Some light is shed by the Boston SAC's response of October 26, 1950:

With respect to the authorization contained in the [October 5, 1950] Bureau letter relating to the contact [One line deleted.] Harvard University in accordance with arrangements [Twelve lines deleted].

[Three lines deleted] would assure that no embarrassment would come to the Bureau by contact [name deleted] inasmuch as [two lines deleted].

The Bureau is assured that every precaution will be exercised in connection with this matter and [half line deleted] under the authority granted in Bureau letter of August 5, 1950, will be exercised only after careful consideration. [Name and title deleted] was assured that any contact for the purpose of obtaining such confidential information from Harvard University files, would be on a selective basis and this policy has been closely adhered to.[26]

The FBI director was pleased that the arrangement precluded the possibility of embarrassment. He replied on November 20, 1950:

Reurlet dated October 26, 1950, which states that you feel the arrangement completed [name and title deleted] assure that no embarrassment would come to the Bureau by contact with [name deleted] inasmuch as [two lines deleted]. You assure that every precaution will be exercised in connection with this matter and contact with [name and title deleted] will only be had after careful consideration.

If at any time in the future, agents of your Office experience impatience, antagonism or any other difficulties in contacts, [name deleted] you should immediately notify the Bureau of this fact. Contacts [name deleted] are to be limited to those absolutely necessary and you should, of course, follow previous Bureau instructions relating to investigations on campuses of colleges and universities.[27]

Confidential National Defense Informants were clearly not people whom the FBI interviewed during routine applicant investigations. Whether they were serving as consultants to sensitive national security agencies (the FBI, CIA, National Security Council, State and Defense Departments) or as FBI sources on the Harvard campus cannot now be resolved. These informants were individuals of importance. Can we, then, obtain information about them, their mission as Confidential National Defense Informants, and their importance in the Harvard hierarchy? At Yale, the cooperation between the FBI and the University existed at a level at least as high as that of provost and secretary of the University, and there was an official administrative position—liaison officer—whose occupant, H. B. Fisher, boasted of supervising relations with the "one hundred and twenty six different investigative bodies who have and are using Yale records and files and faculty for background and information concerning Yale men."[28]

We cannot resolve these questions until all FBI documents have been released (and the extensive deletions filled in) and Harvard releases at least the first of its documents. We do have, though, some information about these informants.

In response to a court suit I have filed against FBI Director William Webster, the FBI has submitted affidavits further detailing its reasons for deletions and for withholding certain documents entirely. Most of the deletions are said to be needed to protect informants. The FBI had several levels of informants, ranging from those who furnished information "during a single interview" to those "from whom information

was regularly received under an expressed assurance of confidentiality."
The latter sources were informants "within the common meaning of that
term and not merely conscientious or cooperative citizens." To protect
their identity, FBI documents cited them by source numbers and not by
their names, and information was obtained from them "only at locations
and under conditions which guarantee the contact will not be noticed."[29]

When justifying its refusal to release certain documents in their entirety, the FBI claimed—as it had in other instances—that these involved
confidential sources "reporting information to the FBI on a regular basis,
the release of which would lead to the sources' identification." Most of
the deletions were made to "protect the name, symbol number, position
and place of employment pertaining to a confidential source reporting to
the FBI on a regular basis." The FBI's justification, required to claim an
exemption under the Freedom of Information Act, has thereby confirmed
that these were the FBI's most important informants—confidential informants who had provided information to the FBI "on a regular basis" and
whose identity was known to FBI personnel only on a "need to know"
basis. Can these informants be identified more precisely?

Attempting to answer this question, I had requested from the FBI all
correspondence pertaining to Harvard University. In explaining why
one document was withheld in its entirety, the FBI claims that it "was
outside the scope of the plaintiff's request because it pertains to an invitation from Harvard graduates to the Director" while my Freedom of
Information Act request simply sought correspondence from Harvard
employees.

In fact, I had not requested only FBI documents relating to Harvard
employees, but *all* documents bearing upon the relationship between
Harvard and the FBI during a specified period. The FBI's response in
this instance indirectly confirms that the documents the Bureau released
to me involved only Harvard employees. We now know, therefore, that
the informants whose names were deleted from this series of released
documents were reporting to the Bureau on a regular basis and were employees of Harvard University—faculty or staff—not students or
alumni.

Can we, nonetheless, ascertain the level at which the Harvard-FBI
"arrangements" were made?

Pursuant to the order of Federal District Judge Carter, on January 7, 1982, the FBI released a second version of a memorandum from which it had originally deleted the name of the referenced Harvard official. That memorandum, dated February 9, 1949, from the Boston SAC to the FBI Director, concerns the Russian Research Center. The Center's work, the memo reports, had "greatly expanded" over the years:

It is believed that the results of the work of the international program and the Russian Research Center can be made available to the Bureau officially through contact with President James B. Conant of Harvard University, who has on occasion indicated his respect for the Bureau's work and his understanding for its many and varied interests in connection with internal security matters. It appears that a presentation of the Bureau's desire to be informed on such matters to President Conant personally would make available the current programs and results of research work of the Center on such basis that the interests of the Bureau would not be revealed to the personnel of the particular program and in that way no possible embarrassment could possibly come as the result of any inquiries being directed in an attempt to obtain material outlines and other items of interest in connection with this matter.

Accordingly, the Bureau is requested to consider the advisability of authorizing this office to discuss this matter with President Conant on a discreet and personal basis to determine his reaction to the suggestion set forth above.

An internal FBI memorandum of May 11, 1949, the same day Hoover wrote to the Boston SAC, confirms that the FBI was not uninterested in the contact with Conant, but rather that it did not feel it necessary to trouble him to obtain all the publications of the Center: "In the event that certain members of the Research Center become subjects of subsequent investigation, it may then be desirable to secure their original efforts for inclusion in their files, but it does not appear that procuring the complete work of the Center is necessary."[30]

FBI officials were particularly interested in Conant's conceptions of the loyalty issue. On January 23, 1948, FBI Director Hoover requested from the Boston SAC a copy of Conant's annual report of 1947 to the Harvard Board of Overseers. The SAC obliged. In that report, Conant had distinguished between government and university employment: "I can imagine a naive scientist or a philosopher with very strong loyalties to the advancement of civilization and the unity of the world who would be a questionable asset to a government department charged with negotiations with other nations; the same man, on the other hand, because of his professional competence might be extremely valuable to a university." Conant's distinction disturbed FBI officials. One wrote on the bottom of the memorandum: "Intellectual freedom is not license and when it is slavery is around the corner." To which Hoover added: "I agree. I can understand now some strange things about Harvard."[31]

On January 9, 1953, when Conant was under consideration for appointment as High Commissioner to Germany, Ogden Reid telephoned FBI Assistant Director Nichols. (President and editor of the *New York Herald-Tribune*, Reid had played a major role in promoting Dwight D. Eisenhower's presidential candidacy.) Reid advised Nichols that Herbert Philbrick, who had recently catapulted to prominence as an FBI undercover informant in the New England area, "was very suspicious of Conant. Reid thought that perhaps we should check our files and if there is evidence indicating any subversive connection with Conant, it should be made known to [President-elect Eisenhower]. I thanked Reid for calling this to our attention [Nichols advised FBI Associate Director Clyde Tolson]. I frankly do not see that there is anything for us to do until we receive some request to investigate Conant, which I doubt we will receive." Hoover, however, scribbled on the bottom of Nichols's memorandum: "We have now received it." Secretary of State-designate John Foster Dulles had requested the usual security investigation; and Hoover responded by directing twenty-three FBI field offices to "conduct thorough investigation as to character, loyalty, reputation, associates, and qualifications of Conant."

The Boston Field Office's January 19, 1953, report stated that "this Office has a file entitled, 'Listed Individuals not to be Contacted by Personnel of this Office.' This list was compiled of individuals who have demonstrated hostility to Bureau Agents or who are Communists or Communist sympathizers. Although Doctor Conant does not appear on this list, it does contain the names of twenty-one faculty members at Harvard University, who are not contacted by Agents doing investigations." The Boston SAC pointed out, moreover, that Conant was listed in the pamphlet "Red-ucators at Harvard," published by the National Council for American Education.[32]

None of the many persons whom the FBI interviewed doubted Conant's loyalty and staunch anti-Communism. Some described him in terms compatible with the hypothesis that the Harvard president might well have seen the necessity to limit the range of political beliefs and associations permitted to faculty members. For example:

Mr. James R. Killion [*sic*], President, Massachusetts Institute of Technology . . . stated that he regards Doctor Conant as a liberal in the sense that he has a strong belief in . . . freeing educational systems of political or governmental influence. . . . Conant was one of the first to express to [Killian] during World War II the opinion that the United States must inevitably oppose the Soviet Union and Communism as well as the Nazis. . . .

Doctor Roger Irving Lee [member of the Harvard Corporation] . . . pointed out that Doctor Conant has described himself for many years as a liberal in that he was very strongly in favor of the principles of academic freedoms. Doctor Lee believes that the appointee is not as liberal at the present time as he was in the late 1930's in this regard.

Mr. Donald Kirk David [dean of the Harvard Business School] . . . stated that Doctor Conant's opposition to Communism is almost violent in its strength. . . . Conant has may times told Doctor David that he believes that no university should have or keep on its staff a known Communist. However, it is Doctor Conant's opinion that no university has a legal right to inquire into a faculty member's political beliefs. Only the Government, he stated, has this right. . . . He also believes that the invocation of the Fifth Amendment by a faculty member constitutes grounds for dismissal of that faculty member.

Mr. Charles A. Coolidge [member of the Harvard Corporation] . . . advised that the appointee has on several occasions declared his opposition to Communism. In this connection Mr. Coolidge pointed out that Granville Hicks, a known Communist, was at one time, in 1938, given a one-year appointment as lecturer at Harvard with the full knowledge and consent of both the appointee and the members of the Corporation. This was done . . . because in 1938 it appeared bigoted and undemocratic not to have had Mr. Hicks explain his views. . . . after the Hitler-Stalin Pact . . . the Communists showed their true colors and since that time Mr. Conant's attitude, once relatively liberal, has undergone a complete re versal with respect to Communists and their beliefs. He is now utterly opposed to them. Mr. Coolidge stated that President Conant expressed to the members of the Corporation his belief that the invocation of the Fifth Amendment by a faculty member constituted grounds for dismissal. . . . He also pointed out that in President Conant's report to the Overseers of Harvard University in January of

1953, he declared his belief that Communists had no place on the staff of a university.[33]

Lee's and Coolidge's statements are particularly important. As members of the Harvard Corporation, their knowledge of Conant's beliefs provide insights into how those views affected university policy. George V. Whitney, whom the FBI identified as a member of the Harvard Board of Overseers from 1932 to 1938 and again from 1947 to 1953, similarly described Conant's views. Conant, Whitney asserted,

did not favor the retention of the University instructors who are members of the Communist Party, that he would favor the retention of those who had formerly been a member of the Communist Party but who had broken with that party; but that University instructors and professors should be allowed to explore Socialist and Communist doctrines so long as they did not openly advocate the overthrow of the government. . . . Conant had taken this stand apparently in the name of the doctrine of 'academic freedom' and while the stand was not as strong as [Whitney] believes the situation warrants, he does not consider that this in any way reflects upon the loyalty of Doctor Conant to this country.[34]

The FBI questioned Princeton University President Harold W. Dodds as to Conant's role in drafting the Association of American Universities (AAU) statement that Communists should not be allowed to become university professors. Dobbs did not know whether Conant had been present at the February 15, 1953 committee meeting when the final resolution was drafted, but "it was his belief that Conant would be in complete accord with the principles as set forth by the Association."[35]

Washington University President Arthur H. Compton, an associate of Conant for more than thirty years, told the FBI that the Harvard president had no "immediate and direct connection" with the AAU statement, which was nonetheless "in accordance with Conant's attitude and thinking; he said that he based this belief on several comments made by Conant in his presence previous to the drafting of the statement." Compton then "voluntarily" added:

Conant had been criticized for having had members of his faculty at Harvard University who have been either former members of the Communist Party, or who have been sympathetic with the Communist line of thinking. Mr. Compton said that he wished to state that in all such cases, it was his belief that Conant was aware of whatever affiliations with the Communist Party any of his faculty members might have had, but not through a direct knowledge. Mr. Compton went on to explain that Conant learned of the affiliations through investigation and only after being fully satisified that all Communist affiliations on the part of any prospective faculty members had ceased, and there was no danger of renewed affiliation, did Conant allow any member of his faculty to be hired.[36]

How could Conant assert that no Communist should be appointed to a teaching position, learn of the affiliations of the faculty "through investigation," and still affirm that, so long as he was president of the university, "there will be no policy of inquiring into the political views of members of the staff"? One possible answer is that the FBI conducted the political inquiry. Conant and other university officials might have sought relief from the bull-in-a-china-shop tactics of congressional committees by cooperating with the FBI, whose discretion they thought to purchase by their display of cooperation.

Whether or not Conant was a major architect of a strategy of university cooperation with the FBI as a defense against accusations by congressional committees, by the 1950s, at least, that had become the apparent policy of Harvard and a number of other universities.

On December 8, 1954, representatives of seven universities, together with two attorneys, met with members of the staff of the Joint Committee on Internal Revenue Taxation. Arts and Sciences Dean McGeorge Bundy represented Harvard. One of the attorneys prepared minutes of that meeting which were sent to members of the "Listening Post," apparently an unofficial committee of university officers. According to the minutes, each of the university spokesmen described how they handled or were prepared to handle loyalty questions concerning present and prospective faculty members.

The minutes summarized these individual reports: (1) no present member of the Communist Party or anyone subject to Communist discipline would knowingly be retained as a faculty member or given scholarships and fellowships; (2) while not in itself a cause for dismissal, use of the Fifth Amendment would precipitate a thorough investigation and review of the user's fitness to teach; (3) these reviews were conducted by faculty members or others having a responsibility to the university; (4) "any derogatory information received by the university [was] a basis for an investigation of some sort"; (5) none of the universities had a regular investigating staff; they "obtain[ed] such information as they can from Governmental investigating agencies but [found] this of limited usefulness because of the refusal of such agencies to disclose sources"; (6) a faculty member under Communist discipline or who refused to be "completely frank" with the university investigating board would not be protected by academic tenure; and (7) as a result of their investigations, some universities had refused to renew contracts of non-tenured faculty members, some had dropped faculty members with tenure, and some were in the process of making investigations.

All the university representatives concurred that since 1939, as a result of greater awareness of the problem of subversion, there had been a fundamental change in "investigating procedures used by the universities." It was agreed that had "present-day investigative procedures . . . been in effect" earlier some of the difficult cases of the time would not have occurred. These recently instituted procedures, moreover, had to be continued to guard against subversion and to retain public confidence "in the integrity of the universities and of the teaching process." In response to a Joint Committee staff member's suggestion that the universities might be helped if there were a statutory oath requiring the affiant to swear he was not a member of the Communist Party or under its discipline—a requirement that "would bring the FBI and the Department of Justice into operations which the universities now have to undertake"—the university representatives pointed out that both the Department of Justice and the FBI "are not today following up and prosecuting cases which the universities have already handed over to them under existing law."[37]

IV

Whether or not the FBI forwarded all its investigative findings to university officials, the Bureau did intensively investigate political activists at fifty-six universities. In a March 26, 1953, memorandum to twenty-four FBI field offices, entitled "Communist Infiltration into Education/Internal Security—C," FBI Director Hoover demanded reports on "subversive . . . persons at a number of universities":

The statement should set out the name of the individual, the position he holds at the institution, a brief summary of the subversive information available, a statement as to whether an investigation has been conducted and whether it is pending or closed, whether the subject is on the Security Index and the Bureau file number, if known.

In order to establish which individuals should be included in the survey, it is suggested that you review the Security Index, your pending security files, and that any confidential informants and established sources which might be expected to have information concerning persons connected with these institutions be contacted.

Individuals and not institutions were to be investigated, though the FBI director did not explain how the distinction could be maintained:

The Bureau does not desire that you conduct any investigation whatsoever concerning the institutions themselves or concerning the extent of Communist infiltration. You are especially cautioned not to make any contacts which might give the impression that the Bureau is conducting any such investigation of institutions of learning.

If you feel that there are any other steps which you should take in addition to the suggestions set out above in order to insure that the surveys include all individuals on whom there exists the type of information as outlined above, you should take these steps on your own initiative provided full security may be maintained in order to prevent any allegation that the Bureau is investigating the educational field. Also, if you feel there are other schools in your territory where information exists which would make such a survey desirable, you should submit such a survey again on your own initiative.

The survey should bear the caption "Communist Infiltration into Education, Survey at ——— (Institution), Internal Security—C." The survey should be submitted within 30 days from the date of this letter.

The universities listed by Hoover were: Bennington, Cornell, Syracuse, Johns Hopkins, Maryland, Boston, Dartmouth, Harvard, Mount Holyoke, MIT, Smith, Wellesley, New Hampshire, Buffalo, Rochester, Duke, North Carolina, Northwestern, Chicago, Illinois (at Chicago), Antioch, Ohio State, Colorado, Michigan, Wayne State, Cal Tech, San Jose State, Stanford, UCLA, Southern California, Fisk, Wisconsin, Minnesota, Princeton, Rutgers, Upsala, Yale, Tulane, Brooklyn, CCNY, Columbia, Hunter, Long Island, NYU, Sarah Lawrence, Carnegie Tech, Penn State, Temple, Pennsylvania, Reed, Contra Costa Junior

College, California (at Berkeley), Washington, Illinois (at Champaign-Urbana), and Howard.

I have requested but have not yet received the full file on this investigation.

V

Research into FBI documents obtained under the Freedom of Information Act has so far produced suggestions, not conclusive findings, especially since many universities are even more reluctant than the FBI to make available the documents needed to confirm or refute statements in Bureau reports.[38] But even tentative suggestions are important, above all when they apparently contradict the consensual understanding that has become the commonsense view of the matter. My preliminary research seriously challenges this commonsense view and suggests that the current consensus is based more on complacency than documentary evidence.

When I began my research, I shared the widely held notion that the universities were powerful sources of opposition to McCarthyism, and that FBI agents and informants were unwelcome visitors on university campuses. Indeed, my thinking was dominated by figures of speech in which the universities, besieged, were surrounded by walls which had to be breeched by an insidious enemy who sought to penetrate the sanctuaries of decency. These metaphors still dominate our views of higher education in the late 1940s and 1950s, but they are more appropriate to self-congratulatory myth than to the analysis of documentary evidence.

Heavily censored and at times self-serving, FBI documents do not conclusively confirm that university administrations during the McCarthy period were avid partners of the FBI in the political purge that was then taking place. Indeed, research that has already been done on universities in Massachusetts, Connecticut, New York, California, Illinois, Washington, and Pennsylvania suggests that the question may fairly be asked: Was there any university in the United States that did not have an undisclosed arrangement with the FBI by which each side traded information with the other? The relationship between the FBI and the universities was not adversarial; the sanctuary did not have to penetrated. The relationship was symbiotic: each tried to get from the other what it felt it needed for survival—the FBI, cooperation from the universities to provide information about selected individuals; the universities, cooperation from the FBI to stave off what officials felt was the even greater threat of congressional committees. The Alexander Meiklejohns, who rejected the philosophical and political grounds for the purge, were few and far between; the James B. Conants separated themselves from the Frank Obers, but their notion of Realpolitik—based in part on their conviction that Communism posed a mortal threat, in part on their concern to safeguard their institutions—required them to proceed part way down the path of the purge to justify not going all the way.[39]

FBI documents emphasize the fact that the relationship between Yale and Harvard—and no doubt other universities—and the FBI did not depend merely upon the personal qualities of the *dramatis personae*; it was institutional in character—officials in high places made policies on the basis of which subordinates gave and received information. Those same documents also show a powerful reluctance on the part of both the FBI and the universities to reveal the existence of that relationship.

Why did not the universities argue that they were simply doing their patriotic duty? Was it because they were uneasily aware that at least to some degree they were violating certain academic and professional norms that, in other contexts, it was their proud boast to have defended? These norms included the principles that students should not be denied knowledge of the ultimate sponsor of their research; that the openness required of a scholarly organization cannot coexist with the dissembling required of an intelligence apparatus; and that the criteria invoked to purge the professorate cannot be reconciled with the idea that scholarly competence alone should govern appointments.

That the universities in the 1940s and 1950s concealed what they were doing is disturbing enough. This concealment can probably be explained by the passions—and fears—of the McCarthy period. More disturbing is the continued unwillingness of many university officials to allow research into university archives regarding the activities of a quarter of a century ago. Even if one believes that the position that the universities took then was the wrong one, it was understandably wrong.

Is whatever damage that might be caused by revelation of historical facts more dangerous than the continuing concealment of the truth?

On December 9, 1977, the very day on which Harvard University opened the papers of former Harvard President A. Lawrence Lowell on the Sacco-Vanzetti case—the fiftieth anniversary of their execution—the Harvard *Gazette* announced that the University had reaffimed its rule barring access to Corporation records for a period of fifty years after their deposit and that, therefore, documents relating to the McCarthy period would remain closed. President Derek Bok has rejected requests from scholars for access to these documents and has even denied permission to quote from his letters to me. I can, however, quote from my April 24, 1980 letter to him:

The judgments of history do not pronounce doom; they allow us to close the case and therefore to get on with the business of living. May I appeal to you, in that spirit, to open the Harvard archives to qualified scholars? In so doing, you would be rendering a service to your university, to your calling, and to your country that would entitle you to—and assure you of—the admiration and respect of all those who place morality above expediency.

What is most disturbing about this earlier relationship between the FBI and the universities is not what historical research reveals about the past, but the persistence into the present of a myth about that relationship—a myth that distorts our knowledge of what we were and what we are, of what we once did and of what we can do, a myth that the FBI and many university officials continue to cultivate and nourish. Compare, for example, the ringing conclusion of Professor Seymour Lipset's study of education and politics at Harvard:

As McGeorge Bundy once explained of Harvard, "the extraordinary feedom . . . was sustained . . . more by the universal commitment to the ideal of excellence," than by anything else—[40]

with the chilling report of the Boston SAC to FBI Director Hoover:

It is noted that as a result of [half line deleted] on this date, arrangements have been completed for a most cooperative and understanding association between the Bureau and Harvard University.[41]

During the height of the Cold War years, this country was the victim of the FBI and the universities' symbiotic relationship. It continues to be the victim of the distortion that comes from the creation of a myth about that relationship. Must we be victimized by both history and historiography?

Contributing powerfully to the creation of that myth is the reluctance, at best, or the refusal, at worst, of its beneficiaries to permit research into the documents that record how the universities responded to political pressures. Twenty years ago, Otto Kirchheimer concluded: "One might nearly be tempted to define a revolution by the willingness of the regime to open the archives of its predecessor's political police. Measured by this yardstick, few revolutions have taken place in modern history."[42]

Kirchheimer's observation should be both qualified and extended. A revolution has not been required to pry from the government's political police at least some of its secrets; only passage of the Freedom of Information Act. But the rage for secrecy that Kirchheimer found characteristic of political regimes seems, in this case, to be even more characteristic of its private partners.

Notes

1. *New York Times*, June 9, 1949, p. 1.
2. *Harvard Crimson*, June 9, 1949, p. 4.
3. *Harvard Crimson*, June 23, 1949, p. 1.
4. Sigmund Diamond, "God and the F.B.I. at Yale," *Nation* 230 (April 12, 1980): 422–28, and "More on Buckley and the F.B.I.," *Nation* 231 (Sept. 13, 1980): 202, 206.
5. The quotations are from "Rules and Regulations on Conduct of Interviews," Section 87, Security Investigations, paragraph 5A: "Restrictions upon . . . investigations and interviews with individuals connected with institutions of learning."
6. Memo, SAC, Boston to FBI Director, Dec. 31, 1948, FBI 100–360557–X1.
7. Memo, SAC, Boston to FBI Director, Jan. 27, 1949, FBI 100–360557–X2.
8. Memos, SAC, Boston to FBI Director, Feb. 25, 1949, FBI 100–

360557–9; SAC, Boston to FBI Director, May 5, 1949, FBI 100–360557–14.

9. Memo, SAC, Richmond to FBI Director, May 1, 1951, FBI 100–360557–33.

10. Memo SAC, Richmond to FBI Director, May 24, 1951, FBI 100–360557–36.

11. Memos, SAC, Boston to FBI Director, May 29, 1952, FBI 100–360557–46; FBI Director to SAC, Boston, June 11, 1951, FBI 100–360–557–36; FBI Director to SAC, Boston, June 20, 1952, FBI 100–360557–46.

12. Memos, SAC, Boston to FBI Director, Aug. 17, 1951, FBI 100–360557–39; SAC, Boston to FBI Director, Oct. 27, 1952, FBI 100–360557–52.

13. Memo, SAC, Boston to FBI Director, March 12, 1953, FBI 94–1–1005–148X/C. Since at least 1947, the FBI had investigated Harlow Shapley, director of the Harvard Observatory. As part of this investigation the FBI wiretapped Shapley's conversations. FBI Director Hoover reported on two of these conversations to President Truman's aides, Harry Vaughan and George Allen, disguising the information as having been "furnished to the Bureau by a reliable confidential source." Letters, FBI Director Hoover to George Allen, Feb. 6, 1947, Truman Papers, PSF–FBI–N; and FBI Director to Harry Vaughan, Nov. 20, 1947, Truman Papers, PSF–Personal–FBI; both in Harry S. Truman Library.

14. Memo, Nichols to Tolson, Dec. 29, 1954, FBI 94–1–1005–156.

15. Memo, SAC, Boston to FBI Director, Jan. 7, 1954, FBI 100–335070–19.

16. Memo, SAC, Boston to FBI Director, July 28, 1954, FBI 100–335070–26.

17. Memo, SAC, Boston to FBI Director, Nov. 8, 1948, FBI 100–[undecipherable].

18. Memo, Thomas McLaughlin, Jr. to SAC, Boston, Feb. 16, 1949, FBI 100–22311–16.

19. Memo, Brenton Gordon to SAC, Boston, April 12, 1949, FBI 100–22311–36.

20. See Memos, Brenton Gordon to SAC, Boston, April 12, 1949, FBI 100–22311–41 and the use of this claim to justify deletions from SAC, Boston to FBI Director, Feb. 11, 16, and 25, 1948; March 2, April 12, May 5, June 11, and August 18, 1951; and March 12 and May 5, 1952.

21. Memo, SAC, Boston to FBI Director, June 19, 1950, FBI 66–2542–3–5–852.

22. FBI Director Hoover was enraged by what he considered at least as in-

solence in DeVoto's article on the FBI. He raised this issue in connection with the program *Yale Daily News* editor William F. Buckley, Jr., was arranging in support of the FBI. Hoover feared that Yale Law School Professor Thomas I. Emerson might attack the FBI as had DeVoto. See, Diamond, "God and the FBI and Yale," *op. cit.* But who raised the issue of DeVoto's article in the discussion between the FBI agent and the Harvard official, and why? That discussion occurred in June 1950, a full eight months after publication of the article. The FBI agent might have been sensitive to the issue because aware of Hoover's concern. But what would have led the Harvard official to raise the issue?

23. Memo, FBI Director to SAC, Boston, July 31, 1950, FBI 2542–3–5–856.

24. Letter, SAC, Boston to FBI Director, Aug. 28, 1950, FBI 2542–3–5–893.

25. Letter, FBI Director to SAC, Boston, Oct. 5, 1950, FBI 66–2542–3–5–893.

26. Letter, SAC, Boston to FBI Director, Oct. 26, 1950, FBI 2542–3–5–899.

27. Letter, FBI Director to SAC, Boston, Nov. 20, 1950, FBI 66–2542–3–5–897.

28. Letter, H. B. Fisher to J. Edgar Hoover, "Personal and Confidential," Oct. 27, 1949, FBI Yale University File. In this letter, Fisher discussed William Buckley, Jr. at length, assuring the FBI director that Buckley approved the Yale-FBI relation: "This, of course, includes the record of the Bureau in our mutual relationships and problems and also Mr. Buckley's growing admiration for Yale University in meeting all of these issues by having such an animal as am I in this position." Apparently, Fisher was not acting on his own authority. In an April 15, 1949 memo to FBI Director Hoover, the New Haven SAC reported on his recent meeting with Yale Provost Edgar S. Funiss. He quoted Furniss as stating that all Yale University undergraduate deans have "made it plain that they would oppose and fight to the limit the appointment of any known Communist or known fellow traveler to the faculty of Yale University." He then added: "This, of course, is not for public consumption, but it is believed it reflects a rather interesting light to [*sic*] a statement recently made by President Charles Seymour of Yale University . . . in which President Seymour was quoted as saying that 'there would be no witch hunt for Communists at Yale.' The position of Yale University is aparently swinging around to the point which [half line deleted] that it is much better to look men over and know exactly what they are before they are appointed, and that it is much easier to get rid of them then by not appointing them than after they have once been appointed." This information was to be kept

confidential: "It is not desired that any of the confidential information concerning trends at Yale University [several words deleted] be furnished to any outside agency." Memo, SAC, Boston to FBI Director, April 15, 1949, FBI 100-3-71.

29. Affidavit of Special Agent David L. Smith, *Sigmund Diamond v. FBI et al.*, Ca 79-C-3770, U.S. District Court, Southern District of New York, pp. 48–50.

30. Memos, SAC, Boston to FBI Director, Feb. 9, 1949, FBI 100-360557-15; FBI Director to SAC, Boston, March 9, 1949; Whitson to Fletcher, May 11, 1949, FBI 100-360557-16.

31. Memo, M. A. Jones to L. B. Nichols, re: James B. Conant, Research, March 12, 1948, FBI James B. Conant File.

32. Letter, FBI Director to SACs, March 27, 1953, FBI James B. Conant File.

33. FBI Special Inquiry on James Bryant Conant, Boston, April 3, 1953, FBI James B. Conant File. Ironically, the FBI had investigated James Killian's attitudes toward security matters and concluded that these "investigations of him have been favorable except the following: In April, 1947, he opposed establishment of a Massachusetts Committee on Subversive Activities and opposed asking the Massachusetts Attorney General to compile a list of subversive or Communist front organizations, stating this would jeopardize our civil liberties. In February, 1948, he, with other college presidents, opposed Massachusetts legislation designed to bar Communists from teaching in public and private schools. In April, 1949, Dirk Struik, MIT professor, was named as a secret member of the Communist Party. Killian refused to remove Struik from his teaching post, stating that this action would be a violation of academic freedom." Brief for Use of the [FBI] Director in Appearance before the Presidential Board to Review Periodically U.S. Foreign Intelligence Activities, Jan. 20, 1956, pp. i–ii, folder 149, *O&C.*

34. FBI Special Inquiry on James Bryant Conant, New York, April 3, 1953, FBI James B. Conant File.

35. FBI Special Inquiry on James Bryant Conant, Newark, April 6, 1953, FBI James B. Conant File.

36. FBI Special Inquiry on James Bryant Conant, Cleveland, April 7, 1953, FBI James B. Conant File.

37. Memorandum to the Members of the Listening Post, Report of December 8, 1954, Meeting with Staff of Joint Committee on Internal Revenue Taxation, pp. 1–6, Records of the University, Columbia University Files, Low Library, New York, N.Y. (I am greatly indebted to the authorities of Columbia University for access to this and other University documents.) By the 1950s, many university officials had apparently abandoned their earlier opposition to inquiries into

their faculties' political activities. I have cited in note 28 the change in the position of Yale University President Charles Seymour. By 1951 MIT President James Killian had also abandoned the principled opposition he had voiced from 1947 to 1949 concerning inquiries into the political activities of his faculty. An FBI document reports that "Killian spoke with [FBI Assistant Director] Nichols in March, 1951, concerning security at MIT. No assistance was given him. The [FBI] Director has commented that Killian was [half line deleted]. Killian was quoted May 29, 1955 in the 'Washington Star' as stating that 'present security procedures may be among the most hazardous threats to our loyalty defense.' " Brief for Use of the [FBI] Director in Appearance before the Presidential Board to Review Periodically U.S. Foreign Intelligence Activities, Jan. 20. 1956, p. ii folder 149, *O&C*.

38. "Admittedly, it is difficult to scrutinize an organization from either the information with which it is willing to part, or from those effects of its activities which by sheer accident become a matter of public knowledge." Otto Kirchheimer, *Political Justice: The Use of Legal Procedure for Political Ends* (Princeton: Princeton University Press, 1961), p. 204 n61.

39. The strategy had precedent. Concern with finding a "right way" to counter the "wrong way" to fight Communism led many during the late 1930s and early 1940s to see in the intelligence work of the FBI a less obnoxious alternative to the rampaging anti-Communism of the Dies Committee. Outright repression was one thing; identification and surveillance seemed quite another. "More than any single circumstance, the acceptance of political identification by a substantial consensus as a necessary governmental function diminished challenge to the bureau's emergence as a political police force. Even those in positions of power with reservations did not dare oppose this development, if for no other reason than to demonstrate that they could be as realistic as their adversaries." Frank J. Donner, "How J. Edgar Hoover Created His Intelligence Powers," *Civil Liberties Review* 3(1977): 46. If political identification was "a necessary governmental function," surely good citizenship required cooperation with the agency performing that function. See also Mary Sperling McAuliffe, *Crisis on the Left: Cold War Politics and American Liberals, 1947–1954* (Amherst: University of Massachusetts Press, 1978), for a discussion of how the same problem was perceived and responded to by such organizations as the CIO, the ACLU, the American Committee for Cultural Freedom, and Americans for Democratic Action.

40. Seymour Martin Lipset and David Riesman, *Education and Politics at Harvard* (New York: McGraw-Hill, 1975), p. 256.

41. Memo, SAC, Boston to FBI Director, June 19, 1950.

42. Kirchheimer, *Political Justice*, p. 204.

10

The FBI, the Congress,
and McCarthyism

Kenneth O'Reilly and Athan G. Theoharis

Historians and political scientists have written extensively about the Congress during the Cold War years, focusing almost exclusively on three themes: Congress's role in the rise of McCarthyism, Congress's part in the shaping of United States foreign policy and, in turn, the responses of conservative congressmen to national security issues (loyalty/security at home, and the Soviet Union abroad). The sharpened anti-Communist obsessions of the Cold War years, many scholars have emphasized, partially explain why Congress abrogated its traditional foreign policy role, deferring instead to increasing presidential claims of "inherent powers," and led either to the enactment of legislation or tolerance for executive procedures that violate constitutional liberties.[1]

Although having intensively researched congressional anti-Communism, historians and political scientists have not explored the FBI's relationship with congressional practitioners of McCarthyite politics. This neglect resulted in part from FBI Director Hoover's success in denying access to FBI files. With the enactment of the Freedom of Information Act of 1966—as substantively amended in 1974—such research can now be initiated.

The collection of essays in *Beyond the Hiss Case* suggests the magnitude of the FBI's contribution to McCarthyite politics. Dating at least from an executive conference decision of February 1946, the FBI initiated an "educational" campaign through "available channels" about the "basically Russian nature of the Communist Party in this country": the American public was to be alerted to the serious internal menace of Communism, which Hoover and other FBI officials defined as including liberal and radical demands for political and economic reform. FBI officials resorted to two tactics to shape public opinion and

national policy: they (principally FBI Assistant Directors Louis Nichols and Cartha DeLoach) leaked information from FBI files to cooperative reporters, and assisted the McCarthyites in the Congress—notably Karl Mundt, Joseph McCarthy, Richard Nixon, the Senate Internal Security Subcommittee, and the House Committee on Un-American Activities. In a 1947 statement, FBI Director Hoover aptly characterized Congress's helpful role: "Committees of Congress have served a useful purpose in exposing some of these [subversive] activities which no Federal agency is in a position to do, because the information we obtain is either for intelligence purposes or for use in prosecution, and committees of Congress have a wider latitude."[2]

FBI leaks of derogatory information to conservative reporters did not begin with the now-infamous Counterintelligence Programs (COINTELPROs) of the late 1950s and 1960s. For example, in 1955 FBI Assistant Director Louis Nichols advised *New York Herald-Tribune* Washington bureau chief Don Whitehead that the FBI would help him write a history of the Bureau. Over the next year, the FBI's Crime Records Division, under Nichols's careful supervision, spoon-fed FBI documents that Whitehead relied on to write *The FBI Story*. Not surprisingly, Whitehead's unofficially commissioned study eulogized Hoover and the FBI, and acclaimed the Bureau's successful battle during the Cold War years against the "Red" threat to American society. FBI officials were not content merely to assist and direct Whitehead's research; through the FBI Recreation Association, they purchased copies of the book to boost sales and distribution.[3]

Nichols similarly assisted Hearst reporter Jim Bishop, then researching the Julius and Ethel Rosenberg atomic espionage case. For FBI officials, publicity about the Rosenberg case could confirm the seriousness of Communist spying on behalf of the Soviet Union.

FBI documents record both the Bureau's assistance to Bishop and federal judge Irving Kaufman's intercession to ensure this help. (Presiding judge during the Rosenberg trial, Kaufman, in an emotional verdict, had handed down the death penalty.) On May 1, 1958, Kaufman contacted the Special Agent in Charge (SAC) of the New York City Field Office. Kaufman was concerned over Bishop's slow progress in completing the study and attributed it to the fact that whereas, under Nichols, the FBI

had initially been "supplying [Bishop] with information" that "BEN POLLICK of the Department of Justice is [now] working with BISHOP on the book and that POLLICK has been supplying [Bishop] with information."

The New York SAC contacted FBI Inspector Cartha DeLoach on May 2, 1958. "The Bureau has been working with BISHOP in connection with this book and has been steadily supplying him with information," DeLoach responded. The New York SAC should "inform Judge KAUFMAN of the fact that officials of the Bureau [have] been working with BISHOP concerning the story, and [have] been providing him with every possible assistance; however, . . . there is no way that the Bureau can bring any pressure to bear on BISHOP to devote additional time to the story."[4]

This May 14, 1958 memorandum documents that Cartha DeLoach had assumed Nichols's role as chief FBI "leaker." More aggressive than Nichols, DeLoach continued to assist, for example, radio commentator Fulton Lewis, Jr., and Hearst reporter Dave Sentner with the understanding that the FBI's "name, of course, will not be used." Consistent with this misison, DeLoach was a particularly effective leader within the American Legion (as *Chicago Tribune* reporter Walter Trohan approvingly wrote Hoover) "writing speeches for prominent [American Legion] orators, drafting resolutions and sparking the show generally."[5]

The FBI's cooperative relationship with conservative reporters was potentially threatened by rules changes announced by Attorney General Elliot Richardson on August 8, 1973. Simultaneous with the announcement of these rules, Richardson had stated that he was "considering" another rule which would require the attorney general's approval before the FBI could question or subpoena a journalist and that all FBI contacts with reporters were to be recorded in writing. FBI officials immediately, and eventually successfully, obtained clarification of the requirement that all FBI media contacts be recorded in writing. Thus, on December 14, 1973, FBI Director Clarence Kelley advised all Special Agents in Charge that the new rule governing FBI contacts with reporters applied:

only when the news representative involved is suspected of an offense "committed in the course of, or arising out of, the coverage or investigation of a news story, or while engaged in the performance of his official duties as a member of

the news media." Accordingly, we may continue contacts with the news media as before unless the news media representative becomes a suspect.[6]

The House Committee on Un-American Activities (HUAC),[7] however, was the principal recipient of FBI assistance. Whether by servicing HUAC requests for specific files, providing FBI reports to HUAC members and staff, or channeling HUAC investigators to prospective witnesses or to public source information, FBI officials furthered the Committee's politics of exposure. FBI assistance started at least in August 1938 (when the Bureau leaked information to HUAC chairman J. Parnell Thomas regarding Paul Edwards, the New York City director of the Works Art Project) and continued until at least November 1969 (when HUAC chief counsel Donald Sanders, a former FBI agent, received from the Crime Records Division "blind" memoranda—not traceable to the Bureau—on two Security Index subjects). Other FBI leaks to HUAC involved Bertolt Brecht, Larry Parks (in Parks's case, the FBI prepared for HUAC Chairman Thomas a list of questions he might ask), and the National Committee to Secure Justice for the Rosenbergs and Morton Sobell. FBI officials both directed HUAC staff to undercover FBI operatives and even pressured reluctant informers to testify publicly before the Committee.[8] The FBI's responses to HUAC's critics highlight the scope and nature of the Bureau's relationship with the Committee.

Recently-released FBI files on the National Committee Against Repressive Legislation (NCARL), formerly the National Committee to Abolish HUAC (NCAHUAC), confirm that the FBI covertly leaked to HUAC derogatory information regarding NCAHUAC at least twenty different times.[9] HUAC, in turn, widely publicized this information, received either on an ad hoc basis or as part of the FBI's formal counterintelligence program against the Communist Party (COINTELPRO-CPUSA).[10] The FBI's admitted purpose for this covert assistance was to "expose, discredit, or disrupt" NCAHUAC.

NCAHUAC was founded in 1960 by retired Wall Street banker James Imbrie, ex-New Dealer Aubrey Williams, civil libertarian Alexander Meiklejohn, and American Friends Service Committee chairman-emeritus Clarence Pickett. The sole purpose of the Los Angeles-based

Committee had been to abolish HUAC. FBI Director Hoover immediately ordered the Los Angeles field office to "expedite" an investigation of NCAHUAC even before its existence was publicly announced. All reports submitted to FBI headquarters were to include memoranda "suitable for dissemination."

These memoranda were at least disseminated to HUAC. In late August 1960, for example, FBI Assistant Director Cartha DeLoach forwarded information gathered by FBI informants "to his sources at HCUA." In addition, in articles reporting the establishment of the National Committee, *Los Angeles Examiner* reporter E. F. Tompkins and the American Legion's *Firing Line* characterized the new organization as a "communist front." Their source for this charge apparently was information from FBI files. Three weeks later and in response to a HUAC press release to the UPI based on leaks from FBI files, conservative reporters Fulton Lewis, Jr. and Jack Lotto reiterated this communist front charge. Within the next nine months, the FBI disseminated at least twenty-three investigative reports and letterhead memorandums in addition to the FBI Crime Records Division's sizeable number of leaks to its "contacts."[11]

The Bureau's investigaiton of NCAHUAC was ostensibly initiated to ascertain whether the organization should be required to register as a Communist-front organization under provisions of the Internal Security Act of 1950. The Department of Justice consistently rejected FBI recommendations for such a listing (in 1962, 1963, 1964, 1966, and 1972). "The evidence is insufficient," Department of Justice officials concluded, to initiate legal proceedings against NCAHUAC either as a Communist-front or a Communist-infiltrated organization. The FBI had provided "no indication . . . that . . . the CP, USA and its leaders have influenced the operations of the NCARL [formerly NCAHUAC] or that the organization has conducted its activities primarily to advance the objectives of the CP, USA, or the world Communist movement." As early as July 1963, Assistant Attorney General J. Walter Yeagley directed the FBI to discontinue submitting "prospective summary reports" on NCAHUAC (between February 20, 1962, and June 18, 1963, the Bureau had forwarded twelve summary reports and memoranda to the Department).

Yeagley's order reduced the flow of FBI reports to the Justice Department. Unresigned to the Department's decision not to initiate Subversive Activities Control Board (SACB) hearings, FBI surveillance of NCAHUAC intensified. Field offices were chastised for their reports' "paucity of information," and FBI officials demanded detailed and thoroughly analyzed memoranda suitable for dissemination outside the Bureau.[12]

FBI Director J. Edgar Hoover never intended FBI surveillance to be confined to ascertaining whether HUAC's opponent came under the provisions of the Internal Security Act of 1950. A target of the Bureau's COINTELPRO-CPUSA almost from its inception, NCAHUAC and its sponsors were also subjected to numerous disruptive actions on an ad hoc basis.[13] Intended in every case to "expose, discredit, or disrupt" NCAHUAC, the vast majority of FBI leaks to HUAC were recorded in the FBI's file on the organization, and not in the Bureau's COINTELPRO-CPUSA file. It is not surprising, therefore, that the most thorough investigation of the FBI's COINTELPROs, conducted by the Church Committee in 1975–1976, erroneously concluded that the FBI had conducted only 1,388 COINTELPRO-CPUSA disruptive actions from 1956 to 1971.[14] There may have been 1,388 FBI actions filed as COINTELPRO-CPUSA; nonetheless, as confirmed by the case of NCAHUAC, the FBI's more than five hundred thousand case files would have to be searched to determine the total number of COINTELPRO kinds of actions that the FBI instituted during this period against organizations defined by Bureau officials as Communistic.[15]

From the beginning, Frank Wilkinson was the FBI's primary COINTEPRO target within NCAHUAC. Throughout the 1950s, Wilkinson unsuccessfully attempted to organize a broadly based, national, and liberal coalition against HUAC.[16] In response, HUAC subpoenaed Wilkinson in 1958, *after* his arrival in Atlanta to protest a roving HUAC subcommittee's hearings. Cited and ultimately convicted for contempt of Congress for declining to answer HUAC's questions, Wilkinson served nine months of a one-year prison sentence. Following his release from federal prison, FBI officials widely circulated a "blind" memorandum reporting that "Wilkinson was publicly identified as

having been a Communist Party (CP) member in California at some time during the period from 1951 to 1955 by [FBI informer] Anita Belle Schneider who testified at HCUA hearings which were held in San Diego in 1958."[17]

As NCAHUAC's field representative, Wilkinson criss-crossed the country during the 1960s, sometimes speaking ten or more times a week at churches and on college campuses. Complying with procedures outlined in the FBI *Manual of Instructions* concerning "public appearances of Party Leaders," FBI agents sent "URGENT" teletypes detailing Wilkinson's movements and promising to be alert for counterintelligence opportunities. FBI informers routinely photographed and secretly taped Wilkinson's lectures, while FBI agents brought his itinerary to the attention of local police "Red Squads." Agents received standing instructions to "give careful consideration to possible counter-intelligence plans to disrupt the schedule of Wilkinson. The utmost discretion will be necessary to avoid any basis for allegations that the Bureau is conducting investigations on college campuses, or interfering with academic freedom."[18]

During his speaking engagements, Wilkinson was invariably asked if he was a Communist, or some other "embarrassing" question. The FBI apparently inspired these queries. An April 1962 Omaha Field Office report on a debate at Drake University between Wilkinson and a Birch Society spokesman noted that, during the question and answer period following the debate, a member of the audience (apparently an FBI plant) *"had been able* to ask WILKINSON if he . . . was a Communist [emphasis added]."[19]

In May 1962 the Detroit SAC reported that, even after Michigan State University and Wayne State University officials had apprised University of Michigan administrators of Wilkinson's background (the FBI had leaked derogatory information about Wilkinson to an undisclosed source at Wayne State), Wilkinson was allowed to speak on the Michigan campus. When approving Wilkinson's appearance, the Detroit SAC reported: "University of Michigan authorities decided that rather than give cause of 'violation of academic freedom' propaganda and 'martyrdom' propaganda, it was decided in the University's best interest to permit the speech, without publicity, in limited University space."

That same month, the Washington, D.C., Field Office recommended the stationing of a "friendly newspaperman" at the entrance to the church where Wilkinson and Carl Braden (another HUAC witness recently released from prison for contempt of Congress) were scheduled to speak against HUAC on May 4. The "inquiring reporter" could ask persons entering the church for their names and addresses in a not-too-subtle effort to dissuade them from attending the meeting rather than risk "exposure in the press." "The Washington, D.C., area is a particularly sensitive area," the SAC observed, "with regard to publicity for organizations in opposition to HCUA and possible affiliation with organizations which are tinged by Communist infiltration." This disruptive action was apparently implemented. The SAC's airtel recommending this operation contains a notation under Cartha DeLoach's initial indicating that something was "handled" on May 4. DeLoach's specific reference, however, is unclear.

In May 1964, the Cincinnati SAC advised FBI headquarters that University of Cincinnati officials had cancelled Wilkinson's scheduled talk. In November 1965, the Omaha SAC reported that the Executive Committee of Local 46, United Packinghouse Workers had withdrawn its sponsorship of Wilkinson's appearance. Union officials did not know of Wilkinson's subversive background, the SAC reported, until publication of two exposé articles in the *Waterloo* (Iowa) *Courier*.[20] The FBI's precise role in Wilkinson's scheduling difficulties cannot presently be determined because released FBI documents contain extensive deletions, and other referenced FBI documents have not yet been released.

In addition, the FBI purposely attempted to create dissension within NCAHUAC's many local affiliates and other anti-HUAC organizations.[21] Richard Criley, director of the Chicago Committee to Defend the Bill of Rights (CCDBR), was a frequent target of such FBI efforts. "The success of a good counterintelligence operation on an organization," the Chicago SAC wrote in April 1962, "depends to a large degree in being able to decipher for public consumption the direction and control of the CP." Because Criley had been identified as a Communist before the Dies Committee in 1938, and had testified before HUAC in 1959, the FBI concentrated on him. HUAC only summoned Criley and an associate, however, four weeks after all other HUAC subpoenas had been

served and after eight thousand leaflets opposing HUAC's forthcoming Chicago hearings had been mailed under their signatures. The Chicago SAC pointedly described Criley as "probably the only Communist of importance in Chicago who will do battle with anyone, government or press, as a means to publicize his fight for civil rights," at the same time attributing his frequent deviation from the Communist Party "line" to his being a member of the "left wing faction." In fact, the FBI knew that Criley had already left the Party.[22]

The FBI's disruptive actions included preparing a list of questions to be asked by Mike Douglas during an anticipated May 1962 TV interview with Criley and Wilkinson. An established source at the Cleveland television station, KYW-TV, was to handle this COINTELPRO. Before approving the recommendation, FBI officials ordered the Cleveland SAC to determine whether Douglas would be involved with the programming, and, if so, to "furnish background information on him." For whatever reason, this particular recommendation was not implemented on the Mike Douglas show, but during a videotaped interview with Wilkinson for the noon news instead.[23]

To isolate Criley from the "liberal element," during the next month, two FBI agents interviewed a CCDBR board member, who promptly resigned when informed of Criley's allegedly subversive intentions. The Bureau also mailed (in a "commercially purchased envelope," and under the name of "True believers in democratic and constitutional process") a five-page FBI-authored document ("What is the Chicago Committee to Defend the Bill of Rights?") to over twenty members of the CCDBR's Board of Directors. (To monitor responses to this mailing, the Chicago Field Office had originally proposed that a post office box be rented under false pretenses—"If for some reason the application for the box was subpoenaed." COINTELPRO supervisors rejected the proposal because "too many unforeseen and uncontrollable factors arise in such a procedure.") The mailing, the Chicago Field Office subsequently concluded, had undercut the CCDBR's fund-raising efforts, and had "been instrumental in keeping members away from meetings, thereby depriving Criley of the services of those liberals and possibly the use of their names in the future."

In 1962 the FBI also mailed an anonymous statement characterizing

Criley as the "propaganda commissar of the Illinois CP," to Arnold Rosenzweig, Chicago publisher of the *National Jewish Post and Opinion*, and to Illinois State Senator Paul Broyles. Rosenzweig, a frequent recipient of COINTELPRO leaks, was selected because he was "an orthodox Jew who equates Communism with Nazism in its dangers to the Jewish community"; Broyles was chosen because he had headed the Illinois Seditious Activities Investigation Commission during the 1940s, a "little HUAC" popularly known as the Broyles Commission. Broyles might place the FBI's characterization of the CCDBR, the Chicago Field Office hoped, "in the hands of the press, raise the issue on the Senate floor, or perhaps cause [a State Senate] investigation of the CCDBR."[24]

To neutralize NCAHUAC and its affiliates, FBI officials regularly forwarded field office reports to the Immigration and Naturalization Service, and to the Internal Revenue Service's Special Service Staff. Other federal intelligence agencies investigated anti-HUAC activists at the FBI's request. The CIA, for example, opened Richard Criley's mail, and in 1968 informed the FBI of the Communist Party membership of the parents of a young activist working to establish an anti-HUAC committee at Oberlin College.[25]

In addition, FBI agents carefully monitored meetings between NCAHUAC members and the congressmen who opposed, or were thought likely to oppose, HUAC's continuation. Owing to their sensitivity, FBI records of this surveillance were generally filed separately, or were destroyed to prevent public disclosure. Of the FBI's released files on NCAHUAC, moreover, those recording contacts with congressmen have been heavily deleted, many in their entirety. A Chicago Field Office letterhead on "Anti-HUAC activities in relation to the 88th Congress" was one such heavily deleted document. FBI agents would monitor a NCAHUAC-sponsored demonstration in front of the White House, a December 1960 Washington Field Office airtel reported, but would not monitor "by physical surveillance" a meeting between picketers and congressmen later that day "because of the possibility of embarrassment." The next paragraph (deleted in its entirety) and other FBI documents, however, indicated that an FBI informant had "covered" this meeting.

These extensively deleted documents suggest that FBI surveillance and related covert attempts to neutralize HUAC's critics extended to the House of Representatives. Concerned about NCAHUAC efforts to "influence various Congressmen to vote against the HCUA's appropriation," FBI officials demanded full coverage of all debates involving HUAC. The Los Angeles Field Office (the office of origin in the case) was specifically ordered in 1962 to report any "action taken by Congress regarding the House Committee on Un-American Activities." To discredit liberal Congressmen James Roosevelt and John Conyers, the FBI disseminated the congressmen's opinions on HUAC. The FBI also followed the anti-HUAC activities of former congressmen, including Maury Maverick and Charles O. Porter.

FBI agents were further ordered to determine NCAHUAC's legislative representative Donna Allen's "pertinent activities . . . but also . . . what further counterintelligence activities we will be able to utilize as a disruptive measure." Anticipating Frank Wilkinson's visit to the nation's capitol, the Washington SAC reported that the Washington, D.C., Field Office was "considering [the] possibility of counterintelligence activity in connection with [Wilkinson's] presentation of [anti-HUAC] petitions to Congressman CARLTON SICKLES." Not satisfied with this single proposal, on November 30, 1964, FBI officials ordered that the Washington SAC "immediately consider possible counterintelligence action in an effort to expose, discredit or disrupt Wilkinson's activities. . . . [Y]ou should consider furnishing data to cooperative news media sources of your office or at [FBI headquarters] . . . and to the HCUA through the Bureau." DeLoach did brief HUAC. The SAC, however, could not fully comply with this order, because Wilkinson "held no public meetings [while contacting congressmen on Capitol Hill] and no situation arose which would offer an opportunity to employ counterintelligence measures."[26]

To deter other congressmen from challenging HUAC, the FBI leaked derogatory information about NCAHUAC to the Committee and to cooperative reporters. After the New York Field Office discovered, for example, that the plates used to address copies of the *Daily Worker* were also used by NCAHUAC's local affiliate, suggesting a close tie between the Communist Party and the New York Council to Abolish the Un-

American Activities Committee (NYCAUAC), the SAC recommended furnishing this "material" "through appropriate liaison channels to the House Committee on Un-American Activities." "This publicity," Internal Security section chief F. J. Baumgardner hoped, could be "arranged [by the Crime Records Division] prior to the reconvening of Congress on 1-3-61," and thereby "discredit the [NCAHUAC] and weaken its attack on the HCUA." Ordered by Hoover to "get this out," DeLoach promptly leaked the information to HUAC and to Fulton Lewis, Jr.— and both beat Baumgardner's deadline. On December 27, Lewis reported on his nationally syndicated radio program NYCAUAC's use of the *Worker*'s addressograph plates; the next day, HUAC chairman Francis E. Walter issued a special wire release. Summarizing the "tangible results" of this COINTELPRO, FBI officials stressed the "increasing public support of the HCUA" which had resulted from the "current publicity showing communist activity in the movement to abolish HCUA." FBI officials were also pleased that "Congressman James Roosevelt (the most active congressman behind the movement to abolish the HCUA) has retreated from his former position of calling for the abolition of HCUA to a less drastic position of calling for a reduction in the appropriation granted to the HCUA."[27]

In December 1961, DeLoach gave Fulton Lewis, Jr. another report (or perhaps a letterhead memorandum) on a NCAHUAC national committee meeting, containing data on six congressmen who recently voted against HUAC's appropriation, and a list of the congressmen whom the NCAHUAC proposed to lobby during the current congress. (An FBI informer had apparently turned over the minutes of the meeting to the Bureau.) Because released FBI files have been extensively deleted, we cannot determine what information Lewis received. Hoover had specifically approved the leak and urged that "DeLoach should try and get this widely exposed."

The FBI's covert assistance to Fulton Lewis was part of a more general COINTELPRO operation to disrupt NCAHUAC's attempt to establish a legislative office in Washington. Similar information on NCAHUAC strategy, and on congressional anti-HUAC resolutions was apparently supplied to Paul Harvey and other media "friends." To gather data for these leaks, the FBI carefully followed the activities of

HUAC's liberal congressional critics William F. Ryan, Philip Burton, and Don Edwards. For example, in November 1962, Internal Security section chief Baumgardner advised FBI Assistant Director Sullivan of Ryan's anticipated anti-HUAC meeting in Los Angeles with recently elected Democratic congressmen Roosevelt, Edward R. Roybal, George E. Brown, Jr., and Augustus F. Hawkins. DeLoach was then directed "to alert his sources at HCUA but on a confidential basis." Another FBI report of 1969 identified the Democratic congressmen—including Burton, Thomas S. Foley, Bob Eckhardt, William L. St. Onge, and Allard Lowenstein—who had attended a NCAHUAC-sponsored reception.[28]

In "URGENT" January 1965 teletypes to FBI headquarters and to the Los Angeles, New York, Chicago, Philadelphia, and San Francisco Field Offices, the Washington Field Office identified thirteen congressmen who supported HUAC's abolition.[29] Learning that Edwards and Burton planned to introduce anti-HUAC resolutions, FBI informants secured and forwarded a draft copy of Edwards's resolution to FBI contacts, even before the resolution was introduced in the House. With Hoover's approval, DeLoach forwarded this political intelligence to HUAC staff director Francis J. McNamara. In 1967, another "informant" reported that Congressman Edwards had written twenty-five colleagues, urging them to speak out against HUAC. The Washington Field Office also covered a meeting the next year between anti-HUAC activists and newly elected Republican Congressman Gilbert Gude; the widely disseminated report on this meeting noted that Gude supported procedural reform but not HUAC's abolition. Gude had also indicated to the anti-HUAC delegation his receptivity to having HUAC's duties transferred to the Judiciary Committee.[30]

The FBI dissemination list periodically included the White House. In November 1960, and again in January 1961, FBI Director Hoover advised Dwight D. Eisenhower's aide Wilton B. Persons of NCAHUAC plans to picket the White House and lobby individual congressmen. Three years later, the FBI director apprised Lyndon Johnson's aide, Marvin Watson, of NCAHUAC opposition to HUAC's anticipated investigation of the Ku Klux Klan—a probe that the President and Vice President Hubert Humphrey both supported. Again in 1964, the FBI briefed presidential assistant Walter Jenkins of NCAHUAC plans to

invite twenty-five congressmen and senators to a March 16, 1964 luncheon honoring civil rights activist and NCAHUAC founder Aubrey Williams. Four FBI field offices investigated the anticipated luncheon, which was "covered" by at least one FBI "informant." Once again, DeLoach briefed HUAC staff director McNamara.[31]

FBI surveillance of NCAHUAC declined after 1967, owing to FBI officials' changed priorities (occasioned by the initiation of the FBI's "New Left" and "Black Hate Group" COINTELPROs).[32] After 1967, FBI offiicals also formally ceased briefing HUAC on NCAHUAC activities. "Our relations with the House Committee on Un-American Activities," Domestic Intelligence Division official Charles Brennan explained, "have been strained and the Director has instructed that no contact be made with it." Hoover's order, however, seems to have been intended to create a "paper record" of disapproval (much like the FBI director's July 19, 1966 directive prohibiting "black bag jobs"). Bureau officials continued to share with HUAC (and its successor, the House Committee on Internal Security) political information gathered through the Bureau's investigations of other organizations and individuals.[33]

Key congressmen not only collaborated with the FBI in McCarthyite politics but sought to preclude any intensive public or congressional inquiries into FBI practices. Until the Church Committee hearings of 1975, the Congress had investigated neither the legality of FBI activities nor the possibility that FBI officials had abused the broad discretionary authority granted under vaguely worded executive directives and "antisubversive" legislation. Congress had had numerous opportunities to conduct such investigations dating from the infamous Palmer Raids of 1920 and subsequent revelations of the Bureau's other post–World War I abuses. FBI investigative abuses were again brought to public attention during the Judith Coplon trial of 1949–50. The National Lawyers Guild and the *Washington Post* publicized these disclosures, demanding an independent investigation of FBI practices. Rather than investigating the FBI, Congress (through HUAC) instead investigated the National Lawyers Guild. Responding in 1974 to admittedly sketchy revelations about the FBI's questionable COINTELPRO activities, HUAC's successor, the House Internal Security Committee (HISC), initiated public hearings into the FBI's investigative authority. HISC's intent, however,

was not to ascertain whether the FBI had exceeded its authority but whether legislation was needed to legalize FBI investigations of dissident activities.[34]

Events occurring in 1971, however, provided the most serious prospect that Congress would initiate an investigation of FBI priorities and political activism. The surfacing of an FBI memorandum recording the Bureau's surveillance of the front-running aspirant for the Democratic presidential nomination, Senator Edmund Muskie, and others attending an Earth Day environmental rally had embarrassed the Bureau despite White House press secretary Ronald Ziegler's brazen attempt to dismiss the resultant publicity as "blatantly political." Ziegler was right: a Nixon aide had specifically requested a report on the Earth Day affair.[35] More troubling to FBI officials was a burglary of the FBI's resident agency in Media, Pennsylvania committed by the Citizens' Commission to Investigate the FBI. The Citizens' Commission had obtained approximately one thousand FBI documents that starkly revealed the FBI's investigative priorities and compromised one of the FBI's so-called counterintelligence programs. In response, Hoover officially terminated all COINTELPRO operations for "security reasons."[36]

Assisted by their allies in the press and in the Congress, FBI officials successfully precluded a meaningful congressional inquiry into FBI activities and frustrated Senator Sam Ervin and the few other elected officials who half-heartedly attempted to gain access to FBI files. Not everyone, however, was willing to look the other way.

Writing in the February 8, 1971 *Nation*, H. H. Wilson of Princeton University's Politics Department called for a conference on the FBI; during the spring and summer of 1971 the Committee for Public Justice (CPJ)—whose founding members included former Attorney General Ramsey Clark, New York University Law School Professor Norman Dorsen, Princeton University Politics Department chairman Duane Lockard, Yale Law School Deputy Dean Burke Marshall, Blair Clark, and the playwright Lillian Hellman—began organizing. (The CPJ was a national civil liberties organization which had been formed in 1970.) Funded by the Field Foundation and the New World Foundation, the conference attracted fifty writers, panelists, and participants and was held at Princeton University on October 29 and 30, 1971, jointly spon-

sored by the CPJ and the Woodrow Wilson School of Public and International Affairs. Doubleday later published the edited version of the papers presented at the conference.[37]

With Robert Sherrill, Vern Countryman, Fred Cook, Aryeh Neier, Thomas Emerson, Victor Navasky, Frank Donner, and others scheduled to present papers, the FBI decided, in the words of FBI Director Hoover, to "handle" this "group of anti-FBI bigots."[38] On May 5, 1971, Inspector Bowers of the Crime Records Division briefed HISC chairman Richard Ichord on the "subversive affiliations" of several CPJ members. The FBI later furnished more detailed information to HISC's chief counsel, former FBI agent Donald Sanders, and Ichord pledged to be alert for "an appropriate occasion . . . whereby he or some other member of the Committee could make use of it."[39]

On two such occasions, October 28 and November 29, 1971, Ichord described Lillian Hellman's association with "about 100 different" Communist fronts, Frank Donner's "convenient" reliance "on the fifth amendment when questioned about his connection with the Communist Party," and Telford Taylor's history of representing "Communist Party members before congressional committees." The HISC chairman went on to complain about "a whole gaggle of the beautiful people [who] have flocked to the Committee for Public Justice"—specifically, Jules Feiffer, Shirley MacLaine, Candice Bergen, Mike Nichols, and Arthur M. Schlesinger, Jr.—and the likelihood of "extensive coverage from the practitioners of the new journalism, the east coast version."[40]

FBI efforts escalated during the month preceeding the conference. After receiving two CPJ letters in confidence from William O. Bittman, a former Justice Department attorney who had been invited to attend the Princeton conference, the Crime Records Division began "preparing a detailed brochure-type memorandum concerning this conference which will include summary memoranda on 39 individuals mentioned in Bittman's two letters plus the members of the [CPJ] executive committee." Hoover ordered the Crime Records Division to "expedite" this project, and when it was completed, authorized the following actions: (1) disseminating FBI-authored "speeches to some of our good friends on the Hill"; (2) discreetly suggesting to HISC chairman Ichord that he should "release appropriate material" on CPJ members; (3) orally briefing

"some of our good friends in the news media such as Victor Riesel, Bob Allen, Ed O'Brien, Ray McHugh, etc."; and (4) cultivating "Bittman so that we will be immediately advised of any further developments." (Bittman was also given "a detailed briefing regarding the individuals involved.")[41]

All of these proposals were subsequently "handled." After contacting Ray McHugh of the Copley News Service, for instance, Crime Records Division Chief Thomas E. Bishop reported to FBI Assistant Director W. Mark Felt:

I asked McHugh if he would be so kind to write a column on this matter which would clearly reflect the biased nature of [the CPJ]. Enclosed herewith is a copy of a column by McHugh which appeared in . . . the [October 24, 1971] . . . issue of all newspapers in the Copley chain. . . . Steps are being taken to have a copy of this column placed in The Congressional Record.[42]

The Bureau arranged to place the McHugh column in the *Congressional Record* by handing it, together with "background information," to Jack Cox, administrative assistant to Congressman Barry Goldwater, Jr. (R., Cal.), on November 1, two days after the Princeton conference concluded. (Hoover also thanked Congressman Floyd D. Spence, a Republican from South Carolina whose name graced the FBI's "Special Correspondents List," for his "thoughtfulness" in placing William F. Buckley, Jr.'s column on the CPJ in the *Congressional Record*.) The next day, Goldwater made a short speech on the Committee for Public Justice.[43]

Also on November 2, Republican Congressman John E. Hunt, a former New Jersey state policeman, contacted FBI Inspector Bowers. Bowers, who had already discussed the Princeton conference with Hunt and "furnished copies of the columns by William Buckley, Robert Allen, and Alice Widener," then met in Hunt's office with the following individuals: Hunt and his assistant, Ken Bellis; Ed Turner, an aid to Congressman Dan Daniel (D.,Va.); Ronald Dear, an aide to Congressman Bill Archer (R.,Tex.); Jerry Janes, an aide to Congressman Spence; Sid Hoyt, an aide to Congressman Samuel L. Devine (R.,Ohio); Don Joy, an aide to Congressman Edward Derwinski (R.,Ill.); Congressman Lawrence Hogan (R., Md.); and Jay Parker of the Friends of the FBI. This group

decided that Hunt would "take a 'special order' of one hour for himself and other Members to make remarks concerning the conference." Following the meeting, the FBI provided Hunt (at his request) "public source information concerning various individuals participating in the conference." Hunt then disseminated the information "to the appropriate people without the FBI being identified with it."[44]

On November 9, 1971, Hunt, Spence, Hogan, Joe D. Waggoner (D., La.), William M. Colmer (D., Miss.), William L. Dickinson (R., Ala.), and Jerry L. Pettis (R., Cal.) spoke briefly on the Princeton conference. (Other congressmen who had made commitments to "join in" were apparently prevented from doing so because the first seven speakers used up Hunt's allotted hour.) Collectively, the speakers defended the FBI's apolitical image, critiqued the various papers presented at the conference, and linked the participants to some type of liberal-subversive plot. For example, Hunt noted that Lockard "had his two daughters go to Cuba," and described Sherrill simply "as the Washington editor of the Nation"— as if no more need be said. Others (Vern Countryman and I. F. Stone) were identified as having been active in the campaign to abolish HUAC and its successor, HISC.[45]

Annual appropriation hearings on the proposed FBI budget had provided congressmen with another oversight opportunity. Yet, excepting the radical Congressmen Vito Marcantonio and a few liberals—such as James Roosevelt, Don Edwards, and William Ryan—most congressmen uncritically deferred to the conservative congressional leadership. Conservative leader saw no need to ascertain how the FBI was operating, in part because they allowed their power of oversight to be neutralized by the Bureau itself. To improve the investigative expertise of the staff of the House Committee on Appropriations, for example, FBI agent (and later FBI assistant director) Hugh Clegg was assigned to the committee's staff in 1943. Then, in 1945, FBI officials provided "materials" to Appropriations Committee chairman John Kerr, which Kerr used in a speech to the Congress to "get some things over to the public" about the Bureau's appropriations request. In 1944, Senator Styles Bridges consulted with FBI Assistant Director D. M. Ladd over whether to change his committee assignment from the Subcommittee on War Department Appropriations to the Subcommittee on State and Justice Departments

Appropriations so that "he could do the Bureau some good." Bridges acceded to FBI Director Hoover's encouragement that he seek this transfer.

Not surprisingly, FBI Director Hoover's appearances before congressional committees often resembled proceedings at a royal court—with Hoover the revered monarch and congressmen the appropriately deferential courtiers. Congressman Glenard Lipscomb's comments at the conclusion of Hoover's 1968 testimony before the House Committee on Appropriations effectively capture this obsequiousness: "Mr. Director, it is a real privilege to listen to your testimony. It is always an outstanding presentation. . . . The high regard that the American people have for the FBI and its integrity and the job it is doing is certainly a credit to your leadership and your associates' dedicated efforts."[46]

Investigative hearings initiated in 1964 and 1965 by the Subcommittee on Administrative Practice and Procedure of the Senate Committee on the Judiciary, under the chairmanship of Senator Edward Long (the so-called Long Committee), provided another occasion when the Congress could have discovered, if inadvertently, the FBI's far-reaching abuses of power. When beginning public hearings in 1965, the Long Committee had two complementary, but somewhat distinct purposes. The first was to draft legislation requiring departments and agencies to "publish information necessary to persons having business with Government agencies, including the organization of each department and agency, their general rules and policies issued for the guidance of the public, their public procedures, and agency decisions of precedential significance." (These hearings eventuated in the Freedom of Information Act of 1966.) The second was to draft legislation to amend the investigative provisions of the Administrative Procedure Act of 1946—specifically "the extent that highly sophisticated electronic eavesdropping equipment is used by the Federal agencies both internally and in dealing with the public." Having learned that federal agencies, such as the Internal Revenue Service, had expended large sums of money to purchase eavesdropping equipment, in September 1964, Subcommittee staff sent a comprehensive questionnaire to "the departments and agencies in an effort to develop as many facts as possible on this subject."

Among the Long Committee's questions to federal agencies and departments were: Had they ever surreptitiously installed or monitored a

telephone tap? Had they requested the assistance of another federal, local, or state agency in the installation or monitoring of a tap? Would they enumerate these requests for fiscal years 1959–64? Had they purchased bugs and closed circuit TV equipment? How many had been purchased? Had they requested mail covers be placed by the Post Office Department? Would they enumerate such requests and their purposes? The Long Committee further requested copies of all agency and department rules (both written and oral) governing wiretaps, bugs, and mail covers.[47]

The questionnaire, unknown to the Subcommittee staff and to Chairman Long, threatened to disclose some of the FBI's abusive practices and procedures: these included the FBI's extensive use of warrantless wiretaps and bugs during so-called intelligence (that is, non-criminal) investigations; resort to break-ins either to install bugs or to secure the correspondence, membership rolls, and subscription lists of targeted individuals and organizations; and separate filing and record destruction procedures (the "Do Not File" system for break-in documents; the "June mail" system for wiretap and break-in reports; rules stipulating that copies of letters intercepted under either the FBI's or the CIA's mail programs were to be filed separately in a "special file room", the use of Letterhead Memoranda [so-called LHMs] to disguise the fact that forwarded information had been obtained from illegally installed wiretaps or bugs; and the use of "administrative pages" for forwarding "potentially embarrassing" information).

Accordingly, FBI Assistant Director Cartha DeLoach and another ranking FBI official visited Senator Long to convince him not to investigate FBI wiretapping and bugging activities.[48] Long emphasized that he was being pressured to investigate FBI practices. The Senator, DeLoach suggested, "might issue a statement reflecting that he had held lengthy [sic] conferences with top FBI officials and was now completely satisfied, after looking [sic] into FBI operations, that the FBI had never participated in uncontrolled usage of wiretaps or microphones and that FBI usage of such devices had been completely justified in all instances." Long agreed, having made a "commitment that he would in no way embarrass the FBI." When the Senator pleaded an inability to word such a statement, DeLoach agreed to prepare it. DeLoach's prepared press release affirmed

that, "after exhaustive research into the activities, procedures, and techniques of this agency[FBI]," the Subcommittee concluded that FBI electronic surveillance had been conducted properly and lawfully. Long decided against issuing this press release, but agreed not to call FBI witnesses.[49]

The Long Committee's public inquiry, nonetheless, threatened to expose the FBI's (and the CIA's) mail programs. During its February 1965 hearings, the Committee specifically demanded that Chief Postal Inspector Henry Montague name those subjected to mail covers—including "national security" mail covers—during the two preceding years. This request posed delicate security problems.

The Johnson Administration quickly moved to avert the public disclosure of the mail programs. Attorney General Katzenbach, Vice President Hubert Humphrey, (possibly) President Johnson, and Senate Judiciary Committee chairman James Eastland (who had been personally contacted by FBI Director Hoover) pressured Long to exclude "national security" programs from the Subcommittee's public investigative hearings.[50]

Bowing to these pressures, the Long Committee did not investigate the FBI. In introductory comments at the February 18, 1965 hearing, Senator Long conceded the preliminary nature of the Subcommittee's investigation, adding that the Subcommittee had not yet investigated the "surveillance techniques of such agencies as the FBI, CIA, military intelligence, and so forth. I am not saying that such an investigation should not or will not be made, only that it has not been made and our findings must be interpreted accordingly."

The hearings' restricted focus continued to pose problems. Thus, Post Office Inspector Montague initially refused to comply with the Committee's demand for the names of all those subjected to a mail cover for the period January 1, 1963 to February 1965. As justification, Montague cited three reasons: confidentiality, the effect of disclosure on privacy and law enforcement, and "national security." Long assured Montague that "The committee is as concerned as you are over national security and certainly in the consideration of this list we would be as concerned as you are about it. The committee knows of these problems: we know of the sensitive areas in Government. But we feel that there is the responsibility

that we look into this matter further." Responding to Montague's observation that "some of the law enforcement agencies have been exempt from this hearing," Committee counsel Bernard Fensterwald admitted that: the "so-called security agencies" fell into this category. During another round of questions, Fensterwald cautioned Montague that "if these questions have national security implications I do not want you to answer them."

The Committee nonetheless insisted upon the list. Montague again demurred, and, at the March 2, 1965 hearing, produced instead a March 1, 1965 letter from Postmaster General John Gronouski. "We know from discussions we have had with officials of the Air Force, the Central Intelligence Agency, the Army Intelligence Corps, and other agencies of Government," Gronouski explained, "that they use mail covers in cases involving espionage, sabotage, and other threats to our national security. It is apparent that international conflict could arise and this country's security could be placed in jeopardy from disclosure of the names covered in these cases." Once again, when interrogating Attorney General Katzenbach about the number of wiretaps he had approved, Long and Fensterwald were both properly deferential about presumed "national security" considerations.[51]

Constrained because of hesitation to challenge broad "national security" claims, the Long Committee in effect averted the discovery of FBI abuses of power. The Subcommittee's interrogation of Postal Inspector Montague on the Post Office Department's mail cover procedures ironically highlighted one consequence of this self-imposed limitation: having obtained copies of postal forms 2008 (used by agencies to request mail covers), and 2009 (used by the Post Office to forward information obtained through mail covers), the Subcommittee became apprised about a Post Office record destruction procedure. The following notation was printed on the bottom of form 2008: "Under no circumstances should the addressee or any unauthorized person be permitted to become aware of this action [mail cover]. Destroy this form [2008] at the end of period specified [two years]. Do not retain any copies of form 2009." Such record destruction requirements ensured that defense attorneys could not subsequently ascertain whether their clients had been subject to mail covers, Fensterwald stressed. He then asked Montague whether any other agency resorted to such practices, and, as a counter-example of an agency that did not, cited the FBI's record retention practices.[52] Ironically, the Post Office practice strikingly resenbled the FBI's Do Not File procedure for break-ins. The Long Committee never learned that its commendation of FBI record maintenance practices was totally unfounded.

Although FBI officials had neutralized the Long Committee investigation, FBI Director Hoover concluded that continued use of illegal investigative techniques was too risky politically. Accordingly, in 1965 and 1966, Hoover imposed numerical limits on the installation of wiretaps and bugs, and prohibited break-ins, mail covers/intercepts, and trash covers. In addition, in 1967 the FBI formally severed its covert relationship with HUAC—in fact, the leaks continued more circumspectly.[53]

The Long Committee's hesitancy to meet its oversight responsibilities in the "national security" area was not exceptional. In 1955, Senator Mike Mansfield introduced a resolution to establish a joint congressional oversight committee on the CIA. Under Mansfield's resolution, the proposed joint committee would have a broad mandate to study CIA activities, problems relating to the gathering of national security intelligence, and the coordination and use of the intelligence.

Initially co-sponsored by thirty-four senators, and having received an almost unanimous Rules Committee report on February 23, 1956, the Mansfield Resolution was nonetheless defeated on April 9 by a vote of 27 to 59, with ten senators not voting. The conservative congressional leadership was instrumental in ensuring this defeat. The Senate should allow the CIA to continue with its work "without being watchdogged to death," Senator Carl Hayden argued. In tandem, Senator Richard Russell emphasized that "if there is one agency of the Government in which we must take some matters on faith without a constant examination of its methods and sources, I believe this agency is the Central Intelligence Agency." The resolution's opponents specifically maintained that the effectiveness of Appropriations and Armed Services Committees' oversight obviated the need for a special oversight committee. Inadvertently, Senator Leverett Saltonstall described how these committees operated: "It is not a question on the part of CIA officials to speak to us," Saltonstall affirmed. "Instead it is a question of our reluctance, if you will, to seek information and knowledge of subjects which I personally as a member of Congress and as a citizen, would rather not have."[54]

Either because of the Congress's hesitant oversight or the FBI's resort to separate filing procedures, FBI officials during the Cold War years were not deterred from attempting to promote McCarthyite politics. Congress never learned the scope of the FBI's illegal investigative activities, whether in 1920, 1924, 1950, 1956, 1965, or 1974—and, as a part of these activities, the Bureau's covert efforts to discredit dissident political activists. Research into FBI files, recently accessible under the Freedom of Information Act, therefore, will not merely extend our understanding of the origins of McCarthyism; this form of citizen oversight could supplement the oversight responsibility that Congress has so unwillingly exercised until recently and could thereby deter FBI officials from renewing their abuse of civil rights.

Notes

1. Studies dealing with these themes include Justus Doenecke, *Not to the Swift: The Old Isolationists in the Cold War Era* (Lewisburg: Bucknell University Press, 1979); Robert Griffith, *The Politics of Fear: Joseph R. McCarthy and the Senate* (Lexington: University of Kentucky Press, 1970); Griffith, "Old Progressives and the Cold War." *Journal of American History* 66 (Sept. 1979): 334–47; Athan Theoharis, *The Yalta Myths: An Issue in U.S. Politics, 1945–55* (Columbia, Mo.: University of Missouri Press, 1970); Theoharis, *Seeds of Repression: Harry S. Truman and the Origins of McCarthyism* (Chicago: Quadrangle, 1971); Richard Fried, *Men against McCarthy* (New York: Columbia University Press, 1976); Alonzo Hamby, *Beyond the New Deal: Harry S. Truman and American Liberalism* (New York: Columbia University Press, 1973); Hamby, *The Imperial Years: The U.S. Since 1939* (New York: Weybright and Talley, 1976); Alan Harper, *The Politics of Loyalty: The White House and the Communist Issue, 1946–52* (Westport: Greenwood, 1969); Ronald Caridi, *The Korean War and American Politics: The Republican Party* as a Case Study (Philadelphia: University of Pennsylvania Press, 1968); Robert Carr, *The House Committee on Un-American Activities, 1945–50* (Ithaca: Cornell University Press, 1952); Donald Kemper, *Decade of Fear: Senator Hennings and Civil Liberties* (Columbia, Mo.: University of Missouri Press, 1965); Walter Goodman, *The Committee* (New York: Farrar, Straus and

Giroux, 1968); Earl Latham, *The Communist Controversy in Washington from the New Deal to McCarthy* (Cambridge, Mass.: Harvard University Press, 1966); Herbert Parmet, *Eisenhower and the American Crusades* (New York: Macmillan, 1972); Cabell Phillips, *The Truman Presidency: The History of a Triumphant Succession* (New York: Macmillan, 1966); Arthur Schlesinger, *The Imperial Presidency* (Boston: Houghton Mifflin, 1973); Raoul Berger, *Executive Privilege: A Constitutional Myth* (Cambridge, Mass.: Harvard University Press, 1974); H. Bradford Westerfield, *Foreign Policy and Party Politics: Pearl Harbor to Korea* (New Haven: Yale University Press, 1955); Eric Goldman, *The Crucial Decade—And After* (New York: Vintage, 1960); Norman Graebner, *The New Isolationism: A Study in Politics and Foreign Policy Since 1950* (New York: Ronald, 1956); Ross Koen, *The China Lobby in American Politics* (New York: Harper and Row, 1974); Ron Lora, *Conservative Minds in America* (Chicago: Rand McNally, 1971); James Patterson, *Mr. Republican: A Biography of Robert A. Taft* (Boston: Houghton Mifflin, 1972); Daniel Bell, ed., *The Radical Right* (Garden City: Doubleday, 1964); and Lawrence Wittner, *Cold War America* (New York: Praeger, 1974).

2. The Hoover quote is cited in U.S. *Congressional Record*, 93d Cong., 2d sess., 1974, vol. 120, p. 8936. For representative examples of FBI leaks to congressmen and reporters, see *SDSR*, pp. 140–41, 161, 174–79, 182, 219–20; *IARA*, pp. 11, 15–16, 89, 221 n65, 222–23, 222 n69, 241–47, 280. In *The Bureau: My Thirty Years in Hoover's FBI* (New York: Norton, 1979), former FBI Assistant Director William Sullivan recounts the FBI's assistance to Senator McCarthy during the Truman and Eisenhower years. See pp. 45–46.

3. The FBI's COINTELPROs are surveyed in Athan Theoharis, *Spying on Americans: Political Surveillance from Hoover to the Huston Plan* (Philadelphia: Temple University Press, 1978), pp. 133–55; *SDSR*, pp. 3–223; and Frank Donner, *The Age of Surveillance: The Aims and Methods of America's Political Intelligence System* (New York, Knopf, 1980), pp. 177–40. Sanford Ungar, *FBI* (Boston: Atlantic Monthly/Little, Brown, 1975), pp. 124, 277, 373–74.

4. Assigned to the Crime Records Division, DeLoach was appointed FBI assistant director in charge of the Crime Records Division in 1959, two years after Nichols's retirement. Ungar, *FBI*, p. 283; Donner, *Age of Surveillance*, pp. 254–55. Memo, SAC, New York to File, May 14, 1958, FBI 100-107111-2985-A, FBI Rosenberg/Sobell Committee Files, J. Edgar Hoover FBI Building. This document, originally not recorded (that is, serialized), had been filed in the 62-11957 file; it was later transferred to the central files and serialized 100-107111-2985-A.

5. Memo, C. D. DeLoach to Mr. Mohr, Dec. 23, 1960, FBI 100-3-104-2173, COINTELPRO-CPUSA. Letter, Walter Trohan to "Comrade" [J. Edgar Hoover], Sept. 24, 1964, Walter Trohan Papers, Herbert Hoover Presidential Library, West Branch, Iowa. For DeLoach's American Legion activities, see also Ungar, *FBI*, pp. 282–83. The FBI had very close relations with *Reader's Digest, Look Magazine*, and Scripps-Howard editors. Included among the recipients of FBI leaks were: Fulton Oursler, Michael Cowles, Paul Palmer, Leo Rosten, Dan Mitch, Ed Nellor, Courtney R. Cooper, Drew Pearson, Walter Winchell, Jimmy Ward, Frederick Woltman, Gene Strul, Willard Edwards, Ralph deToledano, Karl Hess, George Sokolsky, Walter Trohan, Lyle Wilson, Victor Riesel, Paul Harvey, Ron Koziol, Westbrook Pegler, Jeremiah O'Leary, Ed Montgomery, Charles McHarry, Howard Rushmore, Thomas Lubenow, Ray McHugh, Ed O'Brien, Ed Mowery, Bob Allen, Gordon Hall, and Ray Cromley. See, *LN*; Sullivan, *The Bureau*, pp. 93–95; Theoharis, *Spying on Americans*, pp. 164–65; Donner, *Age of Surveillance*, pp. 93, 111–14, 182, 186, 208–9, 213, 215–16, 224, 233–34, 237–40, 256, 490 n23; and Drew Pearson, *Diaries, 1949–59*, ed. Tyler Abell (New York: Holt, Rinehart and Winston, 1974), pp. 58–60, 119.

6. *New York Times*, August 9, 1973; Memo, Legal Counsel to FBI Director, August 15, 1973; Memo, FBI Director to All SACs, August 23, 1973; Memo 35–73, August 28, 1973; and Memo 55-73, December 4, 1973; all in 66-19022 file.

7. FBI officials also worked closely with HUAC's Senate counterpart, the Internal Security Subcommittee, See Memos, A. H. Belmont to L. V. Boardman, April 4 and May 15, 1958. Because they described FBI efforts to discredit lawyers who had defended Communists, these memoranda were not recorded; the originals were held in the 62-38217 file and carbon copies were to be "filed with this memorandum rather than in individual case files [of the lawyers whose names were leaked to the Senate Subcommittee]." Other FBI documents, for example on Yale Law Professor Thomas Emerson's testimony before the Senate Subcommittee, further confirm the closeness of this relationship. Memo, Nichols to Tolson, June 17, 1953; Memo, Laughlin to Belmont, June 18, 1953; Memo, Nichols to Tolson, January 25, 1954; all in FBI 101-33156. See also, Donner, *Age of Surveillance*, pp. 143, 149–50, 191, 403–4.

8. Memo, P. E. Foxworth to FBI Director, Aug. 16, 1938, FBI 61-7582-12, FBI HUAC files; airtel, FBI Director to SAC New York, November 12, 1969, FBI 100-358086-34-75, FBI Security Index files; Memo, SAC New York to FBI Director, June 3, 1955, FBI 100-107111-1735, FBI Rosenberg/Sobell Committee files; Memo, FBI Director to SAC Los Angeles, October 31, 1958,

FBI 100-3-104-777, COINTELPRO-CPUSA files; and Victor S. Navasky, *Naming Names* (New York: Viking, 1980), p. 317n. For a more detailed discussion of the FBI-HUAC relationship, see Kenneth O'Reilly, "The Bureau and the Committee: A Study of J. Edgar Hoover's FBI, the House Committee on Un-American Activities, and the Communist Issue" (Ph.D. diss., Marquette University, 1981).

  9. For leaks to HUAC, see Memo, F. J. Baumgardner to A. H. Belmont, Aug. 25, 1960, FBI 100-433447-14; Memo, C. D. DeLoach to Mr. Mohr, Dec. 29, 1960, FBI 100-433447-81; Memos, F. J. Baumgardner to W. C. Sullivan, July 16, 1962, FBI 100-433447- [not recorded]; Sept. 4, 1962, FBI 100-433447-23; Nov. 23, 1962, FBI 100-387548-434; Jan. 29, 1963, FBI 100-387548-442; Jan. 30, 1963, FBI [deleted]; Feb. 17, 1964, FBI 100-433447-433; Feb. 20, 1964, FBI 100-433447-435; Feb. 26, 1964, FBI 100-433447-444; Nov. 3, 1964, FBI 100-433447-?; Nov. 20, 1964, FBI 100-433447-563; Dec. 14, 1964, FBI 100-433447-571; and Jan. 13, 1965, FBI 100-433447-582; Airtels, SAC, Los Angeles to Director, Jan. 3, 1963, FBI 100-433447-321; Jan. 10, 1964, FBI 100-433447-415; Jan. 15, 1964, FBI 100-433447-412; and Feb. 25, 1964, FBI 100-433447-442; Airtel, SAC, Pittsburgh to Director, Jan. 23, 1964, FBI 100-433447-437; Memo, SAC, Chicago to Director, Dec. 8, 1964, FBI 100-433447-568; Airtel, SAC, Washington, D.C., to Director, Jan. 11, 1965, FBI 100-433447-579; all in *NCARL*. FBI memoranda do not always specify the information forwarded to HUAC. In many cases, the FBI considered HUAC members and staff "confidential informants," and has therefore claimed the right to exempt reports detailing these contacts from disclosure under the Freedom of Information Act. For instance, a handwritten note on a Jan. 10, 1964 airtel (FBI 100-433447-415) from the Los Angeles SAC indicates only that on Jan. 27 something was "handled with [HUAC staff director Francis J.] McNamara."

  10. The FBI did not rely exclusively on informers to obtain information on NCAHUAC. In January 1966, FBI agents burglarized at least one NCAHUAC affiliate, the Chicago Committee to Defend the Bill of Rights, to photocopy a list of that organization's contributors. NCARL's Los Angeles office, moreover, was burglarized on August 17, 1969. Following publicity of FBI break-on practices in 1973, NCARL officials suspected that the FBI might have conducted this unsolved burglary. The FBI's Los Angeles field office, however, assured the FBI Director that there was "no evidence" to support NCARL's claim. *Chicago Sun-Times*, Feb. 3, 1979, p. 10 and Feb. 5, 1979, p. 29. Memo, Chicago Committee to Defend the Bill of Rights and marked "Not for File," Chicago SAC, Jan. 10, 1966. This break-in authorization memo was produced during

discovery in *A. C.L. U. et al. v. City of Chicago et al.*, Ca 75-C3295 and *Alliance to End Repression et al. v. James Rochford et al.*, Ca 75-C3268. Memo, SAC, Los Angeles to FBI Director, Sept. 10, 1973, FBI 100-433447-?, *NCARL*.

11. Airtel, SAC, Los Angeles to Director, June 16, 1960, FBI 100-433447-?; Airtel, Director to SAC, Los Angeles, June 23, 1960, FBI 100-433447-?; Memos, F. J. Baumgardner to A. H. Belmont, Aug. 25, 1960, FBI 100-433447-14; Nov. 3, 1960, FBI 100-433447-?; and May 22, 1961, FBI 100-433447-129; Los Angeles Field Office Report, Nov. 30, 1960, FBI 100-433447-?; all in *NCARL*. HUAC's Oct. 9, 1960 press release on the NCAHUAC prompted a Justice Department official to remark, "The HCUA is really on top of this outfit" (Memo, Herbert E. Bates to Waterman and Strother, Oct. 10, 1960, *NCARL*). For NCAHUAC's and other organized attempts to abolish HUAC (notably by the ACLU's southern California branch, the New York-based Emergency Civil Liberties Committee, and the Los Angeles Citizens Committee to Preserve American Freedoms, which were all subjects of FBI surveillance), see Jerold Lee Simmons, "Operation Abolition: The Campaign to Abolish the House Un American Activities Committee, 1938–65" (Ph.D. diss., University of Minnesota, 1971).

12. Memo, Thomas E. Marum to Oran H. Waterman, June 11, 1962; Memos, F. L. Williamson to Oran H. Waterman, Sept. 20, 1963; March 19, 1964; and Feb. 23, 1966; Memo, Robert A. Crandall to Oran H. Waterman, Oct. 18, 1972; Memo, J. Walter Yeagley to Director, July 12, 1963; Memo, Director to SAC, Chicago, July 23, 1963, FBI 100-433447-?; Airtel, SAC, Los Angeles to Director, June 21, 1962, FBI 100-433447-?; Airtel, Director to SAC, Chicago, May 10, 1966, FBI 100-433447-?; Airtel, Director to SAC, Memphis, April 27, 1971, FBI 100-433447-?; all in *NCARL*. The Justice Department considered initiating proceedings against *NCARL* only in December 1970 when Assistant Attorney General Robert C. Mardian requested an interview with several FBI informers and inquired about their "availability" for public testimony at a SACB hearing (Memo Mardian to Director, Dec. 2, 1970, *NCARL*). Mardian's interest arose in part from the Nixon Administration's aborted attempt to reinvigorate the SACB.

13. The FBI's disruptive activities against the late Martin Luther King were also not carried out under any formal COINTELPRO. See *SDSR*, pp. 63, 131–84; U.S., Department of Justice, *Report of the Department of Justice Task Force to Review the FBI Martin Luther King, Jr., Security and Assassination Investigations* (Washington, D.C.: 1977), pp. 132–42.

14. Formal counterintelligence actions were not aimed exclusively at Communist party members or alleged Communists. In March 1960, the FBI's

COMINFIL program (targeting alleged Communist-infiltrated organizations) was expanded to prevent Communist party members from infiltrating non-Communist organizations. These "legitimate mass organizations" ranged from NCAHUAC to the NAACP and even a local boy scout troop. In many cases, the non-Communist organization itself was targeted. See SDSR, pp. 4–5, 17–18.

15. Former FBI Assistant Director William C. Sullivan claims that the Bureau's resort to disruptive actions dated at least from 1941. These informal counterintelligence activities continued after COINTELPRO-CPUSA was formally initiated in 1956 and also after FBI Director Hoover formally terminated all COINTELPROs in 1971 (except "in exceptional circumstances"). Hoover's termination order stipulated that henceforth field office counterintelligence proposals were to be filed either under the organization's or the individual's case caption. SDSR, p. 13; IARA, p. 66.

16. ACLU official Irving Ferman duly reported Wilkinson's recruitment effort to the FBI. See Letter, Ferman to L. B. Nichols, March 13, 1957, FBI 61-190-652; Memo, G. A. Nease to Mr. Tolson, July 29, 1958, FBI 61-190-[not recorded], FBI ACLU Files, J. Edgar Hoover FBI Building.

17. Memo, F. J. Baumgardner to W. C. Sullivan, Oct. 12, 1962, and accompanying blind memo regarding Frank Byron Wilkinson, FBI 100-3-104-52-4, NCARL. For Wilkinson's contempt of Congress case, see Wilkinson v. United States, 365 U.S. 399 (1961).

18. Teletype, SAC, Baltimore to Director, June 24, 1964, FBI 100-433447-513; Airtel, Director to SACs, Chicago, Cincinnati, Cleveland, Detroit, Los Angeles, Milwaukee, Newark, New York, Washington, April 30, 1962, FBI 100-433447-196; Airtel, Director to SACs, Chicago, Detroit, Indianapolis, Los Angeles, Milwaukee, Springfield, Sept. 27, 1962, FBI 100-3-3-104-9-80; Airtel, Director to SACs, Los Angeles, Minneapolis, Omaha, Oct. 9, 1962, FBI 100-3-104-26-52; Airtels, SAC, Los Angeles to Director, Sept. 19, 1963, FBI 100-433447-?; Jan. 6, 1964, FBI 100-433447-?; Feb. 5, 1963, FBI 100-433447-330; April 1, 1963, FBI 100-433447-?; April 16, 1964, FBI 100-433447-?; March 25, 1965, FBI 100-433447-?; July 20, 1965, FBI 100-433447-?; Sept. 15, 1965, FBI 100-433447-?; Nov. 10, 1965, FBI 100-433447-?; Feb. 17, 1966, FBI 100-433447-?; Nov. 8, 1966, FBI 100-433447-?; and Nov. 18, 1966, FBI 100-433447-?; Airtel, SAC, Buffalo to Director, April 29, 1964, FBI 100-433447-?; Airtel, SAC, Pittsburgh to Director, April 30, 1964, FBI 100-433447-?; Airtel, SAC, New York to Director, June 17, 1964, FBI 100-433447-?; Minneapolis Field Office Report, July 31, 1962, FBI 100-433447-?; Memo, SAC, Detroit to Director, Nov. 4, 1963, FBI 100-433447-?; all in NCARL.

19. Omaha Field Office Report, April 4, 1962, FBI 100-433447-?, *NCARL*. A Dec. 5, 1966 airtel from the SAC, Detroit to the Director, cross-referenced to a Nov. 8, 1966 airtel from the SAC, Los Angeles recommending disruption of Wilkinson's schedule, reported: "FRANK WILKINSON did not speak at Albion College as scheduled on Nov. 17, 1966." From released documents we cannot ascertain the FBI's particular role.

20. Airtels, SAC, Detroit to Director, May 22, 1962, FBI 100-433447-205; May 22, 1962, FBI 100-3-104-3765; Airtel, SAC, Washington to Director, May 2, 1962, FBI 100-433447-198; Memo, SAC, Cincinnati to Director, May 19, 1964, FBI 100-433447-?; Airtel, SAC, Omaha to Director, Nov. 2, 1965 (see also accompanying letterhead memorandum), FBI 100-433447-?; all in *NCARL*.

21. These included the Wisconsin Committee for Constitutional Freedom, the Women's International League for Peace and Freedom, Citizens for Constitutional Rights, the Washington Area Committee to Abolish HUAC, the Minnesota Committee to Defend the Bill of Rights, and the NYCAUAC. Airtel, Director to SAC, Milwaukee, Dec. 21, 1960, FBI 100-3-104-2132; Memo, F. J. Baumgardner to A. H. Belmont, Jan. 11, 1961, FBI 100-3-104-2229; Memos, SAC, Cleveland to Director, July 13, 1961, FBI 100-3-104-2712; July 31, 1961, FBI 100-3-104-?; Memo, W. C. Sullivan to A. H. Belmont, July 21, 1961, FBI 100-3-104-2748; Airtels, Director to SAC, Cleveland, Feb. 21, 1963, FBI 100-3-104-11-72; Oct. 8, 1963, FBI 100-3-104-11-108; Memos, SAC, Cleveland to Director, March 14, 1963, FBI 100-3-104-11-76; Oct. 11, 1963, FBI 100-3-104-11-109; Memo, F. J. Baumgardner to W. C. Sullivan, Oct. 7, 1963, FBI 100-3-104-53-?; Memo, Director to SAC, New York, Sept. 18, 1962, FBI 100-3-104-34-280; all in *COINTELPRO-CPUSA*. Airtel, SAC, New York to Director, Dec. 16, 1960, FBI 100-433447-57; Memo, W. D. Griffith to Mr. Tamm, Dec. 21, 1960, FBI 100-433447-80; Memo, F. J. Baumgardner to A. H. Belmont, Dec. 22, 1960, FBI 100-3-104-2177; Memo, C. D. DeLoach to Mr. Mohr, Dec. 29, 1960, FBI 100-433447-81; all in *NCARL*. Bureau officials ordered investigations of all anti-HUAC committees, including the fifty abolition committees formed in congressional districts in eighteen states, and file checks on virtually everyone on the NCAHUAC's mailing list. See Memo, Director to SAC, Los Angeles, Aug. 14, 1962, FBI 100-433447-220; Airtel, SAC, Cincinnati to Director, Oct. 12, 1962, FBI 100-433447-261, *NCARL*.

22. Memos, SAC, Chicago to Director, June 21, 1962, FBI 100-32864-1196; April 23, 1962, FBI 100-32864-1145, *Criley*.

23. Airtel, SAC, Chicago to Director, May 14, 1962, FBI 100-32864-1165, *Criley*. Memo, SAC, Cleveland to Director, May 22, 1962, FBI 100-3-104-11-

30; Memo, F. J. Baumgardner to W. C. Sullivan, May 16, 1962, FBI 100-3-104-11-25; Airtel, Director to SAC, Cleveland, May 15, 1962, FBI 100-3-104-11-22; Airtel, SAC, Cleveland, to Director, May 9, 1962, FBI 100-3-104-11-22; all in *COINTELPRO-CPUSA*.

24. Memos, SAC, Chicago to Director, June 21, 1962, FBI 100-32864-1196; Aug. 3, 1962, FBI 100-32864-?; Aug. 31, 1962, FBI 100-32864-1236; July 18, 1962, FBI 100-32864-1200; and Nov. 15, 1962, FBI 100-32864-1302; Memo, [F. J. Baumgardner?] to [W. C. Sullivan?], July 6, 1962, FBI [deleted]; Memos, Director to SAC, Chicago, June 7, 1962, FBI 100-32864-1180; July 9, 1962, FBI 100-32864-1208; Aug. 20, 1962, FBI 100-32864-1228; and Sept. 6, 1962, FBI 100-32864-1239; Airtel, SAC, Chicago to Director, May 14, 1962, FBI 100-32864-1166; all in *Criley*. These anonymous mailings were meticulously executed. For example, the Chicago Field Office was ordered to mail their characterization of the CCDBR and Criley from a place "where a formerly active Communist Party member, such as [deleted], would normally deposit his mail and at a time he could reasonably be expected to do so."

25. See Los Angeles Field Office Reports of July 25, 1967, Jan. 22, 1968, Sept. 29, 1971, Oct. 10, 1972, May 24, 1973; Form letter request for FBI reports, Paul H. Wright, Special Service Staff (IRS) to FBI, Oct. 16, 1970, FBI 100-433447-[not recorded]; Memo, SAC, New York to Director, April 22, 1963, FBI 100-?; all in *NCARL*. Formally established in 1969, the IRS's Special Service Staff received COINTELPRO documents from the FBI and had a particularly close working relationship with HISC, HUAC's successor. See *SDSR*, pp. 876–90; U.S., Senate, Committee on the Judiciary, Subcommittee on Constitutional Rights, *Political Intelligence in the Internal Revenue Service: The Special Service Staff*, 93d Cong., 2d sess., 1974; U.S., Joint Committee on Internal Revenue Taxation, *Investigation of Special Service Staff of the Internal Revenue Service*, 94th Cong., 1st sess., 1975; and Special Service Staff Files, Center for National Security Studies, Washington, D.C.

26. Airtels, SAC, Washington to Director, Nov. 30, 1964, FBI 100-433447-?; Dec. 15, 1960, FBI 100-433447-?; Nov. 25, 1964, FBI 100-433447-?; and Jan. 11, 1965, FBI 100-433447-579; Chicago Field Office Letterhead Memoranda, Jan. 22, 1963, FBI 100-433447-?, and April 8, 1965, FBI 100-433447-?; Memo, Director to SAC, Los Angeles, Oct. 15, 1962, FBI 100-433447-242; Airtel, SAC, San Antonio to Director, April 27, 1964, FBI 100-433447-?; Los Angeles Field Office Report, July 20, 1965, FBI 100-433447-?; Memos, F. J. Baumgardner to W. C. Sullivan, Jan. 30, 1963, FBI 100-?; Jan. 10, 1962, FBI 100-433447-?; Memo, F. J. Baumgardner to A. H. Belmont, May 22, 1961, FBI 100-433447-129; all in *NCARL*.

27. Airtel, SAC, New York to Director, Dec. 16, 1960, FBI 100-433447-57; Memo, W. D. Griffith to Mr. Tamm, Dec. 21, 1960, FBI 100-433447-80; Memo, F. J. Baumgardner to A. H. Belmont, Dec. 22, 1960 (see also accompanying blind memorandum), FBI 100-3-104-2177; Memo, C. D. DeLoach to Mr. Mohr, Dec. 29, 1960, FBI 100-433447-81; all in *NCARL*. Memo, F. J. Baumgardner to A. H. Belmont, Jan. 16, 1961 (see also HUAC chairman Francis Walter's accompanying press release), FBI 100-3-104-2233, *COINTELPRO-CPUSA*. NCAHUAC and its New York affiliate did not always agree, though the FBI never doubted that they were both following the Communist party "line." For the Bureau's account of factionalism within the anti-HUAC movement, see the New York Field Office Report of Sept. 24, 1964, FBI 100-433447-?. This was not the first use by HUAC of the matching addressograph technique. A 1956 Committee report had also noted that the National Committee to Secure Justice for Morton Sobell had used the same addressograph plates as the *National Guardian*. U.S., House, Committee on Un-American Activities, *Trial by Treason: The National Committee to Secure Justice for the Rosenbergs and Morton Sobell*, 85th Cong., 1st sess., 1956, p. 39. Whether the FBI tipped off HUAC in 1956 is not known—it should be noted, however, that in 1960 the FBI had to conduct laboratory tests to establish that the NYCAUAC had used the *Daily Worker*'s plates.

28. Memos, F. J. Baumgardner to W. C. Sullivan, Dec. 14, 1961, FBI 100-433447-157; Jan. 10, 1962, FBI 100-433447-158; Airtel, SAC, Washington to Director, Jan. 8, 1962, FBI 100-433447-156; Airtel, SAC, Chicago to Director, Dec. 19, 1961, FBI 100-433447-?; Washington Field Office Letterhead Memoranda, Jan. 16, 1963, FBI 100-433447-?; March 14, 1969, FBI 100-433447-?; and March 27, 1969, FBI 100-433447-?; all in *NCARL*.

29. The anti-HUAC congressmen were: Edwards, Hawkins, Burton, Roosevelt, Ryan, Robert L. Leggett (D., Cal.), Benjamin S. Rosenthal (D., N.Y.), Leonard Farbstein (D., N.Y.), Joseph Y. Resnick (D., N.Y.), John V. Lindsay (R., N.Y.), Charles C. Diggs, Jr. (D., Mich.), John Conyers, Jr. (D., Mich.), and William S. Moorhead (D., Pa.). William A. Barrett (D., Pa.) was later added to the FBI's list. See Memo, F. J. Baumgardner to W. C. Sullivan, Jan. 13, 1965, FBI 100-433447-582; Teletype, SAC, Washington to Director and SACs, Los Angeles, New York, Chicago, Philadelphia, San Francisco, Jan. 7, 1965, FBI 100-433447-581, *NCARL*.

30. Memo, F. J. Baumgardner to W. C. Sullivan, Jan. 13, 1965, FBI 100-433447-582; Washington Field Office Letterhead Memoranda, Jan. 11, 1965, FBI 100-433447-579; Dec. 29, 1966, FBI 100-433447-?; Washington Field Office Report, May 4, 1967, FBI 100-433447-?; all in *NCARL*.

31. Letters, [J. Edgar Hoover] to Wilton B. Persons, Jan. 3, 1961, FBI 100-433447-?; [J. Edgar Hoover] to Marvin Watson, April 12, 1964, FBI 100-433447-?; and [J. Edgar Hoover] to Walter Jenkins, Feb. 28, 1964, FBI 100-433447-?; Airtel, Director to SAC, Atlanta, Jan. 24, 1964, FBI 100-433447-?; Airtel, SAC, Los Angeles to Director, Jan. 30, 1964, FBI 100-433447-?; Airtel, SAC, New York to Director, Jan. 31, 1964, FBI 100-433447-?; Airtel, SAC, Washington to Director, March 9, 1964, FBI 100-433447-?; Airtel, SAC, Pittsburgh to Director, Jan. 23, 1964, FBI 100-433447-437; Memo, F. J. Baumgardner to W. C. Sullivan, Feb. 26, 1964, FBI 100-433447-444; Washington Field Office Report, April 21, 1964, FBI 100-433447-?; all in *NCARL*. President Johnson was a friend of Williams and had earlier presented the Presidential Freedom Award to another NCAHUAC founder, Alexander Meiklejohn. There was at least one FBI leak to HUAC concerning Meiklejohn. See Memo, F. J. Baumgardner to W. C. Sullivan, Nov. 3, 1964, FBI 100-433447-[?], *NCARL*.

32. At least one COINTELPRO-New Left operation involved NCAHUAC. Airtel, SAC, Boston to Bureau, June 2, 1970, FBI 100-449698-?, *NCARL*.

33. C. D. Brennan to W. C. Sullivan, Jan. 4, 1967, FBI 100-433447-?, *NCARL*; *HIA*, Vol. 6, Federal Bureau of Investigation, p. 359. One such briefing occurred following Martin Luther King's death in April 1968. Having learned in March 1969 of congressional plans to declare King's birthday a national holiday, Cartha DeLoach recommended that the FBI brief several HISC members on King's allegedly subversive background since they could "keep the bill from being reported out of committee" if "they realize King was a scoundrel." Conceding the delicacy of this matter, DeLoach was nonetheless confident that he could handle it. Hoover concurred but admonished that "it must be handled *very cautiously*." *SDSR*, p. 183.

34. This hesitancy to investigate the FBI was consistent with the historic relationship between HUAC and the FBI. For example, when Committee chairman Martin Dies concluded in 1941 that HUAC's troubles stemmed from the "incompeten[ce]" of its counsel and membership, he consulted with FBI officials on the hiring of "competent counsel." See Dies Committee folder, *LN*.

35. *New York Times*, April 17, 1971, p. 1; *SDSR*, p. 551.

36. *IARA*, p. 285; *HIA*, Vol. 6, Federal Bureau of Investigation, p. 605.

37. H. H. Wilson, "The FBI Today: The Case for Effective Control," *Nation* (Feb. 8, 1971), pp. 169–72; Arlie Schardt, "FBI Conference: A Crack in Hoover's Fortress," *Nation* (Nov. 22, 1971), pp. 526–30; Pat Watters and Stephen Gillers, eds., *Investigating the FBI* (Garden City, N.Y.: Doubleday, 1973), pp. vii–ix.

38. Routing slip, n.d., FBI 62-113909-6, *CPJ*. Invitations to participate in the conference were rejected by Attorney General John Mitchell, the Society of Former Special Agents of the FBI, and FBI Director Hoover. When drafting Hoover's letter of regret to Duane Lockard, the Crime Records Division summarized "at some length . . . many of the major accomplishments of this Bureau since the Director took over and state[d] them in a manner which we believe will commend itself to readers among the American public." By publicizing the Hoover-Lockard correspondence, the FBI hoped "to pull the teeth of the conference," to "*force* the conference, if that can be done at all, to recognize the overall worth of this Bureau" (Memo, D. J. Dalbey to Mr. Tolson, Oct. 6, 1971, FBI 62-113909-7, *CPJ*). For the Hoover-Lockard correspondence, see Watters and Gillers, eds., *Investigating the FBI*, pp. 464–77; *Congressional Record*, 92d Cong., 1st sess., Nov. 2, 1971, pp. 38792–94.

39. Memos, M. A. Jones to Mr. Bishop, May 5, 1971, FBI 62-113909-3; Oct. 1, 1971, FBI 62-113909-8, *CPJ*.

40. *Congressional Record*, 92d Cong., 1st sess., Oct. 28, 1971, pp. 38091–92; Nov. 19, 1971, p. 42222.

41. Memos, M. A. Jones to Mr. Bishop, Sept. 28, 1971, FBI 62-113909-10; Oct. 1, 1971, FBI 62-113909-8, *CPJ*. The thirty-nine individuals mentioned in Bittman's letters included, among others, Blair Clark, Ramsey Clark, Fred J. Cook, Robert Coles, Vern Countryman, Frank Donner, Norman Dorsen, Thomas Emerson, Richard Falk, Lillian Hellman, Bourke Marshall, Victor Navasky, Aryeh Neier, Robert Sherrill, and I. F. Stone.

42. Memo, T. E. Bishop to Felt, Oct. 29, 1971, FBI 62-113909-54, *CPJ*.

43. *Congressional Record*, 92d Cong., 1st sess., Oct. 28, 1971, p. 38169; November 2, 1971, pp. 38917–20; Memo, M. A. Jones to Mr. Bishop, Nov. 3, 1971, FBI 62-113909-43, *CPJ*; and Letter, Hoover to Spence, Nov. 1, 1971, FBI 62-113909-44, *CPJ*. In the Senate, Strom Thurmond (R., S.C.), an occasional beneficiary of FBI leaks, put the Buckley column and Robert Allen's FBI-assisted column into the *Congressional Record* (92d Cong., 1st sess., Oct. 27, 1971, pp. 37686–87).

44. Memos, M. A. Jones to Bishop, Nov. 3, 1971, FBI 62-113909-43; Nov. 9, 1971, FBI 62-113909-52, *CPJ*.

45. *Congressional Record*, 92d Cong., 1st sess., Nov. 9, 1971, pp. 40073–79.

46. Walter Pincus, "The Bureau's Budget: A Source of Power," in Watters and Gillers, eds., *Investigating the FBI*, pp. 70–78; *IARA*, pp. 29, 277–81; *SDSR*, pp. 70–73, 140–41; U.S., House, Committee on Internal Security, *Hearings on Domestic Intelligence Operations for Internal Security Purposes*,

Pt. 1, 93d Cong., 2d sess.; Donner, *Age of Surveillance*, pp. 24, 44–45, 48–49, 103–4; Hugh Clegg, John Kerr, and Styles Bridges folders, *LN*.

47. *SAPP, Hearings on Administrative Procedure Act*, 89th Cong., 1st sess., 1965, pp. 195, 198–99, 202–3, 206; *Senate Report No. 119*, March 10, 1965, p. 7; *Senate Report No. 1053*, March 4, 1966, p. 4; *Senate Report No. 21*, Feb. 1, 1965, p. 4; *Senate Report No. 518*, July 28, 1965, pp. 2–3; *Hearings on Invasion of Privacy (Government Agencies)*, 89th Cong., 1st sess., 1965, pp. 1–3, 5, 8–12.

48. The FBI did not confine its containment efforts to lobbying Long, Senate Judiciary Committee chairman James Eastland, and Johnson Administration officials. Memoranda on all the members of the Long Committee were compiled and filed in Hoover's Official and Confidential file. See *HIA*, Vol. 6, Federal Bureau of Investigation, p. 477.

49. *SDSR*, pp. 307–10; *IARA*, p. 278.

50. *SDSR*, pp. 588, 595, 609, 637–38, 661, 665–68, 676–77; *HIA*, Vol. 6, Federal Bureau of Investigation, pp. 830–35; *IARA*, pp. 286, 286 n80.

51. *SAPP, Hearings on Invasion of Privacy (Government Agencies)*, 89th Cong., 1st sess., 1965, pp. 2, 97–99, 110, 211–12, 217–18; *Hearings on Invasion of Privacy (Government Agencies)*, Pt. 3, 89th Cong., 1st sess., 1965, pp. 1163, 1641.

52. *SAPP, Hearings on Invasion of Privacy (Government Agencies)*, 89th Cong., 1st sess., 1965, pp. 90–91.

53. *SDSR*, pp. 302, 310, 365, 562, 634, 661, 668–70, 676, 931, 972. See also the documentation cited in footnote 33. The Long Committee had discovered that the Post Ofice had provided HUAC with a list of individuals receiving Communist literature. The Committee protested this favoritism when challenging the Department's "national security" rationale for not releasing the mail cover list.

54. Harry Howe Ransom, *The Intelligence Establishment* (Cambridge, Mass.: Harvard University Press, 1970), pp. 163–72.

Index